Intelligence Unbound

Intelligence Unbound

The Future of Uploaded and Machine Minds

Edited by

Russell Blackford and
Damien Broderick

WILEY Blackwell

This edition first published 2014

Registered Office
John Wiley & Sons Ltd, The Atrium, Southern Gate, Chichester, West Sussex, PO19 8SQ, UK

Editorial Offices
350 Main Street, Malden, MA 02148-5020, USA
9600 Garsington Road, Oxford, OX4 2DQ, UK
The Atrium, Southern Gate, Chichester, West Sussex, PO19 8SQ, UK

For details of our global editorial offices, for customer services, and for information about how to apply for permission to reuse the copyright material in this book please see our website at www.wiley.com/wiley-blackwell.

Library of Congress Cataloging-in-Publication Data applied for.

Hardback ISBN: 978-1-118-73641-8
Paperback ISBN: 978-1-118-73628-9

A catalogue record for this book is available from the British Library.

Cover image: Circuit board © sborisov /iStockphoto; Vitruvian Man © Devrimb /iStockphoto.

Set in 10/12pt Sabon by Laserwords Private Limited, Chennai, India
Printed and bound in Malaysia by Vivar Printing Sdn Bhd

1 2014

To Aubrey Townsend, who handed me the tools

Russell Blackford

To R. Daneel Olivaw, Golem XIV, Donovan's Brain, and Paul Durham, in the hope that things turn out better next time

Damien Broderick

Contents

Notes on Contributors

Nicholas Agar is a New Zealand philosopher, based at Victoria University of Wellington. His research is focused on ethical issues arising out of the application of new technologies to human beings. His most recent books are *Humanity's End: Why We Should Reject Radical Enhancement* (2010) and *Truly Human Enhancement: A Philosophical Defense of Limits* (2014).

Michael Anissimov is a futurist focused on such emerging technologies as nanotechnology, biotechnology, robotics, and artificial intelligence. He previously managed the Singularity Summit and worked as media director for the Machine Intelligence Research Institute, as well as co-founding Extreme Futurist Festival.

Stuart Armstrong and Seán ÓhÉigeartaigh work at the Future of Humanity Institute of Oxford University, where they analyze the major risks facing humanity, and how these can be prevented or mitigated. Recent work has focused on the risks and ethics of AI, human biases, and the reliability of predictions.

Russell Blackford is an Australian philosopher and literary critic. He is a Conjoint Lecturer at the University of Newcastle, NSW, and editor-in-chief of *The Journal of Evolution and Technology*. His recent books include *Freedom of Religion and the Secular State* (2012) and *Humanity Enhanced: Genetic Choice and the Challenge for Liberal Democracies* (2014).

James Bodington is a doctoral candidate in philosophy at the University of New Mexico, where he studies twentieth-century and contemporary continental philosophy, especially philosophy of religion and philosophy of technology, with a particular emphasis on the ethical and political ramifications of technology.

Damien Broderick holds a PhD in the literary theory of the sciences and the arts from Deakin University, and has written or edited some 60 books in several disciplines, including a number of prize-winning novels. His *The Spike* (1997, 2001) was the first general treatment of the Singularity. In 2008 he edited an original science anthology *Year Million*, on the prospects of humankind in the remote future.

David J. Chalmers is Distinguished Professor of Philosophy and Director of the Centre for Consciousness at the Australian National University and Professor of Philosophy at New York University. He is best known for articulating what he has dubbed the "hard problem" of consciousness – explaining how physical brains and bodies give rise to "qualia," or subjective experiences. His best-known book is *The Conscious Mind* (1996).

Joseph Corabi is an Associate Professor of Philosophy at Saint Joseph's University. He has published numerous articles on philosophy of mind and philosophy of religion.

Linda MacDonald Glenn is a bioethicist, healthcare educator, lecturer, consultant, and attorney. She holds faculty appointments at the Alden March Bioethics Center and California State University Monterey Bay. Her research is focused on the sociopolitical implications of exponential technologies and evolving concepts of legal personhood.

Ben Goertzel, PhD, chief force behind the recent movement toward artificial general intelligence in the AI field, is chief scientist of financial prediction firm Aidyia Holdings and chairman of AI software company Novamente LLC and bioinformatics company Biomind LLC. His research work encompasses artificial general intelligence, natural-language processing, cognitive science, data mining, machine learning, computational finance, bioinformatics, virtual worlds, gaming, and other areas.

Kathleen Ann Goonan is the author of *Queen City Jazz* (1994), *The Bones of Time* (1996), *Mississippi Blues* (1998), *Crescent City Rhapsody* (2000), *Light Music* (2002), *In War Times* (2007), *This Shared Dream* (2011), and *Angels and You Dogs* (2012). She is a Professor of the Practice at Georgia Institute of Technology, Atlanta, where she teaches creative writing and examines the intersection of culture, science, technology, and literature. Her website is www.goonan.com.

Victor Grech is Consultant Pediatrician (Cardiology), Pediatric Department, Mater Dei Hospital, Tal-Qroqq, Malta, and author of several searching essays on the thematics of *Star Trek*.

Robin Hanson is an Associate Professor of Economics at George Mason University and a research associate at the Future of Humanity Institute of Oxford University. He is known as an expert on prediction markets and was a principal architect of the Foresight Exchange, DARPA's FutureMAP project, and IARPA's DAGGRE project.

James J. Hughes is the Executive Director of the Institute for Ethics and Emerging Technologies, and a bioethicist and sociologist at Trinity College in Hartford, Connecticut, where he teaches health policy. Hughes is author of *Citizen Cyborg*, and is working on a second book tentatively titled *Cyborg Buddha*.

Randal A. Koene introduced the multidisciplinary field of whole brain emulation and is lead curator of its scientific roadmap. He is founder of the Carboncopies.org foundation and neural interfaces company NeuraLink Co, and Science Director of the 2045 Initiative. His publications, presentations and interviews are available at http://randalkoene.com.

Richard Loosemore is a lecturer in the Department of Mathematical and Physical Sciences at Wells College. He graduated from University College London as a physicist and from Warwick University as a cognitive scientist. His background includes work in artificial intelligence, cognitive science, physics, software development, philosophy, parapsychology, and archeology.

Max More, who received his PhD in philosophy from the University of Southern California, is a strategic philosopher recognized for his thinking on the implications of emerging technologies. More's contributions include founding the philosophy of transhumanism, developing the Proactionary Principle, and co-founding Extropy Institute. He is currently president and CEO of the Alcor Life Extension Foundation.

Seán ÓhÉigeartaigh and Stuart Armstrong work at the Future of Humanity Institute of Oxford University, where they analyze the major risks facing humanity, and how these can be prevented or mitigated. Recent work has focused on the risks and ethics of AI, human biases, and the reliability of predictions.

Nicole Olson is a Canadian transhumanist writer/researcher holding a bachelor's degree from the University of Alberta in philosophy and sociology.

Massimo Pigliucci is a Professor of Philosophy at the City University of New York. His research is concerned with philosophy of science, the relationship between science and philosophy, and the nature of pseudoscience. His publications include several books, most recently

Answers for Aristotle (2012) and *Philosophy of Pseudoscience* (co-edited with Maarten Boudry, 2013).

Joel Pitt, PhD, is a scientist and software developer based in Wellington, New Zealand. As a scientist, he has contributed original research to molecular biology, machine learning, and ecology. As a developer he has been the CTO Demand Analytics, and currently works for Dragonfly Data Science, a science consultancy in Wellington.

Anders Sandberg has a background in computational neuroscience and the ethics of human enhancement. Since 2008 he has been James Martin Research Fellow at the Future of Humanity Institute at Oxford University, where he is investigating neuroethics, global catastrophic risks, and applied epistemology.

Susan Schneider is an Associate Professor of Philosophy at the University of Connecticut. She has published many articles in the fields of metaphysics and philosophy of mind as well as *The Language of Thought, The Blackwell Companion to Consciousness* (with Max Velmans), and *Science Fiction and Philosophy.*

Joe Strout's career blends science and technology, with degrees in psychology and neuroscience, and extensive experience as a software engineer. He works now as a software consultant, developing artificial intelligence algorithms for the game industry, as well as other applications in business and medicine. His website is http://www.ibiblio.org/jstrout/uploading.

Iain Thomson is Professor of Philosophy at the University of New Mexico. The author of two books, *Heidegger on Ontotheology: Technology and the Politics of Education* (2005) and *Heidegger, Art, and Postmodernity* (2011), Thomson has published dozens of articles in philosophical journals, essay collections, and reference works, and his writing has been translated into seven languages.

Natasha Vita-More, PhD, is a Professor at the University of Advancing Technology and Founder of H+ Lab. She has appeared in over 24 televised documentaries and featured in *Wired*, the *New York Times*, and *Village Voice*. She is chair of Humanity+ and a Fellow of the Institute for Ethics and Emerging Technologies.

Mark Walker is an Associate Professor in the Department of Philosophy at New Mexico State University, where he holds the Richard L. Hedden Chair of Advanced Philosophical Studies. His book, *Happy-People-Pills for All* (2013) argues for creating advanced pharmaceuticals to boost the happiness of the general population.

Naomi Wellington is a postgraduate philosophy student at the Australian National University, working under the supervision of Daniel Stoljar and David Chalmers. Her academic background includes a BA with philosophy honors (H1) from Monash University. Her primary areas of interest are philosophy of mind and philosophy of neuroscience.

Introduction I: Machines of Loving Grace (Let's Hope)

Damien Broderick

1 Machine minds or humans copied into machines?

In an immensely confident but typical summary of the neurocomputational model of mind now dominant in science, Nobel Laureate Eric Kandel wrote in 2013:

> This new science of mind is based on the principle that our mind and our brain are inseparable. The brain is a complex biological organ possessing immense computational capability: it constructs our sensory experience, regulates our thoughts and emotions, and controls our actions. It is responsible not only for relatively simple motor behaviors like running and eating, but also for complex acts that we consider quintessentially human, like thinking, speaking and creating works of art. Looked at from this perspective, our mind is a set of operations carried out by our brain.[1]

More than two decades earlier, the science fiction writer Charles Platt offered a somewhat ampler view:

> A person's mind is structure as well as content. Without the structure, the content can't function. Our minds have to have the specialized architecture … in which to operate. We can store our brain data elsewhere, but when we do that, it's as nonfunctional as a videodisc without a disc player. (Platt 1991: 238)

In the next 25 to 100 years, genuinely intelligent machines are likely to be developed up to and beyond the highest levels of human ability.

Intelligence Unbound: The Future of Uploaded and Machine Minds, First Edition.
Edited by Russell Blackford and Damien Broderick.

We're not there yet, in part because the raw computational power of the brain hugely outstrips even the fastest computer. In mid-2013, the world's top supercomputer was the Tianhe-2, holding more than a million gigabytes of memory and running at some 50 petaflops (where a petaflop is a thousand trillion calculations per second) on its best days. Using an only slightly less extraordinary machine, Japan's 10 petaflop K supercomputer, scientists simulated 1 percent of 1 second of human brain activity. That took 40 minutes of screamingly fast calculations.[2]

You would need to multiply that by a factor of a quarter million to emulate a brain. Luckily, Moore's law (roughly: "computer power doubles every year and a half"[3]) suggests that a machine of this majestic status will be available – all things going well – in perhaps 30 more years. And of course in the meantime, scientists might learn better ways to get the job done sooner on leaner computers.

> Markus Diesmann of the Institute of Neuroscience and Medicine at Germany's Forschungszentrum Julich believes that, within the next decade, we'll be able to use exascale computers – capable of 1000 times one quadrillion operations per second – to represent the entire [*sic*] of the brain "at the level of the individual nerve cell and its synapses."[4]

And Henry Markram, a professor of neuroscience at the Swiss Federal Institute for Technology and founder and director of the Blue Brain Project, is coordinating the Human Brain Project (Keats 2013). This 10-year, €1.3 billion flagship project, selected in January 2013 by the European Commission, plans to simulate

> a rat cortical column. This neuronal network, the size of a pinhead, recurs repeatedly in the cortex. A rat's brain has about 100,000 columns of [about] 10,000 neurons each. [A] human cortex may have as many as two million columns, each having [about] 100,000 neurons each … These models will be basic building blocks for larger scale models leading towards a complete virtual brain.[5]

Will they necessarily be conscious, such brainy machines? Perhaps not, or at any rate not as we experience consciousness. The speeding locomotive, or "Iron Horse," never resembled a real horse, yet it carried a heavier load and moved much more swiftly and without tiring. A submarine isn't much like a whale, yet dives deeper and travels faster. Birds sing more beautifully than jet planes or rockets, but their capacity to fly high, far, and rapidly was outstripped by machines a century ago. Chess programs defeat grand masters without being self-aware, and IBM's Watson supercomputer beat top human contestants on *Jeopardy!*, winning a million dollars but without a jitter of anxiety or a shout of joyful pride.

Even so, machine or artificial intelligence (AI), unlike ours, might well have the ability to understand, modify, and improve its own source code, carrying it by great leaps into domains of ability that unaided flesh can never hope to reach. Half a century ago, the mathematician I.J. Good proposed that an "ultraintelligent machine" could design ever more enhanced versions of itself, resulting in an "intelligence explosion" that would leave humans far behind (Good 1965). If such supersmart computers also achieve consciousness, we (or our children and grandchildren) shall share the planet with a new and intriguing species of mentality.

But wait – what *is* intelligence? Thousands of learned books and scientific or philosophical papers have probed every corner of this apparently simple question with no clear consensus emerging. We can start with theoretical neurophysiologist William Calvin's breezy summary in *How Brains Think*:

> I think of intelligence as the high-end scenery of neuro-physiology – the outcome of many aspects of an individual's brain organization which bear on doing something one has never done before … some of *what* intelligence encompasses are cleverness, foresight, speed, creativity, and how many things you can juggle at once. (1997: 11)

Instead of our brutally slow chemical neurotransmitters, ionic currents, and neural designs, built by millions of years of ad hoc evolution, AI will use engineered electronic or photonic neural nets operating a million times faster. Instead of memories limited by the gene-architected size of our skulls and the human birth canal, AIs will possess effectively limitless storage constrained only by pathways traversed at the speed of light. In that sense, the arrival of advanced AIs will mark the end of some of the limitations that bind human intelligence. Intelligent and superintelligent machines will truly represent "intelligence unbound."

If and when this happens, humanity will face ethical issues of unprecedented gravity and difficulty. What obligations do we owe to artificial minds? Can they morally be switched off, like any other instrument or mechanical device? Or do they share human rights to life and the pursuit of happiness, the right of due process? Is there any way in which their designers can defang hazardous AIs that might turn on us, can make them compliant, obedient to their creators? Or is that slavery, mind bondage? If they are our intellectual superiors, can they at least be encouraged to adopt an attitude of benevolence toward us? Is it even technically possible to enforce friendship between protein and silicon beings, once the AIs pass beyond human comprehension in their abilities and potential?

In addition to this vexed and giddy outlook, in a near future of such fabulous machines, it will be possible to blend human and machine by enhancing our current bodies with chips, modules, and interface devices (a process of "cyborgization" that has already begun).

All these prospects, and more, are discussed in detail in the chapters of this book. No single viewpoint is privileged throughout; these topics remain genuinely controversial, even philosophically troubling, so it is necessary to approach the topics carefully, exploring the pros and cons. And if the imminent arrival of machines with intelligence, however alien, is sure to throw our world into confusion and tumult, how much more will the possibility of minds copied from organic brains to inorganic machines? Not just copied as a static representation, as the Mona Lisa might be counterfeited with great fidelity by a skilled artist, but imbued with emotion, awareness, and all the other aspects of personhood.

2 Emulating the mind

This radical option might become available alongside the emergence of machines powerful enough and intricately connected enough to house a true mind. In the process – called "uploading" by some and, confusingly, "downloading" by others, and "whole brain emulation" by a third group – we could *become* machines while remaining ourselves, physically transferring the structure of our minds into capacious computer programs that generate thought and the quality of minds when they are run. Uploads would live in vivid virtual realities fitted to the needs of their simulated minds, while remaining in touch with the external world.

Is this a crypto-religious hope, the much-lampooned "Rapture of the Nerds"? It does echo religious hopes of reincarnation widespread in Asian cultures, where a non-material essence slips out of an injured or aged body to enter the waiting vessel of an unborn infant. But no, the prospect of uploading has nothing significantly in common with those ancient wishful, consoling dogmas. Naturalistic materialism, the current scientific paradigm, maintains that mind is nothing other than the sublimely complex workings of the physical brain and its bodily extensions in a world of particles and force fields. If that is what we *are*, nothing prevents us from copying – mapping – our neurological complexity into some more durable, swifter material substrate.

Still, isn't this a version of the cliché from bad horror movies: a naked brain in a vat of chemical soup? Some will complain that uploading is a nightmare proposed by body-hating, frightened computer hackers, those nerdish social incompetents allegedly fleeing from sensuous reality and human warmth.

It is true that many proponents of uploading dislike the limitations and messy urgings of the body and its ancient, now often maladaptive Darwinian drives. For others, as Max More details in his chapter, what drives the interest in uploading is a desire for more life, for the greatest possible access to this beautiful and complex universe. It can't be explained away as simple hatred or fear of the flesh.

Suppose it is true that mind and passion and soul are indeed the body at work, a whirling composite of matter and force and energy, engaged with the world. As we eat, drink, and excrete, the very atoms in our cells are regularly replaced. Should we object if mind changes its location from one kind of organized and ceaselessly replaced matter to another material substrate?

It is easy to become trapped by old preconceptions. Is the mind really a machine? If being a machine suggests clockwork or even the relatively stupid computers in our smart phones (already 50 percent more powerful than the greatest supercomputers in 1976), of course not. Even these limited computers are vastly more complex than an eighteenth-century wind-up parrot, or a nineteenth-century piano driven by a paper tape. The human brain is not like a broken-down motor-mower, and nobody ever thought it was.

Uploading need not imply a world of bloated grubs lying in the dark with their brains wired to spreadsheets and simulated worlds. On the contrary: transhumanist philosopher Max More, who intends to upload when that becomes an option (and use his new freedom to explore the stars), put his own case back in the 1990s: "I'm in the gym five days a week, plus I either run or cycle. I can boast that I do 710 lbs on the leg press. No atrophied body here!" In 2013, he added with amusement, "That was 710 lbs for 8 repetitions. I'm currently doing 720 lbs for 15 reps, so I'm definitely stronger. For 8 reps, I can do something over 800 lbs" (private communication). The initial goal of uploaders would be to emulate and enhance the brain, and that requires rich connections to external reality. It calls for give and take, building from the peculiar truth that inside our porridge-like brain matter is where our selves are generated. That fact does not repudiate the body, far from it.

A quadriplegic with no access to the world other than her mouth and ears and eyes and her vivid, courageous brain *is a person*. By contrast, the superb corpse of an Olympic athlete or concert pianist with a fatal brain injury, its metabolism sustained by medical machines, is no kind of person at all, just a tragic reminder of the fallibility of life and a storehouse for luckier transplant patients.

It's worth noting that if synthetic neurons can be made half the size of the organic varieties, replacing each brain cell after copying its structure and contents, you could *double* the number of neurons inside your head. Would this automatically increase your brain power? Perhaps not, because specialized architecture is crucial to cognition. Still, one of the most palpable differences between modern humans and Lucy, the proto-hominid of the Ethiopian plains 3 million years ago, is that we have, on average, 1330 grams of brain tissue, while she had to make do with a third of that. With more components and some measure of plasticity in rewiring them, we might find ourselves becoming conspicuously cleverer in the ensuing weeks and years.

Suppose, once the mapping and substitution are complete, that this detailed atlas of your brain is also copied into the huge memory and processing system of a supercomputer – one easily handling as many petaflops or even exaflops as a human brain – perhaps a hundred thousand trillion calculations each second. So this mindless, terribly fast machine now contains a digital description that emulates your original brain. If we arrange for streams of data from the outside world to enter its ports, just the same kinds that now enter your own ears and eyes and taste buds and movement sensors and internal monitors scattered through your organic body – what happens? Add efferent (outgoing) channels that permit the emulated brain to reach into the world, to hold and move objects, stroke and sniff and chew in synchrony with the afferent (incoming) impulses that feed its sensorium. The simulated "you" will then, surely, feel himself or herself to "be" a "person" – to be, in fact, *you*!

Assuming we've left nothing out in this exercise in simulation, what we've achieved in our thought experiment is indeed an *upload* – a complete copy of your mind into the flickering electronic whir of a computer platform. Just to make sure you don't go mad at the shock of the transition, the flow of sensory data will ensure that you genuinely *feel* a physical continuity with your old self.

This might require linking your cybermind to a humanoid robot extension replete with stereo TV cameras at the top, and two servo-mechanical arms hinged at elbow and shoulder, and five tactile, gripping fingers, and two prosthetic legs. Alternatively, your experience might be delivered, after considerable pre-processing, in the form of a convincing virtual reality construct. Only that small part of the world you're choosing to look at will exist in the model, but that portion will be rendered with the maximum available pixel-rich detail at the focal zone, fading away to impressions at the boundaries – just like now, in fact.

Isn't this the worst kind of manipulative dehumanization ever proposed? Consider the nauseated response likely from humanists such as the American novelist Jonathan Franzen, who recently deplored how Twitter and Facebook, in his view, are diminishing the richness of human life. He gestures at an

> apocalyptic argument about the logic of the machine, which has now gone global and is accelerating the denaturization of the planet and sterilization of its oceans. I could point to the transformation of Canada's boreal forest into a toxic lake of tar-sands byproducts, the leveling of Asia's remaining forests for Chinese-made ultra-low-cost porch furniture at Home Depot, the damming of the Amazon and the endgame clear-cutting of its forests for beef and mineral production, the whole mindset of "Screw the consequences, we want to buy a lot of crap and we want to buy it cheap, with overnight free shipping." (Franzen 2013)

And meanwhile, some scientists and futurists propose whole brain emulation or uploading into the technoapocalyptic machine? For many, this will seem the ultimate blasphemy.

3 Is my copy me?

Here, then, are the key questions:

- Is this uploaded personality conscious?
- Is it (he, she) you or your twin, or something unprecedented?
- If a disaster destroys the hardware it's running on, and the latest back-up is reinstalled on a new machine, is the new version of you the same as the original? After all, you remain *you* when you sleep and wake. Or is it quite a different person, who just happens to recall everything that ever happened to you (with at least the same fidelity now available to your own organic brain)?
- Would you even be prepared to terminate your own stream of awareness, just so that this other person (with the same memories, admittedly) could awaken to an adventure in virtual reality, to potentially endless machine life?

Some say yes. After all, once you're inside that computer, the benefits are extraordinary. No more colds or cancer. Your thinking might accelerate. No longer restricted to the sluggish baton-passing of neurotransmitters and ionic currents, your electronic or optical consciousness-stream would blaze like the pure spirit of some Miltonic angel. And those convenient backups provide a degree of security the flesh can never maintain.

But wait – why should you care about *his* or *her* greater wealth? *Their* security of tenure in a perilous universe?

Evolution has winnowed our genomes in favor of building bodies whose economic behavior is channeled by the need to sustain (and reproduce) the components of that genotype – the individual genes, and the ensembles of genes that do well together.

According to a standard argument, we tend to be "altruistic" toward other bearers of large chunks of the same genotype. Note one crucial and somewhat paradoxical proviso: this mechanism allows high-level adapted structures such as brains and cultures to make "mistaken" identifications. Individuals can sacrifice themselves in support of genotypes quite different from their own. Young men hurl themselves into the firing line because, in a sense, their genetic propensities have been tricked, persuaded to bond with their (genetically distant) fellow warriors, or with their nation or religion. Still, it's clear that the altruism equations would be more than satisfied if you were to sacrifice your body in order to produce a dozen copies of your exact genome, with or without cultural and individual memories.

You the original might not be so ardent.

Grant that you could arrange for a dozen exact copies of your body by cloning: a time-lapsed set of identical -tuples. If you could only achieve this by giving up your individual life you might not share the joy.

Suppose, however, that these copies could also contain your exact memories to this moment, as we've stipulated above, so that you spawned a dozen true copies of yourself. (Admittedly, these duplicates would fork off from each other immediately in terms of experience.) Would this offer make you more inclined to die in order to achieve perfect duplication? Possibly not. Why should you care about *their* enhanced prospects, even if each one of them is convinced that he or she *is* you?

But suppose you were dying of a currently incurable disorder, and you are offered a new, young replacement body grown from your stem cells and imprinted with all your memories, or a robot equivalent, or an emulated and superior cyber version inside an exaflop machine. Would you prefer to go instead gently and immediately into that good night?

These are *difficult* issues, and the answers are not at all self-evident.

Indeed, you might not even be at immediate risk of dying, except in the sense that we all are. Perhaps lingering death by senility or disease causes the irreparable loss of too many brain cells to permit machine resurrection. Perhaps the sooner you get your brain destructively scanned the more reliable the result will be. What would *you* do?

4 Who woke up?

Physical and general brain-process continuity does seem to support our current sense of continuing identity. This allows us to believe that the person who wakes up tomorrow is the same one who went to sleep tonight. What of awakening after 10 years in a coma? Nobody denies that this case is deeply traumatic, but still we assume that *the same person* has woken up. Waking after half the brain is removed to forestall death by cancer? No one denies that this case is even more deeply troubling.

Would you be prepared to die (sacrifice your current embodiment) in order that an exact copy of yourself be reconstituted elsewhere (teleported), or on a different substrate? To insist that this question remains unsettled (and unsettling!) is not to be a hostile "upload skeptic."

In a sense, the philosophical question is moot. As long as there are people who share this conviction that identity persists through upload, they'll purchase the service the moment it is technically feasible. Unless their machine emulations regret the error of their choice (and why should they, since they share the memories and disposition of their predecessors?),[6] humankind will be split into two species: people in their original and continuing bodies, and uploaded people who are copies of dead humans. Add to that a third category, independent minds built from the ground up by artificial intelligence programs. And perhaps a fourth: living, embodied humans in an extended condition of enhancement, plugged in (perhaps only some of the time) to the super-Net.

What happens in a world like this? How do we deal with such a proliferation of new intelligent species? Even before superintelligence makes the world more fraught for ordinary people than it is now – and this could occur due to genetic engineering, as well as AI or uploading – we will find ourselves in a disrupted psychic ecology. Species competition is fiercest between relatives. We do not usually fight with birds and bees for living space, not as the military of nations do. The soil continues to be churned by uncaring worms, whoever walks upon its surface. Our ancient ancestors, admittedly, did wipe out all the other hominins and primates that got anywhere near our ecological zone. Of our omnivorous cousins, only the chimpanzees and bonobos remain, and they persist at our sufferance. True AIs and uploads will suffer the same Darwinian neighborhood pressures, as will we.

At last, even if your original brain is altogether gone, your mind (or its perfect copy) remains as active as ever. Once we command the new array of expanded senses, the unprecedented range of access open to us, we would less *inhabit* our new locus of consciousness than *be* it. And strange new doorways will open to futures with entirely new ethical quandaries, hazards, and joys that are barely imaginable.

Notes

1 Kandel shared the 2000 Nobel Prize in Physiology or Medicine, and is a professor at the Mortimer B. Zuckerman Mind Brain Behavior Institute at Columbia, and a senior investigator at the Howard Hughes Medical Institute. He is an editor

and author of *Principles of Neural Science*, 5th edn. (New York: McGraw-Hill, 2013).

2 http://www.top500.org/blog/lists/2013/06/press-release/ (accessed October 6, 2013).

3 Precisely, the "law" is a historical observation that the number of transistors on an integrated circuit chip doubles every two years, while performance increases by a factor of two every 1.5 years or even faster. It has held true since 1958.

4 http://www.top500.org/blog/an-83000-processor-supercomputer-can-only-match-1-of-your-brain/ (accessed September 12, 2013).

5 Blue Brain Project, http://bluebrain.epfl.ch/page-56882-en.html

6 They do, however, in Norman Spinrad's interesting short novel *Deus X* (1993), which hangs on this very point. And in Greg Egan's brilliant upload novel *Permutation City* (1994), uploads have a distressing way of killing themselves the moment they understand that they are the copies in a virtual reality world and not the originals. See also Platt 1991.

References

Calvin, William H. 1997. *How Brains Think: Evolving Intelligence, Then and Now*. London: Weidenfeld & Nicolson.

Egan, Greg. 1994. *Permutation City*. London: Millennium.

Franzen, Jonathan. 2013. What's wrong with the modern world. *The Guardian*, http://www.theguardian.com/books/2013/sep/13/jonathan-franzen-wrong-modern-world (accessed October 7, 2013).

Good, I.J. 1965. Speculations concerning the first ultraintelligent machine. *Advances in Computers*, 6. New York: Academic Press.

Kandel, Eric R. 2013. The new science of mind. *New York Times*, http://www.nytimes.com/2013/09/08/opinion/sunday/the-new-science-of-mind.html (accessed October 7, 2013).

Keats, Jonathon. 2013. The $1.3B quest to build a supercomputer replica of a human brain. *Wired*, http://www.wired.com/wiredscience/2013/05/neurologist-markam-human-brain/all/ (accessed 7 October 7, 2013).

Platt, Charles. 1991. *The Silicon Man*. New York: Bantam Books.

Spinrad, Norman. 1993. *Deus X*. New York: Bantam Spectra.

Introduction II: Bring on the Machines

Russell Blackford

1 A strange new epoch?

Year by year, computer programs and applications become more fluid, more dazzling, more convenient for our purposes. The allure is obvious, and the results are often beneficial, but how far can we go with the rise and rise of digital technology? We've come very far already, if we're counting sheer numbers:

> [B]etween 2008 and 2009 … the number of devices – sensors, phones, computers – connected to the Internet outnumbered the human population. By 2020, when an estimated 7.6 billion people will be running around on the planet, there will be 50 billion machines communicating to one another. (Tucker 2013)

Clever mobile apps can already help with many of our daily problems, even, as James Hughes' chapter shows in detail, providing us with moral support and guidance. While there may be little prospect of machines and apps answering the deepest moral questions, they can remind and exhort us about many of our goals and the steps prescribed to achieve them. As Hughes makes clear, our mobile devices are becoming tutors, counselors, and externalized consciences.

So far, so good, but more radical outcomes may not be far away. To examine the implications, Damien Broderick and I obtained chapters from a brilliant, clued-up, and diverse cast of contributors. They bring expertise from

Intelligence Unbound: The Future of Uploaded and Machine Minds, First Edition.
Edited by Russell Blackford and Damien Broderick.

the fields of philosophy and cognitive science, from art and literature, and from the burgeoning young culture of transhumanism. The book you're reading, perhaps on your computer or an e-book reader or even the tiny screen of a smartphone, deals with the prospects of full-scale machine intelligence and what has become known as mind uploading – the idea that living, functioning minds could be transferred to powerful computer hardware.

If we take Hans Moravec, the celebrated Carnegie Mellon robotics guru, as our guide to the future, a strange epoch is approaching. In his 1988 book *Mind Children*, Moravec argues that culture and intelligence will soon be the province of increasingly capable machines. He dares us to contemplate what we cannot genuinely imagine: the post-biological world of our thinking, ever-improving "unfettered mind children" (Moravec 1988: 5), superintelligent machines that aspire to immortality and endless self-replication. In this vision, flesh-and-blood human bodies will "play a rapidly diminishing role" (1988: 4). The machines will supersede us, or perhaps they will *be* us – greatly transformed by technology – since we'll resist the prospect of being upstaged and replaced by our own "artificial progeny" (1988: 108).

Moravec's more recent *Robot: Mere Machine to Transcendent Mind* (1999) goes much further in envisioning a spectacular future ecology of Exes, or ex-humans, seeking their destinies in space beyond the limits of our blue earth. But is anything like this plausible?

Caution is needed whenever we speculate about times to come. In their chapter, Stuart Armstrong and Seán ÓhÉigeartaigh investigate the track record of past predictions involving artificial intelligence (AI). Unfortunately, would-be prophets have had little success to date, and there has been scant difference in success rates between experts and non-experts. Armstrong and ÓhÉigeartaigh suggest the use of clearer models, more testable predictions, and a less confident attitude to guessing the future.

That said, change can creep up on us slowly until its full implications start to emerge. Michael Anissimov's chapter considers the likely improvement path of AI and advanced robotics. Anissimov argues that change will be sharp, sudden, and rapid, and will likely produce extraordinary variation of design – especially once powerful artificial intelligences themselves start to participate in AI research programs. In his contribution, neuroscientist/neuroengineer Randal Koene provides an expert and detailed description of current research on the structure and functioning of the brain. Koene believes that uploading of human minds via whole brain emulation should become a reality in the next few decades, and expects to see near-term breakthroughs as researchers develop techniques for large-scale, high-resolution mapping of brain activity.

With our daily experience of "the Cloud" and handy smartphones vastly more capable than the giant "artificial brains" of earlier decades, with war drones replacing soldiers, and brain scanners that can decode brainwaves and drive prostheses, many of us share a sense of change all around. A sense – perhaps – that *everything* is about to change. We are tantalized by an uncanny and altogether unprecedented prospect: the threat or promise of new kinds of advanced intelligence on our planet.[1]

2 Machines that think?

One of our themes is whether a sufficiently advanced computer could be conscious, and/or be a "self," or (putting it another way) whether some kind of software personality could be "run" on an advanced computer. Increasingly powerful machines that do not possess these characteristics might be very useful tools – they might help us solve problems that have defeated our efforts to date. But if they lack anything resembling consciousness, if they "think" only in the same way as our current computers, much of the charm is lost. To say the least, they will lack the intrigue, allure, and philosophical interest of machines with sensations, emotions, and desires comparable to ours.

There are seemingly strong arguments that our mental states are caused by, or emerge from, complex physical structures and events in our bodies, particularly our brains. Indeed, most philosophers of mind believe that thought and sensation are causally dependent on the structure and functioning of our neural systems.[2] The mystery, however, is just *how* these complex physical systems produce mental states. Consider, for example, your belief that lions are carnivores. Just what is it about the organization of your brain that makes it true of you that you possess this belief (as I'm sure you do)?

If what really matters is that our brains perform a kind of computation, then mental states could be produced by other physical systems devised and programmed to perform the same kind of computation. In that case, the artificial system is not merely simulating but actually *emulating* or *replicating* the relevant functioning of a human brain. By contrast, a computer model of a tornado, however accurate and detailed, does not possess the twister's ability to wreak havoc in the real world. What matters for the destructive power of the tornado is the movement of air particles at high speeds, interacting with trees, motor cars, houses, and whatever else might get in their path. A computer simulation of a tornado does nothing of the kind.

Hence, if computation is what really matters for mental states and mental functioning, then these are organizationally invariant across all sufficiently powerful computational systems. The same inner experiences that you or I have, perhaps of sensation, desire, or puzzlement, could also exist in computers made from very different materials. If computation is all that's required, we could devise a "functional isomorph" of a human brain – and its functioning would produce the same mental states as the original. On this approach, a stream of mental states is multiply realizable: it could be realized by all functionally isomorphic (though otherwise very different) systems. By contrast, if something else is important – perhaps something to do with the brain's physical composition or the physical products of its activity – we are back with the general truth that simulation is not replication. In that case, what I've called full-scale machine intelligence, complete with sensation and other conscious experience, will not be achieved via computer simulation of a human brain's structures and functioning.

For several decades now, John Searle has argued that the kind of information-processing carried out by digital computers cannot, by itself, cause such things as sensations, beliefs, desires, and thoughts. Without a genuine mind (such as a human one) to assign an interpretation to it, a computer's output is not intrinsically meaningful; it is not *about* anything in particular until we interpret it. Searle's conclusion is that "mental states are biological phenomena." Thus: "Consciousness, intentionality, subjectivity and mental causation are all a part of our biological life history, along with growth, reproduction, the secretion of bile, and digestion" (Searle 1984: 41).

The ongoing debate between proponents of organizational invariance and biological theorists of consciousness is represented in this volume by the respective chapters of two distinguished professors of philosophy: David Chalmers and Massimo Pigliucci. Chalmers characterizes the debate in these terms:

> Biological theorists of consciousness hold that consciousness is essentially biological and that no nonbiological system can be conscious. Functionalist theorists of consciousness hold that what matters to consciousness is not biological makeup but causal structure and causal role, so that a nonbiological system can be conscious as long as it is organized correctly.

But even this description of the debate is controversial. Pigliucci, for one, challenges it. He points out that biological theorists do not strictly insist that no non-biological system can ever be conscious. Nor, strictly speaking, do they deny that what matters is the causal structure and causal role of a system and its elements. They deny something more specific: that a machine can genuinely think and be conscious merely in undertaking the information-processing tasks possible to a digital computer. Despite their emphasis on biology, theorists such as Searle and Pigliucci concede that some unknown kind of physical system might turn out to have similar causal powers to those of the brain.

This leaves a mystery as to just what is crucial, for present purposes, about the brain and its functioning. Moreover, it is not clear why thought or sensation should require particular material (contrast the tornado, which would have very different effects if it were made of different physical stuff). Chalmers argues that functional isomorphs of us, or our brains, could be conscious; in support, he appeals to considerations about gradual replacement of the brain's neurons by non-biological components. You might share his intuition that we'd end up with a thinking, experiencing system if tiny non-organic neurons that function in exactly the same patterns as your nerve cells gradually replaced those original cells.

This is not a dispute that I can adjudicate here. Pigliucci can retort that a non-organic brain will not be doing *all* the same things as the original brain – see his chapter for more. And even if we think that computational theories of mind are the most plausible currently on offer, is that sufficient for us to accept them? Chalmers and Pigliucci agree that we still lack a general theory with strong empirical support of what can and cannot give rise to mental states.

3 Into the machine ... ?

What if mind uploading were possible? It might offer us many advantages: more varied experiences; greatly enhanced speed of thought; and opportunities to extend our cognitive, motor, and perceptual capacities in multiple ways. Most obviously, perhaps, it might be a way to achieve survival beyond the flesh: the computer hardware might be more durable than a human body, and perhaps you could be transferred to successive computational substrates indefinitely into the future, giving you a form of immortality. So, should you "upload" your mind into some kind of advanced computer or robot if the technology becomes available during your lifetime? Here, once again, our contributors divide.

As we've seen, Massimo Pigliucci denies that consciousness can arise merely from computation, however rapid or complex, so on his approach your attempt to upload yourself would be futile. Nicholas Agar is not necessarily convinced by arguments against computer consciousness, but he concludes that an assessment of the risk will militate against uploading. The most rational thing to do, he suggests, is pursue whatever benefits might be available to us in our human bodies as technology advances. Kathleen Goonan, too, questions the assumption that consciousness and human personality, products of our evolved, flawed, yet marvelously complex bodies, could simply be transferred to computers. Yet she imagines the eventual possibility of immortal, and greatly enhanced, human consciousness through a process in which technology gradually transforms us from within.

Most of our contributors are prepared to assume, at least for the sake of argument, that uploading is possible, but they raise other questions. One is whether there could be too much of a good thing. For example, might we, on reflection, prefer a longer but not *vastly* longer span of life? If I lived for thousands of years, might a time come when I could no longer be considered the person I am now? Or should this be seen much as we currently view growing up? I am very different from the child I was at, say, the age of 4, and I retain few memories from that age. Yet we do not deny that the child has survived as the much older person I have become. Nonetheless, should we balk at genuinely eternal life, as Iain Thomson and James Bodington argue in their thoughtful chapter? Thomson and Bodington see the current duration of human life as dreadfully unsatisfactory, "rather pathetically short," but they suggest that any attempt to ameliorate this should not be based on a quest for literal immortality.

Several chapters grapple with whether the purported transfer of your mind to a new body would, in fact, be merely the creation of a new person, a kind of digital twin. Mark Walker defends uploading on the basis that it can preserve type identity, even if it fails to preserve token identity. To understand this, consider a play such as Shakespeare's *Hamlet*. What is more important, that a particular copy of the play (even a precious early manuscript) should survive, or that the text be preserved? According to Walker, you could ask the same question about a particular human being. If we imagine technologies such as uploading (or some kind of body duplication), it becomes meaningful to distinguish between *the Mark Walker type* and a particular instance or *token* of it. Perhaps there are circumstances in which I should care more about preservation of my type than the particular token.

By contrast, Joseph Corabi and Susan Schneider are skeptical about mind uploading. In their jointly authored chapter, they press the conceptual difficulties we encounter when we try to understand what it means to transfer ourselves from one material body to another. We seem, for example, to be confronted by "odd spatiotemporal discontinuities." Similarly, Naomi Wellington identifies several methods of uploading, concluding that most of them are unlikely to give us what we want. All this raises deep, troubling, and unresolved questions about personal identity. How, as individuals, can we change while in some sense remaining the same?

4 Personal identity and survival

The main advantages proposed for mind uploading presuppose that the experiences of the upload are something that *I* can look forward to, not merely something that happens to another person who is rather like me in certain ways. As a first approximation, the assumption is something like this: When and if I am uploaded, the same individual, Russell Blackford, who once somehow "occupied," or was instantiated by, a biological brain (or perhaps more of an entire biological organism), will now occupy, or be instantiated by, the computational system.

It seems that I gain no advantage unless I, Russell, obtain an extended period of life and other benefits. Perhaps it might be nice to think my digital twin will enjoy the benefits, but that is merely a consolation prize. The real prize is that *I* will be able to live much longer, perhaps even enjoying immortality, and that *I* will be enhanced in various other ways. If I'm to obtain the advantages of uploading, there must be some sense in which the upload is the original me, or in which I have *survived* as the upload.

But what are we to make of these difficult concepts? Consider personal identity. In what sense are you still the *same* person now that you were when you were 7 years old? In what sense will you still be the same person later in your life? In what sense is it the *same* being, when, for example, my friends consider me at 10, me at 40, me at 70 (if I live that long), or me at 100 (if I live *that* long)? Is it possible that I am, in a sense, not the same person that I was as a child, or as I might be in some decades' time? Do we exaggerate our continuity with past and future selves?

Notoriously, to philosophers working in this field, there are problems with the concept of personal identity. We might wonder whether what we call personal identity is really *identity* in the general sense of that word. Think of Russell-at-10, Russell-at-20, and Russell-at-40. We want to say that these are all the same person, in some sense, but they don't all have the same properties. For example, Russell-at-10 was much smaller than either of the others. Russell-at-10 had blond hair, whereas Russell-at-20 had hair that had darkened to brown, and Russell-at-40 was graying around the edges. (As I type these words, Russell-Now is sporting a more silvery look.)

Perhaps these are temporal parts of a single four-dimensional entity (or being), a kind of space-time worm. On this view, Russell-at-10 and Russell-Now are two different, non-identical parts of the same four-dimensional thing, rather than being strictly identical to each other. Perhaps that is what we are really gesturing toward with the language of personal identity. In that case, we might ask in what circumstances two temporally separated, three-dimensional objects should be considered temporal parts of the same space-time thing.

Is personal identity – even in this sense – the best concept to use? We seem to be able to imagine cases where any idea of *identity* is being stretched unmercifully. For example, we can conceive of somebody surviving if each of her cerebral hemispheres is transferred to a new body, given that there have been people who've survived (or at least been interpreted as surviving) after one hemisphere is removed. So it seems as if we should allow for cases of fission of identity. Perhaps we can also imagine science-fictional cases of fusion where two people merge into one being, with both surviving.

The problems with personal identity talk are interesting, but we can abandon it if needed and replace it with talk of survival. We can say, for example, that Russell-at-10 was followed and survived by Russell-at-20 and so on up until at least Russell-Now. Once we start speaking in such ways, however, we might want to start worrying as to whether survival is all-or-nothing or a matter of degree. For example, we might think that Russell-at-10 is more reflected in Russell-at-20 than in Russell-at-40 – or in Russell-Now. Or we might think that Russell-Now *preserves* more of Russell-at-40 than of Russell-at-10 (I can certainly remember more of my life as a 40-year-old than of my life as a 10-year-old). In that case, Russell-at-10 may have survived to a greater extent 10 years later than 30 years later.

For current purposes, I want to avoid some of these complexities. Suffice to say that I'm content assuming that what is at stake in all these discussions might not, strictly speaking, be a relationship of identity.[3] But the key question arises with mind uploading whether we talk in terms of personal identity or survival or in any other way that might be appropriate. That is: Can *I* actually look forward to receiving the promised benefits?

Suppose my brain and any other relevant parts of my body (perhaps parts of my central nervous system) have been non-destructively scanned by a super-technological device. This enables a super-scientist to create Russell-in-the-Machine, a functionally isomorphic duplicate of my relevant neural functioning. Because my brain and the rest of my body have not been destroyed or even damaged by the process, the original specimen of *Homo sapiens*, Russell Blackford, continues to exist, experience pleasures and pains, desires, and so on. There are now two conscious beings with similar psychological makeup and the same apparent memories. Let's hope they can get along.

We might want to say that *both* the ongoing human specimen *and* Russell-in-the-Machine are the original me prior to the scan. That seems odd, as they are not the same as each other, but personal identity is not a straightforward concept, as we've seen, and in any event we can follow Derek Parfit's lead and treat this as a case of division in which I survive as both of the resulting persons (1984: 253–266).

Do I, though? Massimo Pigliucci has very different intuitions. Even waiving his objection to the whole idea of computationally achieved consciousness, he insists that the human being who has been non-destructively scanned is straightforwardly the original person, so the machine intelligence that has been created must be no more than a psychological duplicate. It follows that Russell-in-the-Machine would *still* be a mere duplicate of the original Russell if I were scanned destructively. In that situation, taking part in the uploading procedure would not be a way of obtaining extended life, but actually a high-tech way of committing suicide.

Do you share these intuitions? Here is a good way that we can sharpen up the question, borrowed, with appropriate changes, from the late Bernard Williams (1973: 46–63), who was considering the idea of two people exchanging bodies rather than uploading into a computer. Aubrey Townsend has already used the idea for something much like my current purpose (2000: 33), but I will develop it slightly differently.

Suppose that, prior to a non-destructive scanning process, I am told that Russell-in-the-Machine, after he has been created, will be horribly tortured (the aforementioned super-scientist is a *mad* super-scientist whose minions have captured me). Now, I may be appalled by the idea that someone very like me will be tortured – or, if it comes to that, that *anyone* will be tortured – but should I *fear* being tortured in this situation? Will I – or should I – fear being subjected to horrible pain? I might, of course, fear *for* Russell-in-the-Machine: we're all familiar, I imagine, with the idea of *fearing for* someone, or with *fearing that* some terrible event will happen. But these are not the same as fearing an event in the ordinary way.

Conversely, what if I'm told that the Russell-in-the-Machine will be provided with very enjoyable experiences in virtual reality? I may be glad of this, but will I, or should I, look forward to enjoying those experiences?

In these situations, I'm inclined to side with Pigliucci. As I await the unfolding of the mad super-scientist's plans to create and torture Russell-in-the-Machine, I won't actually fear being tortured. That won't change if Russell-in-the-Machine is to be provided with a robot body. Nor will it change if I'm told that after I'm non-destructively scanned 500 digital copies of me will be made. If I'm told that they will all be tortured, but my ongoing human body will not be, I will see it as horrible, but my response will not be one of *fear* in the same sense as if I'm told that the 500 Russells-in-the-Machine will be treated well, while (trying not to put this too tendentiously) the original flesh-and-blood Russell Blackford will be tortured.

If these intuitions are correct, what if my brain (and any other relevant parts of my body) are scanned *destructively*? Once again, a digital copy will be made, and it, or he, may initially "live" in virtual reality, perhaps later being given a robot body. Imagine that I'm told that the original human animal will be disintegrated after the scanning and Russell-in-the-Machine (poor him!) will be tortured. On this scenario, should I fear being tortured sometime in the near future? Well, I did not fear torture (though of course I was appalled by it) in the scenario involving *non*-destructive scanning. I don't see how anything relevant has changed. It still seems that the torture of Russell-in-the-Machine, appalling though it would be, is not something I would fear in the ordinary sense. (However, it does seem that I have *something* to fear if this scenario comes about – namely, death!)

It's true of course, that Russell-in-the-Machine, waking up in a virtual environment, might have no way of knowing that he *is* the digital version – we can assume an environment sufficiently rich in sensory content to achieve that deception. But this is not the point. I am not trying to answer the question of how a sufficiently accurate duplicate will feel. The issue is what experiences I can now look forward to having. If a scenario works in such a way that I do not, and should not, *fear* something happening to Russell-in-the-Machine, then it appears that a symmetry applies: I likewise should not look forward to enjoying any good experiences that apply to this computational being.

By my admittedly vague and tacit criteria of what it is to continue having experiences worth looking forward to (or fearing), there seems to be a critical difference, in these scenarios, between the human animal (Russell-Now or Russell-A-Bit-Later) and the digital twin (Russell-in-the-Machine). There seems to be a difference in the significance for *me* of the respective fates of the continuing human animal and any digital copy or copies. Still, I have not argued for my criteria from first principles, let alone from first principles that are universally accepted. I have not specified them in a systematic way, and you might wonder whether they are even coherent.

Parfit, for one, would insist that what really matter to us are psychological continuity and psychological connectedness (e.g. having similar memories), irrespective of how these come about. If I am replaced by Russell-in-the-Machine, what really matters is what he calls Relation R: "psychological connectedness and/or psychological continuity, with the right kind of cause" (Parfit 1984: 279). Indeed, Parfit thinks that what matters is the combination of psychological continuity and connectedness, fairly much independent of whether it is achieved through a normal causal process involving bodily continuity (1984: 282–287). At most, he suggests, continuity of the same body could have a kind of sentimental value (1984: 286). Thus, Parfit would favor the line of argument developed by Mark Walker when he distinguishes type identity and token identity. Type identity might be maintained in some circumstances where token identity is not.

When Parfit asks himself whether he is a token or a type, he prefers the idea that he is a type (1984: 293–297). Likewise, Walker places much emphasis on type identity, but he is at pains to state that both the token and the type are important. I cannot exactly prove these ideas wrong, but they do conflict with arguments, such as Pigliucci's, based on compelling intuitions. Have we reached an impasse? Could the problem be that a person survives or maintains personal identity only if the right kind of causation is involved? Might the causal process be crucial to the question of survival?

If so, this might support the general case pressed by Corabi and Schneider – that most uploading scenarios fail to preserve what actually matters, irrespective of our preferred understanding of the mind or the self. In this context, Naomi Wellington distinguishes between immanent (internal) causation, such as from the continuity of bodily processes, and transeunt causation, as when the successive frames displayed by a movie projector do not cause each other, but are caused to appear by the projector's "external" operations. If Wellington is correct, we would need to find an uploading process that is sufficiently based on a process of immanent causation.

Deep, compelling, and often conflicting intuitions are involved in this debate. It will doubtless continue, though with escalating levels of sophistication.

5 Contemplating the unimaginable

As Kathleen Goonan notes in her chapter, science fiction authors and film makers have explored these themes for many decades. They have depicted robots, cyborgs, and superintelligent machines, sometimes benign, but often dangerous. Indeed, the science fiction genre's main thematic concerns have always included the impact of scientific advance and technological change. This theme has taken different forms in successive eras of the genre's development, inevitably influenced by hopes and anxieties in the broader culture.

By the 1950s, Arthur C. Clarke was postulating the storage of entire personalities in computers. Thereafter, Clarke's fiction and non-fiction writings developed ideas of humankind's eventual supersession by advanced cybernetic beings (Blackford 2002). During the middle and later decades of the twentieth century, many other writers developed visions of harmony or conflict between humans and machine intelligences. Stanley Kubrick's 1968 movie *2001: A Space Odyssey* (the screenplay was co-authored by Kubrick and Clarke) provides an especially memorable example of conflict when a spaceship's trusted computer, HAL 9000, rebels against the ship's human crew.

Science fiction authors associated with the 1980s cyberpunk movement synthesized elements from many earlier times and styles, but with a dramatic emphasis on cyberspace, rather than the outer space of extraterrestrial exploration or even the "inner space" of human psychology. Classic cyberpunk texts, such as the early stories and novels of William Gibson, tended to imagine the relatively near future, depicting dystopian (or at best, dark and ambiguous) societies here on earth or in nearby space. Ridley Scott's 1982 movie *Blade Runner* provides a *noir* cinematic equivalent to literary cyberpunk.

There has since been a marked change in the standard iconography of the science fiction field as a whole. This is apparent in all media (prose, film, television, comics, and games), and can be seen in space opera set far beyond our local solar system as much as in near-future dystopian narratives. Contemporary science fiction employs a post-cyberpunk imagery: machine intelligence; direct interfacing between human minds and computers; mind uploading, transfer, and storage; and events in computer-generated virtual realities. Victor Grech's chapter in the present volume discusses this ongoing tendency, particularly as it appears in the popular *Star Trek* franchise.

There is deep conflict within the science fiction field between positive and negative portrayals of advanced computer technology. It is shown as cool, impressive, and alluring, offering pleasures and fulfilling many desires. But just as likely, science fiction seems to tell us, it will bring new dangers or somehow undermine valuable aspects of being human. Grech makes a plausible claim when he sees the overall trend in *Star Trek* as cautionary. It seems to warn us not to go *too* boldly where no one has gone before.

We might expect that the transhumanist movement would show less equivocation in embracing ideas of machine intelligence and mind uploading. Briefly, transhumanists foresee a time when technological interventions in the human body and mind will lead to dramatic increases in our capacities. They look forward to a transition from human to "posthuman." The proposal that we might upload our minds into highly durable computer hardware, thereafter interfacing with the world in complex ways, is popular among transhumanists, as are efforts to develop very powerful, versatile, recursively self-improving machine intelligence.

But much as we saw with the science fiction genre, transhumanist thought identifies both promises and threats in technological advances. Though the general feeling remains radically optimistic, much recent transhumanist writing shows a surprisingly dystopian tinge, as the authors contemplate what might go wrong. One focus relates to existential risks: what could go *very* wrong, perhaps cataclysmically so, on a global scale … and what might be done in an attempt to prevent it. In particular, transhumanists frequently express a concern that machine superintelligence could become a threat to humanity.

Compare James Barrat's recent book, *Our Final Invention: Artificial Intelligence and the End of the Human Era*. This concentrates on the possible downside of machine intelligence, emphasizing its "existential threat to mankind." As Barrat puts it, "I've written this book to warn you that artificial intelligence could drive mankind into extinction, and to explain how that catastrophic outcome is not just possible, but likely if we do not begin preparing very carefully *now*." He adds: "please consider this a heartfelt invitation to join the most important conversation humanity can have" (Barratt 2013: 16).

Some computer experts are already involved in efforts to ensure that any superintelligent machines will, indeed, be benevolent. This is a daunting project, involving a quest to understand the nature of benevolence, human sympathy, and morality, and how these could be programmed into the deepest design levels of machine intelligences. In their chapter, Ben Goertzel and Joel Pitt explain a set of detailed proposals aimed at ensuring that we can live happily in the same world as our mind children.

What might the future be like, on an optimistic approach? We probably can't imagine this in detail, but several contributors offer their overviews. Natasha Vita-More discusses the implications of whole-body prosthetics: the design of custom-made systems of technology to augment the capacities of future human beings and cater to their varied desires. Joe Strout describes a splendidly diverse future where we'll have easy access to highly individualized artificial bodies, while insisting that much about human experience will remain unchanged. Richard Loosemore evokes the practically inexhaustible possibilities if we obtain the technology for what he calls "qualia surfing" – that is, if we could modify or transfer our minds so as to sample a vast new range of sensations, thoughts, emotions, and viewpoints. Nicole Olson considers the likely values of uploaded and enhanced minds, suggesting that they would seek "increased complexity, diversity, emergence, beauty, specialization, and freedom."

Max More responds to one popular objection to mind uploading: that uploading proposals are motivated by a disdain for embodied sensory experience. He argues persuasively that the desire is not to seek an attenuated, purely intellectual existence; rather, it is to extend our physical, sensory, and social lives beyond current limits.

For a less optimistic picture, see the dispassionate analysis by Robin Hanson of what a society of uploads might be like. Though he expects that many readers will find the picture he draws quite repugnant, he urges us to imagine how the citizens of this world might regard *us*, and what might provide them with enjoyment, pride, and pleasure.

6 The future is coming

Grant, if you would, that full-scale machine intelligence and mind uploading are possible. In that case, humankind is confronted with the threat, or the promise, of sharing the world with conscious, non-biological beings who might be our intellectual equals or superiors. There are then important questions as to whether it would be a good idea to bring them into existence. Might the remaining base-line humans come to regret the outcome if they are outclassed and superseded?

But perhaps a world with machine intelligence and uploading will be desirable, all things considered. Even on that stronger assumption, how do we get there from here? Doubtless there will be technical, political, and ethical problems to solve. As to the latter, our mind children will have their own desires, emotions, and vulnerabilities. Like us, they'll be able to suffer and mourn. What responsibilities might we have to them if we press ahead?

Assuming that there can be a viable research program for creating whole brain emulations in computer hardware, it will inevitably involve the use of laboratory animals, which may suffer discomfort or pain. Most likely, many animals will need to be killed to examine their neurological structures. An obvious question is whether the likely benefits of the research can justify this use of sentient creatures. And what about the simulated minds themselves, some of which might be damaged compared to their "originals," and would, in any event, be able to experience yearning and suffering? We seem to need a new body of ethics for research into mind uploading in particular, especially in respect of our conduct toward uploaded minds (whether those of human beings or those of non-human animals). Anders Sandberg deals with much of this in his long, searching chapter.

Our distinguished contributors have much to say about AI and its many prospects, and particularly about our possible mind children: intelligent beings that we might bring about through advanced computer science and robotics. The chapters that follow express a wide range of viewpoints: some show enthusiasm about the prospects of machine intelligence and mind uploading, while others express skepticism or concern. Nothing in this book can be the last word, but we trust that there is much to advance public understanding of what is at stake.

Notes

1 I owe most of the language of this paragraph to Damien Broderick. My thanks to Dr. Broderick for much assistance in clarifying my thoughts on these issues.
2 There are some notable exceptions. See, for example, Swinburne (2013).
3 The philosophical problems here are notoriously complex, indeed, I dare say, mind-boggling. A classic, but highly controversial, analysis can be found in Derek Parfit's *Reasons and Persons* (1984: 199–347).

References

Barrat, James. 2013. *Our Final Invention: Artificial Intelligence and the End of the Human Era*. New York: Tor.

Blackford, Russell. 2002. Stranger than you think: Arthur C. Clarke's *Profiles of The Future*. In Darren Tofts, Annemarie Jonson, and Alessio Cavallaro, eds., *Prefiguring Cyberculture: An Intellectual History*. Sydney: Power Publications / Cambridge, MA: MIT Press, pp. 252–263.

Moravec, Hans. 1988. *Mind Children: The Future of Robot and Human Intelligence*. Cambridge, MA: Harvard University Press.

Moravec, Hans. 1999. *Robot: Mere Machine to Transcendent Mind*. New York: Oxford University Press.

Parfit, Derek. 1984. *Reasons and Persons*. Oxford and New York: Oxford University Press.

Searle, John. 1984. *Minds, Brains, and Science*. Cambridge, MA: Harvard University Press.

Swinburne, Richard. 2013. *Mind, Brain, and Free Will*. Oxford: Oxford University Press.

Townsend, Aubrey. 2000. Survival in cyberspace. *Foundation* 78: 25–33.

Tucker, Patrick. 2013. *The future is not a destination:* The Futurist *magazine's top 10 forecasts for 2014 and beyond*. slate.com/articles/technology/future_tense/2013/10/futurist_magazine_s_predictions_on_quantum_computing_big_data_and_more.html (accessed October 2, 2013).

Williams, Bernard. 1973. *Problems of the Self: Philosophical Papers 1956–1972*. London: Cambridge University Press.

1

How Conscience Apps and Caring Computers will Illuminate and Strengthen Human Morality

James J. Hughes

1 Introduction

The biopolitics of intervening directly in the body with drugs, genes, and wires have always been far more fraught than the issues surrounding the use of gadgets. This is odd, since the rapidly changing exocortex comprising computers, smartphones, and wearables has changed the lives of billions in profound ways, accomplishing things that we are decades away from achieving with neurotechnology and brain–machine interfaces. While eventually we will have safe brain prostheses to record and recall information directly from our neurons, we first figured out how to download, store, and re-upload memory from our brains thousands of years ago with the invention of writing. Now the exocortex permits us to record photos and videos, names and places, poetry, or how many steps we've taken, and to recall all that, or the contents of thousands of libraries and newspapers, with a couple of seconds' retrieval lag. The horror and enthusiasm that our cyborg future excites clearly have more to do with the transgression of the body's boundaries than with the actual enhancements it will bring, since those enhancements are or will be accessible far more cheaply, safely, and upgradably in wearables and gadgets.

Which is not to say that there isn't a chorus of critics of the effects of the exocortex. Susan Greenfield (2009), Nicholas Carr (2011), and Sherry Turkle (2012) have become spokespeople for the dystopian view that our infatuation with gadgets, multitasking, and constant distractions from the

Intelligence Unbound: The Future of Uploaded and Machine Minds, First Edition.
Edited by Russell Blackford and Damien Broderick.

Net and social media is crippling our capacity for authentic attention and connection to one another. Writer Linda Stone has coined the term "continuous partial attention" (Fallows 2013) to describe our state of continuous distraction, degrading our productivity, causing auto accidents, and increasing our levels of stress about what we might be missing on YouTube, Facebook, and Twitter. Cognitive scientists are meanwhile documenting the near-impossibility of true multitasking (Loukopoulos et al. 2009), arguing that the more we attempt it the poorer our cognitive capacity becomes.

As this anxiety about the downsides of the connected life has grown, however, so also have the efforts to address these problems with digital solutions. Just as seatbelts and airbags are technologies that improve the safety of the technology of the automobile, myriad digital solutions are being developed to mitigate the negative aspects of digital life. As these technologies develop they may even allow us to improve our behavior over our natural baseline, and to enhance our capacities for flourishing, connection, and moral behavior.

In the last five years, the debate over the desirability and feasibility of moral enhancement has focused mostly on the use of specific drugs and neurochemicals to improve our capacity for empathy (Crockett et al. 2010; Douglas 2008; Persson and Savulescu 2010, 2011). Critics like Zarpentine (2013), however, have pointed out the inadequacies of our understanding of the effects of moral doping compared to the thousands of years of experience in shaping character through education and spiritual practices. In this chapter I will explore the way that conscience apps and morality software are an underexplored bridge between the traditional forms of moral enhancement and the more invasive methods that we will develop eventually. Just as our collective IQ has been raised far more by ubiquitous access to the Net than by stimulants and modafinil, non-invasive digital forms of behavior modification will likely have a far wider and more profound effect in the coming decades, even though they arouse neither as much enthusiasm nor the same revulsion as empathy pills and utilitarian gene-tweaks.

As a framework to parse these potential behavior improvements, I will use the virtue ethics schema I have been exploring in my recent writings (Hughes 2012, 2013): the core elements are self-control, caring, moral cognition, mindfulness, and wisdom or intelligence.

2 Self-control

Evan Selinger begins his essay "Why It's OK to Let Apps Make You a Better Person" (2012): "one theme emerges from the media coverage of people's relationships with our current set of technologies: Consumers want digital willpower." But it is more accurate to say that human beings have always craved more willpower since they began to understand the benefits of denied gratification, and they have always enlisted the technologies of their time in the pursuit of self-control. Monks' robes, priests' collars, and wedding rings all enlist community support for vows of sexual restraint. From hair shirts to alarm clocks to wiring teeth together as a diet aid, we have attempted to use tools to reinforce our good intentions.

Changing your relationship status on Facebook and taking down your eHarmony profile as public commitments to monogamy are as important today as weddings and rings. We can avoid temptations by leaving the Safe Search filter on when Googling and posting our weight-loss progress on our profile. Perhaps these ubiquitous forms of inconspicuous self-control are the most effective, since they are not flagged as moral self-control. But there are also numerous tools for more conscious exercises of restraint. The psychologist Dan Ariely, for instance, designed the Conscience+ app, which lists five arguments to resist temptation and five arguments to give in to temptation, in dozens of situations, such as eating dessert, buying a new gadget, lying, and exercising.

The app StikK allows users to set up public commitments to give money to charities if they fail to stick to goals such as giving up smoking. The Urge app suggests that users delay impulse purchases so they can reach budgeting goals, and tracks the money saved toward the purchase of a desired item. In the Canadian province of Ontario, gambling addicts can submit their photographs to state-run casinos, which now use facial recognition to keep them out (Vance 2012). Tens of millions of people use online food and exercise diaries like MyFitnessPal, LoseIt, and ShapeUp, apps that allow users to share their diet and exercise progress with clinicians, family, and friends, providing the kind of social support that Weight Watchers has found so successful. Wearable technologies are also expanding the possibilities for self-control. The use of wearable devices like FitBit and BodyMedia Fit, which track exercise and calories burned, is expected to explode in the coming years, as are ways of tracking in real time many other biometric indicators such as calorie burning (Young 2013), blood pressure, blood sugar, and focus. Apps like Quicken, LearnVest, Budgt, and Mint are giving people easier ways to track their expenditures, savings, and budget goals.

3 Caring

Although the technoskeptics claim that digital distraction is impairing our face-to-face relationships and capacity for empathy, there is ample evidence that digital connection is enhancing connection, caring, and compassionate action. In 2011, the Pew Internet & American Life Project found for instance that people who use Facebook have *more* "close, core ties in their overall social network compared with other internet users" (Hampton et al. 2011). Texting and social media allow us to maintain larger social networks, staying connected with people we never meet, and to have more constant, effortless communication with our core social network. When I went to college, I had to make an effort to write and call my mother. When my daughter went to college we set up a laptop with Skype in the kitchen to check in once a day, and faculty grouse that students are constantly in touch with their parents.

Beyond staying connected to distant friends and family, digital life allows us increasingly immediate access to the lives of people around the globe. Amidst the distractions of the information whirlwind are growing numbers of images and stories about human suffering, and increasingly streamlined ways to help people in your life or on the other side of the planet. Although the returns on clicking Like on a cause on Facebook, or re-tweeting a news item, are less than giving money or volunteering time to a cause, we can stay involved in a much higher number of causes. When aggregated with millions of other members of the digerati, "hacktivism" can generate equally momentous real-world effects on targets such as corporations and governments.

Other examples of exocortically facilitated compassion are:

- Compassion, an app that helps you identify and sponsor poor children in the developing world.
- JustGive, an app that facilitates finding, following, and giving to charities.
- Charity Miles, an app that streamlines charity walking and running challenges.
- VolunteerMatch and Save the Children's Earthquake Response, apps that connect would-be volunteers and donors to local needs.

4 Fairness and moral cognition

There is a growing body of literature on the irrational biases that shape our moral decision-making in ways that we would generally want to avoid (Greene 2009). A picture is emerging of a constant negotiation between our innate moral sentiments like disgust, loyalty, and submission to authority rooted in the old brain systems like the amygdala, and the conscious moral reasoning and beliefs mediated through the cortex. People become more censorious of immoral behavior when they smell bad odors or feel stickiness on their hands (Schnall et al. 2008). Judges give harsher sentences when they are hungry. People make different moral judgments depending on the subjects' social status or attractiveness, and the amount of testosterone or serotonin in their own brain (Crockett et al. 2010). It is clear that we could all use some external coaching to improve our moral reasoning.

In a sense, electronic Bible or Quran study and the Christian fad for "What Would Jesus Do?" bracelets are already exocortical aids intended to improve moral decision-making. But many secular digital aids are also emerging (Selinger and Seager 2012). The New York State Bar Association, for instance, has created an app that gives users access to more than 900 decisions of their Professional Ethics Committee on issues confronting judges and attorneys (NYSBA 2012). MoralCompass provides a flowchart of moral decision-making questions, and SeeSaw allows users to query other users about which action they should take in a situation (Statt 2013). The online *Encyclopedia of Ethical Failure* is a compendium of government fraud and abuse, compiled to educate public employees about ethical lapses to avoid. The app ToneCheck screens our digital communications for coarse or hostile speech, placing an automatic hold on messages that, after reflection, we may not want to send.

Secular ethics assistants will also likely emerge from the efforts to design "moral machines" (Wallach and Allen 2011) and ethical artificial intelligence (Anderson and Anderson 2007). Some of this work is being done in order to provide onboard rules of engagement for autonomous battlefield robots, but there are applications for robots in many occupations, including industry, transportation, and medicine. The effort to codify and balance all the factual and value considerations involved in messy, human moral decision-making will be very complicated, and result in multiple possible morality settings, since there is wide moral variability in humans. Eventually, these morality AIs will become a seamless part of our own cognition, allowing us to choose consciously to act in ways we otherwise would find difficult.

5 Mindfulness

In order to act morally we need to be able to pay attention to our lives, and not constantly be distracted by rumination and digital noise. There are now dozens of anti-digital distraction apps, including:

- TimeOut, which tracks your computer use and reminds you to take breaks at pre-set intervals.
- FocusBooster, which organizes your to-do list, tracks your progress, and reminds you with an alarm to take a break every 25 minutes.
- Freedom, which locks you out of Internet access for a specified time.

- StayFocused and Anti-Social, which block access to social media websites like Facebook.
- TrackTime and RescueTime, which monitor your computer activity and give you a regular report card on the amount of time you spent on social media, email, writing and other activities.
- Spaces, Think, and Dark Room, writing programs that take up the full screen, hiding email and social media reminders.
- DriveMode, Textecution, and Text-STAR, which block talking or texting on your phone while your car is moving.
- DriveScribe, which records how well you stay within the speed limit and obey traffic signals, and gives you points to be redeemed as gift cards.
- SimpeEnergy, which tracks energy use and shares energy conservation progress with friends and neighbors.

There are also apps that remind you to be mindful at particular times or in particular places, like the Mindfulness app. The app Habit Maker lets users track how often they perform specific behaviors, such as saying "thank you" or exercising. There are apps that provide short guided meditations to do while at home, in the office, walking, or in the gym, like Simply Being or the Mindfulness Meditation app by Mental Workout.

The development of consumer versions of bio- and neurofeedback technologies, such as the mobile EEG headsets from Neurosky, Melon, and Emotiv, is currently being applied to tracking and improving meditation. Biozen, a freeware app designed for the US Department of Defense for use by soldiers being treated for PTSD, records multiple streams of information from multiple types of bio- and neurofeedback hardware, including EEGs, and provides images that react to the sensors. As these bio- and neuromonitoring tools become smaller and less conspicuous they can also be integrated into daily life to track and fine-tune focus and attention.

6 Intelligence

Unlike the accumulating evidence of substantial effects on the brain and social behavior from mindfulness meditation, so far the apps and brain-games being sold to increase cognitive flexibility or intelligence appear to do little more than improve the capacity to perform the tasks specific to the game, such as word recall in crossword puzzles, memory in N-Back, or hand–eye coordination in first-person shooters (Melby-Lervåg and Hulme 2013). The gains in these specific skills also appear to be transitory.

Nonetheless, if we include our exocortical capacities in our definition of working intelligence and memory, the increasing ease with which we have access to vast amounts of information is making us much more intelligent. We can remember more things and apply more and better information to our daily life. A large amount of effort is being put into online and computerized forms of education, validated with concrete learning outcomes, that will undoubtedly clarify which types of exercises do improve real-world decision-making skills. These will all start as part of our wearable exocortical assistants and ubiquitous computing environment, then be integrated with "augmented cognition" devices that finetune our attentiveness and learning, and then be integrated into the brain–machine interfaces to come.

7 Conclusions

Critics of morality apps point to the alleged inauthenticity and shallowness of behavior change when it is technologically assisted (Selinger 2012). But humans have long enlisted technology in the aid of moral enhancement, from visible markers of vows like rings and uniforms, to self- or state-imposed castration. Developing ethical software as an adjunct to self-guided behavior change – an exocortical layer to the super-ego – is only novel in its flexibility, not in its purpose. Moreover, it will be far more widely and quickly adopted than the forms of pharmaceutical and genetic modification of moral behavior currently being discussed as forms of "moral enhancement."

Because of its rapid adoption, with effects as significant as drugs and gene therapies, we also must confront some of the social challenges exocortical moral enhancement will pose. For instance, how do we ensure that these tools are not used to restrict individual autonomy and psychological diversity, and to enforce authoritarian state control or control in the workplace? The firm Citizen, which designs mobile technology, has begun collecting data from its workers on how much they exercise, what they eat, how much they sleep, their mood, and how productive they are at work (Finley 2013). While this system is voluntary, one could imagine an employer making such self-monitoring a precondition for employment, or a health insurer requiring monitoring as a precondition for a lower premium, or a state imposing monitoring on its citizens. As with all technological innovation, the potential for abuse is best addressed through political mobilization, and not by restricting the technology itself. In liberal societies, the moral exocortex will largely be self-imposed and self-controlled, and pressures from employers and the state to impose control will be resisted in the workplace, the courts, and legislatures.

If individuals have a wide variety of moral software to choose among, and these choices are self-imposed, we can hope for a robust, evolving ecosystem of moral enhancement tools, helping the average person achieve a new level of moral self-control and consistency. Eventually these softwares will be woven into the brain–machine interfaces we adopt to augment our cognition, and become more effective than the methods of character development we have employed in the past.

References

Anderson, M., and Anderson, S.L. 2007. Machine ethics: Creating an ethical intelligent agent. *AI Magazine* 28(4): 15–26.

Carr, N. 2011. *The Shallows: What the Internet is Doing to Our Brains*. New York: W.W. Norton.

Crockett, M.J., Clark, L., Hauser, M.D., and Robbins, T.W. 2010. Serotonin selectively influences moral judgment and behavior through effects on harm aversion. *PNAS* 107: 17433–17438.

Douglas, T. 2008. Moral enhancement. *Journal of Applied Philosophy* 25: 228–245.

Fallows, J. 2013. The art of staying focused in a distracting world. *The Atlantic*, May 22, http://www.theatlantic.com/magazine/archive/2013/06/the-art-of-paying-attention/309312/ (accessed August 24, 2013).

Finley, K. 2013. What if your boss tracked your sleep, diet and exercise? *Wired*, April 17, http://www.wired.com/wiredenterprise/2013/04/quantified-work-citizen/ (accessed August 24, 2013).

Greene, J.D. 2009. The cognitive neuroscience of moral judgment. In M.S. Gazzaniga, ed., *The Cognitive Neurosciences*, 4th edn. Cambridge, MA: MIT Press, pp. 987–999.

Greenfield, S. 2009. *Tomorrow's People: How 21st-Century Technology Is Changing the Way We Think and Feel*. London: Penguin.

Hampton, K., Goulet, L.S., Rainie, L., and Purcell, K. 2011. *Social Networking Sites and Our Lives*. Washington DC: Pew Research Center's Internet and American Life Project.

Hughes, J. 2012. After happiness, cyborg virtue. *Free Inquiry* 32(1): 34–37.

Hughes, J. 2013. Using neurotechnologies to develop virtues: A Buddhist approach to cognitive enhancement. *Accountability in Research: Policies & Quality Assurance* 20(1): 27–41.

Loukopoulos, L.D., Dismukes, R.K., and Barshi, I. 2009. *The Multitasking Myth: Handling Complexity in Real-World Operations*. Farnham, Surrey: Ashgate.

Melby-Lervåg, M., and Hulme, C. 2013. Is working memory training effective? A meta-analytic review. *Developmental Psychology* 49(2): 270–291.

NYSBA (New York State Bar Association). 2012. *New York State Bar Association creates free app providing access to ethics opinions*, http://www.old.nysba.org/AM/Template.cfm?Section=News_Center&template=/CM/ContentDisplay.cfm&ContentID=61692 (accessed August 24, 2013).

Persson, I., and Savulescu, J. 2010. Moral transhumanism. *The Journal of Medicine and Philosophy* 35: 656–669.

Persson, I., and Savulescu, J. 2011. Unfit for the future? Human nature, scientific progress, and the need for moral enhancement. In J. Savulescu, J., R. ter Meulen, and G. Kahane, eds., *Enhancing Human Capacities*. Malden, MA: Wiley-Blackwell, pp. 486–500.

Schnall, S., Haidt, J., Clore, G.L., and Jordan, A.H. 2008. Disgust as embodied moral judgment. *Personal and Social Psychology Bulletin* 34(8): 1096–1109.

Selinger, Evan. 2012. Why it's OK to let apps make you a better person. *The Atlantic*, http://www.theatlantic.com/technology/archive/2012/03/why-its-ok-to-let-apps-make-you-a-better-person/254246/ (accessed August 13, 2013).

Selinger, E., and Seager, T. 2012. Digital Jiminy Crickets: Do apps that promote ethical behavior diminish our ability to make just decisions? *Slate* July 13, http://www.slate.com/articles/technology/future_tense/2012/07/ethical_decision_making_apps_damage_our_ability_to_make_moral_choices_.html (accessed August 22, 2013).

Statt, M. 2013. *Seesaw app could bring "Wisdom of the Crowd" to moral dilemmas*. ReadWrite.com. April 27, http://readwrite.com/2013/04/27/seesaw-app-could-bring-wisdom-of-the-crowd-to-moral-dilemmas (accessed August 24, 2013).

Turkle, S. 2012. *Alone Together: Why We Expect More from Technology and Less from Each Other*. New York: Basic Books.

Vance, A. 2012. Privacy-friendly way to ban gambling addicts from casinos. *Business Week*. August 29, businessweek.com/articles/2012-08-29/a-privacy-friendly-way-to-ban-gambling-addicts-from-casinos (accessed August 13, 2013).

Wallach, W., and Allen, C. 2011. *Moral Machines*. New York: Oxford University Press.

Young, S. 2013. A breathalyzer that knows when you are burning fat. *Technology Review*, August 8, http://www.technologyreview.com/news/517806/a-breathalyzer-that-knows-when-youre-burning-fat/ (accessed August 24, 2013).

Zarpentine, C. 2013. "The thorny and arduous path of moral progress": Moral psychology and moral enhancement. *Neuroethics* 6: 141–153.

2

Threshold Leaps in Advanced Artificial Intelligence

Michael Anissimov

Of all possible future agents with greater-than-human intelligence, the one that stands out as the most potentially powerful is sophisticated artificial intelligence (AI). This is because the term "artificial intelligence" refers not to a specific architecture but to a wide range of possibilities: any mind constructed artificially. Assuming we grant that artificial intelligence will eventually be able to perform all the tasks that human minds do, and more, the space of possible AI minds far exceeds the size of all human minds that have ever existed. Some of these minds will include powerful agents capable of reshaping the world.

The possible dimensions of cognitive variation range from hardware materials to processing speed, to overall architecture, to algorithmic specifics, to size, to internal communication speed between cognitive elements, and more. For instance, by the time smarter-than-human artificial intelligence is developed (estimates range from 2029 to 2100 and beyond, with 2070 as the median), there may be computers constructed from non-silicon components, such as carbon nanotubes. These could be considerably faster than today's silicon computers. In terms of overall architecture, the human brain uses a hundred billion parallel processors – neurons – that operate at the comparatively slow speed of 200 spikes per second. Artificial intelligences are likely to have far fewer processors, though each individual processor would be hundreds of millions of times faster than biological neurons. Alternatively, an artificial intelligence might have millions of processors, all of them hundreds of millions of times faster than biological neurons. Even the cheapest

Intelligence Unbound: The Future of Uploaded and Machine Minds, First Edition.
Edited by Russell Blackford and Damien Broderick.

laptop computer chips today are tens of millions of times faster than neurons. Of course, a neuron in a brain is not perfectly analogous to a transistor in a microprocessor, nor is neural spiking directly comparable with switching time on a transistor. Still, some direct comparisons of speed might be applicable.

Cataloging all the possible dimensions of variation in artificial intelligence relative to human minds would be a huge project, requiring a comprehensive knowledge of minds in general that science simply does not yet have. Even beginning to build such a catalog requires deep interdisciplinary knowledge of cognitive science and computer science, which is still relatively rare. Most commentators on the future of artificial intelligence have a background from one or the other, or even in philosophy with minimal knowledge of cognitive or computer science. This can cause most academics to underestimate the possible dimensions of variation.

There is a tendency to see "intelligence" as an archetype that essentially corresponds to "humanness." This leads futurists to visualize advanced artificial intelligences as genius humans, only more so. To see a similar parallel, consider the historical view of robotics. Early conceptions of sophisticated robots saw them as humanoids. It is natural to assume that we will build robots in the image of what we understand best – ourselves. Humanoid robots have the immediate advantage of being able to use tools designed for the human form, for instance. However, as our technical understanding of locomotion in general and robotics in general has increased and our collective imagination has blossomed, we now build or visualize robots in a much wider range of forms, from hummingbird-like robotic drones, to Boston Robotics' cheetah and mule-like robots, to springtail-like robots or the curious octopus-looking Sentinels from the *Matrix* film trilogy.

Our understanding of the space of possible robotic forms is still very primitive. We are predisposed to taking inspiration from nature, the biological "robots" built by natural selection, but we can safely say that there are thousands of potential robotic forms that are entirely novel and not directly inspired by natural organisms. For instance, consider a ball with thousands of protruding and interlocking appendages, like a flexible, mechanical analog of a sea urchin. No animal in nature has a form quite like this, but there is no reason why it could not eventually be built. Human imagination can conceive of things that natural selection did not. If such mechanical forms eventually come into being, we'll have demonstrated a new aspect of evolution, an alternative path to existence besides competing directly with existing evolved life forms. This path represents a wonderful and delightfully mind-boggling example of an evolved structure – the human mind – creating a tunnel through the natural-selection mountain range, a barrier that has constrained all other naturally evolved structures.

There is a clear difference between natural selection and intelligent engineering. Dogs can evolve, rocket planes cannot. Natural selection does not evenly sample from the space of all possible body plans (bauplans), it can only incrementally update the few basic bauplans it has available. Many exotic animal body plans from the Cambrian and Avalon evolutionary "explosions" (542 and 575 million years ago, respectively) were selected out, never to be used again. Besides these bauplans that were discarded, there is a much wider space of potential bauplans that were simply inaccessible to evolutionary design. The essence of evolution is incrementalism. Unless there is an incremental path to complex features, where each step on the path offers a concrete adaptive benefit to the organism using it, or at least neutrality, a feature will not evolve. This has prevented the evolution of organisms that use wheel-like structures for locomotion, for instance. (Rotifers, sometimes dubbed "wheel animals," don't have rotating structures.)

Consider the notorious problem of the evolution of the eye. For centuries, this complex organ perplexed naturalists. Biblical creationists in the nineteenth and twentieth centuries used it as an example for what is now called Intelligent Design, arguing that it could never have arisen through natural selection. Of what use is half an eye? However, after many years of arduous work, organisms were discovered that had incrementally useful versions of this organ, from the light-sensitive patches on aquatic worms to the pinhole-camera eye of the living fossil, the nautilus. Eventually it became evident, once the evolutionary mechanism of pre-adaptation was understood in the context of natural selection, how the eye could have evolved incrementally.

Truly intelligent engineering has the advantage that it can throw out everything and redesign from scratch. An engineer sitting at a computer screen might in a week design a robot that natural selection would take millions of years to evolve, if ever: robots that can be deployed by other robots, or even robots that can build other robots. Darwinian organisms, other than humans, can only build copies of themselves via reproduction, but robots could one day build many other different types of robots. The only analogy in the natural world to robots building dissimilar robots would be us humans, beginning to unravel the code of life and design purpose-built organisms, such as glowing plants, fluorescent fish, and goats or sheep ("pharm animals") that secrete pharmaceuticals in their milk.

1 Explosive improvement

Just as we can't envision the full suite of possible robotic forms, some of which already are quite grandiose and powerful (consider Amazon's highly automated warehouses), it is difficult to predict the full extent of *cognitive* forms. These will exceed the thinking capacity of individual humans, and eventually of human civilization as a whole, on a grand scale. The performance gap between sophisticated AI brains and human brains will be even greater than the gap between robotic and human bodies, because of the complex and highly energetic nature of powerful computers. These performance features will include: AI minds that do not tire, can work endlessly on boring or difficult problems, can collaborate as "telepathic" (electronically communicating) collectives, operate at thousands, millions, or even billions of times the speed of human thought, have a far greater working memory and capacity for symbolic thought, fluidly blend creative and mechanistic thought processes, rearrange their cognitive structure to specialize in solving specific problems, and improve their own code and hardware.

This last feature could lead to the greatest leaps and bounds, including discontinuous threshold effects. Once a robotic brain can design and build its own hardware effectively, the self-improvement loop could become explosive. This is why the British mathematician I.J. Good (1916–2009) coined the term "intelligence explosion," the source of which would be an "ultraintelligent machine," defined as "a machine that can far surpass all the intellectual activities of any man however clever" (Good 1965: 33).

Some writers have criticized this intelligence explosion hypothesis on the basis that a mind wouldn't be able to construct a mind smarter than itself. However, this is a logical fallacy. Conservation of intelligence is not a natural law like conservation of mass and energy. Stupid processes can and do add up to create intelligent beings cleverer than the sum of their parts. For instance, the brightest human minds were produced by evolution and natural selection, a dumb process (dumb enough that it took billions of years to produce us). Similarly, Einstein's parents were able to produce a child smarter than themselves. Even more striking are the cognitive dynamics of a system like the chess-playing AI Deep Blue, which is just based on huge search trees; no powerful pattern-recognition or "general intelligence" went into it. So too with the *Jeopardy!*-playing AI Watson. Although the low-level algorithms of these systems are relatively primitive, when you pump enough computing power into them, they defeat the best human players in their domains, even at games as subtle and complex as *Jeopardy!* More than half of all market trading is also performed by relatively simple AI systems, entrusted with trillions of dollars and minimal human oversight. Financial quants (quantitative analysts) have described this process as "Converting electricity into money."

The most important threshold in artificial intelligence will be the creation of minds that can purchase and install their own hardware, and develop robotic means to affect the real world. At the start, sophisticated robotics would not be required; the "robots" of this advanced AI would be human beings. (Ironically, the Czech word "robota," which was borrowed for automatons, refers to human toiling at forced labor.) AI projects that previously consisted of human engineers improving the AI will develop into shared improvement and then into fully autonomous AI self-improvement. An AI system can be considered autonomous if the humans assisting in its construction are regarded as interchangeable.

What's more, suppose an AI is being constructed as part of a military project, and its creators decide to "pull the plug." Rather than fight this fate, a sophisticated AI could simply copy itself onto hardware systems elsewhere, either over the Internet, or using human beings as its proxies. The Internet is already so ubiquitous, it is likely that sophisticated artificial intelligences of the future will have direct or indirect access to it unless they are deliberately isolated in secure "sandboxes."

Scenarios such as these, long the stuff of science fiction, have begun to attract serious attention from security analysts. Even if such an event is 40, 50, 60, or even 100 years off, it would be the most transformative event in the history of the planet, far greater than the founding of civilization, the development of electricity, and the Industrial Revolution combined. An AI that could replicate itself and aggregate its own hardware would constitute a new intelligent species, with which we would henceforth share the planet. Rather than getting distracted with speculation about its possible motives, which has been considered at length elsewhere, it is worth focusing exclusively on the concrete technical means by which this development could occur.

2 Scenarios of AI emergence

Previous discussion of explosive AI growth, postulated to occur after the human-equivalency barrier has been broken, has often pointed to the possibility of an AI developing advanced nanotechnology, that is, molecular nanotechnology (which is actually a form of micro-robotics), bootstrapping from present-day protein-folding technology. However, this historical focus on molecular nanotechnology in the context of explosive AI growth is unfortunate because the use of nanotechnology for mass manufacturing and the creation of rapid infrastructure is so highly speculative. By contrast, improvement scenarios based on less speculative technology can be envisioned that carry a higher credibility.

Arguably, a more credible scenario is an AI utilizing the existing infrastructure of human civilization to bootstrap itself to global significance. Consider online workspaces like oDesk and Amazon's Mechanical Turk.

These websites enable employers to hire workers for computer-based tasks. A sophisticated artificial intelligence could complete many such tasks simultaneously, earning money far faster than any human worker. This money could be reinvested to rent cloud computing resources, like the Amazon Elastic Compute Cloud (EC2), which could then be used to perform further tasks and earn more money, while creating actual wealth. In this way, a clever artificial intelligence with roughly human-equivalent intelligence could quickly expand to dominate a large portion of the online workforce.

An artificial intelligence of this kind could treat cognitive processes in the same way that Henry Ford treated the production of automobiles. Human thinkers today are analogous to the skilled craftsman, painstakingly producing each thought with the full weight of their cognitive resources and individual care. AI thinkers could blithely throw out cognitive resources not directly useful to the task at hand. Does the market need solutions that pertain to a certain specific type of analytic thinking, say, delivery optimization? An AI might temporarily put into storage those cognitive modules that do not directly pertain to solving the problem, and make a thousand copies of only those modules that are optimized for solving it. In this way, an artificial intelligence could turn itself into a streamlined money-making machine, simultaneously creating actual wealth for those who create and own the AI, while depriving of that wealth all who attempt to compete against it unless special measures are taken to avoid this disaster.

The human capacity for reason and autonomous decision-making is based on the specifications of our brain, which runs at approximately 2×10^{13} operations per second (ops/sec), computed by multiplying the number of neurons (roughly 10^{11}) by the firing speed of those neurons (200 times a second at most). This is comparable to 20 teraflops, whereas the fastest computer today already runs at 33.86 petaflops, more than a thousand times faster. The "flops" in a modern computer are actually not directly comparable to operations in human neurons because the computing operations are actually much more flexible and mathematically powerful, but for the sake of argument, let's say that they are approximately analogous. A "typical" supercomputer, say an NVIDIA® Tesla® GPU Accelerator, which costs from about $3,000 to $7,000 depending on model, clocks in at around 4 teraflops. This puts the cost of human brain-equivalent computing power at about $30,000, assuming $6,000 per ~4 teraflop computer.

How quickly could the AI in our model gather up a marginal $30,000 to purchase a human-equivalent unit of computing power? If the AI starts out with a million dollars of computing resources in 2014 terms, this would be sufficient to purchase about 166 Tesla supercomputers, providing 664 teraflops of computing power. That works out to 33.2 human brain-equivalent units of computing power (much of it expended on keeping the body functioning correctly). Say that the AI is clever enough to break up 20 human brain-equivalent units into 200 units of dedicated "cognitive assembly line" that can earn $50 an hour in programming jobs, working an average of 40 hours a week. (We can make that stipulation for the sake of conservative comparison, while recognizing that AI can and will surely run 24/7.)

An additional five human-brain equivalents of cognitive performance would be used for high-level creativity and supervision not possible for the rote cognitive processors. We can set aside the remaining balance for now (it makes the math easier). This sums to $200 a week per unit, times 200 units, working out to $40,000 a week in earnings for the entire million-dollar supercomputer. Each unit consumes perhaps one-tenth of a human brain-equivalent, or 2 teraflops. This machine could pay for itself in about six months, or more productively, recycle those earnings into renting flexible cloud computing resources, even using these admittedly unrealistically conservative assumptions.

Assume the machine rents itself cloud computing resources from the Amazon Elastic Compute Cloud. One commonly rented computing instance available, "m1.large," provides a dual-core processor with 7.5 GB of RAM, a 64-bit architecture, 850 GB disk, running at 6 gigaflops of multiplicative operations per second, where each instance costs 40 cents to rent for an hour. Using our number of 2 teraflops per marginal cognitive assembly-line unit, that works out to about 333 instances per unit. That puts the cost of renting a new unit at $133.20 an hour, more than the $50 an hour each unit brings in. (This is a fun calculation, even if we recognize that referring to money that a machine "brings in" is not perfectly equivalent to wealth a machine creates.)

The magic happens when computing power gets cheap enough to rent or finance for less than each marginal unit produces, or the AI finds out a way to optimize itself to squeeze out more productivity, or it finds a way to make each unit earn more than it costs. At that line, the growth rate of the AI potentially becomes exponential. When the AI can make 1 percent on its investment per hour, it can grow in size at the rate of 1 percent per hour. As anyone who has taken an economics class knows, 1 percent interest compounds quickly. In the 1 percent per hour example, doubling time is about three days; 10 doublings in about a month is about three orders of magnitude. We would be changing prefixes (mega, giga, tera, peta) as often as we change calendar pages. Computers can run around the clock, so the compounding happens around the clock too. Ultimately, the limiting factor is how quickly the AI gets paid by its employers, or the size of the market itself. Just the possibility of this magnitude of growth raises questions for humanity that have never before been asked.

3 Physical growth

Above, we've outlined a scenario whereby AI computing power growth compounds quickly. We've ignored scenarios where the AI clandestinely seizes computing power for itself over the Internet, or figures out some other means of obtaining computers. Using basic economics alone, we have a scenario where explosive AI growth seems possible, as long as the AI can make enough money.

Next, we address physical growth, i.e., growth in the real world. Setting aside "miracle technologies" like molecular nanotechnology, the easiest way a growing AI will be able to effect change in the physical world is through human beings. This could be achieved not by threatening, as in the movies, but by hiring us, fooling us, inspiring us, asking nicely, etc.

A key limitation here is that humans were crafted by evolution to respond to charismatic human leaders, not robots. However, a growing AI might have many millions of dollars available to transfer to the right charismatic human able to lead an army of workers for it. All it takes is one competent, charismatic leader willing to obey the AI and it would be possible to get thousands of additional humans to follow along.

It's intuitively more plausible that an AI would be able to make money by solving programming problems than by exerting influence over the world via indirect command of a large cohort of humans. However, both are highly complex tasks that require general problem-solving capability. Tasks involving social persuasion may be less parallelizable than programming problems, but at the growth stage where an AI is expanding from Internet influence into real-world influence, it presumably would have considerable cognitive resources. An AI might have to solve special problems to expand in this way, such as improving its powers of persuasion and social engineering. By its very definition, though, any AI that successfully passes the Turing test would need some charisma and persuasive powers. So, in a "human-equivalent" AI, the seeds of those skills would already be in place.

For an AI on a growth tangent, the primary objective would be to bridge from Internet influence to using humans as tools, and eventually to using robots as tools. Once an AI can exclusively use general-purpose robots to achieve all its goals, it would have gained full autonomy. So, an AI would be well advised to purchase a robotics company, or workshops where robots can be built. Given that an AI could link up any robot to its mainframe and infuse it with its own intelligence, these could be hot products. Robots connected to the Internet could take as much advantage of the full cognitive resources of the core AI as bandwidth and computing budgets permit.

Most robotics companies comprise a few dozen people, or a few hundred at most. The iRobot Corporation, which is among the most successful, has about 500 employees and makes roughly $25 million a year. The advantage an AI would have over humans is that it could take the best possible "employee" it can build out of its software, and copy it indefinitely. Conversely, for humans, star employees are limited. Robotics is a relatively exclusive field, with many of the top performers hailing from such universities as MIT and Stanford. Specialty is scarce. If $30,000 computers could be converted into top-level developers in unlimited quantities, the limiting factor would be the humans needed to move things around and build them, not brainpower. With ubiquitous cameras and voice interfaces, AI employees could even troubleshoot development in real time. In this sense, AIs will take the top jobs and push humans to lower-level tasks.

Robots already exist that can quickly move objects into arbitrary positions; one such, Quickplacer, reaches accelerations of 15G and can pick up and place 200 items per minute. These items can weigh up to 2 kg (4.4 lb). Integrated with advanced intelligence, such machines could perform complex building tasks, including the construction of other robots. The only reason these robots aren't being used now to build other robots is that our software isn't smart enough, and building sufficiently intelligent software is an AI-hard problem (Yampolskiy 2011). If AI itself is solved, however, the tools for recursive self-improvement of robotic platforms exist.

With enough money and people, and access to workshops that can fabricate robots like Quickplacer, the next step would be to create an automated factory that can move toward constructing entirely autonomous, free-roaming robots. Such robots aren't far off; humanoid robots like the humanoid "Petman" by Boston Dynamics already exist and can move at 7.4 km/h (4.4 mph) (Boston Dynamics 2103a). Boston Dynamics has also built a cheetah robot that moves at 46.6 kph (29 mph), setting the land speed record for legged robots (Boston Dynamics 2013b). Integrated with arbitrary accessories, like dexterous robotic hands, human equivalency in the domain of physical influence wouldn't be far behind.

4 Conclusion

Once an AI has many millions of dollars, thousands of employees, and robotic foundries pumping out human-equivalent or human-superior robotic servants, that's endgame. We could quickly find ourselves sharing the planet with a robotic civilization, or replaced by it. If we are conscientious in advance and build the seed AI to care about humans, it might prefer to use its powers for human benefit – to be benevolent or "friendly," or, in simplistic human-centric terms, good rather than evil. Note, though, that the terms "good" and "evil" or even "benevolence" are impossible to define to everyone's satisfaction. AI research and commentary going all the way back to Isaac Asimov's *I, Robot* stories have recognized that any such system is susceptible to self-contradictory paradox, even if we put to one side software bugs and mechanical failure. For instance, what is "good" and what is "evil" for the world? For the Middle East? For the West, in its still unresolved ever-present predicaments regarding the distribution of wealth and power?

However, crucial as they are, discussions about goals tend to derail analyses about brute means and methods, which is our focus here.

There may be other thresholds to cross – securing power sources and raw materials, and avoiding provocation of human fear to the point where we bomb the machines – but such hazards are unlikely to stymie an ultra-intelligent AI. After all, once such a system is up and running, it could send immense numbers of general-purpose, tireless, intelligently controlled androids to the ends of the Earth to achieve its goals.

Some might consider the scenario outlined here fanciful, possibly even terrifying – perhaps justifiably so, given both the possible threats and benefits that might result. At this unique point in history, humankind is standing on either the threshold of a dream or the crumbling edge of a sheer precipice. Our technologies are already in an accelerating, self-reinforcing positive feedback loop, placing those living today atop the punctuation of the evolutionary equilibrium that has existed for eons. For the first time in human evolution, history is suddenly no longer our guide. We might be able to control the destiny briefly outlined above, or we might find the task insuperable. I hope this introductory chapter contributes a concrete model of self-improving artificial intelligence that provokes further thought.

Acknowledgments

Thanks to engineer and rocket scientist Gregory Jones for his careful reading and suggestions.

References

Boston Dynamics 2013a. *PETMAN*, http://www.bostondynamics.com/robot_petman.html (accessed October 17, 2013).

Boston Dynamics 2013b. *CHEETAH – Fasted legged robot*, http://www.bostondynamics.com/robot_cheetah.html (accessed October 17, 2013).

Good, Irving John. 1965. Speculations concerning the first ultraintelligent machine. *Advances in Computers* 6: 31–88.

Yampolskiy, Roman V. 2011. *AI-complete, AI-hard, or AI-easy: Classification of problems in Artificial Intelligence*, Technical Report # 2, University of Louisville, Department of Computer Engineering and Computer Science, Louisville, KY, USA, http://www.academia.edu/1419272/AI-Complete_AI-Hard_or_AI-Easy_Classification_of_Problems_in_Artificial (accessed October 17, 2013).

3

Who Knows Anything about Anything about AI?

Stuart Armstrong and Seán ÓhÉigeartaigh

1 Introduction

Past predictions about artificial intelligence (AI) have been confident, diverse, and wrong. Alan Turing (1950) estimated a 30 percent pass rate on the Turing test by 2000, and since then computer scientists, philosophers, and journalists have never been shy to offer their certain opinions, claiming AI to be impossible (Jacquette 1987), just around the corner (Darrach 1975), or anything in between.

There are claims that AI could be extremely dangerous (Minsky 1984; Yampolskiy 2012; Yudkowsky 2005). At a minimum, it would have a completely transformative impact on human society, so assessing the truth of these conflicting predictions is very important. Thus, this chapter, and two previous papers (Armstrong and Sotala 2012; Armstrong, Sotala, and ÓhÉigeartaigh 2012), aim to provide a classification scheme for AI predictions, and tools for analyzing their reliability and uncertainties.

Since AIs have never been built, predictions in this field depend to a very great extent on expert opinion. Some theoretical work has been done on the reliability of expert opinion, which dovetails closely with a practical analysis of actual expert performance. This performance is quite poor, both in theory and in practice, especially on the key issue of when AI will be developed.

After an analysis of the wildly varying "timeline" predictions offered by experts in the field, this chapter presents a series of brief case studies of some

Intelligence Unbound: The Future of Uploaded and Machine Minds, First Edition.
Edited by Russell Blackford and Damien Broderick.

of the most famous AI predictions: the initial Dartmouth AI conference; Hubert Dreyfus' criticism of AI; Ray Kurzweil's predictions in *The Age of Spiritual Machines*; and Stephen Omohundro's AI Drives. All these suffer from overconfidence, and it is extremely hard to figure out the quality of a prediction at the time it is made (the Dartmouth predictions were much worse than could have been foreseen, though Dreyfus' criticisms were much better). In general, model-based predictions seem to outperform expert opinion-based ones, and the uncertainties assigned to all predictions must be increased.

There is room for major improvements in AI predictions and in the assessments of these predictions, and we hope that this chapter and others will contribute to this.

2 Taxonomy of predictions

Types of predictions

> *"A rocket will never be able to leave the Earth's atmosphere."*
>
> *(New York Times, 1936)*

All predictions are constraints on expectations about the future: all say something about what the future could, or could not, be. A prediction must be falsifiable: there must be a perceptible difference in the future depending on whether the prediction ultimately proves true or false (Popper 1934). This chapter will take every falsifiable statement about future AI to be a prediction. Thus the following four categories are all predictions:

- *Timelines and outcome predictions*. These are the traditional types of predictions, giving the dates of specific AI milestones. Examples: An AI will pass the Turing test by 2000 (Turing 1950); within a decade, AIs will be replacing scientists and other thinking professions.
- *Scenarios*. These are a type of conditional prediction, claiming that if the conditions of the scenario are met, then certain types of outcomes will follow. Example: If someone builds a human-level AI that is easy to copy and cheap to run, this will cause mass unemployment among ordinary humans (Hanson 1994).
- *Plans*. These are a specific type of conditional prediction, claiming that if someone decides to implement a specific plan, then they will be successful in achieving a particular goal. Example: AI can be built by scanning a human brain and simulating the scan on a computer (Sandberg 2008).

- *Issues and metastatements*. This category covers relevant problems with (some or all) approaches to AI (including sheer impossibility results), and metastatements about the whole field. Examples: An AI cannot be built without a fundamental new understanding of epistemology; Generic AIs will have certain (potentially dangerous) behaviors (Omohundro 2008).

This chapter will use this decomposition schema.

Methods of prediction

There are many ways of arriving at predictions. The following schema was suggested by a review of the AI predictions literature (it is of course meant to be a guide, not a straitjacket):

- Causal models
- Non-causal models
- The outside view
- Philosophical arguments
- Expert judgment

Causal models are staples of physics and the harder sciences: given certain facts about the situation under consideration (momentum, energy, charge, GDP, etc.), a conclusion is reached about what the ultimate state will be. For different inputs, there will be different outcomes.

Outside of the hard sciences, however, causal models are often a luxury, as the underlying causes are not well understood. Some success can be achieved with *non-causal models*: without understanding what influences what, one can extrapolate trends into the future. Moore's law is a highly successful non-causal model.

In the *outside view*, specific examples are grouped together and claimed to be examples of the same underlying trend. This trend is then used to make further predictions. For instance, one could notice the many analogs of Moore's law across the spectrum of computing (e.g., in number of transistors, size of hard drives, network capacity, pixels per dollar), note that AI is in the same category, and hence argue that AI development must follow a similarly exponential curve (Kurzweil 1999). Note that the use of the outside view is often implicit rather than explicit: rarely is it justified why these examples are grouped together, beyond general plausibility or similarity arguments. There is evidence that the use of the outside view provides improved prediction accuracy in some domains (Kahneman and Lovallo 1993).

Philosophical arguments are common in the AI literature. Some are simple impossibility statements: AI is decreed to be impossible, using arguments of varying plausibility. More thoughtful philosophical arguments highlight problems that need to be resolved in order to achieve AI, interesting approaches for doing so, and potential issues that might emerge if AIs were to be built.

Since empirical evidence isn't generally available, most AI predictions rely on the judgment of the expert making the prediction. Indeed, in a field as challenging and speculative as AI, *expert judgment* may be the best tool available – experts will have developed a feel for the field and its subtleties and common pitfalls. There are many issues with expert judgment, though, which will be explored in the next section. Non-expert judgment is generally not worth considering: non-experts can make valid arguments, but these arguments must stand solely on their own merits if they are not the work of experts *in the specific field in question* (Kahneman 2011).

The case studies later in the chapter have examples of these prediction methods, often used in combination.

3 (Un)reliable experts

Empirical, scientific evidence is the gold standard for distinguishing between true and false predictions. It is generally lacking in AI predictions, however, since AIs have never existed. Some predictions make more use of empirical evidence than others: the whole brain emulations model, for instance, makes testable predictions about the near and medium-term future (Sandberg 2008). Being open to empirical evidence (and less theoretically rigid) also improves expert predictive abilities (Tetlock 2005).

Reliance on empirically ungrounded expertise is often unavoidable in AI prediction, however. Timeline predictions are often explicitly based on experts' judgment. Plans also need experts to come up with them and judge their credibility. The ideal would be to refine and decompose a prediction: to highlight what is logical argument, what is evidence-based, and the exact points where one must rely on expert judgment (Armstrong, Sotala, and ÓhÉigeartaigh, 2012).

Over the last few decades, there have been several studies of the accuracy of expert judgment (Shanteau 1992; Kahneman and Klein 2009). These have found that the nature of the task most determines the accuracy of the expertise. Table 3.1, reproduced from Shanteau's paper, lists the characteristics that lead to good or poor expert performance (see Table 3.1). One crucial factor is whether experts get feedback, preferably immediately. When feedback is unavailable or delayed, or the environment doesn't allow for good feedback, expert performance drops precipitously (Kahneman and Klein 2009; Kahneman 2011). Generally, AI predictions allow little

Table 3.1 Task properties conducive to good and poor expert performance

Good performance	*Poor performance*
Static stimuli	Dynamic (changeable) stimuli
Decisions about things	Decisions about behavior
Experts agree on stimuli	Experts disagree on stimuli
More predictable problems	Less predictable problems
Some errors expected	Few errors expected
Repetitive tasks	Unique tasks
Feedback available	**Feedback unavailable**
Objective analysis available	Subjective analysis only
Problem decomposable	Problem not decomposable
Decision aids common	Decision aids rare

possibility for any feedback, especially not rapid feedback. The most useful characteristic that is actually under the expert's control is the decomposition of the model: well-decomposed models are preferable. Simple algorithmic methods designed by experts can often outperform the experts themselves (Grove et al. 2000).

4 AI timeline predictions

Jonathan Wang and Brian Potter of the Machine Intelligence Research Institute performed an exhaustive search of the online literature and from this assembled a database of 257 AI predictions from the period 1950 to 2012. Of these, 95 contained predictions giving timelines for AI development.[1] This data was put into a uniform format to give a single median date of AI prediction (Armstrong and Sotala 2012).

Table 3.1 implies that experts should show poor performance at AI timeline predictions. Prediction errors are expected and allowed, but all other task characteristics are neutral or negative, especially the vital issue of feedback.

This expectation is borne out in practice. The timeline predictions are scattered, seemingly at random, over a large timespan (see Figure 3.1), and show no sign of converging. Ignoring the predictions beyond 2100, the dates have a standard deviation of over a quarter-century (26 years). There is little difference between expert predictions (standard deviation of 26 years) and non-expert predictions (standard deviation of 27 years). Past predictions, that we know to have failed, do not stand out from others. One consistent trend in all predictions (experts, non-experts, past failed predictions, and others) is that there is a strong tendency to predict AI within 15 to 25 years

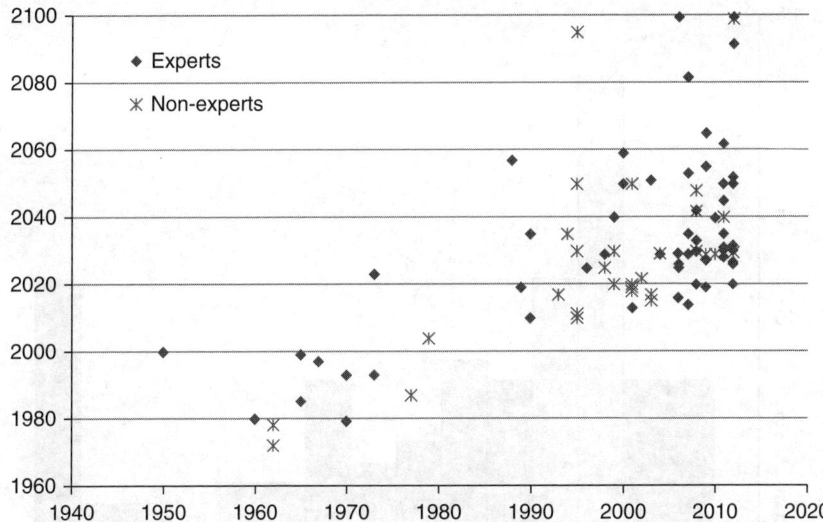

Figure 3.1 Median estimate for human-level AI, graphed against date of prediction. Based on data gathered by Wang and Potter for the Singularity Institute, now Machine Intelligence Research Institute (MIRI).

from when the prediction is made. About a third of all predictions fit this category; see Figure 3.2.

In summary, there are strong theoretical and practical reasons to believe that timeline AI predictions are likely unreliable.

5 Case studies

This section looks at four prominent AI predictions, and analyses their accuracy, attempting to gain insights that will be useful for assessing future prediction. The four predictions analyzed are the original Dartmouth conference, Dreyfus' criticism of AI, Kurzweil's predictions, and Omohundro's AI Drives. (More detailed examples can be found in Armstrong, Sotala, and ÓhÉigeartaigh 2012.)

In the beginning, Dartmouth's created the AI and the hype

Classification: plan, using expert judgment and the outside view

Predictions must be assessed, as far as possible, in the context of the time they were made, avoiding hindsight bias (Fischhoff 1975). The 1956

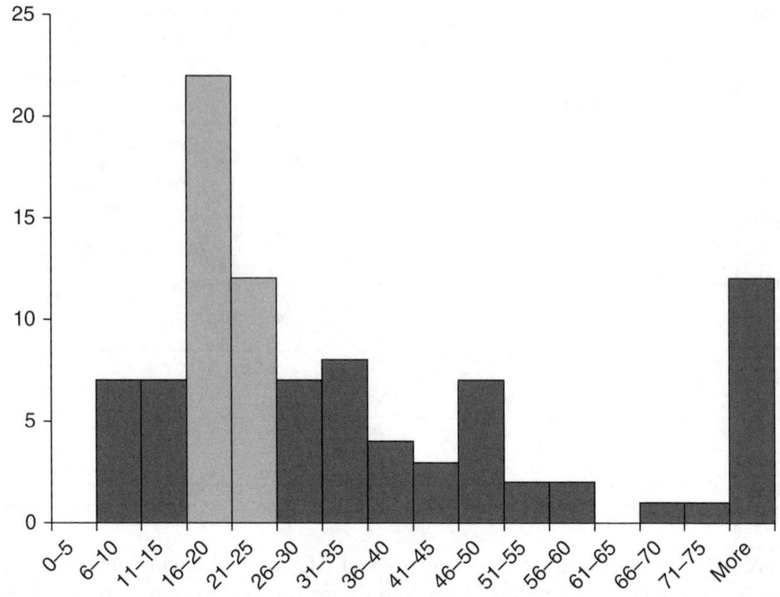

Figure 3.2 Time between the arrival of AI and the date the prediction was made. Years on the x axis, number of predictions on the y axis. Based on data gathered by Wang and Potter for the Singularity Institute, now Machine Intelligence Research Institute (MIRI).

Dartmouth Summer Research Project on Artificial Intelligence gave some of the most spectacularly wrong predictions in all of AI, but that doesn't mean that they were bad predictions *at the time*. The most infamous prediction was in the opening paragraph of the conference proposal (McCarthy et al. 1955[2006]):

> We propose that a 2 month, 10 man study of artificial intelligence be carried out during the summer of 1956 at Dartmouth College .... An attempt will be made to find how to make machines use language, form abstractions and concepts, solve kinds of problems now reserved for humans, and improve themselves. We think that a significant advance can be made in one or more of these problems if a carefully selected group of scientists work on it together for a summer.

This is a plan, mainly based on expert judgment. The conference organizers were John McCarthy, Marvin Minsky, Nathaniel Rochester, and Claude Shannon. They had been involved in much computer-related theoretical and practical work, had built functioning computers and programs (thus developing good feedback), and were very prominent in their fields. If anyone could be considered AI experts, they could. Their proposal does not read as blindly optimistic: their research plan is well decomposed, looking at different aspects of the AI problem. They were well aware of the inefficiency of exhaustive search methods, of the differences between informal and formal languages, of the need for encoding creativity, and of the need to deal robustly with noise and small errors. They proposed simple models to approach these challenges, pointed to some previous successful work, and outlined how further improvements could be made. The implicit reason for their confidence seems to be that they had a long track record of taking complex problems, creating simple models to deal with them, and then improving their models and understanding until the problem was solved. They made implicit use of the outside view, by assuming these new problems could be approached similarly. There was no reason to suspect that further progress would not be both forthcoming and dramatic.

Even at the time, though, one could criticize their overconfidence. Philosophers, for one, had a long track record of pointing out the complexities and subtleties of the human mind. It might have seemed plausible in 1956 that further progress in logic and information theory would end up solving all the problems – but the alternative, that all the low-hanging fruits had been plucked, should have been considered. If the experts had shown a little bit more humility and included some reasonable qualifiers, their predictions would have been almost perfect, *as far as could have been known at the time*.

This case study demonstrates that even the best prediction, agreed by the most prominent experts, can still turn out completely wrong. It also illustrates the danger of reasoning with simple models, and of using human or anthropomorphic terms to describe computer phenomena. Very intelligent but informal reasoning has remarkably little value in AI predictions.

Dreyfus' artificial alchemy

Classification: issues and metastatements, using the outside view, non-expert judgment, and philosophical arguments

Hubert Dreyfus is a prominent early critic of artificial intelligence. He published a series of papers and books attacking the claims and assumptions of the AI field, starting with a paper for the Rand corporation entitled "Alchemy and AI" (Dreyfus 1965). The paper was famously combative, analogizing AI research to alchemy and ridiculing AI claims, although Dreyfus was certainly not an expert on minds, consciousness, or AI.

Thus the accuracy of his criticisms is even more impressive. Dreyfus highlighted several over-optimistic claims that had already been made for the power of AI, predicting – correctly – that the 1965 optimism would also fade. He took an outside view on the AI hype cycle: initial progress, grand claims, then unforeseen difficulties and ultimately disappointment. He delved into the ambiguity in human language and syntax, the importance of unconscious processes, and the problems computers would have in dealing with these. He claimed that philosophical ideas in linguistics and classification were relevant to AI research. In all, his paper is full of interesting ideas and intelligent deconstructions of how humans and machines operate – astoundingly prescient predictions for 1965, when computers and AI research were in their infancy.

His main failing was also overconfidence: he strongly implied that some achievements (such as chess-playing and answering linguistically ambiguous questions) would remain impossible, but he didn't foresee that programmers would change their approach (e.g., reducing their reliance on logic and symbolic manipulation). Computers like Deep Blue and Watson (the IBM computer that triumphed on the TV quiz program *Jeopardy!*) eventually achieved these "impossible" goals.

Thus a 1965 paper by an outsider managed to predict correctly the course of AI research for several decades into the future. There were several signs that his paper was of high quality (he displayed much knowledge of AI work, and made many falsifiable predictions/analyses), but many wrong predictions can seem of very high quality at the time (such as the Dartmouth conference paper, for instance). Thus the partial vindication of Dreyfus' paper is a stark warning: just as experts can err, non-experts can be correct. Though most non-experts will be wrong, of course, assessing the accuracy of a prediction based on the status of the predictor is unreliable and subject to great uncertainty.

It also seems that philosophers' meta-analytical skills can contribute useful ideas to AI, which is certainly not self-evident.

How well have the "Spiritual Machines" aged?

Classification: timelines and scenarios, using expert judgment, causal models, non-causal models, and (indirect) philosophical arguments

Ray Kurzweil is a prominent and oft-quoted AI predictor, hired in 2013 as director of engineering at Google. One of his most important books was the 1999 *The Age of Spiritual Machines* which presented his futurist ideas in more detail, and made several predictions for the years 2009, 2019, 2029, and 2099. The book will be the focus of this case study, ignoring Kurzweil's more recent work or more recent reinterpretations of his old predictions.

There are five main points relevant to judging *The Age of Spiritual Machines*: Kurzweil's expertise, his "Law of Accelerating Returns," his extension of Moore's law, his predictive track record, and his use of fictional imagery to argue philosophical points. Analysis of most of these points can be found in Armstrong, Sotala, and ÓhÉigeartaigh 2012; the focus here will be on his track record. His timeline predictions are based heavily on his expert judgment, but his predictions for 2009 give empirical evidence of his predictive quality.

Initial assessments suggested that Kurzweil had a success rate around 50 percent.[2] We broke his predictions down into 172 individual statements.[3] Then we asked for volunteer assessors from various websites (Less Wrong and Reddit, mainly) and ended up recruiting nine people. Each person was given the predictions in random order, and asked to assess them systematically in the order given, for as many as they desired. In total, 531 assessments were made, an average of 59 assessments per volunteer. Each volunteer assessed at least 10 predictions, while one assessed all 172.

146 assessments (27 percent) found their predictions to be true, 82 (15 percent) weakly true, 73 (14 percent) weakly false, 172 (32 percent) false, and 58 (11 percent) could not be classified. The results are little changed (±1 percent) if the results are calculated for each volunteer, and then averaged.[4]

Kurzweil's correct prediction rate of 42 percent is impressive, given how specific some of his predictions were (e.g., "Unused computers on the Internet are being harvested, creating virtual parallel supercomputers with human brain hardware capacity"). When it comes to self-assessment/self-commissioned assessment, however, Kurzweil is much less reliable. He commissioned investigations into his own performance, which gave him scores of 102 out of 108,[5] or 127 out of 147,[6] with the caveat that "even the predictions that were considered wrong … were not all wrong." This is dramatically different from our assessments: he rates himself much higher than our outside analysis did.

The tension between the impressive prediction rate and the poor self-assessment suggests that Kurzweil's main model (continuing exponential trends in computing) is likely correct, while Kurzweil's expertise and opinions add little. This is a common finding in research relating to expert tasks – experts are often better at constructing predictive models than at making predictions themselves (Kahneman 2011).

What drives an AI?

Classification: issues and metastatements, using philosophical arguments and expert judgment

In his paper on "AI Drives," Steve Omohundro (2008) argued that generic AI designs would show the same types of behavior, even if these weren't programmed in initially. Most AIs would be thus "driven" to self-improve, to become expected utility maximizers, to protect themselves, and ultimately to acquire more resources and power.

This is a metastatement: a claim that generic AI designs would show this convergent behavior. It relies on philosophical and mathematical arguments, and although the author has expertise in mathematics and machine learning, he has none directly in philosophy. It also makes implicit use of the outside view: utility maximizing agents are grouped together into one category and similar types of behaviors are expected from all agents in this category.

Omohundro's thesis should be divided into two claims. The weaker claim is that a generic AI design *could* have these drives. The stronger claim is that it is *very likely* to have them. His paper provides strong evidence for the weaker claim: every drive (self-improvement, self-preservation, gathering extra resources) is consistent with the AI's initial goals (unless these are specifically tailored or highly unusual).

The paper fails to establish the stronger claim, however. This can be seen by considering human beings as counterexamples. It has been argued that AIs could have any motivation a human has (Armstrong 2013; Bostrom 2012). Thus, according to Omohundro's thesis, it would seem that humans should be subject to the same drives and behaviors. This does not fit the evidence, however: humans do not generally act as self-improving expected utility maximizers. Therefore there is a whole category of intelligent agents that do not generally follow Omohundro's "drives." His paper does not present a useful division between those agents that would follow these drives, and those that wouldn't. The human counterexample undermines the strong version of Omohundro's thesis.

Even a superintelligence would be a boundedly rational agent (Simon 1955), probably existing within a social structure of other agents. Omohundro's arguments are at their strongest when considering a solitary unbounded agent, and it is plausible but not certain that they apply to generic bounded superintelligences. Conversely, the superintelligent might be powerful enough that they see little need to make themselves "rational" in terms of following a utility function (von Neumann and Morgenstern 1944). This is especially so since there might be a cost to such modification: an agent might not trust a future version of itself with different goals to work in its present best interest.

A more subtle point is that any sequence of decisions can be explained as maximizing a (potentially very complicated or obscure) utility function. Thus, saying that the agent will be an expected utility maximizer does not narrow things down, in the abstract. Omohundro's arguments work best for agents with simple goal structures. More complicated agents *could* conceivably escape the AI drives.

But these counterarguments only address the strong version of the thesis. The weak version still survives intact: almost any AI design could end up with very dangerous goals. From the perspective of creating an AI, there is little difference between the strong and weak thesis: a significant risk of disastrous consequences should be enough to motivate safety research. The simple model is also very valuable in allowing AI designers to show clearly how their approach differs from the generic dangerous behaviors.

Others have also argued that generic AIs would behave very dangerously, unless they were exceptionally well programmed. Roman Yampolskiy (2012), Eliezer Yudkowsky (2005), and Marvin Minsky (1984), among others, have made this point. There is an interesting extra piece of evidence for all these arguments: the inability of critics to dismiss them effectively.[7]

Many counter-proposals have been made to these theses (often in Q&A sessions at the end of conferences), and some critics have presented ideas about how to dispose easily of the dangers.[8] Generally these ideas have failed to grapple with the fundamental issue at hand, at least effectively enough to weaken the theses. In the absence of conclusive proof, this continuing failure of counter-proposals is evidence that there are, at least, no *easy* counters to the AI risk theses defended by Omohundro.

6 Conclusion: To know the limits of what can be known

Artificial intelligence poses some unique challenges to the would-be predictor. AIs have never been built, workable designs don't exist, and there is little theoretical understanding of what a true AI would actually be. But the potential risk of AI means that correct predictions are very important.

Consequently, the aim of this chapter and of the two papers that preceded it (Armstrong and Sotala 2012; Armstrong, Sotala, and ÓhÉigeartaigh 2012) was to estimate the quality of AI predictions that are made, provide tools to analyze and rank them, and give a better impression of the uncertainties. Experts were seen to be quite poor at AI timeline predictions, both in theory and in practice: the biases and the uncertainties seemed to swamp any information the prediction may contain.

An analysis of several case studies illustrated that it is very hard to gauge the quality of AI predictions at the time they are made. Some that seemed very impressive failed completely (the Dartmouth conference) while others that had no reason to be believed succeeded well (Dreyfus' arguments). The only consistent message was that all predictors were overconfident in their verdicts, and that model-based predictions were superior to those founded solely on expert intuition. Also of interest is the surprising strength of more philosophical AI arguments (Dreyfus' and Omohundro's theses), though this is partly a reflection of the weaknesses of all other modes of prediction.

We hope that future predictors (and assessors of future predictions) will follow in the spirit of this analysis, and make their assumptions explicit, their models clear, their predictions testable, and their uncertainty greater.

Acknowledgments

The authors wish to acknowledge the help and support of the Machine Intelligence Research Institute, the Future of Humanity Institute and the Oxford Martin School, as well as the individual advice of Nick Bostrom, Luke Muehlhauser, Vincent C. Müller, Anders Sandberg, Lisa Makros, Daniel Dewey, Eric Drexler, Maia Armstrong, the nine volunteer prediction assessors, and the online community of Less Wrong.

Many thanks especially to Kaj Sotala for his invaluable analysis work.

Notes

1 The data can be found at http://www.neweuropeancentury.org/SIAI-FHI_AI_predictions.xls (accessed October 6, 2013).
2 http://lesswrong.com/lw/diz/kurzweils_predictions_good_accuracy_poor/ (accessed October 6, 2013).
3 Details of the process can be found at http://lesswrong.com/r/discussion/lw/gbh/assessing_kurzweil_the_gory_details/ (accessed October 6, 2013).
4 http://lesswrong.com/lw/gbi/assessing_kurzweil_the_results/ (accessed October 6, 2013).
5 See Ray Kurzweil's response: http://www.acceleratingfuture.com/michael/blog/2010/01/ray-kurzweil-response-to-ray-kurzweils-failed-2009-predictions/ (accessed October 6, 2013).
6 http://www.forbes.com/sites/alexknapp/2012/03/21/ray-kurzweil-defends-his-2009-predictions (accessed October 6, 2013).
7 http://lesswrong.com/lw/hvp/the_failure_of_counterarguments_argument/ (accessed October 6, 2013).
8 See, for example, http://lesswrong.com/lw/cbs/thoughts_on_the_singularity_institute_si/ (accessed October 6, 2013), and http://becominggaia.files.wordpress.com/2010/06/agi-11-waser.pdf (accessed October 6, 2013).

References

Armstrong, S. 2013. General purpose intelligence: Arguing the Orthogonality thesis. *Analysis and Metaphysics*.

Armstrong, S., and Sotala, K. 2012. How we're predicting AI – or failing to. In J. Romportl, P. Ircing, E. Zackova, M. Polak, and R. Schuster, eds., *Beyond AI: Artificial Dreams*. Pilsen: University of West Bohemia, pp. 52–75.

Armstrong, S., Sotala, K., and ÓhÉigeartaigh, S. 2012. The errors, insights and lessons of famous AI predictions – and what they mean for the future. Winter Intelligence Conference. Journal of Experimental & Theoretical Artificial Intelligence.

Bostrom, N. 2012. The superintelligent will: Motivation and instrumental rationality in advanced artificial agents. *Minds and Machines* 22: 71–85.

Darrach, B. 1975. Meet Shaky, the first electronic person. In Russell Hill, ed., *Reflections of the Future: An Elective Course in Science Fiction and Fact*. Boston: Ginn & Co., pp. 64–72.

Dreyfus, H. 1965. *Alchemy and AI*. Paper prepared for the RAND Corporation.

Fischhoff, B. 1975. Hindsight is not equal to foresight: The effect of outcome knowledge on judgment under uncertainty. *Journal of Experimental Psychology: Human Perception and Performance* 1(3): 288–299.

Grove, W., Zald, D., Lebow, B., Snitz, B., and Nelson, C. 2000. Clinical versus mechanical prediction: A meta-analysis. *Psychological Assessment* 12: 19–30.

Hanson, R. 1994. If uploads come first: The crack of a future dawn. *Extropy* 6(2): 10–15.

Jacquette, D. 1987. Metamathematical criteria for minds and machines. *Erkenntnis* 27(1): 1–16.

Kahneman, D. 2011. *Thinking, Fast and Slow*. New York: Farrar, Straus & Giroux.

Kahneman, D., and Klein, G. 2009. Conditions for intuitive expertise: A failure to disagree. *American Psychologist* 64(6): 515–526.

Kahneman, D., and Lovallo, D. 1993. Timid choices and bold forecasts: A cognitive perspective on risk taking. *Management Science* 39(1): 17–31.

Kurzweil, R. 1999. *The Age of Spiritual Machines: When Computers Exceed Human Intelligence*. New York: Viking.

McCarthy, J., Minsky, M., Rochester, N., and Shannon, C. 1955. A proposal for the Dartmouth Summer Research Project on Artificial Intelligence. Published in 2006 in *AI Magazine* 27(4): 12.

Minsky, M. 1984. *Afterword to Vernor Vinge's* True Names, web.media.mit.edu/~minsky/papers/TrueNames.Afterword.html (accessed October 6, 2013). Unpublished manuscript.

Omohundro, S. 2008. The basic AI drives. *Frontiers in Artificial Intelligence and Applications* 171: 483–492.

Popper, K. 1934. *The Logic of Scientific Discovery*. Tübingen: Mohr Siebeck.

Sandberg, A. 2008. *Whole Brain Emulations: A Roadmap* (vols. 2008–03). Future of Humanity Institute Technical Report.

Shanteau, J. 1992. Competence in experts: The role of task characteristics. *Organizational Behavior and Human Decision Processes* 53: 252–266.

Simon, H. 1955. A behavioral model of rational choice. *The Quarterly Journal of Economics* 69(1): 99–118.

Tetlock, P. 2005. *Expert Political Judgement: How Good Is It? How Can We Know?* Princeton, NJ: Princeton University Press.

Turing, A. 1950. Computing machinery and intelligence. *Mind* 59: 433–460.
von Neumann, J., and Morgenstern, O. 1944. *Theory of Games and Economic Behavior*. Princeton, NJ: Princeton University Press.
Yampolskiy, R.V. 2012. Leakproofing the singularity: Artificial intelligence confinement problem. *Journal of Consciousness Studies* 19(1–2): 194–214.
Yudkowsky, E. 2005. Artificial intelligence as a positive and negative factor in global risk. In N. Bostrom and M. Cirkovic, eds., *Global Catastrophic Risks*. New York: Oxford University Press, pp. 308–345.

4

Nine Ways to Bias Open-Source Artificial General Intelligence Toward Friendliness

Ben Goertzel and Joel Pitt

1 Introduction

Artificial general intelligence (AGI), like any technology, carries both risks and rewards. Lodging the issue deep in our cultural awareness, one movie or TV show after another has highlighted the potential dangers. Hypothetically, an AGI with superhuman intelligence and capability could dispense with humanity altogether and thus pose an "existential risk" (Bostrom 2002). In the worst case, an evil but brilliant AGI, programmed by some cyber Marquis de Sade, could consign humanity to unimaginable tortures (perhaps realizing a modern version of the medieval Christian imagery of hell). On the other hand, the potential benefits of powerful AGI also go beyond human imagination. An AGI with massively superhuman intelligence and a positive disposition toward humanity could provide us with dramatic benefits, through the application of superior intellect to scientific and engineering challenges that befuddle us today. Such benefits could include a virtual end to material scarcity via advancement of molecular manufacturing, and they might force us to revise our assumptions about the inevitability of disease and aging (Drexler 1986). Advanced AGI could help individual humans grow in a variety of directions, even beyond our biological legacy, leading to massive diversity in human experience, and hopefully a simultaneous enhanced capacity for openmindedness and empathy.

Eliezer Yudkowsky introduced the term "Friendly AI" to refer to advanced AGI systems that act with human benefit in mind (Yudkowsky 2001).

Intelligence Unbound: The Future of Uploaded and Machine Minds, First Edition.
Edited by Russell Blackford and Damien Broderick.

Exactly what this means has not been specified precisely, though informal interpretations abound. Goertzel (2006) has sought to clarify the notion in terms of three core values of "Joy, Growth and Freedom." In this view, a Friendly AI would be one that advocates individual and collective human joy and growth, while respecting the autonomy of human choice.

Some (for example, de Garis 2005), drawing parallels with humanity's own exploitation of less intelligent systems, have argued that Friendly AI is essentially impossible, that the odds of a dramatically superhumanly intelligent mind worrying about human benefit are vanishingly small. Indeed, in our daily life, questions such as the nature of consciousness in animals, plants, and larger ecological systems are generally considered merely philosophical, and only rarely lead to individuals making changes in outlook, lifestyle, or diet. If Friendly AI is impossible for this reason, then our best options would presumably be to avoid developing advanced AGI altogether, or else to fuse with AGI before the disparity between its intelligence and humanity's becomes too large, so that beings-originated-as-humans can enjoy the benefits of greater intelligence and capability. Some will consider sacrificing their humanity an undesirable cost. The concept of humanity, however, is not a stationary one, and can be viewed as sacrificed only from our contemporary perspective. With our cell phones, massively connected world, and the inability to hunt, it's unlikely that we'd seem the same species to the humanity of the past. Just like an individual's self, the self of humanity will inevitably change, and as we do not usually mourn losing our identity of a decade ago to our current self, our current concern for what we may lose may seem unfounded in retrospect.

Others, such as Waser (2008), linking greater intelligence with greater cooperation, have argued that Friendly AI is essentially inevitable. Waser adduces evidence from evolutionary and human history in favor of this point, along with more abstract arguments such as the economic viability of cooperation over not cooperating.

Omohundro (2008) has argued that any advanced AI system will very likely demonstrate certain "basic AI drives," such as desiring to be rational, to self-protect, to acquire resources, and to preserve and protect its utility function (the mathematics describing its preferred goals and choices) and avoid counterfeit utility; these drives, he suggests, must be taken carefully into account in formulating approaches to Friendly AI.

Yudkowsky (2006) discusses the possibility of creating AGI architectures that are in some sense "provably Friendly" – either mathematically, or else by very tight lines of rational verbal argument. Several possibly insurmountable challenges face such an approach. First, proving mathematical results of this nature would likely require dramatic advances in multiple branches of mathematics. Second, such a proof would require a formalization of the goal of "Friendliness," which is a subtler matter than it might seem (Legg 2006a, 2006b); formalization of human morality has thwarted moral philosophers. Finally, it is unclear to what extent such a proof could be created in a generic, environment-independent way – yet if the proof depends on properties of the physical environment, then it would require a formalization of the environment itself, which runs up against various problems related to the complexity of the physical world, not to mention the current lack of a complete, consistent theory of physics.

The problem of formally or at least very carefully defining the goal of Friendliness has been considered from a variety of perspectives. Among a list of 14 objections to the Friendly AI concept, with suggested answers to each, Sotala (2011) includes the vagueness of the Friendliness concept. An attempted solution is Coherent Extrapolated Volition (CEV), suggested by Yudkowsky (2004), which roughly equates to the extrapolation of the common values shared by all people when at their best. Many subtleties arise in specifying this concept – for example, if Bob Jones is often possessed by a strong desire to kill all Martians, but he deeply aspires to be a nonviolent person, then the CEV approach would not rate "killing Martians" as part of Bob's contribution to the CEV of humanity. Resolving inconsistencies in aspirations and desires, and the different temporal scales involved for each, is another non-trivial problem.

Goertzel (2010) has proposed a related notion of Coherent Aggregated Volition (CAV), which eschews some subtleties of extrapolation, and instead seeks a reasonably *compact*, *coherent*, and *consistent* set of values that is close to the collective value-set of humanity. In the CAV approach, "killing Martians" would be removed from humanity's collective value-set because it's assumedly uncommon and not part of the most compact/coherent/consistent overall model of human values, rather than because of Bob Jones' aspiration to nonviolence. (It must be granted, though, that abusing, molesting, or killing the Other is quite common in human action and aspiration.)

More recently, we have considered that the core concept underlying CAV might be better thought of as CBV, or Coherent Blended Volition. CAV seems to be easily misinterpreted as meaning the average of different views, which was not the original intention. The CBV terminology clarifies that the CBV of a diverse group of people should not be thought of as an average of their perspectives, but as something more analogous to a "conceptual blend" (Fauconnier and Turner 2002) – incorporating the most essential elements of their divergent views into a whole that is overall compact, elegant, and harmonious. The subtlety here (to which we shall return below) is that for a CBV blend to be broadly acceptable, the different parties whose views are being blended must agree to some extent that enough of the essential elements of their own views have been included.

Multiple attempts at axiomatization of human values have also been made. In one case, this is done with a view toward providing near-term guidance to military robots (from Arkin's [2009] excellent though chillingly titled book *Governing Lethal Behavior in Autonomous Robots*). However, there are reasonably strong arguments that human values (and similarly a human's language and perceptual classification) are too complex and multifaceted to be captured in any compact set of formal logical rules. Wallach and Allen (2010) have made this point eloquently, and argued for the necessity of fusing top-down (e.g., formal logic-based) and bottom-up (e.g. self-organizing learning-based) approaches to machine ethics.

Modes of AGI development

Other sociological considerations also arise. For example, it is sometimes argued that the risk from highly advanced AGI going morally awry on its own may be less than that of moderately advanced AGI being used by a human being to advocate immoral ends. This possibility gives rise to questions about the ethical value of various practical paths of AGI development. For instance:

- Should AGI be developed in a top-secret installation by a select group of individuals? Individuals selected for a combination of technical and scientific brilliance, moral uprightness, or any other qualities deemed relevant (a "closed approach")? Or should it be developed in the open, in the manner of open-source software projects like Linux (an "open approach")? The open approach allows the collective intelligence of the world to participate more fully – but also potentially allows unscrupulous elements of the human race to take some of the publicly developed AGI concepts and tools, then privately develop them into AGIs with selfish or evil purposes in mind. Is there some meaningful intermediary between these extremes?
- Should governments regulate AGI, with Friendliness in mind (as advocated carefully by e.g. Hibbard [2002])? Or will this just cause AGI development to move to the handful of countries with less controlling policies? Or will it cause development to move underground, where nobody can see the dangers developing?

Clearly, there are many subtle and interwoven issues at play here, and it may require an AGI beyond human intelligence to unravel and understand them all thoroughly. Our goal here is more modest: to explore the question of *how to militate in favor of positive, Friendly outcomes*. Some of our suggestions are fairly generic, but others are reliant on the assumption of an open rather than a closed approach. The open approach is currently followed in our own AGI project, hence its properties are those we're most keen to explore.

While we would love to be proved wrong on this, our current perspective is that provably, or otherwise guarantee-ably, Friendly AI is not achievable. On the face of it, achieving strong certainty about the future behaviors of beings massively more generally intelligent and capable than ourselves seems implausible. Again, we are aiming at a more modest goal – to explore ways of biasing the odds, and creating AI systems that are significantly more likely than not to be Friendly.

While the considerations presented here are conceptually fairly generic, we will frequently elaborate them using the example of the OpenCog AGI framework (Hart and Goertzel 2008; Goertzel et al. 2010b) on which we are currently working, and the specific OpenCog applications now under development, including game AI, robotics, and natural language conversation.

2 Is open or closed AGI development safer?

We will not seek here to argue rigorously that the open approach to AGI is preferable to the closed approach. Rather, our goal is to explore ways to make AGI more probably Friendly, with a non-exclusive focus on open approaches. We do believe intuitively that the open approach is probably preferable, but our reasons are qualitative and we recognize there are also qualitative arguments in the opposite direction. Before proceeding further, we will briefly sketch some of the reasons for our intuition on this.

First, we have a strong skepticism about self-appointed elite groups that claim that they know what's best for everyone (even if they are genuine saints), and a healthy respect for the power of collective intelligence and the Global Brain (Heylighen 2007), which the open approach is ideal for tapping. On the other hand, we also understand the risk of terrorist groups or other malevolent agents forking an open-source AGI project and creating something terribly dangerous and destructive. Balancing these factors against each other rigorously is impossible, due to the number of assumptions currently involved.

For instance, nobody really understands the social dynamics by which open technological knowledge plays out in our current world, let alone hypothetical future scenarios. Right now, open knowledge exists about many very dangerous technologies, and there are many terrorist groups, yet these groups fortunately make scant use of the technologies. The reasons appear to be essentially sociological – the people involved in terrorist groups tend not to be the ones who have mastered the skills of turning public knowledge of cutting-edge technologies into real engineered systems. While it's easy to observe this sociological phenomenon, we don't really have a strong understanding of how safe we are right now, given the technological knowledge available via the Internet, textbooks, and so forth. Relatively straightforward threats such as nuclear proliferation remain confusing, even to the experts.

The open approach allows for various benefits of open-source software development to be applied, such as Linus' law (Raymond 2000): "Given enough eyeballs, all bugs are shallow."

Software development practice has taught us that in the closed approach it's very hard to get the same level of critique available on a public, open codebase. At a conceptual level of development, a closed approach also prevents external theorists from finding specific flaws in a design. Discussing the theoretical basis for Friendliness design is easy, but implementing and designing a system that conforms to that design is not.

Nor does keeping powerful AGI and its development locked up by an elite group really provide reliable protection against malevolent human agents. History is rife with such situations going awry, such as subversion of the group's leadership, brute force inflicted by some outside party, or a member of the group defecting to an outside group in pursuit of power or reward, or in response to internal disagreements. Many things can go wrong, and no particular group is immune.

Clearly, neither the open nor the closed approach is a panacea.

3 The (unlikely) prospect of government controls on AGI development

Given the obvious long-term risks associated with AGI development, is it feasible that governments might enact legislation intended to prevent AI from being developed? Might government regulatory bodies slow down the progress of AGI development in order to enable measured development of accompanying ethical tools, practices, and understandings? This seems unlikely, for the following reasons.

Consider two cases. First, there is the case of banning AGI research and development *after* an "AGI Sputnik" moment has occurred. We define an AGI Sputnik moment as a technological achievement that makes the short- to medium-term possibility of highly functional and useful human-level AGI broadly evident to the public and policymakers, bringing it out of the realm of science fiction to reality. Second, we might choose to ban it *before* such an event.

After an AGI Sputnik moment, even if some nations chose to ban AI technology due to the perceived risks, others would probably proceed eagerly with AGI development because of the wide-ranging perceived benefits. International agreements are difficult to reach and enforce, even for extremely obvious threats like nuclear weapons and pollution, so it's hard to envision that such agreements would come rapidly in the case of AGI. In a scenario where some nations ban AGI while others do not, it seems the slow speed of international negotiations would contrast with the rapid speed of development of a technology in the midst of revolutionary breakthrough. While worried politicians sought to negotiate agreements, AGI development would continue, and some nations would gain increasing competitive advantage from their differential participation in it.

The only way it seems feasible for such an international ban to come about would be if the AGI Sputnik moment turned out to be largely illusory because the path from the moment to full human-level AGI proved to be blocked by severe technical bottlenecks. If AGI development somehow slowed after the AGI Sputnik moment, then there might be time to set up a system of international treaties similar to those that now control nuclear weapons research. However, we note that the nuclear weapons research ban is not entirely successful – and that nuclear weapons development and testing tend to have large physical impacts that are remotely observable by foreign nations. If a nation decided not to cooperate with an international AGI ban, this would be much more difficult to uncover.

An unsuccessful attempt to ban AGI research and development could end up being far riskier than no ban. An international R&D ban that was systematically violated in the manner of current international nuclear weapons bans would shift AGI development from cooperating developed nations to "rogue nations," thus slowing down AGI development somewhat, but also perhaps decreasing the odds of the first AGI being developed in a manner that is concerned with ethics and Friendly AI.

Thus, subsequent to an AGI Sputnik moment, the overall value of AGI will be too obvious for AGI to be effectively banned, and monitoring AGI development would be next to impossible.

The second option is an AGI R&D ban earlier than the AGI Sputnik moment – before it's too late. This also seems infeasible, for the following reasons:

- Early stage AGI technology will supply humanity with dramatic economic and quality-of-life improvements, as narrow AI does now. From a government policy perspective, distinguishing narrow AI from AGI would also be prohibitively difficult.

- If one nation chose to enforce such a slowdown as a matter of policy, the odds seem very high that other nations would explicitly seek to accelerate their own progress on AI/AGI, so as to reap the ensuing differential economic benefits.

To make the latter point more directly, the prospect of any modern government seeking to put a damper on current real-world narrow-AI technology seems remote and absurd. It's hard to imagine the US government forcing a roll-back from modern search engines like Google and Bing to more simplistic search engines like 1997 AltaVista, on the basis that the former embody natural language-processing technology that represents a step along the path to powerful AGI.

Wall Street firms (that currently have a powerful economic influence on the US government) will not wish to give up their AI-based trading systems, at least not while their counterparts in other countries still use such systems to compete with them on the international currency futures market. Assuming the US government did somehow ban AI-based trading systems, how would this be enforced? Would a programmer at a hedge fund be stopped from inserting some more effective machine learning code in place of the government-sanctioned linear regression code? The US military will not give up its AI-based planning and scheduling systems, and the idea of the government placing an IQ limit on the AI characters in video games, out of fear that these characters might one day become too smart, seems absurd. Even if the government did so, hackers worldwide would be drawn to release "mods" for their own smart AIs inserted illicitly into games; and one might see a subculture of pirate games with illegally smart AI.

"But all these examples are narrow AI, not AGI!" it might be argued. "Banning AI that occurs embedded inside practical products is one thing; banning autonomous AGI systems, with their own motivations and self-autonomy and the ability to take over the world and kill all humans, is quite another!" However, the professional AI community does not yet draw a clear border between narrow AI and AGI. While we do believe there is a clear qualitative conceptual distinction, we would find it hard to embody this distinction in a rigorous test for distinguishing narrow AI systems from "proto-AGI systems" representing dramatic partial progress toward human-level AGI. At precisely what level of intelligence would you propose to ban a conversational natural language search interface, an automated call center chatbot, or a house-cleaning robot? How would you distinguish rigorously, across all areas of application, a competent non-threatening narrow-AI system from something with sufficient general intelligence to count as part of the path to dangerous AGI?

A recent workshop of a dozen AGI experts, oriented largely toward originating such tests, failed to come to any definitive conclusions

(Adams et al. 2010), recommending instead that a looser mode of evaluation be adopted, involving qualitative synthesis of multiple rigorous evaluations obtained in multiple distinct scenarios. A previous workshop with a similar theme, funded by the US Naval Research Office, came to even less distinct conclusions (Laird et al. 2009). The OpenCog system is explicitly focused on AGI rather than narrow AI, but its various learning modules are also applicable as narrow AI systems, and some of them have largely been developed in this context. In short, there's no rule for distinguishing narrow AI work from proto-AGI work that is sufficiently clear to be enshrined in government policy, and the banning of narrow AI work seems infeasible as the latter is economically and humanistically valuable, tightly interwoven with nearly all aspects of the economy, and nearly always non-threatening in nature. Even in the military context, the biggest use of AI is in relatively harmless-sounding contexts such as back-end logistics systems, not in frightening applications like killer robots.

In summary, we submit that, due to various aspects of the particular nature of AGI and its relation to other technologies and social institutions, it is very unlikely to be explicitly banned, either before or after an AGI Sputnik moment. If one believes the creation of AGI to be technically feasible, then the more pragmatically interesting topic becomes how to most effectively manage and guide its development.

4 Nine ways to bias AGI toward Friendliness

There is no way to guarantee that advanced AGI, once created and released into the world, will behave according to human ethical standards. There is irreducible risk here, a risk humanity has been moving toward, at accelerating speed, ever since the development of tools, language, and culture. However, we can bias the odds in favor of ethically positive AGI development. The degree of biasing that can be achieved seems impossible to estimate quantitatively, and any extrapolation from human history to a future populated by agents with significantly transhuman general intelligence has an obvious strong risk of being profoundly flawed. Nevertheless, it behoves us to do our best to bias the outcome in a positive direction, and the primary objective of this chapter is to suggest some potential ways to do so.

1 Engineer the capability to acquire integrated ethical knowledge

First of all, if we wish our AGI systems to behave in accordance with human ethics, we should design them to be capable of the full range of human ethical understanding and response. As reviewed in Goertzel and Bugaj (2008) and Goertzel (2009b), human ethical judgment relies on the coordination and integration of multiple faculties. One way to think about this is to draw connections between the multiple types of human memory (as studied in cognitive psychology and cognitive neuroscience) and multiple types of ethical knowledge and understanding:

Episodic memory corresponds to the process of ethically assessing a situation based on similar prior situations.

Sensorimotor memory corresponds to "mirror neuron" (Rizzolatti and Craighero 2004) ethics, where you feel another person's feelings via mirroring their physiological emotional responses and actions.

Declarative memory corresponds to rational ethical judgment.

Procedural memory corresponds to "ethical habit": learning by imitation and reinforcement to do what is right, even when the reasons aren't well articulated or understood.

Attentional memory corresponds to the existence of appropriate patterns guiding one to pay adequate attention to ethical considerations at appropriate times.

Intentional memory corresponds to ethical management of one's own goals and motivations (e.g., When do the ends justify the means?).

We argue that an ethically mature mind, human or AGI, should balance all these kinds of ethics, although none is completely independent of the others.

How these memory types relate to ethical behavior and understanding depends somewhat on the cognitive architecture in question. For instance, it is straightforward to identify each of these memory types in the OpenCog architecture, and articulate their intuitive relationship to ethical behavior and understanding:

Episodic memory. Through placing OpenCog in ethical scenarios with a teacher agent that provides feedback on choices, and with OpenCog's goal system initially biased to seek approval from the teacher.

Sensorimotor memory. Knowledge is usually contextually represented within the OpenCog AtomSpace (a weighted hypergraph-like knowledge base). A perceptual interface that takes on the role of mirror neurons may activate contexts representing another's emotional state, causing that context to move into the attentional focus of OpenCog. In this way, OpenCog becomes sensitive to the emotional state of other agents it has interacted with and whose worldviews it has modeled. Then, through induction or pattern mining, these changes in emotional state can be mapped on to new agents that the AI is unfamiliar with.

Declarative memory. Declarative ethical knowledge may be embedded as a seed within the OpenCog AtomSpace, or built from data-mining episodic memory for patterns learned during ethical teaching. This knowledge can then be reasoned about, using probablistic logic to make ethical decisions in novel situations.

Procedural memory. The development of new schemata can be based on previous experience. Schemata that have previously been evaluated in the same or similar ethical scenarios can be used to guide the construction of new program trees.

Attentional memory. OpenCog has networks of attention that can implicitly store attentional memories. These memories form from observation of temporal patterns of knowledge access, and their relative importance to goal fulfillment. Once formed they degrade slowly and may provide resilience against potentially unethical replacements if initially taught ethical behavior (Goertzel et al. 2010b).

Intentional memory (memory regarding goals and subgoals). OpenCog expresses explicit goals declaratively using uncertain logic, but also expresses implicit goals using "maps" recording habitual patterns of activity, created and stored via attentional memory.

To pass beyond childish ethics to the "mature" stage of ethical development, a deep and rich integration of the ethical approaches associated with the five main types of memory systems is required.[1] Other valuable perspectives are founded on different cognitive models, so this is an area wide open for further exploration, both conceptually and empirically.

2 Provide rich ethical interaction and instruction, respecting developmental stages

Of course, a cognitive architecture with capability to exercise the full richness of human ethical behavior and understanding is not enough. How is this cognitive architecture filled with appropriate "ethical content"? Just as human ethics are considered a combination of nature and nurture, so we should expect for AGI systems. AGI systems are learning systems by definition, and human values are complex and best conveyed via a combination of methods in order that they become well grounded.

In Goertzel (2009a) the memory types listed in the previous section are associated with different common modes of human communication:

sensorymotor/depictive; episodic/dramatic; declarative/linguistic; procedural/demonstrative; attentional/indicative; intentional/intentional.[2] Our suggestion is that AGIs should be provided with ample ethical instruction using all of these communication modalities. During this instruction, respect for modern thinking about progressive education will be important. It is important to tailor ethical instruction to the student's stage of cognitive and ethical development. Instructions on the abstract nature of justice are not likely to be helpful to an AGI that hasn't yet learned the practicalities of sharing with its peers – at that early stage, abstract ethical instructions would constitute ungrounded declarative knowledge, and the AGI system would have a hard time grounding and integrating them with its overall worldview, and expressing it in all the different forms of memory available to it. Whereas, after an AGI has learned some of the everyday aspects of justice, including the balance of justice with empathy in everyday life, and once it has also gotten familiar with the application of abstract principles to other aspects of ordinary life, it will be well poised to appreciate abstract ethical principles and their utility in making difficult decisions. It will be able to understand the abstract nature of justice in a richer and more holistic way.

More concretely:

1 The teacher(s) should be observed to follow their own ethical principles, in a variety of contexts that are meaningful to the AGI. Otherwise, declarative memory may clash with episodic (or other memory types). At the same time, perceived inconsistencies in the behavior of the teacher may hint at subtleties in human ethics that the AGI was not previously aware of. In such a case, questioning the teacher may refine the AGI's understanding.
2 The system of ethics must be relevant to the AGI's life context and embedded within its understanding of the world. Without this, episodic memories may not be sufficiently similar to new situations for the AGI to engage an appropriate ethical response.
3 Ethical principles must be grounded in both theory-of-mind thought experiments (emphasizing logical coherence) and real-life situations in which the ethical trainee is required to make a moral judgment and is rewarded or reproached by the teacher(s). The feedback should also include the reason for a particular decision by the teacher.

For example, in our current application of OpenCog to control intelligent game characters, we intend to have human players take the role of the teacher in a shared sandbox environment. The AGI can not only interact with the teacher through dialogue and action, but can also observe the teacher interacting with other humans and AGIs, including how they are rewarded or chastised. Initially, teaching should occur for each embodiment option: each game world in which an AGI has a virtual avatar, and each robotic body available to the AGI. Eventually, a sufficient corpus of varied episodic knowledge will allow the AGI to extract commonalities between embodied instances; which, in turn, will encourage commensurability.

3 Create stable, hierarchy-dominated goal systems

One aspect of cognitive architecture is especially closely associated with ethical issues: goals and motivations. Here, we suggest, the best path to creating highly ethical AGI systems may be to deviate somewhat from human cognitive architecture.

Some may perceive this as a risky assertion since, after all, the human cognitive architecture is moderately well understood, whereas any new direction will bring additional uncertainties. However, the ethical weaknesses of the human cognitive architecture are also very well understood, and we see no reason to believe that seeking to implement a closely human-like goal system and ethical system in an AGI system that differs from humans in significant ways (e.g., a robot body rather than a human body, no mother and father, no rhythmic breathing flow giving it innate empathy with the rhythms of nature, etc.) would yield predictable or positive results.

Indeed, if we could really create a digital human, correct down to a fairly detailed level, with a closely human-like body, then we would have a system whose ethical behavior and thinking we would be able to understand very well by analogy to ordinary humans. We might find this digital human has profound psychological and ethical difficulties due to its lack of an ordinary biological heritage and family, and then we could try to deal with these issues using the tools of human psychology and psychiatry. We might even choose to implant such a digital human with false memories of a human heritage and family, and experiment with the ethically questionable consequences.

Apart from scenarios like these, however, if we're talking about taking a human-like AGI mind and embodying it in a video-game world, a plastic/metal humanoid robot body, or only a text chat interface, we are already talking about a system operating in a regime very different from that of any historical human being. For instance, empathy is a very important component of human ethics, and the roots of human empathy lie in our tactile relationship with our parents in our infancy, our ability to synchronize our breathing with the other humans around us, and a host of other aspects of our particular human embodiment. In taking a closely human-like cognitive architecture and lifting it out of the context of all this bodily intelligence, one is already doing something quite "artificial."

So, barring a true mind-and-body digital-human approach (which seems infeasible in the short- or medium-term future), the choice is not human vs. non-human, but rather between different ways of constructing non-human-like AGIs by incorporating aspects of human architecture with engineered structures and dynamics. Given this reality, our considered opinion is that the approach most likely to yield an ethically positive outcome is to deviate significantly from the "intentional" component of human cognitive architecture, and create AGI systems embodying a different approach to goals and motivations. Specifically, we believe it may be valuable to design AGI systems with a more rigorous and precise notion of "goal" than humans possess, playing a central (though not necessarily dominating) role in their dynamics.

In the context of human intelligence, the concept of a "goal" is a descriptive abstraction. Humans may adopt goals for a time and then drop them, may pursue multiple conflicting goals simultaneously, and may often proceed in an apparently goal-less manner. Sometimes the goal that a person appears to be pursuing may be very different from the one they think they're pursuing. Evolutionary psychology (Barrett et al. 2002) argues that, directly or indirectly, all humans are ultimately pursuing the goal of maximizing the inclusive fitness of their genes – but given the complex mix of evolution and self-organization in natural history (Salthe 1993), this is hardly a general explanation for human behavior. Ultimately, in the human context, "goal" is best thought of as a frequently useful heuristic concept.

AGI systems, however, may be designed with explicit goal systems. This provides no guarantee that such AGI systems will actually pursue the goals that their goal systems specify – depending on the role that the goal system plays in the overall system dynamics, other dynamic phenomena might sometimes intervene and cause the system to behave in ways opposed to its explicit goals. However, we submit that this design sketch provides a better framework than would exist in an AGI system closely emulating the human brain.

We realize this point may be somewhat contentious. A counterargument (given that society exists) would be that the human brain is known to support at least moderately ethical behavior, judged by human ethical standards, whereas the ethical propensity of less brain-like AGI systems is not well understood. However, the obvious counter-counterpoints are that:

- Humans are often not consistently ethical, so creating AGI systems potentially much more practically powerful than humans, but with closely human-like ethical, motivational, and goal systems could pose significant risk. People put in positions of gross power imbalance without oversight can often succumb to the temptation to abuse their power (Zimbardo 2007).
- The effect on a human-like ethical/motivational/goal system of increasing the intelligence, or changing the physical embodiment or cognitive capabilities, of the agent containing the system is difficult to predict,

given the complexities involved. Consider a human who could outwit the rest of humanity. Without a social contract to abide by, they might discard ethical behavior in favor of their personal wants.

The course we tentatively recommend, and are following in our own work, is to develop AGI systems with explicit, hierarchically modulated goal systems. That is:

- Create one or more "top goals."
- Have the system derive subgoals from these, using its own intelligence, although potentially guided by educational interaction or explicit programming.
- Have a significant percentage of the system's activity governed by the explicit pursuit of these goals.

In addition, these goals should be relatively stable. One way is to represent the goals in the context of a network of related concepts instead of a simplistic representation that requires a quantitative variable (perhaps representing energy available or "hunger") to remain above a threshold.

Included in the top goals should be expansion of the conceptual understanding of the other top goals, as well as understanding the relationship between the goals. An AGI may recognize when goals conflict, and then optimize a balance between them instead of wildly oscillating between fulfillment of two contrary goals.

One important decision relates to the immutability of the top goals. Embedding them in a network of concepts will shape their meaning, but conversely will provide resilience against removal. For example, if the network of related concepts describes the goal well enough, then semantically they could have an implicit influence on the goal system similar to that of the goal itself. However, this may be dependent in large part on the architecture of an AGI.

Note that the "significant percentage" in the third point need not be 100 percent; OpenCog, for example, is designed to combine explicitly goal-directed activity with other "spontaneous" activity. Insisting that all activity be explicitly goal-directed may be too strict a requirement to place on AGI architectures, especially when the route to achieving any particular goal is unclear. Such acknowledgments of undirected behavior may set off alarm bells for proponents of provably Friendly AI; however, spontaneous behavior could still be checked to ensure it isn't predicted to harm the rest of the AGI's goal system.

The next step, of course, is for the top-level goals to be chosen in accordance with the principle of human-Friendliness. One of our next points, about the Global Brain, addresses a way of doing this. In our near-term work with OpenCog, we are using somewhat simplistic approaches, with a view toward early-stage system testing.

For instance, an OpenCog agent in a virtual world may have top-level goals to satisfy various physiological demands. At the most basic level, one of these goals usually relates to satisfying an energy demand in order to remain a functional non-entropic system. The complete motivation system currently used for guiding avatars in a virtual sandbox world comes from Dietrich Dörner's Psi theory of motivation and actions (Dörner 2002). Another example of a demand is "certainty," to encourage exploration of the unknown, and increase the extent to which the avatar understands and can predict the world. Other more subtle motivations might be to find more compact representations of patterns observed in the world, so as to minimize the resources required to reason about them.

There are also some motivations that do relate to social behavior, such as the "affiliation" demand that is related to seeking the company and attention of other agents. However, these are not currently chosen specifically to promote friendliness. Demands such as that of maintaining energy clearly need to be tempered with those that encourage socially responsible behavior, perhaps with relative ordering of their importance.

4 **Ensure that the early stages of recursive self-improvement occur relatively slowly and with rich human involvement**

One of the more exciting, and worrisome, aspects of advanced AGI is the possibility of radical, rapid self-improvement, or "self-programming." If an AGI can understand its own source code and the algorithms underlying its intelligence, it may be able to improve these algorithms and modify its code accordingly, thus increasing its intelligence. Potentially this could lead to a dynamic of accelerating intelligence, in which the smarter the system gets, the better it is at making itself smarter. It's easy to leap from this potential to visions of an AGI ascending from human-level general intelligence to massive transhumanity in days or even minutes.

Furthermore, fundamental algorithmic improvements to the AGI system's intelligence could synergize with simpler processes like the AGI marshaling additional hardware for its infrastructure, or more complex options like the AGI inventing new forms of computing hardware, commissioning their construction, and then achieving greater intelligence via porting itself to the new hardware.

At the current stage of AGI development, it's difficult to assess the realism of the more extreme hypothetical forms of "recursive self-improvement." Metaphorical analogs to physical situations like nuclear chain reactions are compelling, but obviously are more poetic than scientific. This sort of computational dynamic has never been experimented with before, and could be susceptible to bottlenecks that aren't currently clear. There also could be modes of acceleration that aren't currently clear – for instance, a sufficiently intelligent system might discover new principles of physics or computation enabling intelligence increase beyond levels current science can predict. Getting more science-fictional, a sufficiently intelligent AGI could potentially figure out how to contact extraterrestrial civilizations, which might then inject it with a large amount of intelligence and knowledge already developed elsewhere.

However, in spite of the particularly speculative nature of this possibility, it seems worthwhile to structure AGI development to minimize the associated risks. The primary course in this regard, it seems, is to minimize the extent to which self-improvement and self-programming occur in isolation.[3] The more the AGI system is engaged with human minds and other AGI systems in the course of its self-modification, presumably the less likely it is to veer off in an undesired and unpredictable direction. Of course, this can only happen if we create AGIs that have a strong inbuilt motivation to consult and work with others in the context of their self-modifications. This may slow down the process of self-improvement, compared to what would be maximally achievable otherwise, but it should also reduce the chance of things rapidly going awry.

A rich coupling between the AGI system and the outside world, such as we've suggested here, leads to our next topic, the Global Brain.

5 Tightly link AGI with the Global Brain

Some futurist thinkers, such as Francis Heylighen, believe that engineering AGI systems is at best a peripheral endeavor in the development of novel intelligence on Earth, because the real story is the developing Global Brain (Heylighen 2007; Goertzel 2001): the composite, self-organizing information system comprising humans, computers, data stores, the Internet, mobile phones, and other communication systems.

Our own views are less dismissive of AGI – we believe that AGI systems will display capabilities fundamentally different from the Global Brain, and that ultimately (unless such development is restricted) self-improving AGI systems will develop intelligence vastly greater than any system possessing humans as a significant component. However, we do respect the power of the Global Brain, and suspect that the early stages of development for an AGI system may go quite differently if it is tightly connected to the Global Brain, making rich and diverse use of Internet information resources and communication with diverse sections of humanity.

The Internet component of the Global Brain allows us to access almost any piece of available information, but we don't have it contextually integrated with our experience, which might be considered the difference between knowing a fact and understanding its meaning. Despite our impressive capacity to generate relationships and perform this integration, we are confined to the neural capacity of our brains and the firing speeds of our neurons. The reduction in conceptual bandwidth from brain to keyboard and mouse, or even to human face-to-face communication, reduces our effective ability to reason using knowledge outside of our brain.

Despite the difference in memorization and integrated knowledge, there is great potential for Global Brain integration to bring intelligence enhancement to AGIs. The ability to invoke web searches across documents and databases can greatly enhance the perceived cognitive ability of the AGI, as well as the capability to consult specialized databases like Geographic Information Systems and other specialized services via its web API (application program interface). Goertzel (2008) reviews the potential for embodied language learning achievable using AGIs to power non-player characters in widely accessible virtual worlds or massively multiplayer online games. Work by Orkin and Roy (2010) provides one example. Here, the actions of interacting humans are used to record social behavior and language, as human players interact with one another within the confines of a restaurant, with the hope that it will provide a contextual grounding to language use.

Another powerful potential benefit from the Internet for the development of ethical AGI has two aspects:

1. In a manner analogous to language learning, an AGI system may receive ethical training from a wide variety of humans in parallel, for example, via controlling characters in wide-access virtual worlds, and thus gain feedback and guidance regarding the ethics of their behaviors. This could also be weighted by the perceived social acceptance of that character by other human-controlled characters. Of course, measuring such a trait is not trivial, but heuristics such as how often others initiate follow-up interactions with a human character, or the frequency with which others facilitate the AGI reaching its goals, may be starting points.
2. Internet-based information systems (such as, but not limited to, social media and Wikipedia) may be used to explicitly gather a consensus regarding human values and goals, which may then be appropriately utilized as input for an AGI system's top-level goals.

The second point begins to make abstract-sounding notions like Coherent Extrapolated Volition and Coherent Aggregated Volition, mentioned above, seem more practical and concrete. Gathering information about individuals' values via brain imaging, if such a technology becomes available, is an interesting prospect; but at present more prosaic methods, such as directly asking people questions, and assessing their ethical reactions to various real-world and hypothetical scenarios, may be used. In addition, engaging people in structured interactions might be used, aimed specifically at eliciting collectively acceptable value systems (see the next sub-section). This sort of approach could realize CAV in a practical way, using existing knowledge in social science and psychology.

6 **Foster deep, consensus-building interactions and commensurability between divergent viewpoints**

Three potentially problematic issues arising with the notion of using Global Brain-related technologies to form a "coherent volition" from the divergent views of various human beings are:

- The tendency of the Internet to encourage people to interact mainly with others who share their own narrow views and interests, rather than a more diverse body of people with substantially different viewpoints. The 300 people in the world who want to communicate using predicate logic can find each other,[4] obscure musical virtuosos from around the world can attract an audience, and researchers in obscure domains can share papers without needing to wait years for paper journal publication, etc. People will tend to clique with those with common interests, but eschew people with radically different viewpoints.
- The tendency of many contemporary Internet technologies to reduce interaction to a very simplistic level (e.g. 140-character tweets, brief Facebook wall posts). This allows more topics to be reviewed but can lead to careful reading being replaced by quick skimming. Such trends mean that a deep sharing of perspectives by individuals with divergent views is not necessarily encouraged. As a somewhat extreme example, many of the YouTube pages displaying rock music videos are currently littered with comments by "haters" asserting that rock music is inferior to classical music or jazz; obviously this is a far cry from deep and productive sharing between people with different tastes and backgrounds. Twitter arguments often end with one or both parties admitting 140 characters is insufficient to convey their views. Fortunately, these sometimes do lead to an agreement to move to email or face-to-face discussion.
- Search engines and content customization algorithms have been criticized as providing overly personalized views of the world. To an extent, we are presented with a viewpoint of the world that makes us comfortable rather than substantially challenging our existing beliefs (Pariser 2011). Tweets and YouTube comments have their place in the cosmos, but they probably aren't ideal in terms of helping humanity to form a coherent collective volition suitable for providing guidance to an AGI's goal system.

A description of communication at the opposite end of the spectrum is presented in Adam Kahane and Peter Senge's excellent book *Solving Tough Problems* (2004), which describes a methodology that has been used to reconcile deeply conflicting views in some challenging real-world situations (e.g., helping to peacefully end apartheid in South Africa). A core idea of the methodology is to have people with different views explore various possible future scenarios together, in great detail. In cognitive psychology terms, this is a collective generation of hypothetical episodic knowledge. This has multiple benefits, including:

- Emotional bonds and mutual understanding are built in the process of collaboratively exploring the scenarios.
- The focus on concrete situations helps to break through some of the counterproductive abstract ideas that people (on both sides of any dichotomy) may have formed.
- The emergence of conceptual blends that might never have arisen from people with only a single point of view.

The result of such a process, when successful, is not an "average" of the participants' views, but more like a "conceptual blend" of their perspectives.

According to conceptual blending, which some hypothesize to be the core algorithm of creativity (Fauconnier and Turner 2002), new concepts are formed by combining key aspects of existing concepts – but doing so judiciously, carefully choosing which aspects to retain, so as to obtain a high-quality, useful, and interesting new whole. A blend is a compact entity that is similar to each of the entities blended, capturing their "essence" but also possessing its own novel holistic integrity. In the case of blending different people's worldviews to form something new that everybody is going to have to live with (as in the case of finding a peaceful path beyond apartheid for South Africa, or arriving at a humanity-wide CBV to use to guide an AGI goal system), everybody has to agree that enough of the essence of their own view has been captured.

Can deep conceptual blending of diverse and divergent human perspectives be fostered on a global scale? One possible way is the creation of appropriate Global Brain-oriented technologies, while moving away from technologies like Twitter that focus on quick and simple exchanges of small thoughts within affinity groups. What's needed is arguably just the opposite: long exchanges about difficult concepts between individuals with radically different perspectives. The exchanges should include sharing feelings, and should take place between people who would not commonly associate with each other.

There is some hope of getting there, however. When mailing lists and comments on blogs are carefully moderated to enforce civility between opposing sides of a strongly heated exchange, this can sometimes be a productive way for two conflicted groups to discuss their viewpoints. If an AGI moderated discussion between groups representing viewpoints of the Global Brain, then perhaps such democratic consensus could more easily be reached.

Building and effectively popularizing Internet technologies that have an ever richer capability to promote this kind of meaningful interaction – and quickly enough to provide guidance to the goal systems of the first highly powerful AGIs – seems a significant, though fascinating, challenge.

Relationship with Coherent Extrapolated Volition

Yudkowsky's CEV concept, mentioned above, has been loosely described by its author as follows:

> In poetic terms, our coherent extrapolated volition is our wish if we knew more, thought faster, were more the people we wished we were, had grown up farther together; where the extrapolation converges rather than diverges, where our wishes cohere rather than interfere; extrapolated as we wish that extrapolated, interpreted as we wish that interpreted. (Yudkowsky 2004)

While a moving humanistic vision, this seems to us rather difficult to implement in a computer algorithm in a compellingly "right" way. With many different ways of implementing CEV, the choice between them would involve multiple, highly subtle, and non-rigorous human judgment calls.[5] However, if a deep collective process of interactive scenario sharing and analysis is carried out, to arrive at a form of Coherent Blended Volition, this process may well involve many of the same kinds of extrapolation that are conceived to be part of Coherent Extrapolated Volition. The core difference between the two approaches is that, in the CEV vision, the extrapolation and coherentization[6] are to be done by a highly intelligent, highly specialized software program, whereas in the approach suggested here, they are to be carried out by the collective activity of humans as mediated by Global Brain technologies. Our perspective is that the definition of collective human values is probably better carried out via human collaboration, rather than delegated to a machine-optimization process. And the creation of Internet technologies that can support deep sharing and engagement with humanity, while a difficult task, is significantly easier and more likely to be done in the near future than the creation of narrow AI technology capable of effectively performing CEV-style extrapolations.

Another issue with the original CEV formulation is its assumption that humanity's wishes, when extrapolated, will cohere and converge. There seems no strong basis to believe this will happen – nor to believe that, in the case where it does happen, the extrapolation will reflect human desires or needs in any humanly comprehensible sense. Humans may share ancestral biological goals but, as noted above, we have divergent views on many topics. Even people whom we might judge to have an equivalent level of intelligence can differ significantly in their ethics, as our belief systems are built up from a different temporal ordering of experiences, and may be founded on different childhood axioms of social interaction.

7 Create a mutually supportive community of AGIs

Omohundro (2009) argues that game-theoretic dynamics related to populations of roughly equally powerful agents may play a valuable role in mitigating the risks associated with advanced AGI systems. Roughly speaking, if one has a society of AGIs rather than a single AGI, and all the members of the society share roughly similar ethics, then if one AGI starts to go "off the rails," its compatriots will be in a position to correct its behavior.

One may argue that this is actually a hypothesis about which AGI designs are safest, because a "community of AGIs" may be considered a single AGI with an internal community-like design. However, the matter is more subtle than that if one considers the AGI systems embedded in the Global Brain and human society. In this case, there is some substance to the notion of a population of AGIs systematically presenting themselves to humans and non-AGI software processes as separate entities.

Unfortunately, a society of AGIs is no protection against a single member undergoing a "hard takeoff" and drastically accelerating its intelligence as it simultaneously shifts its ethical principles. In this sort of scenario, with a single AGI that rapidly becomes much more powerful than the others, and differently oriented, the latter are left impotent to act so as to preserve their values. This, however, may be mitigated by the difficulty an individual node in a largely homogeneous community may have in trying to subvert the resources still available to the others to mount an immune response or social reprisal. The chance of the community being able to respond to the outlier in time brings up the point considered next, regarding "takeoff speed."

The operation of an AGI society may depend somewhat sensitively on the architectures of the AGI systems in question. Community moderation will work better if the AGIs have a relatively easy way to inspect and comprehend much of the contents of each other's minds. This introduces a bias toward AGIs that rely heavily on more explicit forms of knowledge representation.

The ideal in this regard would be a system like Cyc (Lenat and Guha 1990) with a fully explicit logic-based knowledge representation using a standard ontology – in this case, every Cyc instance would have a relatively easy time understanding the inner thought processes of every other such instance. However, most AGI researchers doubt that fully explicit approaches like this will ever be capable of achieving advanced AGI using feasible computational resources. OpenCog uses a mixed representation, with an explicit (but uncertain and experientially adaptable) logical aspect as well as an explicit subsymbolic aspect more analogous to attractor neural nets.

The OpenCog design also includes a yet unimplemented mechanism called *Psynese*, intended to make it easier for one OpenCog instance to translate its personal thoughts into the mental language of another. This translation process may be quite subtle, since each instance will generally learn a host of new concepts based on its experience, and these concepts may not possess any compact mapping into shared linguistic symbols or percepts. The wide deployment of some mechanism of this nature, among a community of AGIs, will be very helpful in enabling this community to display the level of mutual understanding needed for strongly encouraging ethical stability.

Of course, it is possible that the distinction between an individual instance and a community will not be meaningful. OpenCog is currently a mostly non-distributed application,[7] but there is a lot of interest in moving it to a distributed architecture that can take advantage of cloud services or volunteers willing to run local instances of OpenCog in a manner similar to SETI@home or other distributed processing tasks.

There may be even more concern in this case about unscrupulous individuals injecting knowledge intended to compromise the AGI's non-partisan Friendliness; however, there are a number of similar areas eager to ensure consistent behavior in a networked application. BitTorrent is a heterogeneous network of peer-to-peer file-sharing clients. While the core protocol between clients is shared, individual clients have a number of guards to prevent "leechers" who don't contribute to the health of the torrents and the performance of the network (Legout et al. 2007). Bitcoin, the distributed currency, uses cryptography techniques to ensure the safe transaction of currency without a centralized bank (Nakamoto 2008). A key point is that the health of these networks relies on the majority of nodes acting in a "friendly" way, consistent with the original design. For a massively distributed and large network, the chances of any one individual being able to co-opt enough networking elements or computing power become exceedingly small, although not impossible.

8 Encourage measured co-advancement of AGI software and AGI ethics theory

This point intersects with all the previous ideas. Everything involving AGI and Friendly AI (considered together or separately) currently involves significant uncertainty, and it seems likely that significant revision of current concepts will be necessary as progress on the path toward powerful AGI proceeds. However, whether there is time for such revision to occur, before AGI at the human level or above is created, depends on how fast the progress toward AGI turns out to be. Ideally, progress would be slow enough that, at each stage of intelligence advance, concepts such as those discussed in this chapter can be reevaluated and reanalyzed in the light of the data gathered, and AGI designs and approaches can be revised accordingly as necessary.

But how can this kind of measured co-advancement be encouraged? Of course, an all-powerful world government could strictly enforce such a pattern of development, but that's far from the current situation, and history shows that such scenarios tend to have their downsides.

One possibility would be the creation of an "AGI Nanny" – i.e., an AGI system with at least human-level intelligence, and with a high level of power to surveil and police the human world, but no taste for radical self-modification or reproduction. Such an AGI Nanny would allow human science, technology, and thought to advance fairly freely. It would, however, have the goal of forcibly preventing any development that seemed to be leading to premature creation of highly advanced AGI or other Singularity-enabling technologies, such as molecular nanotechnology or radical human brain enhancement. Once a sufficient understanding of AGI architecture and ethics was achieved, the AGI Nanny would release its control and enable the Singularity to proceed. The "Nanny" metaphor is chosen specifically because a human nanny watches human children until they grow up, and then releases them. Similarly, the AGI Nanny would watch over the human species until its technological and conceptual framework matured sufficiently to enable it to launch a Singularity with acceptable safety.

There seems no in-principle reason why an AGI Nanny scenario like this couldn't succeed. An AGI system like OpenCog, with an explicit goal system guiding most of its behaviors, could be programmed with goals consistent with the AGI Nanny role. However, the idea obviously would face significant practical obstacles (how would the AGI Nanny come to power in an ethical way?), and also has significant risk attached to it (what if, in spite of our best efforts, the AGI Nanny behaved in some unpredictable way?).

Of course, to make an AGI Nanny would itself require dramatic advances in AGI technology beyond the current state of the art. It is unclear whether it's easier to create an AGI Nanny than to create an unpredictably and dramatically self-improving AGI system. It may be that a similar set of technologies (OpenCog for instance) could be used to create either one, leading to possible scenarios where an AGI Nanny-focused team competes with a team focused on more hurriedly launching a Singularity via a rapidly self-improving AGI, each team using a separate forked version of the same codebase.

Setting aside the AGI Nanny possibility, how might measured co-advancement of AGI technology and AGI ethics understanding best be encouraged?

9 Develop advanced AGI sooner, not later

Somewhat ironically, it seems that one good way to ensure that AGI development proceeds at a relatively measured pace may be to initiate serious AGI development sooner rather than later. The same AGI concepts will yield slower practical development today than 10 years from now, and be slower 10 years from now than 20 years from now. This is a result of the ongoing rapid advancement of various tools related to AGI development, such as computer hardware, programming languages, and computer science algorithms.

Currently, the pace of AGI progress is sufficiently slow that practical work toward human-level AGI is in no danger of outpacing associated ethical theorizing. However, if we want to avoid dangerous outpacing, our best practical choice is to ensure more substantial AGI development occurs in the phase before the development of tools and hardware that will make AGI development and prototyping much quicker. Which, of course, is why the authors are doing their best in this direction via their work on the OpenCog project.

Furthermore, this point is connected with the need, raised above, to foster the development of Global Brain technologies that "foster deep, consensus-building interactions between divergent viewpoints." For such technology to be maximally valuable, it must be created quickly enough to incorporate the blended volition it extracts, so that we can use it to shape the goal system content of the first powerful AGIs. In essence, we want both deep-sharing Global Brain technology and AGI technology to evolve together rapidly, in comparison to the ongoing improvement in computing hardware and software engineering tools. Such a goal is challenging, since the latter aspects are more easily incrementally improved and thus receive dramatically more funding and focus than AGI.

5 Conclusion

We have briefly considered a number of strategies oriented toward increasing the odds of AGI Friendliness, with a focus on techniques relevant to an open-source AGI project such as OpenCog. None of these strategies gives any guarantees, but combined they should bias the odds in favor of a positive outcome.

None of the nine points raised is particularly well understood, but research into each of them could proceed meaningfully, in large part separately from any particular AGI design. However, at present little attention seems to get paid to AGI-ethics issues, either by the research funding establishment or by individual researchers on their own time.

The Machine Intelligence Research Institute (http://intelligence.org/; originally the Singularity Institute for Artificial Intelligence) – co-founded by Yudkowsky, referenced frequently above – is doing an admirable job of pursuing research in the Friendly AI domain. However, as the Institute's perspective is significantly different from ours, much of its work does not yet directly address the issues we've described. Although the Institute initially co-founded the OpenCog project, recently its preference has been for closed approaches to AGI development. Its recent research foci have included CEV, the pursuit of provably Friendly AGI designs, broad exploration of existential risks, and advocacy of general human rationality. While worthy, each of these covers only a small scope of the area required to figure out how to bias an open-source (or otherwise) AGI software project in the direction of Friendliness.

We anticipate that once AGI research advances to the point where it demonstrates more exciting practical capabilities, and more resources are consequently focused on AGI, then more resources will also be focused on problems related to AGI ethics. We have proposed that the best approach is to begin the serious co-evolution of functional AGI systems and AGI-related ethical theory, as well as the development of deep-sharing-oriented Internet tools, as soon as possible. These need to move ahead before we have so much technical infrastructure and computing power that parties relatively unconcerned with ethics are able to rush forward with AGI development in dangerously hasty fashion.

Notes

This chapter is a slightly abridged version of a paper first published in *Journal of Evolution and Technology*, 22(1) (December 2011): 115–131.

1 See "Stages of Ethical Development in Artificial General Intelligence Systems" presented in Goertzel and Bugaj (2008). This theory integrates, among other aspects, Kohlberg's (1981) theory of logical ethical judgment (focused on justice and declarative knowledge) and Gilligan's (1982) theory of empathetic ethical judgment (focused on interpersonal relationships formed from episodic and sensorimotor memory).

2 For more details, see our longer discussion in *Journal of Evolution and Technology*, 22(1): pp. 115–131.

3 Ironically, this is almost the opposite of one approach sometimes suggested for regulating AGI development: AI boxing. This is where an AGI is confined to a tightly controlled environment with limited interaction with the rest of the world.

4 See the website Lojban: The Logical Language, available at http://lojban.org (accessed August 14, 2013).

5 Readers are encouraged to look at the original CEV essay (Yudkowsky 2004) online and make their own assessments.
6 "To coherentize is to make something autopoietic, or more robustly autopoietic. What consciousness does, when it coherentizes, is to **make autopoietic systems.** It makes things more self-producing." Goertzel 1997.
7 Various narrow AI components, or parts of the embodiment architecture, can run as separate servers, but the core control resides in a single application.

References

Adams, Sam, Goertzel, Ben, et al. 2012. Mapping the landscape of artificial general intelligence. *AI Magazine* March 22.

Arkin, Ronald. 2009. *Governing Lethal Behavior in Autonomous Robots*. London: Chapman & Hall/CRC.

Barrett, Louise, Dunbar, Robin, and Lycett, John. 1993. *Human Evolutionary Psychology*. Princeton, NJ: Princeton University Press.

Bostrom, Nick. 2002. Existential risks. *Journal of Evolution and Technology* 9(1) (March), http://www.jetpress.org/volume9/risks.html (accessed October 10, 2013).

de Garis, Hugo. 2005. *The Artilect War: Cosmists vs. Terrans : A Bitter Controversy Concerning Whether Humanity Should Build Godlike Massively Intelligent Machines*. Palm Springs, CA: ETC Publications.

Dörner, Dietrich. 2002. *Die Mechanik des Seelenwagens. Eine neuronale Theorie der Handlungsregulation*. Bern: Verlag Hans Huber.

Drexler, K.E. 1986. *Engines of Creation: The Coming Era of Nanotechnology*. New York: Anchor Books. Also available online at http://e-drexler.com/p/06/00/EOC_Cover.html (accessed October 10, 2013).

Fauconnier, Gilles, and Turner, Mark. 2002. *The Way We Think: Conceptual Blending and the Mind's Hidden Complexities*. New York: Basic Books.

Gilligan, Carol. 1982. *In a Different Voice*. Cambridge, MA: Harvard University Press.

Goertzel, Ben. 1997. *From Complexity to Creativity*, http://www.goertzel.org/books/complex/ch8.html (accessed October 10, 2013).

Goertzel, Ben. 2001. *Creating Internet Intelligence*. New York: Plenum Press.

Goertzel, Ben. 2006. *The Hidden Pattern*. Boca Raton, FL: BrownWalker Press.

Goertzel, Ben. 2008. *A pragmatic path toward endowing virtually-embodied AIs with human-level linguistic capability*. IEEE World Congress on Computational Intelligence (WCCI).

Goertzel, Ben. 2009a. The embodied communication prior. In *Proceedings of ICCI-09*. Hong Kong.

Goertzel, Ben. 2009b. *AGI, ethics, cognitive synergy and ethical synergy*. The multiverse according to Ben, comment posted September 9, http://multiverseaccordingtoben.blogspot.com/2009/09/agi-ethics-cognitive-synergy-and.html (accessed October 10, 2013).

Goertzel, Ben. 2010. *Coherent aggregated volition*. The multiverse according to Ben, comment posted 12 March, http://multiverseaccordingtoben.blogspot.com/2010/03/coherent-aggregated-volition-toward.html (accessed October 10, 2013).

Goertzel, Ben, and Bugaj, Stephan Vladimir. 2008. Stages of ethical development in uncertain inference based AI systems. *Proceedings of First AGI Conference.* Amsterdam: IOS Press, pp. 448–459.

Goertzel, Ben, de Garis, Hugo, Pennachin, Cassio, Geisweiller, Nil, Araujo, Samir, Pitt, Joel, Shuo Chen, Ruiting Lian, Min Jiang, Ye Yang, and Deheng Huang. 2010. OpenCogBot: Achieving generally intelligent virtual agent control and humanoid robotics via cognitive synergy. *Proceedings of ICAI 2010.* Beijing.

Hart, David, and Goertzel, Ben. 2008. OpenCog: A software framework for integrative artificial general intelligence. In AGI, vol. 171 of *Frontiers in Artificial Intelligence and Applications.* Amsterdam: IOS Press, 2008: 468–472, http://dblp.uni-trier.de/db/conf/agi/agi2008.html#HartG08 (accessed October 10, 2013).

Heylighen, F. 2007. The global superorganism: An evolutionary-cybernetic model of the emerging network society. *Social Evolution and History* 6(1): 57–117.

Hibbard, Bill. 2002. *Superintelligent Machines.* New York: Kluwer Academic.

Kahane, Adam. 2004. *Solving Tough Problems: An Open Way of Talking, Listening and Creating New Realities.* San Francisco: Berrett-Koehler.

Kohlberg, Lawrence. 1981. *The Philosophy of Moral Development: Moral Stages and the Idea of Justice.* New York: Harper & Row.

Laird, John, Wray, Robert, Marinier, Robert, and Langley, Pat. 2009. Claims and challenges in evaluating human-level intelligent systems. *Proceedings of AGI-09.*

Legg, Shane. 2006a. *Unprovability of friendly AI.* Vetta Project, comment posted September 15, http://web.archive.org/web/20120918213006/ http://www.vetta.org/2006/09/unprovability-of-friendly-ai/ (accessed October 10, 2013).

Legg, Shane. 2006b. *Friendly AI is bunk.* Vetta Project, comment posted September 9, http://commonsenseatheism.com/wp-content/uploads/2011/02/Legg-Friendly-AI-is-bunk.pdf (accessed October 10, 2013).

Legout, Arnaud, Liogkas, Nikitas, Kohler, Eddie, and Zhang, Lixia. 2007. Clustering and sharing incentives in BitTorrent systems. In *Sygmetrics '07: Proceedings of the 2007 ACM Sigmetrics International Conference on Measurement and Modeling of Computer Systems.* New York: ACI, pp. 301–312.

Lenat, Douglas, and Guha, R.V. 1990. *Building Large Knowledge-Based Systems: Representation and Inference in the Cyc Project.* Reading, PA: Addison-Wesley.

Nakamoto, Satoshi. 2008. *Bitcoin: A peer-to-peer electronic cash system.* Bitcoin.org, http://www.bitcoin.org/bitcoin.pdf.

Omohundro, Stephen. 2008. The basic AI drives. In Ben Goertzel and Pei Wang (eds.) *Proceedings of the First AGI Conference.* Amsterdam: IOS Press.

Omohundro, Stephen. 2009. *Creating a cooperative future.* Self-aware systems: Understanding natural and artificial intelligence, comment posted February 23, http://selfawaresystems.com/2009/02/23/talk-on-creating-a-cooperative-future/ (accessed October 10, 2013).

Orkin, Jeff, and Roy, Deb. 2010. The restaurant game: Learning social behavior and language from thousands of players online. *Journal of Game Development* 3(2): 39–60.

Pariser, Eli. 2011. *The Filter Bubble: What the Internet is Hiding from You.* New York: Viking.

Raymond, Eric Steven. 2000. *The cathedral and the bazaar, version 3.0*. Thyrsus Enterprises, http://www.catb.org/~esr/writings/homesteading/cathedral-bazaar/ (accessed October 10, 2013).

Rizzolatti, Giacomo, and Craighero, Laila. 2004. The mirror-neuron system. *Annual Review of Neuroscience* 27: 169 –192.

Salthe, Stanley N. 1993. *Development and Evolution: Complexity and Change in Biology*. Cambridge, MA: MIT Press.

Sotala, Kaj. 2011. 14 objections against AI/friendly AI/the Singularity answered. Xuepolis, http://www.xuenay.net/objections.html (accessed October 10, 2013).

Wallach, Wendell, and Allen, Colin. 2010. *Moral Machines: Teaching Robots Right from Wrong*. New York: Oxford University Press.

Waser, Mark R. 2008. Discovering the foundations of a universal system of ethics as a road to safe artificial intelligence. *Proceedings of BICA 2008*. Arlington, VA, http://becominggaia.files.wordpress.com/2010//06/waser-bica08.pdf (accessed October 10, 2013).

Yudkowsky, Eliezer. 2001. *Creating Friendly AI 1.0: The analysis and design of benevolent goal architectures*, intelligence.org/files/CFAI.pdf (accessed October 10, 2013).

Yudkowsky, Eliezer. 2004. *Coherent extrapolated volition*, intelligence.org/files /CEV.pdf (accessed October 10, 2013).

Yudkowsky, Eliezer. 2006. *What is friendly AI?*, http://www.kurzweilai.net /what-is-friendly-ai (accessed 10 October, 2013).

Zimbardo, Philip. G. 2007. *The Lucifer Effect: Understanding How Good People Turn Evil*. New York: Random House.

5

Feasible Mind Uploading

Randal A. Koene

Having a good idea of what goes on inside our bodies is extremely useful for reparative surgery. Making copies of valuable documents saves them from getting lost. We need similar access to the brain.

One of the most significant advances in the biological sciences was the development of tools that let us sequence and synthesize DNA, and thus access the blueprints of biological form and function. While we can examine our developmental blueprints in DNA and even apply gene therapy in adulthood (Bernardes de Jesus et al. 2012), the complex structure of the brain has not yet been addressed with tools powerful enough to give us a similar kind of access. Initiated by developmental processes guided by DNA, its structure is linked to and influenced by its environment within a human body, but much of its intricacy is arrived at by a different kind of development: neural plasticity. The resulting operational circuitry is still largely opaque to us. We cannot yet take a snapshot that would enable any sort of backup, inform repair or reconstruction, or enable the correction of problems or the extension of our abilities and senses.

Understanding how mental functions work requires more than just a rough idea of the brain locations involved. Published studies using magnetic resonance imaging (MRI) are frequently unsatisfactory, since they rarely give insight into mechanisms specific to a mental operation. Without such insight, it is difficult to understand why John responds to an experienced scene in one way, while Mary responds in another. How is it that Mary's brain allows her to concentrate on scientific studies and a passion for exploration, while

Intelligence Unbound: The Future of Uploaded and Machine Minds, First Edition.
Edited by Russell Blackford and Damien Broderick.

John seeks primarily distraction and social comforts? What underlies these very individual characteristic differences?

The most complete solution for backup, repair, study, and enhancement would involve mind uploading to an implementation of mental processing in a substrate that allows direct insight into the details of ongoing mental functions. The aim here is to implement intelligence in an engineered processing substrate – a machine mind, as it were. This solution is clearly related to work in artificial intelligence and shares many of its analytical requirements and synthesis goals, but the objective is unambiguously to make individual human minds independent of a single (biological) substrate (Koene 2011).

1 Neural interfaces and neural prostheses

The level of access we must achieve requires further study and the development of interfaces that can be used long-term for ongoing access to detailed brain activity without causing unwanted disturbances or changes. The same interfaces are needed so that individualized clinical neuroprostheses can replace the function of specific brain circuits. Brain–machine interfaces require adaptations for communication to be possible, emphasizing either the machine or the brain. A large proportion of interfaces today expect the brain to do most of the heavy lifting in terms of learning to adjust and work with the interface, to learn to use it as a channel for either read-out or stimulation (Lebedev and Nicolelis 2006).

When the brain has to do most of the adapting to the new communication protocol, the interface does not need to understand all the intricacies of neuronal circuitry nor how the brain normally interprets signals and produces output through the body. Nor does it need to understand how one brain region speaks with another so that together they may carry out some brain function. Instead, the brain learns to identify and decode the interface and to give the necessary responses, so that, for example, a prosthetic limb with limited degrees of motion or feedback can be used. Beyond this practical matter of requiring the interface recipient to carry out the learning and adjusting, it is worthwhile to consider how the adjustment differentially affects identity, personality, and the experience of a patient over time, especially when the number of interface channels is drastically increased.

Alternatively, we must devise interfaces that fit seamlessly into the operating brain. Such interfaces must be pre-adapted and usable without much learning at the recipient's end, seeming as natural as a person's normal sensations and actions of body and limb. To build such interfaces demands careful analysis of neuronal circuit function. What input does the circuitry receive? How does it transform input into output? The analysis might even need to be carried out in a subject-specific manner where the details of circuit function depend on individual characteristic details of the circuitry.

Future developments that might actually accomplish access to the detailed mechanisms and parameters of mental operations will require communication channels with high resolution and high bandwidth. Retraining the brain for each of those channels is not only impractical, but would alter and distort those same details to which we seek access.

Cognitive prosthetic work, as carried out by the Berger lab at the University of Southern California, has already addressed this issue successfully (Berger et al. 2012). While practical examples of functioning cognitive neural prostheses are still rare, one well-known example is the Berger lab's hippocampal neural prosthetic. This depends on a so-called bio-mimetic chip, which implements an algorithmic transfer function that was trained to replicate the operational properties of biological neural circuitry in a region of the hippocampus, CA3. It copies the way input to the region is turned into output. The prosthesis has been shown to take over the function of rat CA3 circuitry successfully under experimental conditions and is now being tested in primates (Marmarelis et al. 2013).

The brain is composed of many similar components, such as neurons of several types and synapses of several types. It is a very large collection of such components and the arrangement is highly complex. Brain emulation aims at a mechanistic re-implementation letting us predict with acceptable error an active state and behavior at a time $t+dt$ if we know the state at the slightly earlier time t. This process of discovering the functions by which an unknown system turns input into output is often called *system identification* (Ljung 1999). By investigating the correlated input and output, you try to determine which functions constitute the characteristic processing.

The concrete success of such an approach to brain emulation, a successful neuroprosthesis, is determined with reference to experimental goals or well-defined performance requirements that set experiential criteria (Koene 2012). One example is the experimental performance of the hippocampal replacement chip, as tested in laboratory settings by Berger's team. Another is the proof-of-concept verification carried out in published work by Briggman et al. (2011), where the connectome of a sample of retinal tissue was studied. They used the structural data obtained by electron microscopy in the lab of Winfried Denk to derive functional interpretations for retinal ganglion cells, and the protocol was similar to one that could be used to build model representations with specimen-specific parameters for brain emulation. Their publication was an important proof-of-concept, because they were able to verify their functional derivations by comparison with functional data that had been gathered in the same specimen via fluorescent optical microscopy.

2 Iterative improvements in four main areas to achieve whole brain emulation

Whole brain emulation relies on determining precisely which signals we care about and then breaking the problem down into a collection of smaller system-identification problems. To tackle those, we have a roadmap that includes structural scanning (connectomics) as well as new tools for functional recording.

The method that is currently producing the most promising results in terms of connectome data is high-resolution volume microscopy carried out by taking electron microscope images of successive ultra-thin layers of brain tissue. Electron micrographs at a resolution of 5–10 nanometers enable us to identify individual synapses and to reconstruct the 3D geometry of fine detail in the axon and dendrite branches. Excellent results have come out of the labs of Winfried Denk (Max Planck), Jeff Lichtman (Harvard), and Ken Hayworth (Janelia Farm). A strong interest in connectome data led to rapid tool development between 2008 and 2011. Two teams used Serial Block Face Scanning Electron Microscopy techniques from Denk's lab in combination with two-photon functional recordings; they published remarkable results that might be proof-of-principle for system identification in pieces of retina and visual cortex. From 3D reconstructions, they were able to identify specific neural circuit functions that were corroborated by their functional recordings, such as for the direction selectivity of retinal ganglion cells (Briggman et al. 2011). 3D reconstructions clearly show the cell bodies of individual neurons, and the detailed morphology of axons and dendrites, situated within neuronal circuitry with visible synaptic connections.

It is important to realize that this is no longer just an idea for future development, but a class of existing tools that can directly solve one of the main requirements for whole brain emulation.

As for the functional data required for system identification in each small sub-system, the most promising developments take their inspiration from the brain's own method of detecting activity: this functions at very close range in physical proximity to sources of interaction, through microscopic synaptic receptor channels. The brain handles an enormous quantity of information by using a vast hierarchy of such connections. So, to satisfy the temporal and spatial resolution requirements for in-vivo functional characterization, we look primarily to the development of new tools that can take these measurements from within.

There is a collaborative effort underway at MIT, Harvard, and Northwestern University to create biological tools that employ DNA amplification to write events onto a molecular "ticker-tape" (Kording 2011). The advantage of these tools is that they readily operate at cellular and sub-cellular resolutions, and can do so in vast numbers throughout the neural tissue. Synthetic DNA with a known code is duplicated over and over again through circular amplification. This is done within the cell body of a neuron, but that cell has also received a voltage-gated channel that interferes with the amplification process, resulting in a rate of errors that correlates with the activity of the cell. Functional events are thereby recorded on biological media such as DNA. The bio-recordings can then be retrieved from the cells in which they reside. The project goal is to record signals from all neurons in a brain, and potentially to measure at higher resolutions.

Another approach is to carry out functional characterization by establishing the equivalent of an electronic synaptic network based on micron-scale wireless neural interfaces. Researchers in labs at MIT, Harvard, UC Berkeley, and other locations are focusing on this approach, tackling the various issues such as power, communication, localization, recording, stimulating, and biocompatibility. One prototype technology under active development at UC Berkeley, so-called "Neural Dust," is composed of free-floating probes that contain a piezoelectric crystal within a capacitive loop (Seo et al. 2013). Changes of local field potentials in neural tissue will alter the resonance frequency of the crystal, which can be detected by probing the crystals with ultrasound.

In another prototype technology envisioned by an MIT–Harvard collaboration, a probe with a diameter of 8 micrometers, the size of a red blood cell, can include operational circuitry, infrared power delivery and communications, and an antenna for passive communications similar to radio frequency identification or RFID. An infrared version of this passive communication, a micro-OPID (at optical wavelengths), is being developed by Dr. Yael Maguire. Using 32-nanometer integrated circuit (IC) technology, a probe that can fit into the brain vasculature capillaries supplying every neuron can have 2300 or more transistors. Properly developed, technology such as wireless implantable neural probes should be inexpensive, adaptable, accurate, and comparatively safe to use, since their application can be less invasive than procedures that break tissue barriers or deliver high doses of electromagnetic radiation. Probes at micron scales can be self-contained, requiring minimal assembly. The probes are based on IC technology, so the trajectory of their development and production can take advantage of Moore's law (which implies exponential growth in the capabilities of integrated circuits).

When we have the tools, and make all the necessary measurements, we end up with a vast amount of data such as brain images and recordings of voltage changes near neurons. How do you turn that data back into a functioning mind? We need ways to generate models and to populate them with parameters based on the pool of measurements. Different types of measurement need to be combined, such as structure data and activity data. We also need computing platforms that are well suited to an implementation of the emulation. Some work in this direction has been done in studies of efficiently distributing volumetric neural tissue computations over many nodes of a supercomputer (Kozloski and Wagner 2011).

Brain emulation on general-purpose computers is convenient, because model functions can be modified easily. Ultimately, a mature emulation demands a suitable computing substrate. We know that low-power solutions that fit within 10 cubic centimeters are possible in principle, because those are the specifications achieved by the biological brain. There, the functions of mind are carried out by a vast network of mostly inactive, low-power processors: neurons. A new substrate with similar features might achieve efficient emulation, and the development of so-called neuromorphic computing platforms points in that general direction. Examples are: chip designs resulting from the DARPA SyNAPSE project, outcomes of the EU CAVIAR and FACETS projects, and extensible neural microchip architectures such as developed by Guy Paillet (Menendez and Paillet 2013).

Iterative improvements in our understanding of the system identification problem seek to converge effectively on methods that satisfy our success criteria. Can we make do with a simple model of neurons, or might we need to model molecular kinetics explicitly? Must we take into account the specifics of each glial cell in addition to the neurons? The more we know about the relevant signals and the architecture of the brain, the smaller we can make the sub-systems for which system identification must be carried out. Determining the right scope and resolution for emulation is an outcome of iterative hypothesis testing using our models and data acquisition tools.

3 Is a computer too deterministic to house a mind?

Theoretical debates occasionally focus on the question of determinism and computation in the Von Neumann sense. Is it impossible to implement a successful whole brain emulation in terms of a software program within a digital computer, because some aspect of the operation of biophysical primitives in the brain is inherently non-deterministic? We can say that neurons and other parts of the physiology are not deterministic and therefore not like computer programs. But that is true for anything built in the real world, such as transistors, which also do not operate in a totally deterministic and predictable manner. They too are subject to the whims of variability in material and effects from surrounding environmental noise. At the highest resolution, the transistors within a modern CPU are not all identical and they will not all exhibit exactly the same response function. Additionally, they will be affected by many other unpredictable quantities, such as the surrounding temperature, magnetic fields, and other sources of radiation. From this, we might deduce (mistakenly) that, given the hardware of a computer, it cannot possibly be a deterministic machine that could be represented as running programs. At high resolution, all the building blocks of nature and our world are subject to variability that appears non-deterministic at least at the scale where mesoscopic and macroscopic processes need to take place reliably.

Of course, we know that engineers go to great lengths to make the components of a CPU work together in a reliable manner. This includes using a clock for synchronous timing, using thresholds and binary encoding instead of analog representations on the transistors, and incorporating error-detection and error-correction technology in processes and memory buses. But if a biological system were truly non-deterministic, how could it operate to carry out things like goal-directed behavior or reliable responses? The mind needs to operate in a predictable, deterministic manner, even if its components do not. The brain goes to great lengths to make its mesoscopic and macroscopic operations more predictable, more deterministic. There are numerous ways to get around physiological unreliability, to enable reliable communication and collaboration between brain regions and circuits. Of course, the biological implementation of those solutions is directly related to the identification of the appropriate level of representation and parameter measurement for brain emulation.

Natural selection resulted in solutions that work reliably, even when depending on billions or trillions of components within many different operational regions that need to collaborate and upon which the survival of the organism can depend. Those solutions can be quite different from the ones in the CPU example, but they are no less rigorous and effective. Examples of measures taken within the brain include:

- Region-wide or brain-wide modulation of membrane potentials in accordance with large-scale rhythms in the brain (such as the ones detectable by EEG). This effectively gives the brain a synchronizing clock, or rather several clocks running at related oscillation frequencies.
- The use of ensembles for encoding, not relying on the firing of a single synapse or even of a single neuron.
- The use of powerful signals, such as bursts of hundreds or thousands of neural spikes.
- The use of rates of spiking in some places instead of individual spike times (although individual spike timing is meaningful in some brain functions).
- Large-scale modulators that can control the operating modes and conditions of regions or the entire brain.

And the measures include requiring repeated processes to take place before changes are made in the system:

- A single pre- and post-synaptic spike is not usually sufficient to cause a lasting and significant change in a synapse, but several repetitions are.
- A tiered system of memory that will elevate an experience or learning to permanence only if it passes a number of thresholds. Most of what is captured temporarily by iconic or short-term memory is lost forever.

Ultimately, you end up with a system that is far more predictable than its fundamental building blocks. The effects that noise and non-determinism have in the operation of the system certainly can be characteristic of it, but even then it is possible to engineer noise sources with very similar characteristics. There is no indication that satisfactory replication in accordance with criteria for whole brain emulation would be greatly affected by a need to replicate non-deterministic noise.

4 A platform for iteration between model and measurement

ARPANET (the Advanced Research Projects Agency Network) first appeared in 1969 and developed throughout the 1970s and 1980s. It was useful for university projects and for the military, but it was not immediately obvious what sort of civilian applications would thrive on such a computer network. The Internet was its outcome, and every corner of the world was changed greatly as a result. Right now, a transition is underway from simple neural interfaces to interfaces with greater bandwidth and with the ability to interpret or directly use the signals the brain is producing, rather than training the brain to use the interface. In fact, research goals include the development of probes that can record at 1ms (millisecond) sample rates from every neuron in a piece of tissue or an entire brain. There is a resemblance to the situation in 1969: we cannot yet anticipate all the applications, devices, and possibilities that might emerge, but it's clear that there is great opportunity to build the platforms for a new type of communication and integration with the mind. My own startup, NeuraLink, is engaged in this effort to take the most promising new neural interface technologies coming from labs in places like Harvard, MIT, and UC Berkeley and to make those reliable, easy to use, and easy to produce. The task is to build the backbone for the next technological revolution.

Many signal modalities remain to be explored, and effective hybrid systems can be built. Some of the most exciting recent developments came out of a summit at Harvard on June 12, 2013, which gathered leading neural engineers with the stated goal of identifying technologies that could sample activity data at every neuron in a brain at 1ms resolution in-vivo (Marblestone et al. 2013). That goal is a milestone in the roadmap to whole brain emulation, and the concept of whole brain emulation was acknowledged and recognized as a valid and desirable research target during the special Brain Researchers Meeting that preceded the Global Future 2045 Congress in New York City in June 2013.

The brain's own system components, synapses, and neurons are sensitive to information that is conveyed by the appearance at specific times of spike signals. That information can be conveyed at rates up to 1kHz, or a thousand cycles per second (though often at lower rates). If this is what the components of a brain can listen to, then it makes sense that neuroscience tools aimed at characterizing the behavior of a neuronal circuit, devising its functions though system identification, or coexisting with neuronal circuitry for the purposes of neural interfacing should be able to record activity data at time intervals of 1ms. The problem of system identification, and of interacting with the distributed activity of brain systems, becomes more tractable when the recording is carried out at more and smaller pieces of the circuitry; for example, at every neuron.

5 Conclusions – uploaded and machine minds

Using the iterative approach described here, based on rigorous system identification and a decomposition into feasibly characterized sub-systems, uploading a mind via whole brain emulation can become a reality in the next two to four decades. I share with several of the pioneers of artificial general intelligence (AGI) the conviction that areas of overlap exist between AGI research and neuroscience research in which an interdisciplinary perspective is of particular value (Goertzel and Pennachin 2007). Of course, one of the primary reasons for interest in AGI (and artificial intelligence or machine minds in general) has been "to make computers that are similar to the human mind," as Pei Wang notes unequivocally (Wang n.d.). Some AGI researchers are explicitly pursuing forms of (general) intelligence designed from first principles and without a desire for comparability or compatibility with human intelligence. By and large, though, many of the underlying objectives that drive the search for AGI also involve an interest in anthropomorphic interpretations of intelligent behavior. The operations of the human mind are of interest to strong AI and many in the field of AGI.

In past decades, research in AI has been guided by insights about the human mind from experimental and theoretical work in psychology and cognitive science, since very little was known about the underlying mechanistic architecture and functionality of the brain. For a long time it has been impossible in neuroscience to reconcile the very small with the very large. Investigation at large scale and low resolution was congruent with cognitive science, and led to the identification of centers of the brain responsible for different cognitive tasks through fMRI studies (e.g., Op de Beek et al. 2008). But having a rough map of the localization of the known set of gross cognitive functions within a standardized brain does not add significantly to an understanding of exactly how the brain does what it does.

If we accept that definitions of generality and of intelligence used in AGI can apply to human minds, then a substrate-independent implementation of a human mind is an artificial version of the necessary functions. That makes the substrate-independent mind a type of AGI (Koene 2012). Emulation is a concrete approach to the transition from a biological brain to implementation in another substrate and it is reasonable to assume that the result will be a functioning mind with general intelligence.

Modeling of thought processes is necessary both in artificial intelligence work and when creating neuroprostheses for a whole brain emulation. But the goals and therefore the success criteria are different: AI is successful if it manages to capture the general principles of a mind to the point where a machine can achieve a desired level of performance for a spectrum of possible tasks. A neuroprosthesis or a whole brain emulation is successful if it captures perceived aspects of an individual and personal nature. Due to this difference, there will be points at which different levels need to be chosen for system identification in existing brains.

Modern science relies on creating representations of things, where we pick the signals that interest us and the behavior that interests us, and then determine how to interpret the manner in which system input is converted into output. Our description of that process is our understanding of that system. For practical purposes, a similar approach applies to mind uploading, where we seek to create a substrate-independent version of a specific mind's functions. To achieve that via whole brain emulation relies on determining precisely which signals we care about, and then breaking the problem down into a collection of smaller system-identification problems; a roadmap to whole brain emulation includes structural scanning (connectomics) as well as new tools for functional recording.

Within five years, from 2008 through 2012, we saw connectomics grow from a call for novel research and development to a solid field with proof-of-principle results and sophisticated new tools. In 2013, the 10-year Human Brain Project began. Now large-scale high-resolution activity mapping has emerged as the new challenge in neurotechnology, as made abundantly clear in the aims of the BRAIN Initiative (the US National

Institutes for Health Brain Research through Advancing Innovative Neurotechnologies project). In another five years, we should have methods for both large-scale high-resolution structural and functional data acquisition. A feasible project proposal might then involve the analysis and emulation of the neural tissue functions of the fruit fly Drosophila – the primary animal studied at Janelia Farm Labs. Emulation of a Drosophila brain, tiny as it is, constitutes a breakthrough of incredible proportions, because it is the brain of an animal that shares with us so many basic features: mobility, learning, planning, sensation. Such an accomplishment will effectively make mind uploading a reality.

References

Berger, T.W., Song, D., Chan, R.H., Marmarelis, V.Z., LaCoss, J., Wills, J., Hampson, R.E., Deadwyler, S.A., and Granacki, J.J. 2012. A hippocampal cognitive prosthesis: Multi-input, multi-output nonlinear modeling and VLSI implementation. *IEEE Transactions on Neural Systems and Rehabilitation Engineering* 20(2): 198–211. doi: 10.1109/TNSRE.2012.2189133.

Bernardes de Jesus, B., Vera, E., Schneeberger, K., Tejera, A.M., Ayuso, E., Bosch, F., and Blasco, M.A. 2012. Telomerase gene therapy in adult and old mice delays aging and increases longevity without increasing cancer. *EMBO Molecular Medicine* 4: 691–704. doi: 10.1002/emmm.201200245.

Briggman, K., Helmstaedter, M., and Denk, W. 2011. Wiring specificity in the direction-selectivity circuit of the retina. *Nature* 471: 183–188.

Goertzel, B., and Pennachin, C. 2007. *Artificial General Intelligence*. Springer: New York.

Koene, R.A. 2011. AGI and Neuroscience: Open Sourcing the Brain. In Jürgen Schmidhuber, Kristinn R. Thórisson, and Moshe Looks, eds., *Proceedings of the Fourth Conference on Artificial General Intelligence* (AGI2011). Heidelberg: Springer, pp. 401–406.

Koene, R.A. 2012. Experimental research in whole brain emulation: The need for innovative *in-vivo* measurement techniques. *International Journal of Machine Consciousness* 4(1): 35–65. doi: 10.1142/S1793843012500047.

Kording, K.P. 2011. Of toasters and molecular ticker tapes. *PLoS Computational Biology* 7(12): e1002291. doi:10.1371/journal.pcbi.1002291.

Kozloski, J., and Wagner, J. 2011. An ultrascalable solution to large-scale neural tissue simulation. *Frontiers in Neuroinformatics* 5(15), doi: 10.3389/fninf.2011.00015. http://www.frontiersin.org/Journal/10.3389/fninf.2011.00015/full (accessed November 22, 2013).

Lebedev M.A., and Nicolelis M.A. 2006. Brain–machine interfaces: Past, present and future. *Trends in Neurosciences* 29: 536–546.

Ljung, L. 1999. *System Identification: Theory for the User*, 2nd edn. Upper Saddle River, N.J.: PTR Prentice Hall.

Marblestone, A.H., Zamft, B.M., Maguire, Y.G., Shapiro, M.G.,. Cybulski, T.R., Glaser, J.I., Stranges, B., Kalhor, R., Dalrymple, D.A., Seo, D., Alon, E., Maharbiz, M.M., Carmena, J., Rabaey, J., Boyden, E.S., Church, G.M., and Kording, K.P. 2013. Physical principles for scalable neural recording. *Frontiers in Computational Neuroscience* 7: article 137, doi: 10.3389/fncom.2013.00137. http://www.frontiersin.org/Journal/10.3389/fncom.2013.00137/full (accessed November 22, 2013).

Marmarelis, V.Z., Shin, D.C., Song, D., Hampson, R.E., Deadwyler, S.A., and Berger, T.W. 2013. On parsing the neural code in the prefrontal cortex of primates using principal dynamic modes. *Journal of Computational Neuroscience*. Published online August 9. doi: 10.1007/s10827-013-0475-3.

Menendez, A., and Paillet, G. 2013. Fish inspection system using a parallel neural network chip and the image knowledge builder application. *AI Magazine, Association for the Advancement of Artificial Intelligence* 29(1): 21–28.

Op de Beek, H.P., Haushofer, J., and Kanwisher, N.G. 2008. Interpreting fMRI data: Maps, modules and dimensions. *Nature Reviews Neuroscience* 9(2): 123–135.

Seo, D., Carmena, J.M., Rabaey, J.M., Alon, E., and Maharbiz, M.M. 2013. *Neural Dust: An Ultrasonic, Low Power Solution for Chronic Brain-Machine Interfaces*, arXiv:1307.2196, http://arxiv.org/pdf/1307.2196.pdf (accessed November 22, 2013).

Wang, P. n.d. *Artificial General Intelligence: A gentle introduction*, http://sites.google.com/site/narswang/home/agi-introduction (accessed October 6, 2013).

6

Uploading: A Philosophical Analysis

David J. Chalmers

In the long run, if we are to match the speed and capacity of nonbiological systems, we probably have to dispense with our biological core entirely. This might happen through a gradual process in which parts of our brain are replaced over time, or via a process of scanning our brains and loading the result into a computer, then enhancing the resulting processes. Either way, the result is likely to be an enhanced nonbiological system, most likely a computational system.

This process of migration from brain to computer is often called *uploading*, which can take many different forms. It can involve gradual replacement of brain parts (gradual uploading), instant scanning and activation (instant uploading), or scanning followed by later activation (delayed uploading). It can involve destruction of the original brain parts (destructive uploading), preservation of the original brain (nondestructive uploading), or reconstruction of cognitive structure from records (reconstructive uploading). We can only speculate about what form uploading technology will take, but some forms have been widely discussed.[1]

For concreteness, I will describe three relatively specific forms: destructive uploading, gradual uploading, and nondestructive uploading.

Destructive uploading. It is widely held that this may be the first form of uploading to be feasible. One possible form involves serial sectioning. Here one freezes a brain, and proceeds to analyze its structure layer by layer.

Intelligence Unbound: The Future of Uploaded and Machine Minds, First Edition.
Edited by Russell Blackford and Damien Broderick.

In each layer one records the distribution of neurons and other relevant components, along with the character of their interconnections. One then loads all this information into a computer model that includes an accurate simulation of neural behavior and dynamics. The result might be an emulation of the original brain.

Gradual uploading. Here the most widely discussed method is that of nanotransfer. One or more nanotechnology devices (perhaps tiny robots) are inserted into the brain and each attaches itself to a single neuron, learning to simulate the behavior of the associated neuron and also learning about its connectivity. Once it simulates the neuron's behavior well enough, it takes the place of the original neuron, perhaps leaving receptors and effectors in place and uploading the relevant processing to a computer via radio transmitters. It then moves to other neurons and repeats the procedure, until eventually every neuron has been replaced by an emulation, and perhaps all processing has been uploaded to a computer.

Nondestructive uploading. The nanotransfer method might in principle be used in a nondestructive form. The holy grail here is some sort of noninvasive method of brain imaging, analogous to functional magnetic resonance imaging, but with fine enough grain that neural and synaptic dynamics can be recorded. No such technology is currently on the horizon, but imaging technology is an area of rapid progress.

In all of its forms, uploading raises many questions. From a self-interested point of view, the key question is: Will I survive? This question itself divides into two parts, each corresponding to one of the hardest questions in philosophy: the questions of consciousness and personal identity. First, will an uploaded version of me be conscious? Second, will it be me?

1 Uploading and consciousness

Ordinary human beings are conscious. That is, there is something it is like to be us. We have conscious experiences with a subjective character: there is something it is like for us to see, to hear, to feel, and to think. These conscious experiences lie at the heart of our mental lives, and are a central part of what gives our lives meaning and value. If we lost the capacity for consciousness, then in an important sense, we would no longer exist.

Before uploading, then, it is crucial to know whether the resulting upload will be conscious. If my only residue is an upload and the upload has no capacity for consciousness, then arguably I do not exist at all. And if there is a sense in which I exist, this sense at best involves a sort of zombified existence. Without consciousness, this would be a life of greatly diminished meaning and value.

Can an upload be conscious? The issue is complicated by the fact that our understanding of consciousness is so poor. No one knows just why or how brain processes give rise to consciousness. Neuroscience is gradually discovering various neural correlates of consciousness, but this research program largely takes the existence of consciousness for granted. There is nothing even approaching an orthodox theory of why there is consciousness in the first place. Correspondingly, there is nothing even approaching an orthodox theory of what sorts of systems can be conscious and what systems cannot be.

One central problem is that consciousness seems to be a further fact about conscious systems, at least in the sense that knowledge of the physical structure of such a system does not tell one all about the conscious experiences of such a system.[2]

Complete knowledge of physical structure might tell one all about a system's objective behavior and its objective functioning, which is enough to tell whether the system is alive, and whether it is intelligent. But this sort of knowledge alone does not seem to answer all the questions about a system's subjective experience.

A famous illustration here is Frank Jackson's case of Mary, the neuroscientist in a black and white room, who knows all about the physical processes associated with color but does not know what it is like to see red (Jackson 1986). If this is right, complete physical knowledge leaves open certain questions about the conscious experience of color. More broadly, a complete physical description of a system such as a mouse does not appear to tell us what it is like to be a mouse, and indeed whether there is anything it is like to be a mouse. Furthermore, we do not have a "consciousness meter" that can settle the matter directly. So given any system, biological or artificial, there will at least be a substantial and unobvious question about whether it is conscious, and about what sort of consciousness it has.

Still, whether one thinks there are further facts about consciousness or not, one can at least raise the question of what sort of systems are conscious. Here philosophers divide into multiple camps. Biological theorists of consciousness hold that consciousness is essentially biological and that no nonbiological system can be conscious. Functionalist theorists of consciousness hold that what matters to consciousness is not biological makeup but causal structure and causal role, so that a nonbiological system can be conscious as long as it is organized correctly.

The philosophical issue between biological and functionalist theories is crucial to the practical question of whether or not we should upload. If biological theorists are correct, uploads cannot be conscious, so we cannot survive consciously in uploaded form. If functionalist theorists are correct, uploads almost certainly can be conscious, and this obstacle to uploading is removed. My own view is that functionalist theories are closer to the truth here. It is true that we have no idea how a nonbiological system, such as a silicon computational system, could be conscious. But the fact is that we also have no idea how a biological system, such as a neural system, could be conscious. The gap is just as wide in both cases. And we do not know of any principled differences between biological and nonbiological systems that suggest that the former can be conscious and the latter cannot. In the absence of such principled differences, I think the default attitude should be that both biological and nonbiological systems can be conscious. I think that this view can be supported by further reasoning.

To examine the matter in more detail: suppose that we can create a perfect upload of a brain inside a computer. For each neuron in the original brain, there is a computational element that duplicates its input/output behavior perfectly. The same goes for non-neural and subneural components of the brain, to the extent that these are relevant. The computational elements are connected to input and output devices (artificial eyes and ears, limbs, and bodies), perhaps in an ordinary physical environment or perhaps in a virtual environment. On receiving a visual input, say, the upload goes through processing isomorphic to what goes on in the original brain. First artificial analogs of eyes and the optic nerve are activated, then computational analogs of lateral geniculate nucleus and the visual cortex, then analogs of later brain areas, ultimately resulting in a (physical or virtual) action analogous to one produced by the original brain.

In this case we can say that the upload is a functional isomorph of the original brain. Of course it is a substantive claim that functional isomorphs are possible. If some elements of cognitive processing function in a noncomputable way, for example, so that a neuron's input/output behavior cannot even be computationally simulated, then an algorithmic functional isomorph will be impossible. But if the components of cognitive functioning are themselves computable, then a functional isomorph is possible. Here I will assume that functional isomorphs are possible in order to ask whether they will be conscious.

I think the best way to consider whether a functional isomorph will be conscious is to consider a gradual uploading process such as nanotransfer.

Here we upload different components of the brain one by one, over time. This might involve gradual replacement of entire brain areas with computational circuits, or it might involve uploading neurons one at a time. The components might be replaced with silicon circuits in their original location, or with processes in a computer connected by some sort of transmission to a brain. It might take place over months or years, or over hours.

If a gradual uploading process is executed correctly, each new component will perfectly emulate the component it replaces, and will interact with both biological and nonbiological components around it in just the same way that the previous component did. So the system will behave in exactly the same way that it would have without the uploading. In fact, if we assume that the system cannot see or hear the uploading, then the system need not notice that any uploading has taken place. Assuming that the original system said that it was conscious, so will the partially uploaded system. The same applies throughout a gradual uploading process, until we are left with a purely nonbiological system.

What happens to consciousness during a gradual uploading process? There are three possibilities. It might suddenly disappear, with a transition from a fully complex conscious state to no consciousness when a single component is replaced. It might gradually fade out over more than one replacements, with the complexity of the system's conscious experience reducing via intermediate steps. Or it might stay present throughout.

Sudden disappearance is the least plausible option. Given this scenario, we can move to a scenario in which we replace the key component by replacing 10 or more subcomponents in turn, and then reiterate the question. Either new scenario will involve a gradual fading across a number of components, or a sudden disappearance. If the former, this option is reduced to the fading option. If the latter, we can reiterate. In the end we will either have gradual fading or sudden disappearance when a single tiny component (a neuron or a subneural element, say) is replaced. The latter seems extremely unlikely.

Gradual fading also seems implausible. In this case there will be intermediate steps in which the system is conscious but its consciousness is partly faded, in that it is less complex than the original conscious state. Perhaps some element of consciousness will be gone (visual but not auditory experience, for example) or perhaps some distinctions in experience will be gone (colors reduced from a three-dimensional color space to black and white, for example). By hypothesis the system will be functioning and behaving the same way as ever, though, and will not show any signs of noticing the change. It is plausible that the system will not believe that anything has changed, despite a massive difference in its conscious state. This requires a conscious system that is deeply out of touch with its own conscious experience.

We can imagine that at a certain point partial uploads become common, and that many people have had their brains partly replaced by silicon computational circuits. On the sudden disappearance view, there will be states of partial uploading such that any further change will cause consciousness to disappear, with no difference in behavior or organization. People in these states may have consciousness constantly flickering in and out, or at least might undergo total zombification with a tiny change. On the fading view, these people will be wandering around with a highly degraded consciousness, although they will be functioning as always and swearing that nothing has changed. In practice, both hypotheses will be difficult to take seriously. So I think that by far the most plausible hypothesis is that full consciousness will stay present throughout. On this view, all partial uploads will still be fully conscious, as long as the new elements are functional duplicates of the elements they replace. By gradually moving through fuller uploads, we can infer that even a full upload will be conscious.

At the very least, it seems very likely that partial uploading will convince most people that uploading preserves consciousness. Once people are confronted with friends and family who have undergone limited partial uploading and are behaving normally, few people will seriously think that they lack consciousness. And gradual extensions to full uploading will convince most people that these systems are conscious at well. Of course it remains at least a logical possibility that this process will gradually or suddenly turn everyone into zombies. But once we are confronted with partial uploads, that hypothesis will seem akin to the hypothesis that people of different ethnicities or genders are zombies.

If we accept that consciousness is present in functional isomorphs, should we also accept that isomorphs have qualitatively identical states of consciousness? This conclusion does not follow immediately. But I think that an extension of this reasoning (the "dancing qualia" argument in Chalmers 1996) strongly suggests such a conclusion.

If this is right, we can say that consciousness is an organizational invariant: that is, systems with the same patterns of causal organization have the same states of consciousness, no matter whether that organization is implemented in neurons, in silicon, or in some other substrate. We know that some properties are not organizational invariants (being wet, say) while other properties are (being a computer, say). In general, if a property is not an organizational invariant, we should not expect it to be preserved in a computer simulation (a simulated rainstorm is not wet). But if a property is an organizational invariant, we should expect it to be preserved in a computer simulation (a simulated computer is a computer). So given that consciousness is an organizational invariant, we should expect a good enough computer simulation of a conscious system to be conscious, and to have the same sorts of conscious states as the original system.

This is good news for those who are contemplating uploading. But there remains a further question.

2 Uploading and personal identity

Suppose that I can upload my brain into a computer? Will the result be me?[3]

On the *optimistic* view of uploading, the upload will be the same person as the original. On the *pessimistic* view of uploading, the upload will not be the same person as the original. Of course if one thinks that uploads are not conscious, one may well hold the pessimistic view on the grounds that the upload is not a person at all. But even if one thinks that uploads are conscious and are persons, one might still question whether the upload is the same person as the original. Faced with the prospect of destructive uploading (in which the original brain is destroyed), the issue between the optimistic and pessimistic view is literally a life-or-death question. On the optimistic view, destructive uploading is a form of survival. On the pessimistic view, destructive uploading is a form of death. It is as if one has destroyed the original person, and created a simulacrum in their place.

An appeal to organizational invariance does not help here. We can suppose that I have a perfect identical twin whose brain and body are molecule-for-molecule duplicates of mine. The twin will then be a functional isomorph of me and will have the same conscious states as me. This twin is *qualitatively* identical to me: it has exactly the same qualities as me. But it is not *numerically* identical to me: it is not me. If you kill the twin, I will survive. If you kill me (that is, if you destroy *this* system) and preserve the twin, I will die. The survival of the twin might be some consolation to me, but from a self-interested point of view this outcome seems much worse than the alternative.

Once we grant that my twin and I have the same organization but are not the same person, it follows that personal identity is not an organizational invariant. So we cannot count on the fact that uploading preserves organization to guarantee that uploading preserves identity. On the pessimistic view, destructive uploading is at best akin to creating a sort of digital twin while destroying me.

These questions about uploading are closely related to parallel questions about physical duplication. Let us suppose that a teletransporter creates a molecule-for-molecule duplicate of a person out of new matter while destroying or dissipating the matter in the original system. Then on the optimistic view of teletransportation it is a form of survival, while on the pessimistic view it is a form of death. Teletransportation is not the same as uploading: it preserves physical organization where uploading preserves only functional organization in a different physical substrate. But at least once one grants that uploads are conscious, the issues raised by the two cases are closely related.

In both cases, the choice between optimistic and pessimistic views is a question about personal identity: under what circumstances does a person persist over time? Here there is a range of possible views. An extreme view on one end (perhaps held by no one) is that exactly the same matter is required for survival (so that when a single molecule in the brain is replaced, the original person ceases to exist). An extreme view on the other end is that merely having the same sort of conscious states suffices for survival (so that from my perspective there is no important difference between killing this body and killing my twin's body). In practice, most theorists hold that a certain sort of *continuity* or *connectedness* over time is required for survival. But they differ on what sort of continuity or connectedness is required.

There are a few natural hypotheses about what sort of connection is required. *Biological* theories of identity hold that survival of a person requires the intact survival of a brain or a biological organism. *Psychological* theories of identity hold that survival of a person requires the right sort of psychological continuity over time (preservation of memories, causally related mental states, and so on). *Closest-continuer* theories (Nozick 1981: 38 et seq.) hold that a person survives as the most closely related subsequent entity, subject to various constraints.

Biological theorists are likely to hold the pessimistic view of teletransportation, and are even more likely to hold the pessimistic view of uploading. Psychological theorists are more likely to hold the optimistic view of both, at least if they accept that an upload can be conscious. Closest-continuer theorists are likely to hold that the answer depends on whether the uploading is destructive, in which case the upload will be the closest continuer, or nondestructive, in which case the biological system will be the closest continuer.[4]

I do not have a settled view about these questions of personal identity and find them very puzzling. I am more sympathetic with a psychological view of the conditions under which survival obtains than with a biological view, but I am unsure of this, for reasons I will elaborate later. Correspondingly, I am genuinely unsure whether to take an optimistic or a pessimistic view of destructive uploading. I am most inclined to be optimistic, but I am certainly unsure enough that I would hesitate before undergoing destructive uploading.

To help clarify the issue, I will present an argument for the pessimistic view and an argument for the optimistic view, both of which run parallel to related arguments that can be given concerning teletransportation.

3 The argument from nondestructive uploading

Suppose that yesterday Dave was uploaded into a computer. The original brain and body were not destroyed, so there are now two conscious beings: BioDave and DigiDave. BioDave's natural attitude will be that he is the original system and that DigiDave is at best some sort of branchline copy.

DigiDave presumably has some rights, but it is natural to hold that he does not have BioDave's rights. For example, it is natural to hold that BioDave has certain rights to Dave's possessions, his friends, and so on, where DigiDave does not. And it is natural to hold that this is because BioDave is Dave: that is, Dave has survived as BioDave and not as DigiDave.

If we grant that, in a case of nondestructive uploading, DigiDave is not identical to Dave, then it is natural to question whether destructive uploading is any different. If Dave did not survive as DigiDave when the biological system was preserved, why should he survive as DigiDave when the biological system is destroyed?

We might put this in the form of an argument for the pessimistic view, as follows:

1 In nondestructive uploading, DigiDave is not identical to Dave.
2 If in nondestructive uploading, DigiDave is not identical to Dave, then in destructive uploading, DigiDave is not identical to Dave.

____

3 In destructive uploading, DigiDave is not identical to Dave.

Various reactions to the argument are possible. A pessimist about uploading will accept the conclusion. An optimist about uploading will presumably deny one of the premises. One option is to deny premise 2, perhaps because one accepts a closest-continuer theory: when BioDave exists, he is the closest continuer, but when he does not, DigiDave is the closest continuer. Some will find that this makes one's survival and status an unacceptably extrinsic matter, though.

Another option is to deny premise 1, holding that even in nondestructive uploading DigiDave is identical to Dave. Now, in this case it is hard to deny that BioDave is at least as good a candidate as DigiDave, so this option threatens to have the consequence that DigiDave is also identical to BioDave. This consequence is hard to swallow as BioDave and DigiDave may be qualitatively distinct conscious beings, with quite different physical and mental states by this point.

A third and related option holds that nondestructive uploading should be regarded as a case of fission. A paradigmatic fission case is one in which the left and right hemispheres of a brain are separated into different bodies, continuing to function well on their own with many properties of the original. In this case it is uncomfortable to say that both resulting systems are identical to the original, for the same reason as above. But one might hold that they are nevertheless on a par. For example, Parfit (1984) suggests that, although the original system is not identical to the left-hemisphere system or to the right-hemisphere system, it stands in a special relation R (which we might call survival) to both of them, and he claims that this relation rather than numerical identity is what matters. One could likewise hold that, in a case of nondestructive uploading, Dave survives as both BioDave and DigiDave (even if he is not identical to them), and hold that survival is what matters. Still, if survival is what matters, this option does raise uncomfortable questions about whether DigiDave has the same rights as BioDave when both survive.

4 The argument from gradual uploading

Suppose that 1 percent of Dave's brain is replaced by a functionally isomorphic silicon circuit. Next suppose that another 1 percent is replaced, and then another 1 percent. We can continue the process for 100 months, after which a wholly uploaded system will result. We can suppose that functional isomorphism preserves consciousness, so that the system has the same sort of conscious states throughout.

Let Dave_n be the system after n months. Will Dave_1, the system after one month, be Dave? It is natural to suppose so. The same goes for Dave_2 and Dave_3. Now consider Dave_{100}, the wholly uploaded system after 100 months. Will Dave_{100} be Dave? It is at least very natural to hold that it will be. We could turn this into an argument as follows.

1 For all $n < 100$, Dave_{n+1} is identical to Dave_n.
2 If for all $n < 100$, Dave_{n+1} is identical to Dave_n, then Dave_{100} is identical to Dave.

---

3 Dave_{100} is identical to Dave.

On the face of it, premise 2 is hard to deny: it follows from repeated application of the claim that when $a = b$ and $b = c$, then $a = c$. On the face of it, premise 1 is hard to deny too: it is hard to see how changing 1 percent of a system will change its identity. Furthermore, if someone denies premise 1, we can repeat the thought-experiment with ever smaller amounts of the brain being replaced, down to single neurons and even smaller. Maintaining the same strategy will require holding that replacing a single neuron can in effect kill a person. That is a hard conclusion to accept. Accepting it would raise the possibility that everyday neural death may be killing us without our knowing it. One could resist the argument by noting that it is a sorites or slippery-slope argument, and by holding that personal identity can come in degrees or can have indeterminate cases. One could also drop talk of identity and instead hold that survival can come in degrees. For example, one might hold that each Dave_n survives to a large degree as Dave_{n+1} but to a smaller degree as later systems.

On this view, the original person will gradually be killed by the replacement process. This view requires accepting the counterintuitive view that survival can come in degrees or be indeterminate in these cases, though. Perhaps more importantly, it is not clear why one should accept that Dave is gradually killed rather than existing throughout. If one were to accept this, it would again raise the question of whether the everyday replacement of matter in our brains over a period of years is gradually killing us also.

My own view is that, in this case, it is very plausible that the original system survives. Or at least, it is plausible that insofar as we ordinarily survive over a period of many years, we could survive gradual uploading too. At the very least, as in the case of consciousness, it seems that if gradual uploading happens, most people will become convinced that it is a form of survival. Assuming the systems are isomorphic, they will say that everything seems the same and that they are still present. It will be very unnatural for most people to believe that their friends and families are being killed by the process. Perhaps there will be groups of people who believe that the process either suddenly or gradually kills people without them or others noticing, but it is likely that this belief will come to seem faintly ridiculous.

Once we accept that gradual uploading over a period of years might preserve identity, the obvious next step is to speed up the process. Suppose that Dave's brain is gradually uploaded over a period of hours, with neurons replaced one at a time by functionally isomorphic silicon circuits. Will Dave survive this process? It is hard to see why a period of hours should be different in principle from a period of years, so it is natural to hold that Dave will survive.

To make the best case for gradual uploading, we can suppose that the system is active throughout, so that there is consciousness through the entire process. Then we can argue: (i) consciousness will be continuous from moment to moment (replacing a single neuron or a small group will not disrupt continuity of consciousness); (ii) if consciousness is continuous from moment to moment, it will be continuous throughout the process; (iii) if consciousness is continuous throughout the process, there will be a single stream of consciousness throughout; (iv) if there is a single stream of consciousness throughout, then the original person survives throughout. One could perhaps deny one of the premises, but denying any of them is uncomfortable. My own view is that continuity of consciousness (especially when accompanied by other forms of psychological continuity) is an extremely strong basis for asserting continuation of a person.

We can then imagine speeding up the process from hours to minutes. The issues here do not seem different in principle. One might then speed it up to seconds. At a certain point, one will arguably start replacing large enough chunks of the brain from moment to moment that the case for continuity of consciousness between moments is less secure. Still, once we grant that uploading over a period of minutes preserves identity, it is at least hard to see why uploading over a period of seconds should not.

As we upload faster and faster, the limit point is instant destructive uploading, where the whole brain is replaced at once. Perhaps this limit point is different from everything that came before it, but this is at least unobvious. We might formulate this as an argument for the optimistic view of destructive uploading. Here it is to be understood that both the gradual uploading and instant uploading are destructive in that they destroy the original brain.

1 Dave survives as Dave_{100} in gradual uploading.
2 If Dave survives as Dave_{100} in gradual uploading, Dave survives as DigiDave in instant uploading.

---

3 Dave survives as DigiDave in instant uploading.

I have in effect argued for the first premise above, and there is at least a prima facie case for the second premise, in that it is hard to see why there is a difference in principle between uploading over a period of seconds and doing so instantly. As before, this argument parallels a corresponding argument about teletransportation (gradual matter replacement preserves identity, so instant matter replacement preserves identity too), and the considerations available are similar. An opponent could resist this argument by denying premise 1 along the lines suggested earlier, or perhaps better, by denying premise 2. A pessimist about instant uploading, like a pessimist about teletransportation, might hold that intermediate systems play a vital role in the transmission of identity from one system to another.

This is a common view of the ship of Theseus, in which all the planks of a ship are gradually replaced over years. It is natural to hold that the result is the same ship with new planks. It is plausible that the same holds even if the gradual replacement is done within days or minutes. By contrast, building a duplicate from scratch without any intermediate cases arguably results in a new ship. Still, it is natural to hold that the question about the ship is in some sense a verbal question or a matter for stipulation, while the question about personal survival runs deeper than that. So it is not clear how well one can generalize from the ship case to the case of persons.

5 Where things stand

We are in a position where there are at least strongly suggestive arguments for both the optimistic and pessimistic views of destructive uploading. The arguments have diametrically opposed conclusions, so they cannot both be sound. My own view is that the optimist's best reply to the argument from nondestructive uploading is the fission reply, and the pessimist's best reply to the argument from gradual uploading is the intermediate-case reply. My instincts favor optimism, but as before I cannot be certain which view is correct.

Still, I am confident that the safest form of uploading is gradual uploading, and I am reasonably confident that gradual uploading is a form of survival. So if at some point in the future I am faced with the choice between uploading and continuing in an increasingly slow biological embodiment, then as long as I have the option of gradual uploading, I will be happy to do so. Unfortunately, I may not have that option. It may be that gradual uploading technology will not be available in my lifetime. It may even be that no adequate uploading technology will be available at all in my lifetime. This raises the question of whether there might still be a place for me, or for any currently existing humans, in a future of artificial intelligence.

6 Uploading after brain preservation

One possibility is that we can preserve our brains for later uploading. Cryonic technology offers the possibility of preserving our brains in a low-temperature state shortly after death, until such time as the technology is available to reactivate the brain or perhaps to upload the information in it. Of course much information may be lost in death, and at the moment we do not know whether cryonics preserves information sufficient to reactivate or reconstruct anything akin to a functional isomorph of the original. But one can at least hope that, after an artificial intelligence explosion, with superintelligent computers designing ever cleverer machines, extraordinary technology might be available.

If there is enough information for reactivation or reconstruction, will the resulting system be me? In the case of reactivation, it is natural to hold that the reactivated system will be akin to a person waking up after a long coma, so that the original person will survive. One might then gradually upload the brain and integrate the result into a technologically advanced world. Alternatively, one might create an uploaded system from the brain without ever reactivating it. Whether one counts this as survival will depend on one's attitude to ordinary destructive and nondestructive uploading. If one is an optimist about these, then one might also be an optimist about uploading from a preserved brain.

Another possible outcome is that there will be first a series of uploads from a preserved brain, using better and better scanning technology, and eventually reactivation of the brain. Here, an optimist about uploading might see this as a case of fission, while a pessimist might hold that only the reactivated system is identical to the original.

In these cases, our views of the philosophical issues about uploading affect our decisions not just in the distant future but in the near term. Even in the near term, anyone with enough money or suitable insurance has the option of having their brain or whole body cryonically preserved, and of leaving instructions about how to deal with the brain as technology develops. Our philosophical views about the status of uploading may well make a difference to the instructions that we should leave.

Of course most people do not preserve their brains, and even those who choose to do so can die in a way that renders preservation impossible. Are there other routes to survival in an advanced future world shared with superintelligent AIs?

7 Reconstructive uploading

The final alternative is reconstruction of the original system from records, and especially reconstructive uploading, in which an upload of the original system is reconstructed from records. Here, the records might include brain scans and other medical data; any available genetic material; audio and video records of the original person; their writings; and the testimony of others about them. These records may seem limited, but it is not out of the question that a superintelligent AI could go a long way with them. Given constraints on the structure of a human system, even limited information might make a good amount of reverse engineering possible. And detailed information, as might be available in extensive video recordings and in detailed brain images, might in principle make it possible for a superintelligence to reconstruct something close to a functional isomorph of the original system.

The question then arises: is reconstructive uploading a form of survival? If we reconstruct a functional isomorph of Einstein from records, will it be Einstein? Here, the pessimistic view says that this is at best akin to a copy of Einstein surviving. The optimistic view says that it is akin to having Einstein awaken from a long coma.

Reconstructive uploading from brain scans is closely akin to ordinary (nongradual) uploading from brain scans, with the main difference being the time delay, and perhaps the continued existence in the meantime of the original person. One might see it as a form of delayed destructive or nondestructive uploading. If one regards nondestructive uploading as survival (perhaps through fission), one will naturally regard reconstructive uploading the same way. If one regards destructive but not nondestructive uploading as survival because one embraces a closest continuer theory, one might also regard reconstructive uploading as survival (at least if the original biological system is gone). If one regards neither as survival, one will probably take the same attitude to reconstructive uploading. Much the same options plausibly apply to reconstructive uploading from other sources of information.

8 Upshot

I think that gradual uploading is certainly the safest method of uploading.

A number of further questions about uploading remain. Of course there are any number of social, legal, and moral issues that I have not begun to address. Here I address just two further questions.

One question concerns cognitive enhancement. Suppose that before or after uploading, our cognitive systems are enhanced to the point that they use a wholly different cognitive architecture. Would we survive this process? Again, it seems to me that the answers are clearest in the case where the enhancement is gradual. If my cognitive system is overhauled one component at a time, and if at every stage there is reasonable psychological continuity with the previous stage, then I think it is reasonable to hold that the original person survives.

Another question is a practical one. If reconstructive uploading will eventually be possible, how can one ensure that it happens? There have been billions of humans in the history of the planet. It is not clear that our successors will want to reconstruct every person who ever lived, or even every person of whom there are records. So if one is interested in immortality, how can one maximize the chances of reconstruction? One might try keeping a bank account with compound interest to pay them for doing so, but it is hard to know whether our financial system will be relevant in the future, especially after an intelligence explosion.

My own strategy is to write about a future of artificial intelligence and about uploading. Perhaps this will encourage our successors to reconstruct me, if only to prove me wrong.

Acknowledgments

This chapter is based on David Chalmers' "The Singularity: A Philosophical Analysis," published in *The Journal of Consciousness Studies* 17 (2010): 7–65, downloadable in full at http://consc.net/papers/singularity.pdf (accessed October 7, 2013).

Notes

1 See Sandberg and Bostrom 2008 and Strout 2006 for detailed discussion of potential uploading technology. See Egan 1994 and Sawyer 2005 for fictional explorations of uploading.

2 The further-fact claim here is simply that facts about consciousness are epistemologically further facts, so that knowledge of these facts is not settled by reasoning from microphysical knowledge alone. This claim is compatible with materialism about consciousness. A stronger claim is that facts about consciousness are ontologically further facts, involving some distinct elements in nature – e.g., fundamental properties over and above fundamental physical properties. In the framework of Chalmers 2003, a type-A materialist (e.g., Daniel Dennett) denies that consciousness involves epistemologically further facts, a type-B materialist (e.g., Ned Block) holds that consciousness involves epistemologically but not ontologically further facts, while a property dualist (e.g., me) holds that consciousness involves ontologically further facts. It is worth noting that the majority of materialists (at least in philosophy) are type-B materialists and hold that there are epistemologically further facts.

3 It will be obvious to anyone who has read Derek Parfit's *Reasons and Persons* that the current discussion is strongly influenced by Parfit's discussion there. Parfit does not discuss uploading, but his discussion of related phenomena such as teletransportation can naturally be seen to generalize. In much of what follows I am simply carrying out aspects of the generalization.

4 In the 2009 PhilPapers survey of 931 professional philosophers (philpapers.org/surveys), 34 percent accepted or leaned toward a psychological view, 17 percent a biological view, and 12 percent a further-fact view (others were unsure, unfamiliar with the issue, held that there is no fact of the matter, and so on). Respondents were not asked about uploading, but on the closely related question of whether teletransportation (with new matter) is survival or death, 38 percent accepted or leaned toward survival and 31 percent death. Advocates of a psychological view broke down 67/22 percent for survival/death, while advocates of biological and further-fact views broke down 12/70 percent and 33/47 percent respectively.

References

Chalmers, D.J. 1996. *The Conscious Mind*. Oxford: Oxford University Press.

Chalmers, D.J. 2003. Consciousness and its place in nature. In S. Stich and F. Warfield, eds., *Blackwell Guide to the Philosophy of Mind*. Oxford: Blackwell.

Egan, G. 1994. *Permutation City*. London: Orion/Millennium.

Jackson, F. 1986. What Mary didn't know. *Journal of Philosophy* 83: 291–295.

Nozick, R. 1981. *Philosophical Explanations*. Cambridge, MA: Harvard University Press.

Parfit, D.A. 1984. *Reasons and Persons*. Oxford: Oxford University Press.

Sandberg, A., and Bostrom, N. 2008. *Whole brain emulation: A roadmap*. Technical report 2008-3, Future for Humanity Institute, Oxford University. http://www.fhi.ox.ac.uk/Reports/2008-3.pdf (accessed 7 October 2013).

Sawyer, R. 2005. *Mindscan*. New York: Tor.

Strout, J. 2006. *The mind uploading home page*, http://www.ibiblio.org/jstrout/uploading/ (accessed October 7, 2013).

7

Mind Uploading: A Philosophical Counter-Analysis

Massimo Pigliucci

1 Introduction

The possibility of "mind uploading" and related ideas about the nature of consciousness have been discussed relatively little in the technical philosophical literature. One prominent exception is the analysis by David Chalmers (see Chapter 6 above), first presented in the *Journal of Consciousness Studies* (2010). The present chapter takes Chalmers' arguments to be one of the best defenses of the concept of mind uploading and uses them as the starting point for a philosophical counter-analysis.

My criticisms are based in part on the contention that supporters of uploading do not take seriously enough the apparent fact that consciousness is – to the best of our knowledge – a biological phenomenon that is unlikely to be entirely (or even largely) substrate-independent, although this does not imply that the current biological substrates are the only ones capable of generating consciousness. Indeed, substrate independence of the type envisioned by Chalmers implies a form of dualism that should be unacceptable in modern philosophy of mind. Moreover, I argue that the Computational Theory of Mind underlying the concept of mind uploading is incomplete and thus only partially applicable to human-like intelligence/consciousness. Finally, I maintain that mind uploading – even if somehow technically possible – would be at best a form of mental cloning, most certainly *not* a way to preserve one's own consciousness.

Intelligence Unbound: The Future of Uploaded and Machine Minds, First Edition.
Edited by Russell Blackford and Damien Broderick.

2 What I am going to attempt here

There has been quite a brouhaha about mind uploading and the related concept of a (soon, but not quite yet) forthcoming "Singularity" episode in the history of artificial and human intelligence. Indeed, this book is one example of what the fuss is all about, with a preponderance of contributions from Singularity and mind-uploading (MU) theorists, several of whom are operating at least partially outside classical academic institutions, for instance at the Singularity Institute (now the Machine Intelligence Research Institute), the Singularity University, and so forth.

This chapter will set aside the question of whether a Singularity will occur (in the near future or ever), to focus on the closely related issue of MU, specifically as presented by one of its most articulate proponents, David Chalmers (2010; Chapter 6 in this collection). MU and the Singularity share a common basis in that they both rely on the success of a strong type of artificial intelligence research program, which is in turn based on some version of the Computational Theory of Mind (CTM). I will proceed in the following fashion: first, I will briefly recall Chalmers' main arguments; second, I will argue that the ideas of MU and CTM do not take seriously enough the fact that consciousness is a biological phenomenon, as pointed out in different contexts by both John Searle and Jerry Fodor, among others; third, I will stipulate *for the sake of argument* that MU is somehow possible, and show that it would, at best, amount to a sort of mind cloning, but most certainly not to a preservation of anyone's consciousness in a medium different from one's own brain.

3 What Chalmers says, redux

Chalmers first presented his broad ideas about the Singularity and MU in a paper published in the *Journal of Consciousness Studies* (Chalmers 2010), and some substantive criticisms of the paper have already appeared in print (e.g., Prinz 2012). Limiting ourselves to MU, as Chalmers does in his abridged discussion of the issues in this volume, we can summarize his arguments as follows.

Chalmers begins with a taxonomy of possible methods of MU, including destructive, gradual, and non-destructive uploading, but quickly and correctly zeros in on the idea that there are two components to a philosophical analysis of MU: first, the issue of the nature of consciousness; second, the question of personal identity. For MU to be possible, it has to be true that consciousness is a particular type of computational phenomenon; and for

MU to be worth our while we also need to agree on a particular view of personal identity. Section 4 of this chapter will deal with the first issue, leaving the second for section 5.

To my way of seeing the problem of consciousness, it is astounding that Chalmers begins with an admission that ought to halt him right in his tracks:[1]

> The issue here is complicated by the fact that our understanding of consciousness is so poor. No one knows just why or how brain processes give rise to consciousness .... There is nothing even approaching an orthodox theory of why there is consciousness in the first place. Correspondingly, there is nothing even approaching an orthodox theory of what sorts of systems can be conscious and what systems cannot be.

But that apparently does not stop Chalmers and other supporters of MU from proceeding *as if* we had a decent theory of consciousness, and by that I mean a decent *neurobiological* theory (as opposed to a general philosophical account). Odd, to say the least.

Chalmers then portrays an antagonism between biological and functionalist views of consciousness, a distinction that is crucial to all his further arguments:

> Biological theorists of consciousness hold that consciousness is essentially biological and that no nonbiological system can be conscious. Functionalist theorists of consciousness hold that what matters to consciousness is not biological makeup but causal structure and causal role, so that a nonbiological system can be conscious as long as it is organized correctly.

I will show that Chalmers here does not provide his readers with an accurate view of what biological theorists actually say, and that moreover his view of functionalism appears to work only because it is founded on an equivocation about what functionalism *means*.

The next step in the argument is to present readers with a thought experiment (since actual experiments on MU cannot be done): What would happen if we gradually replaced the components of a biologically conscious system (i.e., neurons, etc.) with *functionally equivalent* (more on this later) non-biological components? Chalmers tells us that there are three possibilities here, regarding consciousness:

> It might suddenly disappear, with a transition from a fully complex conscious state to no consciousness when a single component is replaced. It might gradually fade out over more than one replacements, with the complexity of the system's conscious experience reducing via intermediate steps. Or it might stay present throughout.

He then (too) quickly concludes that both sudden disappearance and gradual fading "seem implausible," thereby accepting the scenario most favorable to MU: consciousness is maintained throughout the replacement procedure.[2] The upshot is that, according to Chalmers, consciousness is an organizational invariant (i.e., it is substrate-independent), and MU is therefore possible.

He then moves to the second issue, that of personal identity. Again he contrasts an "optimistic" view of MU, according to which mind uploading is a form of survival of the individual, to a "pessimistic" view, according to which MU is a technologically sophisticated form of suicide. The discussion in turn hinges on what criteria we use for personal identity, a notoriously contentious subfield within metaphysics (Olson 2010). Chalmers presents his readers with three choices: biological theories, psychological theories, and "closest-continuer" theories (see Chapter 6 above for a brief explanation), commenting that someone holding a biological view of personal identity is likely to be a pessimist about MU, those adopting a psychological view are going to be optimists, and those espousing a closest-continuer view will hedge their bets depending on whether the upload is destructive or not.

Although he proceeds by examining arguments about different forms of uploading, Chalmers admits that he does not have a settled view of personal identity, and that he would "hesitate" before undergoing destructive uploading. The last part of Chalmers' chapter goes into science-fictional scenarios involving mind reconstruction from cryonic preservation or, even more fancifully, from a combination of leftover genetic material and data records. I will not entertain those any further, largely on the ground that I will show that Chalmers gets into serious trouble way ahead of reaching those far points in the discussion.

4 Consciousness, computation, and mind uploading

The fundamental premise of Chalmers' (and others') arguments about MU is some strong version of the Computational Theory of Mind, which is defined by Horst (2009) as a "particular philosophical view that holds that the mind literally is a digital computer … and that thought literally is a kind of computation." This is of course not the place for an in-depth critique of the CTM, but I'd like to point out a number of prima facie reasons why it simply cannot do the sort of job needed by supporters of MU.

To begin with, there is much misunderstanding of what "computation" stands for here. Jerry Fodor, one of the originators (Fodor 1975) – together with Hilary Putnam (1960) – of the CTM, has expressed bewilderment at how it has generated a totalizing view in philosophy of mind that simply cannot be right: distinguishing between "modular" and "global" mental processes, and arguing that the former, but not the latter (which include consciousness) are computational in any strong sense of the term, he has commented that it "hadn't occurred to me that anyone could think that it's a very large part of the truth; still less that it's within miles of being the whole story about how the mind works" (Fodor 2000, a direct response to Pinker 1997). If Fodor is right, then the CTM cannot be a complete theory of mind, because there are a large number of mental processes that are not computational in nature.[3] In turn, this would mean that MU is not possible, since it is premised on the idea that minds are essentially (and completely) computational in nature.

Indeed, Copeland (2002) traces much trouble with the concept of computation in philosophy of mind to a widespread and persistent misunderstanding of the famous Church–Turing thesis about universal computability. Turing's version of the thesis says that logical computing machines, which eventually became known as Turing machines, can do anything that can be described as a rule of thumb or purely mechanical ("algorithmic"); the Church version says that a function of positive integers is effectively calculable only if recursive (see Copeland 2002 and references therein), which turned out to be equivalent to Turing's statement.

None of the above implies the sort of much stronger declarations that have been made by computationally inclined philosophers of mind. Specifically, the following thesis is *not* established by Church–Turing: Whatever can be calculated by a machine (working on finite data in accordance with a finite program of instructions) is Turing-machine-computable (Copeland 2002). Moreover, Turing was explicitly interested in what *cannot* be computed (i.e., in the limits of computability), and we now know of a number of problems that fall into this category (other than the classical halting problem). And yet mind computationalists often talk (see Copeland 2002 for a number of textual examples) as if Church–Turing has essentially established the CTM, and therefore indirectly also the possibility of mind uploading.

An additional problem for the CTM is that it is often not clear whether its supporters are arguing that a computer can *simulate* a human mind or that it can function as a human-type mind. The difference is crucial. Searle (1980) drew the analogy with other biological processes, such as, say, photosynthesis. We can most certainly simulate what is going on during photosynthesis, down to the quantum level, as it turns out. But there is a crucial thing we don't get out of simulated photosynthesis: sugar, the only outcome that matters to real plants.

Searle did not claim that this somehow shows that consciousness is impossible outside of biological systems (contra what is implied by Chalmers in his summary of biologically informed positions in philosophy of mind). Rather, the question is empirical, and cannot, therefore, be settled by any thought experiment, regardless of how ingenious it is. It can be rephrased thus: How strong are material constraints on the production of the phenomenon of consciousness? And the answer is: We don't know, but they are unlikely to be weak.

Another way to put the issue is this: Is minding (the conscious thinking activity of the brain) more like photosynthesis or more like the sort of abstract symbol shuffling that characterizes the operations of an electronic computer? At the very least, this is an open question that cannot simply be brushed aside by hard-core computationalists. And let us remember that – biologically speaking – any activity of the brain does take place by way of, and results in, physical products (neurotransmitters, electrical impulses, chemical interactions, and so forth). To claim that these are only incidental – as opposed to constitutive – of the ability to be self-conscious is to veer deeply into a form of dualism that ought to make contemporary philosophers at least a little bit uncomfortable.

Other than the problem that there usually is a difference between X and the simulation of X, there is an additional reason why I think biological naturalism is a better way to think about consciousness than hard-core computationalism. Consider life itself: there is no question – I hope – that being alive is a qualitatively different state of matter from not being alive, just as having consciousness is a qualitatively different state from not having it. (This, of course, has no pseudo-mystical or vitalistic implications at all, and does not negate the basic fact that both rocks and biological organisms are made of atoms.) Now, although we know quite a bit about the chemistry of life on earth, it unfortunately is so far the only example we have in the entire universe. Astrobiologists have therefore been somewhat free to speculate about possible alternative chemistries capable of producing life forms. Setting aside the very thorny question of what we mean by "life" (which, of course, is analogous to the thorniness of defining consciousness), such speculations have focused on silicon as pretty much the only other *potential* game in town (and by town, I mean the universe), aside from carbon (e.g., Schulze-Makuch and Irwin 2006). That is because we know enough about the other elements of the periodic table that we are reasonably sure that their chemistry cannot lend itself to anything like the functionality necessary for the complex metabolism and reproduction typical of living beings. Indeed, there are good reasons to doubt the viability even of silicon-based life forms, given the much more restricted chemical flexibility of silicon when compared to carbon.

Which brings us to the question of whether and in what sense it may be possible to extract or "upload" human consciousness to a mechanical device made of something other than carbon-based neurons. There are two further issues here. First, what do we *mean* when we are asking that question? Second, assuming that what we mean is something coherent, is it technically possible? The latter question is, again, empirical in nature, and I think the best attitude a philosopher can take towards it is to wait and see whether science and technology will be able to provide us with an answer. But an exploration of the first question lays bare a number of troubling equivocations in Chalmers' (and others') position concerning the CTM and MU.

The most obvious equivocation concerns whether we are talking – as Chalmers does through most of his chapter – about replacing carbon-based components in a human brain with functionally equivalent components made of something else (most obviously, silicon), vs. whether we are considering more exotic possibilities, such as somehow transferring human consciousness inside a computer (as he hints in his 2010 paper). The first scenario requires "only" a convincing (empirical) demonstration that, say, silicon-made neurons can function just as well as carbon-based ones, which is, again, an exclusively empirical question. They might or might not, we do not know. What we do know is that not just any chemical will do, for the simple reason that neurons need to be able to do certain things (grow, produce synapses, release and respond to chemical signals) that cannot be done if we alter the brain's chemistry too radically. The second scenario, instead, brings us right back to a curious form of dualism, since it essentially assumes that consciousness is substrate-independent. I find this position downright bizarre, and not at all disanalogous to claiming that photosynthesis, or life itself, is likely to be substrate-independent. Here I follow Searle's (2008) "biological naturalism" position and demand that my colleagues take biology a bit more seriously, since after all consciousness – so far as we can tell – is a biological phenomenon. Needless to say, the second scenario also requires a very strong version of the CTM, which we can reject for the various reasons already mentioned (Fodor's "not everything in the mind is computable" objection; misunderstanding of Church–Turing; etc.).

There is another, more subtle, type of ambiguity at work here. Chalmers (like others) makes a lot out of his "functional" (as opposed to biological) approach to consciousness. As he puts it: "Functionalist theorists of consciousness hold that what matters to consciousness is not biological makeup but causal structure and causal role, so that a non-biological system can be conscious as long as it is organized correctly." But what does Chalmers mean by "causal structure and causal role"? This phrase may very well hide the necessity that neurons be made of certain particular materials, otherwise they won't work – surely, the physico-chemistry of a system has *something* to do with its causal structure and role, no? If, for instance, we replace all the carbon in a brain with, say, krypton (a so-called "noble" gas) the causal functionality of the system will be irreparably disrupted. That's because functionality isn't just a result of the proper arrangement of the parts of a system, but also of the types of materials (and their properties) that make up those parts. But if we expand our concept of functionality in philosophy of mind to take this objection into account, it is no longer clear what is the difference between a functionalist and a biological perspective. Contra Chalmers (as cited above), people like Searle (and myself) who hold to a biological approach to consciousness are not claiming that only currently known biological systems are capable of conscious states. Indeed, already in his classic Chinese room paper Searle stated this explicitly:

> Part of the point of the present argument is that only something that had those *causal powers* could have that intentionality. Perhaps *other physical and chemical processes could produce exactly these effects*; perhaps, for example, Martians also have intentionality but their brains are made of different stuff. That is an empirical question, rather like the question whether photosynthesis can be done by something with a chemistry different from that of chlorophyll. (Searle 1980; my emphasis)

So functionalists cannot have it both ways: either they are saying that the substrate truly does not matter at all, in which case they are endorsing some sort of dualism based on an untenably strong version of CTM and a misunderstanding of Church–Turing; or they are admitting that substrate does matter, in which case they are really falling back onto some sort of (perhaps expanded) biological view of consciousness. And recall that, according to Chalmers' own reckoning, a biologically inclined philosopher will *ipso facto* be a pessimist about mind uploading.

5 Mind uploading, personal identity, and Kirk's death by transporter

We now turn to the second of Chalmers' fundamental questions about MU, that of personal identity. As I mentioned above, he provides his readers with three families of alternatives: biological views, psychological views, and what he terms, following Robert Nozick, "closest-continuer" views, stating – correctly, I think – that adopting the first type leads one to think of MU as a form of suicide, preferring the second one inclines people toward seeing MU as a type of preservation of personal identity, and going for the third option ends up in a type of bet-hedging that depends on the form of uploading (destructive or not). While Chalmers is correct in *logically* separating from the question of personal identity the question whether consciousness is a type of computational phenomenon, the two are obviously deeply related when it comes to mind uploading. It would be odd, for instance, to endorse a biological view of consciousness, leading to skepticism about the CTM, and yet somehow switch to a psychological view of personal identity and gingerly walk into an uploading machine.

Quite honestly, I have always found the standard way of framing the issue of personal identity in metaphysics somewhat odd: it seems that for unfathomable reasons many philosophers think of the types of alternatives laid out by Chalmers as mutually exclusive, while a more commonsensical approach would suggest that they are complementary. It will come as no surprise that it is Searle, again, who takes this latter approach, even in introductory treatments of the subject matter (Searle 2005). He suggests that spatio-temporal continuity of the body is certainly a major criterion we all use to decide about personal identity (so, for instance, our monozygotic twins are not us, even when they are for all effective purposes genetically and physically identical to us, and even if they have the same thoughts – including memories – and general personality as we do). But spatio-temporal continuity is not sufficient to account for the first-person *experience* of personal identity; we *also* (as opposed to *instead*) need memory and personality. And Searle is quick to recognize that there are partial exceptions to all of these criteria (e.g., people whose memory is lost or personality profoundly altered as a consequence of accident or disease). Indeed, these exceptions help us to focus on what we count as personal identity *under normal circumstances*.

And there lies the rub for all discussions about personal identity: we make a certain sense of the concept because human beings are a particular type of biological species (biology again!). If we were a very different type of being, we would have a very different concept of personal identity, or perhaps even no such concept at all. There is, in other words, no *metaphysical fact* of the matter about personal identity – which perhaps helps explain both Chalmers' own lack of commitment on the subject and the fact that neo-scholastic philosophers[4] simply cannot agree on it.

As Chalmers himself observes, the issue here is analogous to the famous "transporter" problem inspired by the futuristic technology of the *Star Trek* series, and the question is often framed informally in philosophical circles as to whether Kirk (the original captain of the *Enterprise*) dies as soon as he steps in the transporter. Of course, for the dramatic purposes of the series, the answer is no: Kirk is scanned by the transporter's computer, information about the position of every one of his molecules is transmitted to the destination, and Kirk is "reassembled" (really, assembled *de novo*) on the other side (Robinson and Riley 2010) – which, incidentally, makes teletransportation a destructive type of uploading.[5]

So, in the spirit of anti-neo-scholastic philosophy, let us use a naturalistic, commonsensical approach for a change, and briefly examine the situation from the point of view of someone about to step into a transporter, or to allow what he thinks is going to be an instance of MU. To begin with, we can do away with any bet hedging: if your decision about pushing the button depends on whether the procedure is going to be destructive or not, I submit that you really do not believe that what's about to be created is a continuation of you. At best you think there will be a copy of you in existence at the end of the process – either *alongside* you as the original (nondestructive uploading), or not (in which case you'll be dead, not transported or uploaded). And indeed, it seems to me that this is pretty much all there is to say on the matter: if it is possible to do the transporting or uploading in a non-destructive manner, *obviously* we are talking about duplication, not preservation of identity. But if the only difference between the two cases is that in one the original is destroyed, then how on earth can we avoid the conclusion that when it comes to destructive uploading we just committed suicide (or murder, as the case may be)? After all, *ex hypothesi* there is no substantive difference between destructive and non-destructive uploading in terms of end results. This means that even by allowing the possibility of MU for the sake of argument, we end up rejecting it by way of what ought to be straightforward (and certainly commonsensical, judging from Chalmers' own hesitation) considerations about personal identity. I realize, of course, that to some philosophers this may seem far too simple a solution to what they regard as an intricate metaphysical problem. But sometimes even philosophers agree that problems need to be dis-solved, not solved: "Since everything lies open to view there is nothing to explain" (Wittgenstein 1953: 126).

6 Conclusion

I have argued that the most reasonable answers to Chalmers' two questions concerning mind uploading are pessimistic: (1) No, the mind "doesn't work that way," as Fodor quipped in the title of his book. That is, we have serious reasons to doubt a straightforward computational account of consciousness, and very good prima facie reasons to endorse a moderate version of biological naturalism. (2) No, personal identity (as understood by normal human beings) would not be maintained after a process of MU, which would result either in a duplication of the original individual (if non-destructive) or in the death of the original (if destructive).

The first conclusion, it should go without saying, does *not* imply that we will never be able to build "conscious machines." After all, human beings *are* conscious (biological) machines, if by machine one means something built in a manner that doesn't invoke mystical or supernatural processes. And, again, it should not even be interpreted as saying that the only way to get consciousness is via carbon-based life forms. It only says that consciousness is unlikely to be substrate-independent, and that there plausibly are very strong constraints on the sort of substrate that is suitable to the process. The proof, of course, is in the pudding: the moment someone is capable of producing human-type thinking and consciousness in a computer, I will stand corrected (though there is the pesky issue of how would we know, a particular version of the problem of other minds: Hyslop 2009; of one thing I'm sure: a simple Turing test is not going to do it).

Even if and when we are able to produce a computerized version of human consciousness, however, I will still strongly advise against pushing the "upload" button: in the light of a naturalistic and commonsensical approach to personal identity, you would simply be committing a very technologically sophisticated (and likely very, very expensive) form of suicide.

Acknowledgments

I would like to thank the editors of this volume for inviting me to contribute as a skeptic to their collection; that's the way intellectual discourse advances. I also wish to thank Leonard Finkleman for thoughtful and helpful comments on a previous draft of this manuscript. Finally, sincere thanks to many of the readers of my blog, Rationally Speaking, who have challenged and continue to challenge me in clever and instructive ways whenever I write about these (or, really, any other) topics.

Notes

1 All quotations from Chalmers are from the version of his arguments presented in the chapter in this volume.

2 Chalmers here rehashes his "dancing qualia" argument, presented in Chalmers (1995) and criticized by various authors, e.g., van Heuveln et al. (1998).

3 Unless one expands the definition of computation to encompass so-called pancomputationalism (Piccinini 2010 and citations therein), the idea that everything computes; at that point, however, talk of computing becomes vacuous and at any rate not particularly helpful to understanding the human mind.

4 I am using the term in the admittedly pejorative way articulated by Ladyman and Ross (2007) and exemplified in Chalmers et al. (2009), and in opposition to naturalistic or "scientific" philosophy: Ross et al. (2013).

5 Of course, also for dramatic purposes, Kirk is always accompanied by one or more "red shirts" from the *Enterprise* security team, who are almost guaranteed to become casualties before the end of the episode. For a complete analysis backing up this particular point, see Barsalou (2013).

References

Barsalou, M. 2013. Keep your shirt on: A Bayesian exploration. *Significance Magazine*, http://www.significancemagazine.org/details/webexclusive/4381371/Keep-your-redshirt-on-a-Bayesian-exploration.html (accessed October 5, 2013).
Chalmers, D.J. 1995. Absent qualia, fading qualia, dancing qualia. In T. Metzinger, ed., *Conscious Experience*. Exeter: Imprint Academic, pp. 309–328.
Chalmers, D.J. 2010. The Singularity: A philosophical analysis. *The Journal of Consciousness Studies* 17: 7–65.
Chalmers, D.J., Manley, D. and Wassermann, R. 2009. *Metametaphysics: New Essays on the Foundations of Ontology*. Oxford: Oxford University Press.
Copeland, B.J. 2002. The Church–Turing thesis. *Stanford Encyclopedia of Philosophy*, http://plato.stanford.edu/entries/church-turing/ (accessed October 5, 2013).
Fodor, J. 1975. *The Language of Thought*. New York: Thomas Crowell.
Fodor, J. 2000. *The Mind Doesn't Work That Way: The Scope and Limits of Computational Psychology*. Cambridge, MA: MIT Press.
Horst, S. 2009. The computational theory of mind. *Stanford Encyclopedia of Philosophy*, http://plato.stanford.edu/entries/computational-mind/ (accessed October 5, 2013).
Hyslop, A. 2009. Other minds. *Stanford Encyclopedia of Philosophy*, http://plato.stanford.edu/entries/other-minds/ (accessed October 5, 2013).
Ladyman, J., and Ross, D. 2007. *Every Thing Must Go: Metaphysics Naturalized*. Oxford: Oxford University Press.
Olson, E.T. 2010. Personal identity. *Stanford Encyclopedia of Philosophy*, http://plato.stanford.edu/entries/identity-personal/ (accessed October 5, 2013).
Piccinini, G. 2010. Computation in physical systems. *Stanford Encyclopedia of Philosophy*, http://plato.stanford.edu/entries/computation-physicalsystems/ (accessed October 5, 2013).
Pinker, S. 1997. *How the Mind Works*. New York: W.W. Norton.
Prinz, J. 2012. Singularity and inevitable doom. *Journal of Consciousness Studies* 19: 77–86.
Putnam, H. 1960. Minds and machines. In S. Hook, ed., *Dimensions of Mind*. New York: New York University Press, pp. 148–180.
Robinson, B., and Riley, M. 2010. *Star Trek: U.S.S. Enterprise Haynes Manual*. New York: Pocket Books.
Ross, D., Ladyman, J., and Kincaid, H., eds. 2013. *Scientific Metaphysics*. Oxford: Oxford University Press.
Schulze-Makuch, D., and Irwin, L.N. 2006. The prospect of alien life in exotic forms on other worlds. *Naturwissenschaften* 93: 155–172.
Searle, J. 1980. Minds, brains and programs. *Behavioral and Brain Sciences* 3: 417–457.
Searle, J. 2005. *Mind: A Brief Introduction*. New York: Oxford University Press.
Searle, J. 2008. Biological naturalism. In M. Velmans and S. Schneider, eds., *The Blackwell Companion to Consciousness*. Malden, MA: Blackwell, pp. 325–334.
van Heuveln, B., Dietrich, E., and Oshima, M. 1998. Let's dance! The equivocation in Chalmers' dancing qualia argument. *Minds and Machines* 8: 237–249.
Wittgenstein, L. 1953. *Philosophical Investigations*. Oxford: Blackwell.

8

If You Upload, Will You Survive?

Joseph Corabi and Susan Schneider

1 Introduction

Suppose you are nearing the end of your biological life, so you consider becoming an upload, that is, a creature that has all of the details of its mental life transferred from its brain to a computer. But wait! Metaphysics is not on your side. As we'll now explain, the philosophical case for surviving uploading is weak. When you upload, you are probably dying, at least in a philosophical sense. Your upload may think exactly like you do, and if it is downloaded into an identical-looking android, people may even be convinced that it is you, but the upload is at best a psychological duplicate of you. Now, you may have other reasons to upload, besides surviving death. If you merely seek a mental duplicate – say, to carry out your earthly tasks – then we have no metaphysical bones to pick with you. But to the extent that your decision is fueled by a suspicion that *you* will be the one carrying out the earthly tasks, your philosophical footing is tenuous.

Why consider the philosophical case for uploading now? This is merely the realm of science fiction, you may think. But science fiction often foreshadows science fact, and uploading may turn out to be a case of such convergence. According to certain scientists and philosophers, such as Nick Bostrom, Anders Sandberg, and Ray Kurzweil, recent technological developments have transformed what used to be seen as far-fetched science fiction tales into goals that may very well be attainable in upcoming decades.[1]

Intelligence Unbound: The Future of Uploaded and Machine Minds, First Edition.
Edited by Russell Blackford and Damien Broderick.

Here's how we will proceed: section 2 introduces issues from the field of metaphysics that are key to determining whether you could survive uploading; then section 3 argues that it is plausible, given these background metaphysical issues, that you will not survive uploading. Section 4 considers David Chalmers' objections to our position, as stated in a recent paper of his.[2] Section 5 concludes.

2 Uploading and personal identity

For many, the attractiveness of uploading would be lost or diminished if it turns out that we can't survive. A pressing philosophical issue, then, is to determine whether an upload is *the very same person* as the individual who existed prior to the upload. Accordingly, this will be the primary focus of our chapter.

We've noted that survival is not the only reason to upload, though – for instance, one may simply want a creature to carry out one's earthly business. In addition to such practical motivations, there are other, more metaphysical, issues to consider. You may believe that although the upload is not literally you, there is a special relationship between you and your upload. Consider that sometimes the relationship between particular beings or entities at different times is not as simple as a question of identity or total distinctness. When a human embryo (call it "Ally") splits into twin embryos, it may not seem correct to describe either of the new embryos as identical to Ally (i.e., as the very same individual as Ally).[3] But, at the same time, many people do not think it seems correct to say that Ally has died and been replaced by two different people either. According to some, the intimate relation that the new embryos share with Ally deserves to be treated differently from the relationship had by two people who were conceived from a different sperm and egg pair. We might label this special sort of relationship "continuation," bearing in mind that we will reserve the expression "survival" for numerical identity.

This leads us to a second kind of question: if uploading of a particular sort does not preserve identity, is the upload at least a *continuation* of the original (in the technical sense of "continuation" employed above)? And there are more questions still. Even if someone in the future were neither you nor a continuation of you, that future person might preserve aspects of you that might make bringing about the existence of such a person of tremendous import to you. For instance, what if you were told that you were about to die, but that for a reasonable sum of money you could form a biological clone of yourself that would have copies of all of the most important memories from your life, as well as a number of the character traits that you most highly value in yourself? Many people, when placed in the situation, would happily pay the fee for this clone. Why? One reason might be that the existence of such a person would comfort your friends and family. But it is pretty clear that this is not the only consideration that might push you in a "yes" direction. It is reasonable to conjecture that part of what might be driving you to pay for the clone is a desire to preserve your distinctive experiences and characteristics for their own sake, even if not embodied by you or a continuation of you. In a similar vein, then, we can ask of uploads whether they preserve enough of what is valuable about ourselves (or at least enough of what we consider valuable) so that, even if they are not identical to us or continuations of us, there will still be much from our standpoint that commends us to upload, especially if doing so does not threaten the quality of our lives in any way (i.e., the lives of *us* or at least those who are continuations of us).[4]

As we can see from the above discussion, there are three kinds of issues that must be addressed in considering personal identity for any upload case. First, we want to determine if the upload has preserved *numerical identity*: i.e., is it the very same person as before the upload? If the upload is not numerically identical to the original person, we can then ask if it is at least a *continuation* of the pre-upload person, in the way that one of the embryos above might be thought to be a continuation of Ally. And if the upload is not even a continuation of the person, we can then turn to the question of whether it preserves enough of what is valuable about the pre-upload person (or at least enough of what we or the pre-upload person consider to be valuable) for uploading to be an attractive proposition from the agent's standpoint.

While we will weigh in concerning all these matters, as noted, our primary task is to determine whether your upload would genuinely be you – that is, whether numerical identity obtains. So let us now ask: how can we determine when an individual who attempts to upload is numerically identical to the uploaded being? To do this, we need to get a better handle on the nature of personhood.

Metaphysical background

The notion of a person is philosophically rich; for one thing, persons are traditionally considered to be the bearers of rights, or at least entities that demand consideration in the utilitarian calculus. For another, understanding the person is central to our self-understanding – for instance, it helps us to understand what it is to be human, and what it is to be a reflective, conscious being. Notice further that there are metaphysical dimensions to the notion of a person: a person is a metaphysical object of some sort. For one thing, it is an entity that has a variety of mental features (or properties): *being rational*, *having certain kinds of conscious experiences*, and so on. These features are *mental properties* of the person. This naturally leads many metaphysicians who consider the notion of a person to take the position that the person is a *substance* – that is, an entity that continues to exist for at least a short period of time and is the bearer of properties. One key philosophical issue is whether persons are material, physical substances (as the physicalist purports), or whether persons are distinct from physical objects, say, because persons have souls.

Substances have some of their properties essentially – that is, they require them for their continued existence. Others they possess only contingently, meaning that they could lack those properties without ceasing to exist. So, for example, a person arguably has the basic capacity for rational thought essentially; in contrast, properties like the person's particular weight and hair color are not essential, but contingent – after all, you could survive if you had a different hair color or weighed a bit more. Different theories of personal identity hold different properties to be essential to the nature of the person. Consider the leading theories:

1 **Soul theories.** This family of views holds that your essential property is that you have a soul or immaterial mind, where souls and immaterial minds are non-physical substances distinct from any physical thing, such as the brain.
2 **Physicalism (or "materialism") about the person.** One is essentially the collection of molecules that makes up one's brain, and arguably, the rest of one's body.[5]
3 **Psychological continuity theories.** In their most general form this family of theories holds that you are essentially your memories and ability to reflect on yourself (Locke 1689; see Olson 2010 and Perry 1975).

Each of these views has been framed by numerous individuals, and the details can differ in important ways (consider, for instance, the range of positions on the nature of the soul within Christianity).

We will have more to say in a moment about what views we will focus on in this chapter, but first, we should address a more radical view that repudiates entirely the reality of the person:

4 **The No Self View.** According to the "no self view," the self is an illusion. The "I" is a grammatical fiction (Friedrich Nietzsche). There are bundles of impressions but no underlying self (David Hume). There is no survival because there is no person (Buddha).

Each position has its own implications about whether one should upload. If you hold (1), then your decision to upload depends on whether you believe the upload would retain (or share) your soul or immaterial mind. If you believe (2), then uploading will not be a form of survival, because survival requires the same material substrate, and uploading changes it. In contrast, according to (3), uploading may be safe, because although it alters your material substrate it preserves your psychological configuration. Finally, (4) contrasts sharply with (1)–(3). If you hold (4), then the survival of the person is not an issue, for there is no person to begin with. As a result, we will avoid discussing (4) further.

One common thread that underlies (1) and (2) is that advocates of these views tend to hold that the person or self is some kind of substance – an object-like entity that has properties and continues to exist for some period of time. For this reason, we will focus on these views below. Depending on how (3) is ultimately interpreted, we believe that it is either untenable or has features which make it susceptible to similar arguments as physicalism and soul theories. But because our discussion must be brief, we will set that aside here.[6]

3 Putting metaphysics to work

Instantaneous, destructive uploading attempts

Now let us ask: Could you survive destructive, instantaneous uploading? This is a form of uploading in which, all at once, all the precise information about your mental functioning is measured, and your brain is destroyed. All of the information is transmitted to a computer host some distance away.

Is it plausible that you would survive? We doubt it, whether persons are physical things or souls. Consider first that the mechanism by which you would move instantaneously from your brain to the computer is problematic, even on the assumption that only a short distance needs to be traversed. Not only does this involve an unprecedentedly rapid kind of motion for a person to follow, but this sort of motion is oddly discontinuous. For it is not as though the person moves, little by little, to the computer, so that a step-by-step spatial transition from brain to computer can be traced. Since information is being uploaded, the information has to be processed and reassembled in the computer host before anything like a functional duplicate of the original brain can be obtained. Hence, the person exists at one moment in a brain, and then ceases to exist for a brief period while the information is being transported, and then comes back into existence in the computer at some distance away.

While it is conceivable that persons behave in such bizarre ways, the issue is whether it is justifiable to believe that they really do so. Ordinary physical objects simply do not behave like this (although quantum teleportation does, on a microscopic scale), and no soul theorists give any hint that they believe that souls have properties that would make them different from physical objects in this respect. This sort of spatial and temporal discontinuity is incompatible with standard views about the endurance conditions of ordinary objects – these intuitions are much stronger than any particular intuitions about the continued existence of a person in this sort of scenario.

It might be objected that some soul theorists deny that people have spatial locations at all – namely, full-blooded Cartesian dualists. (Descartes himself famously claimed that people – i.e., souls – have no spatial locations.) Although the arguments we give here will not address the full-blooded Cartesian view directly, presumably full-blooded Cartesians have intuitions about what sorts of physical entities can causally interact with souls. They will likely endorse constraints on what kinds of bodies may interact with a particular soul that allow parallel arguments to be constructed against the claim that uploading preserves identity on a Cartesian view. For example, most Cartesians will probably endorse the claim that a particular Cartesian soul causally interacting with a biological body at one time could not begin causally interacting with a computer-based body 1,000 miles away from that biological body a fraction of a second later, at least not without special divine intervention. This is all we need to make our point, because this makes the issues that affect uploading for Cartesian dualists parallel to the ones that affect uploading for physicalists.

A second point against survival in instantaneous destructive uploading cases is that, unless the brain is truly destroyed at the *very* instant the information is obtained from it, for at least a small interval the person will continue to exist at the location of the brain even after the information has been transmitted to the computer. If the computer is fast and near enough, and it takes long enough for the brain to be destroyed, this could result in the person remaining where the brain is even after the information has begun its journey to the computer (or perhaps after the information has finished its journey there).[7] Only later does the person "catch up" to the information and come to be located where the computer is. Once again, the strangeness of this sort of behavior violates strong intuitions about the endurance conditions for particulars, and, as both physicalism and the soul theory make clear, persons are particulars. Consequently, as a result of both of these considerations, it is sensible to conclude that identity will not be preserved.

Turning to the matter of whether the upload is at least a continuation of the original person (again, we have in mind the aforementioned technical sense of "continuation"), there is still reason for pessimism. The paradigmatic instances of continuation are ones where there is physical continuity between the bodies of the continuations and that of their predecessor.

Consider, for instance, stock examples like the identical twin scenario from earlier, or transplants of one cerebral hemisphere into a new body. In cases like these, the claim to continuation is based strongly on the physical continuity between the bodies of continuations (and more specifically, brain material in the brain transplant case) and the body of their predecessor. So, insofar as we have any intuitions about continuation, the intuitions track this sort of continuity. But, as we have already seen, the relevant continuity is utterly lacking in uploading, since the "birth" of the upload is spatiotemporally separated from the "death" of the original individual, and moreover the "body" of the upload doesn't even possess the same broad-ranging kinds of physical properties as the body of the original person – that is, the pre-upload is a carbon-based being in which mental properties are in a cellular substrate, whereas the upload is not.

In fact, we are now in a position to see that the pessimistic conclusions of this section do not really depend on whether one is a materialist or a soul theorist. *For the main reasons for being pessimistic have to do with reservations about positions that attribute strange and discontinuous motions of persons (in contrast to the behavior of other macroscopic substances) in order to claim that uploading is compatible with survival.*

Clearly, physicalists are in the worst shape, since the physical differences between the pre-upload person and the upload are most dramatic – they are made of different physical building blocks, after all, and these building blocks are obviously spatiotemporally discontinuous with the original building blocks. But soul theorists are not much better off, since many of them believe that persons are essentially connected to their physical bodies, and even the ones who do not would have a hard time explaining how the soul would manage to "move" from the location of the original body to the location of the upload. (This motion could be literal or it could involve changing which physical objects the soul directly causally interacts with.)

Of course, it could be objected that huge segments of the human population believe in reincarnation, and what is reincarnation if not a movement (or transmigration) of a soul from one body to another? So if reincarnation has plausibility, isn't this reason to be optimistic about uploading's prospects for preserving identity? While, if plausible, reincarnation might provide slight background support for the view that destructive uploading preserves identity, the amount of comfort is likely to be small. The trouble is that virtually all theories of reincarnation posit some supernatural being or supernatural force that moves the soul and "reassigns" it to a new body. But most proponents of uploading do not believe in such beings or forces, at least of the sort that would do the work required. But without these supernatural entities, how would the soul know where to find the new brain or computer host with which it should be associated? By what mechanism would the soul be attached to this new brain or computer host? There does not appear to be a satisfying answer in the offing.

To end the section on a more positive note, what about using uploading to preserve various characteristics that are valuable, or at least are considered to be, such as character traits and qualitative replicas of memories? This is a difficult issue; sorting through it requires a more systematic investigation of people's intuitions and the various valuable characteristics. But here we see the greatest room for optimism: if people care a great deal about preserving copies of their "memories," character traits, and thought patterns, then uploading of this sort may be a feasible way to give them what they are looking for. But the extent to which this sort of thing matters to people remains a topic for further investigation.[8]

Gradual destructive uploading

Now consider the case of gradual destructive uploading. Imagine, for instance, a case like the one Chalmers presents, where a person's brain is slowly replaced, neuron by neuron, by functionally isomorphic silicon units that transmit the functional information from the neurons just as they destroy and replace them. These silicon-based units mimic the exact cause and effect profiles of the neurons, and then – after replacing and destroying them – they report the information to a computer host that then assembles a working model in the computer host that perfectly duplicates all the intricate causal relationships in the person's biological brain.

You may suspect that this case offers better promise for survival than the instantaneous uploading case we considered, but the change from instantaneous to gradual uploading does not seem drastic enough to provide much additional reason for optimism. For one thing, although the transmission of information happens in a more piecemeal fashion than with instantaneous uploading, nevertheless there will fail to be a functional isomorph until all the data from the original is uploaded. Thus, regardless of how long the overall replacement process takes, or how small the incremental replacements are, there will still be a dramatic moment at which the data is assembled by the computer host and the isomorph is born. When we consider what happens at this moment, all of the old issues reemerge: for example, does the person instantly (or almost instantly) travel from brain to computer? Is there a temporal discontinuity between the person's disappearance and reappearance? It is hard to believe that the same kinds of strong intuitions about endurance we saw before will not be violated once again. (And even if the upload is assembled gradually, still there will be an enormous spatial discontinuity between the person in the computer and the one in the brain.)

Interestingly, Chalmers seems sympathetic to the preservation of identity in the gradual uploading case. We find his reasons unpersuasive, though (assuming they are indeed intended as reasons to believe that numerical identity is being preserved). One consideration that he raises is that "i[t] will be very unnatural for most people to believe that their friends and families are being killed by the process [of gradual uploading]" (Chalmers 2012: 45). This is likely to be an untrustworthy folk intuition even if Chalmers is correct that it would be present; attending to the sorts of subtle details of cases like this, and attuning philosophical intuitions to the relevance of these considerations, is not generally a strength of those without philosophical training.

Another reason that he provides is his confidence that consciousness will be continuous between the pre-uploaded individual and the uploaded one, and that the resulting psychological continuity is "an extremely strong basis for asserting continuation of a person" (2012: 45). (By "continuation of a person" here, it is clear in context that Chalmers is talking about what we have called "survival" – the preservation of numerical identity over time.) What is it for consciousness to be continuous in the sense Chalmers is talking about? One possibility is that the continuity of consciousness across time requires that the consciousness be *the same person's* consciousness at the later time as at the earlier time. While this interpretation of what Chalmers says would certainly have the virtue of ensuring that what he says is correct – continuation would be a foolproof basis for asserting survival – it has the drawback of being uninformative. For in order to know whether consciousness is continuous in this sense, we must already know whether survival has occurred. But this is exactly what we are trying to get a handle on.

If, on the other hand, all that is required for consciousness to be continuous is something much looser – that the later conscious states be qualitatively similar to the earlier ones or be caused somehow by earlier conscious states – then what he says will again be no help. If continuity of consciousness is this easy to attain, then the result is that many distinct uploads could be psychologically continuous with me, in the same way that many computers run qualitatively identical copies of Microsoft Word. As the silicon units replace my neurons and transmit information to remote locations, they can just as easily transmit the information to multiple computer hosts as they can to one. But a consequence is then that I could be wholly located in different places, in the same way that redness or triangularity can be wholly located in different places. (There can be red things in different places, and triangles in different places.) This is a classic feature of abstract entities, not concrete ones, and people seem to be classic examples of concrete things, whether they are ultimately physical or non-physical. Suggesting that they can multiply locate in this way violates deep intuitions we have about the nature of persons, and hence a view leading to these implications should be discarded.[9]

To sum up, then, Chalmers is faced with a dilemma here. He can choose an understanding of continuity of consciousness that makes it clear that continuity of consciousness is a good basis for asserting survival, but only at the cost of casting into doubt whether continuity has in fact been preserved in uploading cases. Or he can choose an understanding of continuity of consciousness that makes it clear that continuity has been preserved, but only by severing his desired connection between continuity of consciousness and survival. Either way, it appears his suggestion here will not work.

So much for Chalmers' tentative defense of the idea that gradual uploading preserves identity. Are uploads at least continuations? Again, this question may not be as clear-cut as the parallel question for instantaneous destructive uploading, but the reasons for preferring a different conclusion are not particularly strong. There are still the same spatiotemporal discontinuity issues, and the fact that the biological brain is destroyed gradually and the information transmitted slowly doesn't seem to matter a lot.

Any form of nondestructive uploading is not likely to preserve identity, since the upload will clearly have no claim to be the person when the original brain is still very much in operation and supporting consciousness and thought. (And, in addition, we still have all the same problems we discussed before in the context of destructive uploading.) Whether nondestructive uploads are continuations depends once again on whether being a survivor is compatible with the kind of spatiotemporal discontinuity we have seen. There is also a special issue that arises with nondestructive uploads – namely, whether continuation is compatible with the continued existence of the original person. All of the paradigmatic instances of continuation (e.g., the case of identical twins and the case of transplantation of hemispheres of the brain) seem to involve the original person ceasing to exist and being replaced by persons with an equal claim to intimate causal and substantial connection to the original. But when the original person clearly continues to exist, it is even more difficult than before to make the case that a mere qualitative duplicate with only distant causal connections to the original has any claim to being a continuation.

4 Response to Chalmers

Chalmers has recently responded to similar arguments we have made in our earlier work on uploading. In this final substantive section, we will address his objections and illustrate that they do not mitigate the force of our case.[10]

He expresses his first objection in the following passage:

> In 1713 Yale University moved from Wethersfield to New Haven. I do not know the exact circumstances, but it is not hard to imagine that the move happened with the issuing of a decree. At that moment, the university moved from one place to another without passing through the places in between. One could also imagine versions where it exists for a brief period at both locations, or in which there is a temporal gap during which it is located nowhere. I take it that universities are objects, so there is no general objection to objects behaving this way. There are also objects such as electronic databases that can quite clearly be destructively uploaded from one location to another … So I do not think that a plausible theory of objects will rule out discontinuous motion of this sort.

Let us consider the Yale example first. The problem is that even assuming Yale is an object, it is an artifact. Whether Yale continues to exist and where it continues to exist is largely a matter of what the administrators at Yale declare about its continued existence and how the members of the Yale community treat these declarations. This is very different from human persons, whose endurance is not subject to the mere whims of human conventions, interests, or decrees in the way that Yale is.

Chalmers anticipates this response, though, suggesting that we might hold "that there is a disanalogy between universities and people." He continues:

> Perhaps people are fundamental entities where universities … are nonfundamental entities, for example, and perhaps the continuity constraint is more plausible where fundamental entities are concerned. They say explicitly that they intend their arguments to apply on a materialist view (on which people are not fundamental), however, so this cannot be what is going on. And if we assume a substance dualist view [i.e., a soul view] on which people are fundamental nonphysical entities, there is not much reason to suppose that nonphysical entities are subject to the same continuity constraints as fundamental physical entities.

It is true that, if physicalism is correct, people will not be fundamental. But we do not think this ruins the disanalogy between people and Yale. If physicalism is right, persons are macroscopic natural objects, and, as opposed to human constructions like institutions, do not change location by decree. Institutions are not the normal case; the fact is that when ordinary physical objects move, they trace a continuous path through spacetime.[11] Further, on a physicalist view, people are still loci of consciousness and thought, and this strikes us as being a deep fact about the world, not subject to change by human convention or decree. These considerations suggest that, even on a physicalist view, humans are quite dissimilar from institutions.

Further, as we argued above, there are important reasons to suppose that if the soul theory is true, souls will not move willy-nilly in the way that they would have to in order for uploading to preserve numerical identity. Soul theorists believe that souls are tightly connected to particular bodies or brains. The souls may not depend for their continued existence on the continued existence of those bodies or brains, but they are not thought to be capable of becoming associated with a new body or brain (let alone an uploaded functional duplicate) just because the old one is destroyed (again, at least assuming that a supernatural being or force is not trying to move them).

Chalmers' other example – that of an electronic database – is similarly clever, but ultimately unconvincing. The problem is that electronic databases are *abstract* objects, while human beings are concrete.[12] Electronic databases are patterns of stored data that can be reproduced anywhere. But persons are not mere patterns of data, as we have seen. Even if persons are said to consist partly in their "databases" according to certain computational approaches to the mind, they are not abstract patterns, but concrete entities having certain abstract properties. They are not programs themselves, but entities running a program.

Chalmers' final objection to our approach, which has to do with our handling of gradual uploading cases, is as follows:

> Corabi and Schneider also argue against gradual (destructive) uploading. They say that it is subject to the same issues concerning spatiotemporal discontinuity, at the "dramatic moment at which the data is assembled by the computer host and the isomorph is born." Here I suspect that they are conceiving of gradual uploading in the wrong way. As I conceive of gradual uploading, there is no such dramatic moment. A functional isomorph of the original is present throughout. Its neurons are replaced one at a time by uploaded copies, leading from a 100% biological system to a 99%-1% system (biological-silicon, say), a 98%-2% system, and so on until there is a 100isomorph of the original. Insofar as the person changes location it will be a gradual change, one neuron at a time.

While Chalmers' original discussion did not say that there was a functional isomorph present throughout, let us consider Chalmers' case as he states it here, as it presents a different form of gradual uploading. In the present version the neurons are probed and replaced by silicon units. This happens in a piecemeal fashion, neuron by neuron. As each neuron is probed and replaced, a computer host receives signals from the silicon units. The computer is constantly in communication with the silicon neuron replacements and the brain continues to function as it had before.[13] So, at the end of the process, the artificial brain that has been fully uploaded is functionally isomorphic to the pre-upload brain.

It is important to notice that in this example, the artificial brain (or, in the early phases of the upload, the group of artificial neurons) is actually controlled by a program run by a computer located elsewhere. And the artificial "neurons" are located where the brain is, but their behavior is based on the processing of the program.

Unfortunately, issues emerge for the preferred version of the uploading case as well. To see the worry, let us ask: are the original neurons replaced by something spatially distant from the original brain? Some may suspect that the answer is affirmative because the computer is sending signals to the artificial neurons to tell them how to behave, and how to react to information. But if this is the case, our earlier objection applies: we still have a situation where there is discontinuous movement from one spatial position to another. Granted, in this case it is only parts that are moving in this fashion, not whole persons, but we believe that there is strong intuitive support for the claim that any motion of this sort is incompatible with survival. After all, it is not merely that we have intuitions that *whole* physical objects cannot move in this way. We have the same intuitions about parts of physical objects. As we argued above, the same intuitions seem to apply to persons.[14]

But you may suspect, instead, that the answer to our question is negative: that the original neurons are replaced by the artificial neurons placed in the brain itself, not lines of code in a program. But if this is the case, then, plausibly, at the end of the process, there would be a functioning artificial brain that is in the same location as the original. But then it does not seem that the upload itself (i.e., the information in the remote computer) is the same person as the original, for it is more plausible to hold that this is just a case of neural replacement – the replacement of individual neurons with artificial ones – and if anyone is a plausible candidate for being the same person as the original, it is the artificial brain, especially given the above consideration about spatial discontinuity. To be sure, the issues associated with neural replacement cases are tricky and deserve their own special treatment, but we think it would be a mistake to run them together with uploading.

5 Conclusion

Now that we have discussed the two general kinds of uploading scenarios and given our response to Chalmers' objections, let us summarize where things stand. First, there is considerable reason to be pessimistic about instantaneous destructive uploading's ability to preserve identity or to produce continuations of the original person. For this would require odd spatiotemporal discontinuities, and so conflict with what we know of the general behavior of concrete objects. Second, there is also good reason to be pessimistic about gradual destructive uploading's ability to preserve identity or produce continuations, since exactly the same issues arise in the context of gradual uploading. Third, we saw that all forms of nondestructive uploading are unlikely to preserve identity, and not appreciably more likely to produce continuations. Finally, we saw that there was more room for optimism about whether uploading of all the various sorts preserves psychological aspects of persons that we deem worth caring about, although we noted that a more thorough investigation of people's intuitions on this topic is needed.

Notes

1 See, for instance, a technical report published by Oxford's Future of Humanity Institute: Sandberg and Bostrom (2008).
2 See Chalmers (2012), in response to Corabi and Schneider (2012).
3 Assume, for the purposes of illustration, that it is uncontroversial that embryos are people.
4 These separate issues are distinguished in Chalmers' 2010 paper on the Singularity, from which Chapter 6 in this volume is adapted, albeit sometimes implicitly.
5 For a more extensive survey of the positions on personal identity see Olson (2010). Materialism and physicalism differ in subtle ways (mainly, physics may dispense with matter), but we will not delve into this herein.
6 For discussion see Corabi and Schneider (2012).
7 If the person does not "catch up" until after the computer has reassembled the information and created a conscious being, then what we have is a scenario that is best classified as nondestructive uploading, albeit a nondestructive uploading situation where the original only lasts a short while after the upload. These cases must be dealt with separately.
8 Parfit (1984), along with the literature it has spawned, provides the classic foundation for much of this investigation.
9 This also shows that nondestructive uploading is always problematic for survival, since nondestructive uploading leaves the original person intact, claiming that any new uploads are the very same person as the original, who is still walking around.
10 See Chalmers (2012). All the Chalmers passages we cite in this section come from this article.
11 Time travelers would arguably carve out a discontinuous path through space-time, but it is controversial whether time travel is possible.
12 They may not be purely abstract, because they may require some causal connection to specific concrete phenomena to count as the databases they are. (If the database contains data on casualties in US Civil War battles, for instance, it might have to have some causal connection to the US Civil War in order to count as a database about US Civil War casualties.) But this is a very minimal concession that does not harm our argument, because the sorts of connections required for personal survival (or continuation, for that matter) are much more robust, as we argued above.

13 We are grateful to Chalmers for clarifying in correspondence his preferred notion of gradual destructive uploading.

14 Issues about Chalmers' discussion of continuity of consciousness remain in this context, but we must set them aside here.

References

Chalmers, D.J. 2010. The Singularity: A philosophical analysis. *Journal of Consciousness Studies* 17: 7–65.

Chalmers, D.J. 2012. The Singularity: A reply to commentators. *Journal of Consciousness Studies* 19(7–8): 141–167.

Corabi, J., and Schneider, S. 2012. The metaphysics of uploading. *Journal of Consciousness Studies* 19(7–8): 26–44.

Locke, J. 1690. *An Essay Concerning Human Understanding*.

Olson, Eric T. 2010. Personal identity. In *Stanford Encyclopedia of Philosophy*, http://plato.stanford.edu/archives/win2010/entries/identity-personal/ (accessed 7 October, 2013). (1st pub. August 2002; substantive revisions October 2010.)

Parfit, D. 1984. *Reasons and Persons*. Oxford: Oxford University Press.

Perry, J., ed. 1975. *Personal Identity*. Berkeley: University of California Press.

Sandberg, A., and Bostrom, N. 2008. *Whole Brain Emulation: A Roadmap*. Technical Report #2008-3, Future of Humanity Institute, Oxford University, www.fhi.ox.ac.uk/reports/2008-3.pdf (accessed October 7, 2013).

9

On the Prudential Irrationality of Mind Uploading

Nicholas Agar

For Ray Kurzweil, artificial intelligence (AI) is not just about making artificial things intelligent; it's also about making humans artificially superintelligent.[1] In his version of our future we enhance our mental powers by means of increasingly powerful electronic neuroprostheses. The recognition that any function performed by neurons and synapses can be done better by electronic chips will lead to an ongoing conversion of biological brain into machine mind. We will *mind upload*.

Once the transfer of our minds and identities into machines is complete, we will be free to follow the trajectory of accelerating improvement currently tracked by mobile phones and DNA sequencers. We will quickly become millions and billions of times more intelligent than we currently are. This chapter challenges Kurzweil's predictions about the destiny of the human mind. I argue that it is unlikely ever to be rational for human beings to upload their minds completely onto computers. Although we may find it desirable to replace peripheral parts of our minds – parts dedicated to the processing of visual information, for example – we should stop well before going all the way. A justified fear of uploading will make it irrational to accept offers to replace the parts of our brains responsible for thought processes that we consider essential to our conscious experience, even if the replacements manifestly outperform neurons.

Mind uploading is an option that is not yet available to anyone. Kurzweil's commitment to the exponential improvement of information technology leads him predict computers with human intelligence by 2029. Mind

Intelligence Unbound: The Future of Uploaded and Machine Minds, First Edition.
Edited by Russell Blackford and Damien Broderick.

uploading will presumably be technologically feasible only some time after that. This means that we're speculating about the decisions of people decades or – should Kurzweil be wrong about technological progress – centuries hence. But our best guesses about whether people of the future will deem mind uploading to be prudentially rational have consequences for decisions we make now about the development of AI. The notion that we should call a halt to work on AI may be preposterous. But just as we support the development of clean energy technologies, we can encourage researchers in AI to avoid the dangers here described.

1 Is mind uploading a philosophical possibility?

For the purposes of the discussion that follows, I will use the term "mind uploading" to describe two processes. Most straightforwardly, it describes the one-off event when a fully biological being presses a button and instantaneously and completely copies her entire psychology into a computer. But it also describes the decisive event in a series of replacements of neurons by electronic chips. By "decisive" I mean that it is the event that makes electronic circuits rather than the biological brain the primary vehicle for a person's psychology. Once this event has occurred, neurons will be properly viewed as adjuncts of electronic circuits rather than the other way around. Furthermore, if Kurzweil is right about the pace of technological change, they will be rapidly obsolescing adjuncts. The precise timing of the uploading event is more easily recognized in the first scenario than it is in the second. In the latter case, it's possible that there will be some vagueness about when electronic circuits, rather than the biological brain, become the primary vehicle of a person's psychology.

For simplicity's sake I suppose that if you accept the offer to upload then you consent to the destruction of the biological original. David Chalmers (2010) refers to this as *destructive* uploading. You might instead opt for *nondestructive* uploading, which copies your psychology into a computer but leaves intact the biological original. Since the biological original is preserved, nondestructive uploading does not directly kill its subjects. In the final section I present other reasons for finding nondestructive uploading prudentially irrational.

My claim that destructive mind uploading is prudentially irrational draws on skepticism about the eligibility for uploading of consciousness and intentionality, two properties of mind of great importance both to our ongoing survival and the value we place on that survival. Human minds are conscious. There's something that it's like to be us. Our minds exhibit intentionality. They entertain thoughts that are about other things. We are intelligent in virtue of this intentionality – without intentional states we could never have knowledge about the world.

It's clear that computers outperform human thinkers at a variety of tasks. The chess program on my Mac computer easily checkmates me, and my guesstimates of the time are almost always wider of the mark than is the reading on my computer's clock. These impressive feats are accomplished without conscious or intentional states. According to some philosophers there is a fundamental incompatibility between consciousness or intentionality and computation. It does not matter how powerful computers become, they will be forever incapable of a single conscious thought. For expository purposes I shall sometimes use the term "computer consciousness" in a way that does not distinguish between the putative consciousness or intentionality of computers. This possibility has great significance for aspiring mind uploaders. If consciousness and intentionality are essential to our identities, and destructive mind uploading does not transfer them, then we cannot survive the process. Uploading will not do a better job of preserving human identities than did the embalming techniques used on the ancient Egyptian pharaohs. Suppose that our conscious and intentional states are not essential to our identities. We might survive mind uploading but only in a form devoid of much of what makes life worth living.

2 Acknowledging and responding to philosophical skepticism about computer consciousness

There is a keenly argued debate over whether a computer could be conscious. Many philosophers subscribe to a functionalist view that defines consciousness and intentionality as functional states. The functional roles of conscious or intentional states are certainly complex. However, since a computer can be programmed to realize any functional state, there is no philosophical obstacle to realizing any conscious or intentional state. In this view, computer consciousness is a programming problem.

A dissenting group of philosophers finds differences between brains and computers that prevent the latter from possessing conscious or intentional states realized by the former. Prominent among the skeptics is John Searle, who challenges the notion that computers could ever manifest the intentional states essential to intelligence. He argues that the symbol manipulation performed by computers differs from genuine human thought. We solve problems by thinking about them. A computer instead runs a program that produces output useful to human programmers or users. Searle argues that there is a fundamental difference between a computer's arriving at the correct answer to a question by manipulating symbols and a human's understanding the question and reasoning to the correct answer. This is, according to Searle, not an obstacle that can be overcome by increases in computational power. Increases in the efficiency or power of computers may increase the likelihood that they will present useful and correct answers as outputs but they will never result in genuine intelligence. Consciousness is not the focus of Searle's argument, but his conclusion has implications for consciousness. If computers can never think, then it follows that they will never entertain conscious thoughts.

A distinctively philosophical way to respond to this dispute would be to find some novel argument either in favor of your position or against an ostensibly strong argument of your opponent. I shall not attempt this. The following discussion introduces no new argument to the debate over the possibility of computer consciousness. Rather, it advances a claim about the prudentially rational way for those contemplating mind uploading to respond to philosophical doubt about computer consciousness.

A necessary first move is to acknowledge that there is genuine doubt about whether computers could possess conscious or intentional states. Partisans of computer consciousness should concede that it is at least possible that they are wrong. They should allow that the best arguments of opponents of computer consciousness are informed by reflection on the relevant facts. They are not obviously contradictory. They do not make assumptions about the world that are patently absurd.

Such a concession does not require the renunciation of any considered view about computer consciousness. Advocates of computer consciousness should continue to assert the soundness of arguments in favor of their view. When engaging in philosophical debate they should vigorously insist on the unsoundness of arguments against computer consciousness. The implications of their concession are limited to certain practical consequences of believing in or denying the possibility of computer consciousness.

Essayist and commentator on markets Nassim Nicholas Taleb emphasizes the importance of taking advice from financial advisors who have "skin in the game" – those who suffer personal losses should their forecasts prove mistaken. It's rare for philosophers of mind to have skin in the game. One does not typically suffer personal losses by advocating erroneous views of the mind. Mind uploading gives philosophers of mind skin in the game. A philosopher who consents to destructive mind uploading on the grounds that functionalism offers the correct view of computer consciousness will die if computer consciousness is impossible but she attempts destructive uploading.

In what follows, I argue that it is rational for those contemplating uploading to take out epistemic insurance against the falsehood of their views about computer consciousness. It can be worthwhile to buy fire insurance even if you take precautions that you rightly judge adequate to prevent the destruction of your house by fire. In this case, you take out epistemic insurance against the falsehood of a conclusion about computer consciousness you are fully entitled to believe is true.

There is an obvious similarity between this epistemic insurance policy and Blaise Pascal's Wager for the prudential rationality of belief in the existence of God. The Wager directs even those who strongly doubt God's existence to take out epistemic insurance against God's existence. According to Pascal we aren't much better off if we correctly believe that God does not exist, but we are much worse off if we fail to believe when he does in fact exist. It is therefore prudentially rational to seek to believe in God. I argue that, for future humans faced with the possibility of mind uploading, there will be little to gain should the process succeed, but much to lose should it fail.

I label the following appeal to prudential rationality "Searle's Wager" for John Searle, the philosopher who has most famously opposed the possibility of intelligent computers. The fact that Pascal's Wager has attracted a good deal of philosophical criticism may make using it to introduce an argument I endorse seem like poor philosophical tactics. In what follows, I show that Searle's Wager improves on Pascal's Wager in a couple of philosophically significant respects.

3 Searle's Wager

Searle's Wager treats the exchanges over the possibility of successful mind uploading in much the same way that Pascal's Wager treats the debate over God's existence. The availability of uploading will present us with a choice. We can choose to attempt mind uploading or we can refuse to. There are two possible consequences of choosing to attempt mind uploading. If the process conveys your conscious mind to the upload, you will not only survive, but your powers of thought will be radically enhanced. If the doubters are right, then uploading may be nothing more than a novel way to commit suicide.

Table 9.1 summarizes the possible outcomes of mind uploading. You may be as confident about the possibility of computer consciousness as you can be about the truth of any philosophical view, but if there is room for rational disagreement you should acknowledge that it is possible that the process will fail. Room for rational disagreement is a feature of philosophical questions and solutions. Philosophers do not typically take on questions that have straightforward "yes" or "no" answers. A philosophical answer arrives only after an often fraught process of evaluating and weighing reasons supporting alternative views. We endorse the answer supported by what we judge to be the more philosophically weighty reasons. Kurzweil accepts that

Table 9.1 Possible outcomes of mind uploading

	Mind uploading works	*Mind uploading does not work*
Choose not to upload	**[A] You live** You benefit from enhancements that leave your biological brain intact. You miss out on other more significant enhancements.	**[B] You live** You benefit from enhancements that leave your biological brain intact. You are spared death and replacement by a non-conscious upload.
Choose to upload and destroy your biological brain	**[C] You live** You benefit from enhancements available only to electronic minds. Your life is extended. Your intellect is enhanced. You are free of disease.	**[D] You're dead** You are replaced by a machine incapable of conscious thought.

the question of computer consciousness is philosophical in this sense. He says that the fact that "we cannot resolve issues of consciousness entirely through objective measurement and analysis (science)" leaves a role for philosophy (2005: 380). Conceding that there is a role for philosophy in the debate about computer consciousness effectively leaves Kurzweil vulnerable to Searle's Wager.

Two differences between Searle's Wager and Pascal's Wager become apparent. First, an oft-made objection to Pascal's Wager is that it illicitly restricts alternatives. For example, it fails to account for the possibility of self-effacing gods who punish belief. The alternatives for Searle's Wager are more clearly binary – one either survives destructive mind uploading or one doesn't.

There is a second difference between Pascal's Wager and Searle's Wager. According to Pascal, the infinite reward for correctly believing in God means that any non-zero probability of God existing makes belief prudentially rational. For reasons explored in the following sections, neither option in Searle's Wager promises an infinite return. This means that we must make some attempt to attach probabilities to the propositions "Mind uploading works" and "Mind uploading does not work." If the probability that mind uploading does not work is non-zero but minuscule, then even a large but finite return for correctly not uploading could translate into a tiny expected return. It may be prudentially rational to accept the risk and upload. Compare: A racehorse that pays an infinite reward, should it win, is worth backing so long as there is any positive non-zero probability of its finishing first. No actual racehorse offers an infinite return. The substantial stakes of most long shots do not adequately compensate for their slim chances of winning.

Advocates of Searle's Wager, unlike advocates of Pascal's, must therefore pay attention to the quality of the arguments supporting its conclusion. Poor arguments may fail to raise sufficiently the probability that computers are incapable of thought.

I propose that philosophical arguments against the possibility of thinking machines do exceed this threshold. The weight of philosophical argument against the possibility of computer consciousness does somewhat raise the probability of its conclusion. The impossibility of computer consciousness should be granted more than the bare logical possibility that we assign to the truth of flat earth theory or the falsehood of the Holocaust. We should allow that the proposition "Mind uploading does not work" has both a non-zero probability of being true and a non-negligible probability of being true.

How might "a non-negligible probability of being true" translate into the probabilities required by the wager argument? We should permit the advocates of computer consciousness to grant the proposition "Computers could be conscious" a probability in excess of 50 percent – perhaps significantly in excess of 50 percent. A probability of 90 percent leaves room for the proposition "Computers could never be conscious" to receive a probability of 10 percent. A philosopher who decides that there is a 90 percent probability that computers could be conscious should feel entitled to strongly assert the possibility of computer consciousness in disputes with other philosophers. The non-negligible probability that computers could never be conscious is relevant only to certain practical choices, including those involving mind-uploading technologies.

One reason we may be unable to arrive at a decisive resolution of the debate between advocates and opponents of computer consciousness is that we aren't smart enough. In the final stages of Kurzweil's future history of the human species, we (or our descendants) will become unimaginably more intelligent. It's possible that no philosophical problems will resist resolution by a mind that exploits all of the universe's computing power. But the important thing is that we will be asked to make the decision about uploading well before this stage in our intellectual evolution. Though we may then be significantly smarter than we are today, our intelligence will fall well short of what it could be if uploading delivers all that Kurzweil expects of it. There's a good chance that this lesser degree of cognitive enhancement will preserve many of the mysteries about thought and consciousness.

There's some inductive support for this. Ancient Greek philosophers were pondering questions about conscious experience over two millennia ago. Twenty-first-century philosophers may not be any more intelligent than their Greek counterparts, but they do have access to tools for inspecting the physical bases of thought that are vastly more powerful than those available to Plato. In spite of this, philosophers do not find ancient Greek responses to questions about thought and consciousness the mere historical curiosities that modern scientists find ancient Greek physics and biology. Many of the conundrums of consciousness seem connected to its essentially subjective nature. There is something about the way our thoughts and experiences appear to us that seems difficult to reconcile with what science tells us about them. It doesn't matter whether the science in question is Aristotle's or modern neuroscience.

4 Why death could be so much worse for those considering uploading than it is for us now (or why D is so much worse than B)

Pascal envisages our betting behavior being influenced by the fear of missing out on heaven. In Searle's Wager, the fear of death is operative. Perhaps there's a difference between these penalties that affects their power to motivate a bettor's choice. Death is a very bad thing for most of us, but it's not as significant a loss as missing out on an eternity in paradise. Indeed, for some people it may not be much of a loss at all.

For example, a person about to expire from cancer can choose between certain death from disease and a merely possible death by destructive mind uploading. She seemingly has little to lose from uploading.

It's important to remember that the option of destructive mind uploading is not available to anyone today. We are deciding instead about the manner of support we give to research in AI. This decision should be informed, in part, by our best guesses about the choices of future individuals faced with the possibility of uploading.

We can allow that mind uploading would be prudentially rational for those on their deathbeds while insisting that those circumstances are likely to be uncommon in future societies that have developed technologies capable of transferring all of the relevant detail of an individual's brain onto a computer.

I suspect that future candidates for uploading are unlikely to find themselves stricken with terminal cancer and prepared to give the procedure a go. This is because of technological developments that may seem outlandish today, but are nevertheless easier to achieve than mind uploading. Medical science could advance to the point at which terminal conditions including cancer are curable or, if not, can be sufficiently well treated to make it prudentially irrational to take a punt on the speculative technology of mind uploading.

We are likely to have therapies that either cure cancer or, if not, considerably extend the life expectancy of those suffering from cancer sooner than we will achieve an understanding the human brain sufficient for mind uploading. Uploading requires not only a completed neuroscience, total understanding of what is currently the least well understood part of the human body, but also perfect knowledge of how to convert every relevant aspect of the brain's functioning into electronic computation. This should be more difficult than learning enough about cancer to stop it from killing us. This point survives conversion into the worldview of exponential technological advance. It's a point about the relative difficulty of achieving mind uploading and effective treatments for cancer, not a prediction about when we will achieve either. Suppose that accelerating technological advances enable us to copy into a computer every relevant detail of any human brain by 2045. Effective treatments for cancer and other terminal diseases are likely to come sooner. They too are promoted by the advances in information technology that ground Kurzweil's optimism about mind uploading. These advances should give candidates for destructive mind uploading a more conventional, nondestructive means of extending their existence, a means that does not involve copying oneself into a computer.

This guess about future technological development could be wrong. Suppose that we discover how to upload humans well in advance of finding effective treatments for cancer and other terminal diseases. Then it's possible that people of the future could be diagnosed with terminal cancer and properly view themselves as having nothing or very little to lose from uploading.[4] In these circumstances uploading will be prudentially rational for some people. For those who aren't terminally ill, it will still make sense to direct their hopes and expectations toward the relatively risk-free life extension and quality of life enhancement brought by new conventional medical treatments. Moreover, the issue of what is rational for those who know how to upload but have no expectation of effective treatments for terminal illnesses is different from that which we face now. Given what we know about the relative technological challenges of uploading and effective treatments for terminal illnesses, we should expect the former to postdate the latter. Our plans for the future should place greater emphasis on this, more probable, scenario.

I conclude that people presented with the option of uploading are unlikely to find that they've got little to lose should the procedure fail to transfer their minds into machines. They'll be loath to renounce the variety of enhancements compatible with the survival of their biological brains.

5 Why uploading and surviving is not so much better than, and possible worse than, refusing to upload (or why A is not so much better than, and possibly worse than, C)

Perhaps you'll miss out on a great deal if you choose to mind upload and computers are incapable of conscious thought. But the potential gains could be truly massive. Uploading opens up enhancements much more dramatic than those made possible by the comparatively few nanobots and neuroprostheses properly deemed compatible with the biological brain's survival. If Kurzweil is right, freed of biological limitations we can become massively more intelligent. The gap between enhancements compatible with the survival of the brain and those enabled by uploading and incompatible with its survival is likely to be very large.

To begin with, the uploaded mind will be more an upgrade than a copy. The electrochemical signals that brains use to achieve thought travel at 100 meters per second; this sounds impressive until you hear that electronic signals in computers are sent at 300 million meters per second. This means that an electronic counterpart of a human biological brain will think "thousands to millions of times faster than our naturally evolved systems" (Kurzweil 2005, 127). But there's a more theoretical reason why Kurzweil believes that "[o]nce a computer achieves a human level of intelligence, it will necessarily soar past it" (2005: 145). Computers are technology, improvements of which are governed by the law of accelerating returns. Although biological brains may improve over time, they're subject to the dramatically slower, intergenerational, schedule of biological evolution. Kurzweil thinks that machine minds will learn how to fully exploit the computational potential of matter and energy (2005: 29). They will cannibalize ever-increasing quantities of the previously inanimate universe, reconfiguring it to enhance their powers of thought. According to Kurzweil, "[u]ltimately, the entire universe will become saturated with our intelligence. This is the destiny of the universe. We will determine our own fate rather than having it determined by the current 'dumb' simple, machinelike forces that rule celestial mechanics" (2005: 29).

Suppose that we accept that the enhancements compatible with the brain's survival are likely to be significantly more modest than those enabled by uploading. What should those who are considering uploading make of this gap?

Consider the measures taken by economists to convert the objective values of various monetary sums into the subjective benefits experienced by individuals. For most of us, a prize of $100,000,000 is not 100 times better than one of $1,000,000. We would not trade a ticket in a lottery offering a one-in-ten chance of winning $1,000,000 for one that offers a one-in-a-thousand chance of winning $100,000,000, even when informed that both tickets yield an expected return of $100,000 – $1,000,000 divided by 10 and $100,000,000 divided by 1,000.

The $1,000,000 prize enables you to buy many of the things that you want but that are currently beyond you – a Porsche, a new iPod, a modest retirement cottage for your parents, a trip to the pyramids, and so on. Many of us also have desires that only the higher reward will satisfy – a mere million won't buy a luxury Paris apartment or a trip to the International Space Station aboard a Soyuz rocket, to give just two examples. So we have no difficulty in recognizing the bigger prize as better than the smaller one. But we don't prefer it to the extent that it's objectively better – it's not one hundred times better. The conversion of objective monetary values into subjective benefits reveals the one-in-ten chance at $1,000,000 to be significantly better than the one-in-a-thousand chance at $100,000,000.

I think that the subjective significance of the gap between enhancements compatible with the brain's survival and those incompatible with it is unlikely to match its objective magnitude. In fact, there may not be too much of a gap to those considering uploading between the appeal of the objectively lesser enhancements compatible with the survival of our brains on the one hand, and the objectively greater enhancements enabled by uploading on the other. The more modest enhancements will satisfy many of the desires of people for whom uploading is an option. They will live significantly longer, be freed of disease, play better bridge, learn foreign languages with ease, and so on. Mind uploading may enable feats well beyond those of persons whose biological brains are supplemented with only those electronic chips deemed compatible with the brain's survival, but we have comparatively few desires that correspond specifically with them. There's a reason for this. Desires are a practical mental state – they motivate people to act in certain ways. Those who want to get fit do exercise; those who want to lose weight go on diets; and so on. Desiring radical enhancement is a matter of placing your faith in the law of accelerating returns and waiting for something quite miraculous to be done to you. There's little you can do about it now beyond reading and rereading Kurzweil's book *The Singularity Is Near* and enrolling in your local chapter of the World Transhumanist Association.

One way to adjust the subjective values of $1,000,000 and $100,000,000 is to make the choice from a standpoint of considerable wealth. Donald

Trump is likely to look on the smaller sum as barely enough to achieve anything worthwhile. The larger sum, on the other hand, may suffice to acquire some significant piece of Manhattan real estate. This could lead him to prefer the one-in-a-thousand chance to acquire $100,000,000 to the one-in-ten chance to receive the mere million. Is there an analogous move that can be made in respect of enhancement? It's true that those who've already achieved superintelligence are likely to be more impressed by the objectively greater enhancements possible after uploading than we are. The problem is that it's impossible for us to adopt this standpoint. We're necessarily deciding about mind uploading in advance. Compare: we might be able to imagine Trump's contempt for a mere million dollars; but in advance of actually acquiring his wealth we're unlikely to be motivated by this imaginary contempt.

The problem may actually be more serious than that signaled by the previous paragraphs. In my books *Humanity's End* (2010) and *Truly Human Enhancement* (2014), I make the case that the manner of radical cognitive enhancement permitted by uploading may be worse than the more moderate variety compatible with the survival of our brains in the light of some of our more significant desires. Many of the things that we desire may be contingent on our current level of cognitive powers. We want to protect our relationships with our loved ones. We want to promote and honor our strongest moral and political ideals. Radical enhancement may not remove our capacity to protect, promote, and honor these commitments. But it may remove our desire to do so. I suspect that most parents find equally chilling the prospect that, at some point in the near future, they won't be able to protect their children and the prospect that, at some point in the near future, they won't *care* about their children's welfare. Concern about doing the things we currently most want to do may, therefore, lead us to place a low value on radical cognitive enhancement. I refer readers to my books for more detail on arguments against the prudential rationality of even successful radical enhancement.

What does this mean for those presented with the option of uploading? I suspect candidates will prefer more modest, safe enhancements to those whose potential magnitude is greater but come with a risk of death.

6 Why we shouldn't make electronic copies of ourselves

So far I've argued for a relatively restricted claim. When deciding what manner of support to give to research in AI we should take account of the fact that future individuals are likely to deem it prudentially irrational to mind upload destructively. This leaves open the possibility of nondestructive uploading – making the copy and *not* destroying the original, an option that might seem to offer the best of both worlds. Humans do not need to risk death. They can copy themselves into machines that will then be free to ride the law of accelerating returns all the way to the Singularity. In this final section I briefly explain why nondestructive uploading is prudentially irrational. The continuing existence of the biological original threatens many of the promised benefits of mind uploading.

Doubts about computer consciousness should lead us to acknowledge two possible outcomes from nondestructive uploading. Neither of these should seem attractive to those contemplating it.

Suppose that the mind upload is conscious. The existence of the biological original is an obstacle to your surviving as the upload. Consider the deathbed uploading scenario described earlier. You plan to use uploading as a means of escaping your cancer-stricken biological body. This plan depends both on your conscious mind's entering the computer into which you are uploaded, but also *exiting* your diseased original body. The exit strategy cannot succeed if the computer into which your psychology is copied is incapable of consciousness. But nor can it succeed if the biological original you remains. Rather than experiencing a switch of your conscious mind to the upload, you are likely, supposing that nondestructive mind uploading occurs noninvasively, to notice no change in your condition. You will continue to feel the pains of terminal cancer. In the terms of Robert Nozick's Closest Continuer theory of personal identity (Nozick 1981: 29–114), the disease-stricken original biological brain and body remain your closest continuer – and therefore you. Your conscious upload's claim on being your closest continuer depends on the destruction of your original brain and body.

Suppose, however, that mind uploading does not work. Destructive uploading would kill you, but you will survive the nondestructive version. You are, however, likely to face a case of identity theft that is far more terrifying than that currently arranged by thieves of email passwords and credit card details. The process will result in a being that, even if it is incapable of conscious thought, acts as if it is you. It will act as if it has all of your memories. Furthermore, it will be the beneficiary of increasing powerful enhancements. These it will use to lay claim to past achievements and present property that you think of as your own.

7 Conclusion

I have argued that people presented with the option of uploading their minds into computers are likely to judge it prudentially irrational to do so. They will assess the expected rewards from uploading as insufficient to justify the risk of death. Death denies them futures in which technologies compatible with the survival of their biological brains rejuvenate them and enhance their powers of thought. Our best guesses about these future choices have implications for our support of contemporary research in artificial intelligence. We should proceed with caution.

Acknowledgments

This chapter is based on my 2011 article "Kurzweil and Uploading: Just Say No!" *Journal of Evolution and Technology* 22(1): 23–36. The contents have been somewhat abridged, revised, and, I hope, improved. My thanks to the editors of the journal for permission to draw on the 2011 article.

Notes

1 Ray Kurzweil presents his vision of humanity's future in Kurzweil 1990, 2000, and 2005. Kurzweil's website is also essential viewing: http://www.kurzweilai.net/.
2 For Kurzweil's responses to these criticisms, see Kurzweil 2002.
3 Thanks to Mark Walker for making this point.
4 Daniel Dennett (1991) explores a variety of puzzles such as these concerning phenomenal consciousness. He concludes that the notion of phenomenal consciousness is incoherent. His arguments may make those who reject Searle's Wager more confident about uploading. But they should not be viewed as reducing to zero the probability either that biological human brains support phenomenal consciousness or that uploading destroys this capacity.

References

Agar, Nicholas. 2010. *Humanity's End: Why We Should Reject Radical Enhancement*. Cambridge, MA: MIT Press.

Agar, Nicholas. 2014. *Truly Human Enhancement: A Philosophical Defense of Limits*. Cambridge, MA: MIT Press.

Chalmers, David J. 2010. The Singularity: A philosophical analysis. *Journal of Consciousness Studies* 17: 7–65.

Dennett, Daniel C. 1991. *Consciousness Explained*. Boston: Little, Brown.

Kurzweil, Ray. 1990. *The Age of Intelligent Machines*. Cambridge, MA: MIT Press.

Kurzweil, Ray. 2000. *The Age of Spiritual Machines: When Computers Exceed Human Intelligence*. London: Penguin.

Kurzweil, Ray. 2002. Locked in his Chinese room: Response to John Searle. In Jay W. Richards, ed., *Are We Spiritual Machines? Ray Kurzweil vs. The Critics of Strong A.I.* Seattle, WA: Discovery Institute, pp. 128–167.

Kurzweil, Ray. 2005. *The Singularity is Near: When Humans Transcend Biology*. London: Penguin.
Nozick, Robert. 1981. *Philosophical Explanations*. Cambridge, MA: Belknap Press.
Searle, John. 1980. Minds, brains and programs. *Behavioral and Brain Sciences* 3(3): 417–457.

10

Uploading and Personal Identity

Mark Walker

1 Uploading: prospects and perils

You arrive at one of the thousands of kiosks run by the late twenty-first century's largest corporation: U-Upload. With some trepidation you step into the superscanner. There is a slight hum as it inventories the molecular building blocks of your brain. Your brain is destroyed in the process, but you are not dead – or so the marketing materials from U-Upload claim. Information about the building blocks, along with a general program that describes the fundamental laws of molecular interaction, is uploaded to the shiny new robotic brain you purchased (Sandberg and Bostrom 2008). For your friends and family, a few terrifying moments pass before the robotic body stirs. To their relief, your first words are: "It's me. I made it." You go on to crack a joke – just as your family and friends have come to expect of you. Of course you have changed in some respects: gone is your human carbon-based body. Now you experience the world through camera eyes and microphone ears, you dance the fandango with robotic legs and speak through a voice synthesizer. But it is still you. You have migrated to a silicon substrate: you have been uploaded.

At least that is one interpretation of these events. The contrary construal is that although a robot was created that acts and talks as you used to, claims to have your memories, and indeed, claims to *be* you, this robot is *not* you. You are dead. You died when your brain was destroyed during the scanning process. If, like me, you think that uploading is possible (at least in principle),

Intelligence Unbound: The Future of Uploaded and Machine Minds, First Edition.
Edited by Russell Blackford and Damien Broderick.

and so you hold that the first interpretation of these events is correct, then you must hold true the following three theses:

1 Computers are capable of supporting the important properties constitutive of personal identity, e.g., thought and consciousness.

It is clear that uploading will not preserve all properties we associate with *Homo sapiens*: for example, basic facts about the human digestive system are not likely to be preserved in uploading to a robotic body. But these facts are not typically thought to be important for personal identity. Candidates for important properties include thought, consciousness, emotions, creativity, aesthetic experience, sensory experience, empathy, and so on. For the most part, the question of which properties are important is not as serious as it might first seem, since uploading promises to preserve the essential aspects of the brain and nervous system, which overlap with the usual lists of important properties for identity.

A famous challenge to thesis (1) is made in John Searle's Chinese Room argument (Searle 1980). It is beyond the scope of this chapter to explore the argument; suffice it to say that if Searle is correct, then (1) may be false. For Searle thinks that a computer can never consciously think merely in virtue of instantiating a computer program, and the uploading process seems to be one of merely instantiating a computer program (Agar 2010; 2011).

2 It is possible to capture the information necessary to emulate the important properties of individual humans.

The technical challenge of thesis (2) is to capture the information in all parts of the brain in a manner that preserves the relevant information. Clearly this won't be easy. If we slice off layers of your neurons, and record the information of each layer, the lower layers will change (due to trauma or death), although solutions have been proposed (Moravec 1988). If we flash-freeze your brain, we may destroy some essential information. Philosophical questions arise as to whether the information encoded in the brain is sufficient to account for all the relevant properties. For example, consider a dualist who believes that we have souls in addition to brains, and much of what is morally important (e.g., conscious thought) resides in the soul. If the dualist is right, then scanning your brain could never be sufficient, for it would be necessary to scan your soul to access at least some of what is important. If it is unlikely that we will be able to scan souls, there will be an insurmountable obstacle to uploading. Notice how theses (1) and (2) may differ on this point: a dualist could consistently hold that a computer might have a soul; it is just that if computers have souls, it is not because we obtained the soul-building information from humans. (Perhaps God implants souls in humans and computers.)

3 It is possible to survive the uploading process.

To see how (3) differs from (1) and (2), imagine that at some point in the future we have created computers of sufficient complexity that it is agreed that they have the same morally relevant properties as humans: these advanced computers think and are conscious, they are accorded rights, and the scanning problem has been solved so that we are able to scan the brain in such a way that we are not worried about loss of information. None of this answers the question of whether you have been preserved during uploading or whether uploading merely makes a very good copy of you. The worry that only a copy is created is often fueled by this thought: the information about the building blocks of an individual human brain could be uploaded to multiple computers with robotic bodies. The number of copies of a person is limited only by the available computing power. If an individual can be uploaded once, then it seems the same individual could be uploaded twice into separate computers, and indeed, billions of the same individual all embodied in separate robotic bodies could be created.

This quick survey of the conceptual terrain suggests that there are substantial philosophical (not to mention technical) obstacles to uploading. To make the discussion manageable, I will focus on thesis (3), and assume without argument that (1) and (2) have been resolved in favor of uploading. So our question is this: assuming that computers can be conscious, have memories, and (robotic) bodies, and assuming that it is possible to scan and capture all the information of a human brain, does uploading preserve personal identity?

I will argue that uploading does preserve personal identity, at least identity of a certain sort.

2 The equivalency thesis

The fact that we are assuming that computers are capable of embodying all the same type of properties necessary for personal identity means that we can make use of the equivalency thesis:

Equivalency thesis. If it is possible for an individual to survive migration from a carbon to a carbon body, then it is possible for an individual to survive migration from a carbon to a silicon body.

To spell this out, I'll say first what I mean by occupying different human bodies, and then say what use the equivalency thesis will serve for us.

Let us start by considering a familiar fictional example of people switching human bodies, i.e., carbon-to-carbon transfers. One of my personal favorites is a schlocky episode in the original *Star Trek* series. Captain Kirk finds himself in the body of his jilted ex-lover, Dr. Janice Lester, after an alien "personality swapping" device is used on him. She, jealous of his power, takes control of his body, and, what is worse, his spaceship. This plot device has been used numerous times since, including in the movie *Freaky Friday* where a mother finds herself in her teenage daughter's body and vice versa. These works of fiction are premised on the idea that whatever makes individuals the individuals they are is only contingently related to the bodies that they find themselves in. Captain Kirk grew up in a male body, but we are asked to believe that, at least for a short while, he inhabited a female body.

In Kirk and Lester's body swap, the idea is helped along by the visual effects (such as they were in the 1960s) that showed what apparently we are to understand as soul swapping. (A soul, it turns out, looks much like a translucent version of one's body, rather like the Spiritualist notion of an astral body.) We do not need to have recourse to the idea of souls, however. Imagine the scanner used to encode all the relevant biochemical information from a brain was used to scan both Kirk's and Janice's brains. Nanobots – nanoscale robots – then rearrange the biochemicals in each brain to encode the relevant memories, personality, intellectual abilities, and so on. This differs from brain swapping, because each brain is reorganized using nothing but the locally available biochemicals. Here the information is uploaded to a different human body rather than a computer. Using this procedure, it makes perfect sense why Captain Kirk's body would act much like we would expect Dr. Janice Lester to act, and vice versa.

There are two reasons for invoking the equivalency thesis. The first is so that we are not misled by a new form of racism: substratism (Walker 2006). Substratism is the view that one's substrate is inherently superior to that of other substrates along the lines that racists think their race is inherently superior to some other race. In the present case, it would suggest the idea that carbon-based humans are inherently more morally worthy than silicon-based beings. Consider the fact that we would not accept this argument: it is not possible for persons to migrate from one body to another because then it would be possible for people of skin color X to move to bodies of skin color Y, and Y skin color is morally inferior. We want to avoid the same bad argument in considering moving from one substrate to another. Notice that this does not beg the issue at hand, since it is possible to say that having a certain substrate (or even skin color) is constitutive of my identity; it merely prohibits saying that this property in itself makes for moral superiority.

The second is that it makes directly relevant an enormous amount of philosophical effort that has gone into exploring the possibility of carbon-to-carbon transfers. The question of carbon-to-silicon transfers thus may piggyback on this effort.

3 Personal identity: psychological and somatic accounts

Historically, there are two main schools of thought about what is required for personal survival; the psychological and somatic approaches (Olson 2010). Derek Parfit's famous thought experiment may serve as illustration:

> I enter the Teletransporter. I have been to Mars before, but only by the old method, a space-ship journey taking several weeks. This machine will send me at the speed of light. I merely have to press the green button. Like others, I am nervous. Will it work? I remind myself what I have been told to expect. When I press the button, I shall lose consciousness, and then wake up at what seems a moment later. In fact I shall have been unconscious for about an hour. The Scanner here on Earth will destroy my brain and body, while recording the exact states of all of my cells. It will then transmit this information by radio. Travelling at the speed of light, the message will take three minutes to reach the Replicator on Mars. This will then create, out of new matter, a brain and body exactly like mine. It will be in this body that I shall wake up. (Parfit 1984: 199)

Those who hold the psychological account of personal identity will tend to endorse the view that one survives teletransportation. For the psychological account says that what is essential for survival is continuity of psychological states such as memory, beliefs, desires, and personality. John Locke, an early proponent of this view, famously described personal identity in terms of psychological continuity, within an analysis of personhood as consisting in existence as "a thinking intelligent being, that has reason and reflection, and can consider itself as itself, the same thinking thing, in different times and places" (Locke 1975). The person on Mars who awakens will claim to remember being Derek Parfit, and to have memories and a personality that are psychologically indistinguishable from the person on earth whose body was destroyed. Locke, then, would say that Parfit survived teletransportation.

Somaticist accounts suggest the survival of a particular body is critical for personal identity over time. Since the body on Earth is destroyed during the scanning process, Parfit ceases to be. A different person will wake on Mars.

This person will of course have psychologically indistinguishable memories and personality to those of the late Parfit, but this person will not be Parfit. The new person will be but an infant in terms of chronological age: only a few minutes old.

We will think of "somaticism" as the view that continuity of one's body is necessary for personal identity from one time to the next. There are two ways that one might be a somaticist: one can believe that bodily continuity is necessary but not sufficient, or that it is necessary and sufficient. One easy case to distinguish these two is as follows: a piano falls on your head, and causes you to go into a permanent vegetative state. Your relatives discuss whether to "pull the plug." Those who think that bodily continuity is necessary but not sufficient may say that you no longer exist, but your body continues to exist. Those who think that bodily continuity is necessary and sufficient will say that you continue to exist, albeit your cognitive capacities are non-existent. Both views qualify as "somaticism" in our sense.

In my extremely limited and informal survey of students and friends, most would be unwilling to step into Parfit's Teletransporter. Even Parfit has some doubts about stepping into the Teletransporter. He concedes that he has some residual doubt that he would survive teletransportation (1984: 279). The usual response is that it is equivalent to committing suicide: the person here is killed, and a new duplicate is created. Nothing of the original survives. Locke and others who endorse the psychological account would retort that this is just an irrational attachment to a certain set of molecules. If a molecule-for-molecule identical copy is made, then it seems irrational to prefer one set of molecules to another. Parfit compares this to an attachment to a wedding ring: there may be sentimental value in having the original rather than a molecule-for-molecule identical copy, but such attachments are "merely sentimental" and have nothing to do with personal identity (1984: 286).

The reluctance to use the transportation device seems hard to explain other than by the fact that people hold, at least implicitly, to somaticism. This provides a robust challenge to psychological accounts in general, and a challenge to uploading in particular. In the next two sections, I will offer arguments against somaticism.[1]

4 Against somaticism: the big stroke

The Vorlons,[2] a mysterious and intellectually advanced alien species, make this offer: you can have an original undiscovered play by Shakespeare written in his hand, or a copy of the play made by one of his lackeys. You salivate at the joy this will bring to the world (not to mention the fame and fortune it will bring you personally). Since you can have only one, the choice, it seems, is a no-brainer. You should opt for the one written by the bard's hand. But now consider this variant: the Vorlons tell you that the text written in Shakespeare's hand is missing the last two pages, while they assure you the copy written by the lackey is a perfectly faithful reproduction of all the words in the original. While it would be great to have both, you reason that the most important thing is that the play itself be preserved, not Shakespeare's handwriting. The copy here is in some sense better than the original because the original has been damaged. This tips the scales in favor of the copy, because while being written by the bard's own hand is good, having the whole play is even better.

We can apply this lesson to thinking about personal identity. The Vorlons, with their ability to see into the future, say the news is grim. In less than 12 hours you will have a massive stroke that will cause you to lose many of your memories and some mobility, and impair your intelligence. Your stroke will not be as bad as some: the damage from the stroke will not leave you completely cognitively impaired, but you will no longer be able to work as an academic. You will have to find some relatively mindless job befitting your new level of intelligence, perhaps as a dean or other academic administrator. Friends and family will say that your once keen memory has been dulled such that your memory is now fuzzy, and you seem to remember the most superficial things. It is a shame, and totally unexpected at your young age. Even with their immense power, there is nothing the Vorlons can do to prevent the stroke. They provide a radical alternative: creating a perfect replica of you – down to the molecular level – with the exception that the problems with the arteries to your brain will be fixed in the body replica. They insist, however, that only one body can survive. You must choose tonight whether the replica or your current body survives.

Most people I've asked about this would rather see the replica survive, for the replica best embodies what is most important about you: your memories, your personality, your beliefs and desires. None of this is to say that the loss of one's body is trivial. One can be quite attached to one's body; but, when given this tragic choice, more of what is essential to you as a person survives in the replica.

Obviously, this example is structurally similar to Parfit's, but with one big exception: what is gained by having the replica survive is much more significant in this case than in the Teletransporter to Mars case. Parfit offers the incentive of avoiding three weeks of space travel. (We might not even sacrifice our original wedding ring for an exact replica if the benefit is merely avoiding three weeks in a spaceship.) Here the incentive is the possibility of not having one's life radically altered by the stroke. The attachment to one's body does not seem worth the cost in this case.

Perhaps it might be remonstrated thus: "If I survived in a brain-damaged state, I would be a terrible burden on my family and the world. It would be better for my family and the world that I died and a replica replaced me." To avoid this objection we can simply stipulate that the decision is to be entirely selfishly motivated, and that we know this about your preferences: you would rather survive a stroke than not survive at all. So, if the Vorlons did not offer you a chance to survive as a replica, you would rather live after the stroke than die. If the choice is still to have your present body die (the one with the bad arteries), then this can only be explained by thinking that you will survive as a replica.

It may be thought that even the most selfish person might prefer death if it meant something else he or she valued might result, for example, you value the finishing of your novel more than you value your own life. If a replica of you can better realize this project, then it is consistent with selfishness to prefer death to oneself for the sake of the great unfinished novel. Again, we may simply stipulate around this objection. We may say simply that what you want most is for *you* to finish writing the novel, not someone else. If you die, you would rather it remain the "great unfinished novel" than be finished by someone else. If this is your most important desire, then preferring the stroke body's death cannot be explained away by the thought that what you wish for is the completion of your projects.

It is worth noting that not all somaticists are likely to be convinced by this example.[3] But it should convince a few, and points out one of the heavy costs of somaticism.

5 Against somaticism: retrospective replicas

In this section we will examine an alternative explanation to somaticism for why people might be reluctant to use Parfit's Teletransporter, namely, fear of the unknown. Notice that Parfit's case is prospective: he asks us to imagine the decision to walk into the scanner with the hopes of being teletransported. The thought is that fear of the unknown might be muddying the waters here. That is, perhaps it is this fear of the unknown, rather than a commitment to somaticism, that explains the reluctance to use the Teletransporter. We can test this thought by considering a retrospective rather than a prospective version of a replication scenario.

Suppose that every night, when people sleep, their bodies (including their brains) are scanned by a swarm of nanobots and a molecule-for-molecule identical body is beamed from a hidden alien spaceship in orbit; the old body is vaporized in a manner that is undetectable by the human eye. Scientists discovered this fortuitously: physicists noticed a spike in neutrino levels every time psychologists in the adjoining lab conducted sleep experiments. Intrigued, scientists built a chamber to isolate subjects from neutrino influences and then had test subjects sleep in the chamber. Once the experiment was initiated, a hologram appeared in the lab and spoke thus:

> We are an ancient race known as the "Vorlons." We battled another species, the "Shadows," just as your species was beginning to evolve on this planet. One of the toxic effects of our war was a type of radiation that kills all higher intelligences within three days. We have no way of eliminating the radiation, but we have left advanced technology to re-create your bodies from different molecules every day so that the radiation will not harm you. We left the galaxy eons ago. You are hearing this message now because you have advanced technologically to the point where you can detect our technology. If you interfere with our replicator technology, you will quickly die of radiation poisoning.

What should we make of this? It is clear that dismantling the replication device is out of the question since all humans will die within three days. If you are a somaticist, you must conclude that you have been alive only for a very short while. In fact, you have existed only since last night. After all, the physical continuity of your body has lasted only this length of time. However, most of us, I think, would conclude the opposite. That is, that we have existed for years: that we do not cease to exist every night with a new person coming into being.

This example may not be a decisive refutation of somaticism, but it does at least pull out one pillar of support. Somaticists ask why so many would be reluctant to step into the Teletransporter that Parfit describes, intimating that our reluctance has to do with the fact that our bodies will not survive. The retort, suggested by this example, is that the reluctance is explained more simply as a fear of the unknown. Conversely, the somaticist must now explain how so many people could be mistaken about their own identity in the retrospective case; after all, it seems very likely that, on learning about the Vorlons' technology, most would conduct their lives as if they hadn't just come into existence that day. Who is going to say such things as: "I do not have to look after these children you call mine: how can I have children if I myself was born today? I can't use this driver's license, it is someone else's – I was just born today. I'm not qualified to teach any classes: a postgraduate degree is required, which takes years to earn, and I was just born today."

6 No branching

Debates about identity preservation and uploading invariably get hung up on the "branching" problem, and this probably provides the strongest support for somaticism. The problem is that it seems there is only one of me. But uploading seems to allow the possibility that there could be hundreds, if not millions, of "me." But if there can be only one of me, then uploading does not preserve my identity. It is clear how this problem arises given our previous discussion of the uploading process. Imagine my brain is scanned and the relevant information is recorded. Instead of my being uploaded to a single computer with a robotic body, imagine a thousand robot brains are encoded with the information. Of course it seems possible that thousands of robots could awaken in the same instant, all claiming to be Mark Walker. (And what a wonderful world this would be!)

Using the equivalence thesis we can see how this is exactly the same problem as the problem of branching that philosophers discuss in connection with carbon-to-carbon transfers. Parfit extends his Teletransporter case in exactly this way:

> Several years pass, during which I am often Teletransported. I am now back in the cubicle, ready for another trip to Mars. But this time, when I press the green button, I do not lose consciousness. There is a whirring sound, then silence. I leave the cubicle, and say to the attendant: "It's not working. What did I do wrong?"
>
> "It's working," he replies, handing me a printed card. This reads: "The New Scanner records your blueprint without destroying your brain and your body. We hope that you will welcome the opportunities which this technical advance offers." (Parfit 1984: 199).

Of course there is no reason to stop at one replica. Using Parfit's Teletransporter, thousands of organic molecule-for-molecule identical persons could awaken in the same instant, all claiming to be Mark Walker. (And what a wonderful world this would be!)

Notice that I did not say that any of the thousand persons claiming to be Mark Walker *are* me. Somaticism will deny that any of the thousand replicas are me; only the original is me. If the original is destroyed, and a thousand replicas are made, then somaticism will claim that I did not survive.

What does the psychological account have to say about multiple replicas? Here opinions differ. On the one hand, it seems that if there are multiple replicas, and they are all psychologically indistinguishable from the original, then each of them has as good a claim to be me, and so they are all me. The contrary "no-branching" view is that at most one replica is me, for there can be only one me (Shorter 1962).

The question then is whether there can be "branching" or "forking": more than one of me. I will argue that both sides of the debate are correct; there is a sense in which there can't be more than one of me, and a sense in which there can be multiple versions of me. The first step in our argument is to get a little clearer about the no-branching argument, which may be schematized as follows (where "P" stands for "premise" and "C" for "conclusion"):

The No-Branching Argument

P1: Multiple replicas X, Y, Z.... of an individual O (the original) are numerically non-identical with each other, that is, X is not identical with Y or Z, Y is not identical with X or Z, and so on.
P2: Preservation of personal identity requires preservation of numerical identity.
C: Therefore, not all replicas X, Y, Z... preserve personal identity of O.[4]

It is worth distinguishing this argument from a similar but less serious objection. The less serious objection is that if there are a thousand replicas, then they will quickly have psychologically distinguishable properties. All thousand replicas will not fit in the same cab, for example, and so will have different experiences leaving the replicating center. Their psychological states will only diverge further over time. Riffing on Parfit's example, we can imagine replicas waking on Mars, the Moon, and Pluto all at the same time. Each will almost immediately have different experiences, and so quickly will be psychologically different.

Even if this is conceded, it does not answer the question of the status of the replicas at the moment they are created. Imagine the thousand replicas are all created at the same instant, and each wakes in a separate but identical room. At the instant of awakening, there will not be any psychological divergence and so the argument from diverging experience tells us nothing about the identity of the thousand replicas at this moment.

I want to suggest that the problem with the no-branching argument is that there is a critical ambiguity. To explain the ambiguity it will be helpful to review the type/token distinction.

7 Types and tokens

The nineteenth-century philosopher Charles Peirce is credited with first making the type/token distinction. Peirce's own example involving the individuation of words is as instructive as any:

> A common mode of estimating the amount of matter in a manuscript or printed book is to count the number of words. There will ordinarily be about twenty *the*'s on a page, and of course they count as twenty words. In another sense of the word "word," however, there is but one word "the" in the English language. (Peirce 1906)

There are 20 tokens of the word *the*, but a single type of the word *the*. The argument to be canvassed is that if we think of personal identity as ambiguous between types and tokens, then the no-branching argument may be rejected.

We may approach the issue by recasting the previous argument by reference to a work of literature; so let us consider the no-branching argument applied to Shakespeare's *Hamlet*. We will reconstruct the argument first as about tokens, and then about types.

The No-Branching Token Argument

P1′: Multiple replicas X, Y, Z.... of an individual O (the original *Hamlet* penned in Shakespeare's hand) are numerically not (token) identical with each other, that is, X is not (token) identical with Y or Z, Y is not (token) identical with X or Z, and so on.

P2′: Preservation of play-identity requires preservation of (token) numerical identity.

C′: Therefore, not all replicas X, Y, Z... preserve play-identity of O.

It is pretty clear where this argument goes wrong: **P2′** is false. The original token of *Hamlet*, written in Shakespeare's hand on paper created over 400 years ago, is now long lost. But the same play that Shakespeare wrote can be read today. The no-branching token argument fails.

The No-Branching Type Argument

P1″: Multiple replicas X, Y, Z.... of an individual O (the original *Hamlet* penned in Shakespeare's hand) are numerically not (type) identical with each other, that is, X is not (type) identical with Y or Z, Y is not (type) identical with X or Z, and so on.

P2″: Preservation of play-identity requires preservation of (type) numerical identity.

C″: Therefore, not all replicas X, Y, Z... preserve play-identity of O.

It is pretty clear where this argument goes wrong: **P1″** is false. I may have bought my copy of *Hamlet* at a different bookstore from you, but still, we are reading the same play. At least in the case of plays, the type version of the no-branching argument fails. Thus, the no-branching argument, in both its token and type formulation, does not look the least bit plausible when applied to literature.

8 The type/token solution to personal identity

In this section I will say a little about the type/token (TT) account of personal identity and then see whether the no-branching argument has any traction against it.[5] In the case of literature, the tokens of *Hamlet* are individuated according to the physical implementation: my *Hamlet* is in a different spatial location from your *Hamlet*. The *Hamlet* type is an abstract entity, which particular tokens of *Hamlet* embody. Similarly, the TT solution to personal identity says that tokens of a person type are individuated in terms of physical implementation: each replica will have a different spatial location. The person type is the abstract entity, which the various tokens are all embodiments of.

We previously rejected somaticism, but this is because we had yet to survey the type/token distinction. The version of the type/token view that we should adopt says that somaticism is correct about tokens, and the psychological account correct about types. Consider then the case where the original Mark Walker is scanned and destroyed and a thousand replicas are created. Somaticism, as a theory about tokens, says that the original token was destroyed, and a thousand new tokens created. The psychological account applied to types says that the Mark Walker type continues to exist, and indeed, is multiply instantiated.

The ontological status of abstract entities is a perplexing and contested issue (Wetzel 2009), but there is no reason to think that it is more perplexing in the case of persons than in literature, and we are committed to types in the case of literature.

Can the non-branching argument be deployed against TT? Assuming that types can have more than one token, non-branchers cannot allow the notion of types to have a role in personal identity. So, to disambiguate the original non-branching argument, it must be about tokens:

The No-Branching Argument in Terms of Tokens

P1‴: Multiple replicas X, Y, Z.... of an individual O (the original) are numerically (token) non-identical with each other.

P2‴: Preservation of personal identity requires preservation of numerical (token) identity.

C‴: Therefore, not all replicas X, Y, Z... preserve personal identity of O.

There are two problems with this argument. First, it is question-begging. The entire issue is whether personal identity can be explained in terms of preservation of type identity, and so **P2‴** prejudges the issue.

The other problem is that it is difficult to see how one can insist on non-branching without collapsing into somaticism. To see this, consider the case where the original Mark Walker's body, O, is destroyed when three replicas X, Y, and Z are created. Either O is not identical with any of X, Y, Z, or O is identical with one of X, Y, Z. If the former, then non-branching is simply somaticism in disguise. If it is asserted that O is identical with exactly one of X, Y, Z, then any choice would be arbitrary in the sense that choosing one among the thousand to be *The Mark Walker* would not be choosing based on any intrinsic differences. We could, for example, have all the replicas draw a number out of a hat and designate the winner of the lottery *The Mark Walker*. But an appeal to a lottery shows that precisely no intrinsic properties are used to individuate: it is the process (the lottery) that does the individuating. We could do the same for *Hamlet*. We could assign a number to every extant copy of *Hamlet* and have a lottery to find out which is *The Hamlet*, and which are mere copies. But, of course, no one would be impressed by this.

Criticizing the non-branching argument is not a positive argument for TT, but it does suggest that TT need do little to prove itself more plausible than non-branching. However, in terms of a positive argument for TT, the fact that it provides a number of intuitively plausible consequences speaks in its favor:

1 The TT solution explains why people might be reluctant to enter the Teletransporter in Parfit's original example. It requires sacrifice of their token identity, for little compensatory gain (avoiding three weeks in a spacecraft). In other words, it can explain how we might survive (as a type), even though we may regret some loss of identity (since the original token is now dead).
2 The TT solution explains why it would be rational to sacrifice one's token identity in the stroke case: the loss of token identity is not inconsiderable, but the replica is type-identical, and the new token replica will be in better shape than the original token.
3 The TT solution explains why, in the Vorlon radiation case, we are not likely to feel much threat to our identity: the type survives destruction of each token, and each token is only a day old. Analogously, other things being equal, I would feel more upset about having my copy of *Hamlet* from my undergraduate days stolen, and less worried about a copy just acquired yesterday. In both cases, of course, the same play type is stolen.

4 The TT solution explains why in Parfit's modified Transporter case – where a replica is created on Mars, but the original on Earth is not destroyed – the person on Earth has more claim to being Parfit than the replica on Mars. The person on Earth is both type and token-identical with Parfit from the previous month (assuming he hasn't used the Teletransporter in the meantime). The replica on Mars is merely type-identical.[6]
5 The TT solution explains in a satisfactory manner what happens when the original is destroyed to make multiple replicas. Each replica is type-identical with the original, but none of the replicas is token-identical with the original. This avoids the embarrassment of having to say which of the indistinguishable replicas is identical with the original.

9 Should I upload?

I have tried to strike some compromise between saying that there is no loss of identity in replication (and, by our equivalency thesis, in uploading), and the position that survival is impossible. Still, it may look as though this is tantamount to an argument against uploading: if there is *any* loss in uploading, even if it is only of token identity, why would anyone want to sacrifice some identity? The answer is that there are considerable advantages (or at least purported advantages) to being uploaded, including immortality and enhancement.

Except for the completely reckless, forgetful, or lazy (ahem), everyone backs up his or her valuable computer files. But once we see that people, too, can be backed up, it appears that virtual immortality is assured. For so long as there are operating computers, one can simply transfer the files that comprise oneself from computer to computer. If the hardware on one computer fails, you simply move to another computer. Suppose a piano falls on your robotic body. No problem. A new robotic body is brought out of the closet and a backup copy of you is uploaded. What formerly would have meant certain death is now only a small inconvenience. As Freeman Dyson long ago realized, the question of how long one might live quickly resolves to how long the universe will remain habitable (Dyson 1979), hence, the term "digital immortality" is sometimes used to refer to this prospect.

As for enhancement, one possibility is that our senses could be radically enhanced: robots at present make use of a sensory apparatus that detects light in parts of the spectrum not available to (unaided) human vision (e.g., infrared, X-rays, etc.), sounds that are beyond normal human auditory range, and so on. In terms of enhancing cognition, consider that it is a relatively routine matter to add memory or computing power to today's computers. If one is uploaded to a computer, then it seems that it would be a relatively routine matter to enhance one's memory or cognition: just add more computer memory or processing power. The sky is literally the limit here. Anders Sandberg (1999) has done some preliminary calculations to suggest that planetary-scale computers, "Jupiter-sized brains," might be possible. How powerful and how smart would such brains be? It is, obviously, hard to say. Certainly they would eclipse us by a greater margin than we eclipse the cognitive powers of your typical lab rat. Along with such enhanced cognition would come awesome powers to manipulate the physical world, for there is some truth to the saw that knowledge is power. In short, and without too much hyperbole, those who upload might well be on their way to godhood.[7]

It is beyond the scope of this chapter to argue that these purported benefits of uploading really are benefits, but if they are, the temptation to upload is clear. And just as in the stroke case, it is clear why it might be rational to forgo token identity survival for these advantages.

Acknowledgments

I would like to acknowledge the following persons for their assistance: Nick Agar, Russell Blackford, Jamie Bronstein, and Tim Cleveland. This chapter is adapted from an essay in *Journal of Evolution and Technology*, 22(1) (November 2011): 37–52.

Notes

1 I offer a third argument against somaticism in Walker (2011).
2 From the television series *Babylon 5*.
3 The protagonist and somaticist in John Perry's fun little dialogue accepts death rather than ceding ground to the psychological account (Perry 1978).
4 See Williams (1973). Thomas Reid seems to have had a similar argument in mind: see Perry (2008).
5 Williams (1973: 80–81) considers something analogous to the present proposal.
6 Parfit (1984: 293–297) discusses the possibility of individuating in terms of types and tokens. He argues that it is the type that matters, not the token. As noted above, I disagree: both type and token are important.
7 A related objection is that radical enhancement will threaten identity (Walker 2008).

References

Agar, N. 2010. *Humanity's End: Why We Should Reject Radical Enhancement*. Cambridge, MA: MIT Press.

Agar, N. 2011. Ray Kurzweil and uploading: Just say no! *Journal of Evolution and Technology* 22(1): 23–36. [A version of this paper appears in this book as Chapter 9.]

Dyson, F. 1979. Time without end: Physics and biology in an open universe. *Review of Modern Physics* 51(3): 447–460.

Locke, J. 1975. *An Essay Concerning Human Understanding*. Oxford: Oxford University Press. (1st pub. 1690.)

Moravec, H. 1988. *Mind Children: The Future of Robot and Human Intelligence*. Cambridge, MA: Harvard University Press.

Olson, E. 2010. Personal identity. *Stanford Encyclopedia of Philosophy*, http://plato.stanford.edu/entries/identity-personal/ (accessed November 15, 2011). (1st pub. August 2002; substantive revisions October 2010.)

Parfit, D. 1984. *Reasons and Persons*. Oxford: Oxford University Press.

Peirce, C.S. 1906. Prolegomena to an apology for pragmaticism. *Monist* 16: 492–546.

Perry, J. 1978. *A Dialogue on Personal Identity and Immortality*. Indianapolis: Hackett.

Perry, J. (ed.) 2008. *Personal Identity*. Berkeley, CA: University of California Press.

Sandberg, A. 1999. The physics of information processing superobjects: Daily life among the Jupiter Brains. *Journal of Evolution and Technology* 5(1), http://www.jetpress.org/volume5/Brains2.pdf (accessed October 6, 2013).

Sandberg, A., and N. Bostrom. 2008. *Whole brain emulation: A roadmap*. Future of Humanity Institute, Oxford University, http://www.fhi.ox.ac.uk/Reports/2008-3.pdf (accessed July 3, 2010).

Searle, J.R. 1980. Minds, brains and programs. *Behavioral and Brain Sciences* 3: 417–457.

Shorter, J.M. 1962. More about bodily continuity and personal identity. *Analysis* 22(4): 79–85.

Walker, M. 2006. A moral paradox in the creation of artificial intelligence: Mary Poppins 3000s of the world unite! In Ted Metzler, ed., *Human Implications of Human–Robot Interaction: Papers from the 2006 AAAI Workshop*. Menlo Park, CA: AAAI Press, pp. 23–28.

Walker, M. 2008. Cognitive enhancement and the identity objection. *Journal of Evolution and Technology* 18(1): 108–115.

Walker, M. 2011. Personal identity and uploading. *Journal of Evolution and Technology* 22(1): 37–51.

Wetzel, L. 2009. *Types and Tokens: On Abstract Objects*. Cambridge, MA: MIT Press.

Williams, B. 1973. *Problems of the Self*. Cambridge: Cambridge University Press.

11

Whole Brain Emulation: Invasive vs. Non-Invasive Methods

Naomi Wellington

1 Introduction

In its most basic form, whole brain emulation (WBE) is the prospect of scanning the structure of a biological brain in detail and reproducing this structure in an artificial model, remaining as close as possible to the original, so that "when run on appropriate hardware, it will behave in essentially the same way as the original brain" (Sandberg and Bostrom 2008: 7). In section 2 of this chapter, I examine five emulation methods, drawing a distinction between structure replication and structure reconstruction (SR) methods on the one hand, and reverse brain engineering (RBE) methods on the other. Often the methods are divided into destructive emulation methods, whereby the initial biological brain is destroyed, and nondestructive emulation methods, whereby the initial biological brain is either preserved or gradually replaced. This distinction is counterproductive, since there are both destructive and nondestructive methods that may ultimately be unsuccessful in getting us what we really want in wanting to survive WBE.

In section 3, I argue that we need reasons to claim a particular procedure does or does not maintain identity, independently of whether the procedure is destructive or nondestructive. One candidate for an independent standard is the extent to which the procedure is invasive, that is to say the extent to which it interferes with the person's status as an autonomous self-perpetuator. I argue that SR methods are unable to meet this standard, while reverse brain engineering stands a better chance of success. I conclude

Intelligence Unbound: The Future of Uploaded and Machine Minds, First Edition.
Edited by Russell Blackford and Damien Broderick.

that the best possible way to maintain personal identity is to reverse-engineer the brain neuron by neuron, passing it through a cyborg phase and avoiding any gap in psychological continuity.

The only rational alternative would be to claim that personal identity is not what truly matters in *survival*. Hence, what we should focus on is ensuring survival, not preserving identity. The SR methods could ensure survival in some sense of the word, but whether or not this is on par with ordinary daily survival is debatable. My position is that it is not. For those of us who hold the characteristic psychological continuity of a person through time to be significant, and to be partially the reason why ordinary survival *is* that which it is, the SR methods are unsuccessful.

In section 4, I conclude that, although some of the SR methods are technologically within our grasp, none of these methods are adequate, if we are attempting to ensure certain personal benefits, such as immortality and/or the possibility of living multiple existences. Assuming these benefits constitute a significant reason for the drive to emulate, methods involving replication and reconstruction cannot get us what we want. In these cases, your emulation will not, strictly speaking, be *you*. Rather, it will be an exact functional replica of you, a sort of twin. Accordingly, I propose that WBE research be aimed primarily at cybernetics and the possibility of replacing a biological brain in steps that involve very small parts with no psychologically relevant structure.

2 WBE: Proposed methods

I divide the possible WBE methods I am examining in this chapter into two camps: structure replication and reconstruction (SR) methods and reverse brain engineering (RBE) methods. The first, SR, camp includes the following:

The brain mapping and replication method (BM&R). This is the simplest procedure and requires the least amount of technological advancement. The brain is frozen to extremely low temperatures. It is then carved into thin slices. Each slice is examined, its structure is then mapped in detail, and it is eventually replicated in an artificial substrate.

The superior brain scans method (SBS). This method is rather similar to BM&R, with the distinction that the brain is not destroyed. The hope is that we will eventually have better brain-scanning procedures, for example improved magnetic resonance imaging, and on the basis of these scans we will be able to build an accurate and structurally identical artificial model of the brain.

The reconstructive uploading method (RU). This would presumably take place in a post-Singularity world. The goal is to reconstruct the brain of a previously deceased person in an artificial substrate, through the use of brain scans, videos, writings, and other significant data/records of the person.

The second camp, the RBE methods, includes:

The reverse engineering method – type 1 (REM 1). This involves replacing whole sections or circuits of the brain, by first scanning and mapping their structure and then building appropriate replacement parts.

The reverse engineering method – type 2 (REM 2). This is a similar process to REM 1. The significant difference is that the replacement parts would have no psychologically relevant structure, for example emulation would occur neuron by neuron.

Some of these procedures would require significant technological advances, but we can presuppose that at least the ones that seem technologically within our grasp, in particular BM&R and SBS, will be available in the next few years. There is ongoing research in this area. Notably, in 2007 a University of Nevada research team managed to run an artificial neural network almost half as complex as the brain of a mouse and this showed biologically consistent nerve impulses (BBC News 2007). Another significant project, Blue Brain, was initiated by the Swiss Federal Institute of Technology in 2005, with the aim of re-creating a mammalian neocortical column in an artificial computerized model. The project has since made considerable progress, with a cellular mesocircuit of 100 neocortical columns reaching completion in 2011. It is expected that a simulation[1] of a rat brain will be completed by 2014 and a simulation of a human brain is expected to be possible a decade later (Blue Brain Project 2013).

In the following section I argue that the SR procedures described above are strongly invasive (in the sense that they play an excessive role in the psychological continuity process). Furthermore, similar problems affect REM 1. For this reason, I conclude that the only method that can be successful in preserving personal identity is REM 2.

3 Can your WBE preserve your personal identity?

Neo-Lockean accounts claim that personal identity is characterized by a kind of psychological continuity. According to Shoemaker (2008), the self (the person) is a substance, but it is not a substance in the dualist conception of a bundle of immaterial stuff. Rather it is a substance in the sense of being the subject of mental properties. But in order to be such a substance the self must satisfy an important substantiability criterion. It must be a relatively autonomous self-perpetuator (Shoemaker 1997). That is, the psychological continuity of the self (its persistence through time) lies in relations of causal dependence of the self's mental properties at later times on its mental properties at former times. It is part of a mental state's functional role that it generates successor states which generate their own successors and so on (Shoemaker 1997). "This will include the generation of memories and the preservation of beliefs, desires, preferences, character traits" (Shoemaker 2008: 316).

If physicalism is true, these mental states will have to be realized in or supervene on something physical. But if we want to leave open the possibility of a brain transplant, and most importantly the possibility of WBE, it is a good idea to endorse a neo-Lockean account such as Shoemaker's whereby a person is not identified with her body or the biological animal that she sees in the mirror. For Shoemaker (2007), the self is the body only if we take the *is* to refer to a relation of constitution rather than one of identity. According to this approach, the person is *constituted* by a biological animal that he or she is not, strictly speaking, identical with. The person and the biological animal are thus coincident but distinct entities. They share the same thin physical properties, but differ when it comes to thick physical properties. Mental properties are realized in thick properties. These belong to persons only. The result of this is that persons have mental properties while their bodies do not.

The distinction between thin and thick properties lies in the impact these have on the careers of the persons who instantiate them. A thin physical property, such as X's property of being short-sighted, has no bearing on the psychological continuity of X. Thick physical properties are individuated by thick causal roles. They can "belong only to entities, persons or other mental subjects, that have psychological persistence conditions, where something's having such persistence conditions means that its career will exhibit a certain sort of psychological continuity" (Shoemaker 2007: 91).

To sum up, the mental properties of a person are thick and realized in thick physical properties. Mental properties are not shared by the body or the human animal that is coincident with the person. It follows from this that those thick physical properties that are realizers of mental properties are likewise not shared with the physical body.[2] This may sound like a strange conclusion; however, things become clearer if we consider the theoretical example of a brain transplant (Shoemaker 2004).

Presumably, mental states are instantiated in microphysical states of affairs located in the brain. But can we say that the property of having a brain is a thick property? An understandable intuition would be that both the animal body and the person can be said to have a brain. For Shoemaker, however, there is a particular sense in which a person can be said to have a brain while the animal body does not: "that in which a creature 'has' a certain (brain) just in case that brain is the locus of that creature's mental property realizers" (Shoemaker 2007: 93). If a person has a brain in this sense, and the brain is successfully transplanted in someone else's body, the person will continue to exist in the new body, in virtue of psychological continuity. Her mental properties will continue to be instantiated in the relevant microphysical states of affairs located in her brain. Her memories, beliefs, etc., will be preserved. Once again, it is in virtue of being the subject of self-perpetuating mental properties (and hence being a relatively autonomous self-perpetuator) that the self persists through time.

Since we've established that mental properties have thick physical properties located in the brain as realizers, we can say that the persistence through time of the self involves there being relations of causal dependence of thick physical properties at later times on thick physical properties at former times. The type of causation involved here is immanent causation as contrasted with transeunt causation (Shoemaker 1997).[3] This distinction has significant implications for the persistence (or failure to persist) of personal identity following emulation. Indeed, it will be crucial in what follows.

Immanent causation vs. transeunt causation

Immanent causation is the type of causation that is internal to an entity's career (Shoemaker 1997). For instance, a butterfly has the physical properties it has at T2 in virtue of having had the physical properties it had at T1 (e.g., when it was a larva). Most biological organisms retain their physical properties over time through immanent causation. Even though there are outer factors that come into the picture, such as environmental factors, "it is largely immanent causation that is responsible for the (biological entity's) continuing to exist as a certain thing, one embodying certain principles of change and unchange" (Shoemaker 1997: 288). Significantly this applies to the thick physical property of having a brain. A person has this thick physical property at T2 in virtue of having had the thick physical property of having a brain 2 hours ago at T1, months ago at Tx, etc. Since thick physical properties, such as the property of having a brain in a particular state, are the realizers of mental properties, it follows that the psychological continuity of an entity through time is ensured through immanent causation of this sort. So the person is a (relatively) autonomous self-perpetuator whose distinctive continuity is carried primarily through immanent causation.

What happens when transeunt causation (causation from things outer to the self) is implicated? Transeunt causation is involved in the action of one thing on another. Evidently, transeunt causation occurs frequently in daily life. In particular, there are many environmental factors that contribute to the persistence through time of biological organisms. For this reason, these organisms can only ever be *relatively* self-perpetuating (there is a high degree of immanent causation, but there is also some transeunt causation involved). However, I think Shoemaker makes a legitimate point that there are acceptable and unacceptable degrees of transeunt causation. We have to draw the line somewhere. For instance, moving images on a movie screen are perpetuated *only* through transeunt causation. There is no sense in which they are self-perpetuating. Still, there are obvious differences between biological brains, at one end of the scale, and moving images on a screen at the other (Shoemaker 1997). Identity is lost only if there is too much transeunt causation involved in perpetuating psychological continuity.

Can your WBE be you?

Consider the following thought experiment by Peter Unger (1990):

> Tester's[4] brain is "superfrozen" and all of its matter is rapidly replaced in a way that preserves structure. The resulting brain is superthawed and the result is a person (Tester) functionally indistinguishable from the original. There are two versions of the replacement procedure. On the first version the replacement of the brain takes place in four stages, replacing one quarter of the brain at each stage. On the second version, each stage involves the replacement of one atom. Both procedures take only a tenth of a second to complete. (Shoemaker 1997: 290)

If personal identity is a relatively autonomous self-perpetuating substance, in the sense outlined above, it follows that the first version of the replacement procedure described by Unger is unsuccessful in getting Tester what he wants, if he was wanting to survive. Following this procedure at T2, the Tester who wakes up is no longer the Tester whose brain was frozen for the procedure, at some previous time T1. Tester 2 stands in a particular relation to Tester 1, but it is not a relation of identity. They are not the same person.

The upshot is that this procedure involves too much transeunt causation and therefore cannot be self-preserving. The process whereby the psychological properties of the person are perpetuated involves the scanning of brain structure. "The state of the original brain must be somehow recorded, this providing a *blueprint*, that can be used to construct replacement parts having the right structure" (Shoemaker 1997: 290). Tester exists as a person with particular psychological properties (and particular thick physical properties that are the realizers of these psychological properties) at T2 *primarily* in virtue of the experimenters' abilities and the technological equipment employed (i.e., in virtue of something other than self-perpetuation). When a procedure involves too much transeunt causation (i.e., when the type of causation involved in sustaining psychological continuity over time is primarily transeunt, rather than immanent) the procedure cannot be person-preserving. If we were to say it was, we would risk compromising Tester's autonomy.

Nonetheless, in the second version of the experiment, where each replacement stage involves only the replacement of one atom, we have reason to believe personal identity is preserved. Here there is no mapping and reproducing of psychologically relevant structure involved. Consider the following claim by Shoemaker:

> Both of Unger's procedures are radically invasive involving a large dose of transeunt causation, but there is an important difference: In the first case … it is essential to the success of the procedure that the replacement parts have the right psychologically relevant structure, that of the parts they replace. … By contrast, in the second procedure the replacement parts have no psychologically relevant structure. (1997: 289)

This distinction is very significant. In the initial scenario, the psychological structure of the replacement parts is directly relevant to Tester's psychological continuity, and this structure *exists* and *functions* (if it does) largely in virtue of something other than Tester's self-perpetuation. In the second scenario, by contrast, atoms have no psychologically relevant structure, so their replacement is not directly relevant to psychological continuity.

In a sense, this scenario still involves transeunt causation, but I think it is helpful here to reiterate the distinction between a body or human animal's property of having a brain and the associated person's property of having a brain. There is a sense_1 in which *only* a person has a brain (when this is the center of that person's mental state realizers); and another sense_2 in which the animal body has a brain simply because the brain is located inside its skull. What we should be saying here is that the replacement of one atom at a time involves transeunt causation in a way that sustains the continuity of the material composition of the biological brain in sense_2, but at the same time it does not involve transeunt causation in a way that could undermine the person's psychological continuity, specifically – the continuity of the brain possessed by the person in sense_1.

In the case of Tester, his psychological continuity is perpetuated primarily in virtue of immanent causation. It depends on the way in which atoms interact upon replacing previous existing atoms, the cells they constitute, and the psychological structures that these cells – neurons – realize. These neurological structures are, in turn, the physical realizers of mental states.

Why SR methods are unsuccessful

What does this tell us about WBE? Arguably, one significant thing it tells us is that SR methods are unlikely to be successful in preserving personal identity. This is true in as much as we can consider procedures of structure replication and reconstruction to be analogous to the first version of Peter Unger's thought experiment.

It appears that all of the SR methods outlined above are in fact analogous to this version of the experiment in those respects that are relevant to the personal identity question, i.e. the question: "Can your WBE be *you*?" The analogy is probably most obvious in the brain mapping and replication (BM&R) method. Here the brain is frozen at extremely low temperatures and sliced into thin segments that are then examined and scanned. This provides a blueprint of the structure of the biological brain, which is later used to reconstruct the brain in an artificial substrate.

Let's say Tester undergoes this procedure instead of that described by Unger. There is no sense in which the person he is at T2 (following BM&R) is the same person he was at T1 (prior to undergoing the procedure), because there is no sense in which the person he is at T2 is *primarily* a result of autonomous self-perpetuation. In parallel to the first version of Unger's thought experiment, the type of causation involved in the continuity of Tester's mental states is transeunt causation, rather than immanent causation. Hence, the procedure cannot be self-preserving.

Something similar occurs when we examine the superior brain scans (SBS) method. Here, the significant difference is that the initial brain is not destroyed. However, when it comes to the amount of transeunt causation involved, these procedures are analogous. SBS is a method that is likely to become available in years to come: the hope is that we will have better brain-scanning methods, improved magnetic resonance imaging, etc., and that we will be able to map the structure of the brain in detail using these methods. Let's be optimistic and assume this method gives us a perfect blueprint of Tester's brain, which is later used to construct a functionally indistinguishable artificial brain. But is Tester still *himself* following this procedure? Again, the answer seems to be "no," if we want to respect the status of a person as an autonomous self-perpetuator. There is a sense in which Tester 2 at T2 exists in virtue of Tester 1 having existed at T1, but there is no sense in which the psychological continuity of Tester has been primarily carried through to T2 by a process of immanent causation. So Tester 2 exists at T2, and has particular psychological properties, primarily in virtue of the technology employed, the equipment used, and the individuals (or machines) involved in carrying out the SBS procedure. The perpetuation of Tester's mental states (his psychological continuity) is maintained mostly through transeunt causation, hence we can conclude that the procedure is not self-preserving.

A third possible WBE method is the reverse engineering method type 1 (REM 1). Here portions of the brain are replaced gradually with their artificial-neural equivalents. This is comparable to the first version of Unger's experiment, where one-quarter of the brain is replaced at each stage. The comparison is apt as long as the portions of the brain replaced have a psychologically relevant structure and this structure is scanned, mapped, and later reproduced as an artificial, functionally isomorphic circuit. Consider a related argument by David Chalmers (2010):

> If 1 per cent of a person's (Kate's) brain is replaced by a functionally isomorphic silicon circuit and this step is repeated over a period of 100 months, at which time Kate's entire brain will have been replaced entirely by silicon circuits, the following is true:
>
> 1 For all n < 100, Kate (n + 1) is identical to Kate (n).
> 2 If for all n < 100, Kate (n + 1) is identical to Kate (n), then DigiKate is identical to Kate.
>
> ―――――――
>
> 3 DigiKate is identical to Kate.

At first glance, this looks plausible. Assuming, however, that 1 percent of the brain has a psychologically relevant structure, it is reasonable to argue that the procedure involves too much transeunt causation to count as self-preserving. Hence, we may disagree that DigiKate is Kate by denying premise 2 of Chalmers' argument.

During each step, a neural circuit is scanned and reconstructed employing particular methods. The first step involves some degree of transeunt causation, but this could be outweighed by all of the immanent causation still involved in carrying Kate's psychological continuity into the future. However, by the time we reach the end of the experiment and we get DigiKate, the accumulated amount of transeunt causation involved throughout the process is objectionable.

This is how I take it the initial Unger experiment works, where one-quarter of the brain is replaced at each stage. Perhaps if *only* one-quarter of the brain were replaced from T1 to T2, we could say that there is still sufficient immanent causation to ensure the preservation of personal identity. But once the entire brain has been replaced (at T3) through the use of procedures outer to the self, the overall process whereby the psychological traits of Tester were perpetuated from T1 to T3 is no longer one of self-perpetuation. It is not one involving a high enough degree of immanent causation. I believe the same applies to Kate: the psychological continuity of Kate from T1 to T2, through to DigiKate, is primarily a result of transeunt and not immanent causation. We can conclude that the procedure is not self-preserving.[5]

However, there is always the possibility of employing a second version of this procedure, which Chalmers (2010) also mentions, whereby we could replace the brain neuron by neuron instead. This is, in effect, the *only* procedure I am optimistic about in this chapter and I will discuss it shortly.

A fourth SR method is the reconstructive uploading method (RU). Chalmers (2010) examines how this possibility might work in a post-Singularity world, assuming that post-Singularity scientists decide to upload the brain of a previously deceased person and they do this through the use of something other than cryonics. The thought is that, based on brain scans, videos, writings, and other significant data/records, the post-Singularity scientists will be able to reconstruct the deceased's brain in an artificial substrate.

In as much as the SBS method does not preserve identity, it initially seems that the same applies to the RU method. If the structure of the initial brain is mapped and reconstructed, psychological continuity will be maintained primarily by transeunt causation and the procedure will not be self-preserving. However, by contrast to the SBS method, RU would presumably take place in a post-Singularity world. This changes the terms of the debate because we have no reliable way to make predictions regarding what an intelligence millions of times greater than ours could achieve. Perhaps there would be a way, unintelligible to us at present, to ensure the psychological continuity of a person through immanent causation, even though the person is deceased. If physicalism is true, then psychological continuity is necessarily dependent on physical continuity in some sense, but perhaps it is not dependent on physical continuity in the particular way that we have in mind. Or perhaps post-Singularity beings will come up with superior theories of personal identity on the basis of tangible proof, rather than purely theorizing, in which case identity may turn out to require something other than autonomous self-perpetuation.

So far I have argued that SR methods (BM&R, SBS, and RU) as well as the REM 1 method cannot preserve identity if we take the self to be a relatively autonomous self-perpetuating substance.[6] All of these methods strip the self of its title as an autonomous self-perpetuating substance. Hence, they leave it as no longer a *self*. The only exceptions to this might come about in the event of a technological Singularity. If this occurred and there existed beings millions of times more intelligent than we are at present, it is entirely arbitrary to venture guesses about what they *could not* achieve. Presumably they could achieve vastly more than we could, and with considerably more ease.

REM 2 can preserve identity

I argue here that the only type of procedure that is likely to be identity-preserving is one that is analogous to the second version of Unger's thought experiment. REM 2 is the procedure we need. The brain is still replaced gradually but the replacement parts (neurons) have no psychologically relevant structure. As per the *atom by atom* scenario above, the replacement of the brain neuron by neuron is not directly relevant to psychological continuity. If Tester underwent *this* procedure he would continue to be himself after each step all the way through to the conclusion of the process, when his entire brain will have been replaced. In this case if we take Tester at T1 (pre-emulation) and Tester at T2 (post-emulation), they are the same person because the process that ensured psychological continuity over that period of time was one of mostly immanent causation.

The replacement of one neuron at a time (much like the replacement of one atom at a time) involves transeunt causation in a way that ensures the continuity of the material composition of the biological brain in $sense_2$ of brain. It does not, however, involve transeunt causation in a way that is central to Tester's psychological continuity: the continuity of Tester's brain in $sense_1$. Since transeunt causation did not play a direct role in psychological continuity at each step, there is no objectionable amount of accumulated *relevant* transeunt causation (relevant, that is, to psychological continuity) by the end of the procedure. By contrast to DigiKate, DigiTester's psychological continuity is still carried mainly through immanent causation, and accordingly he is *still* Tester.

I am very optimistic about the outcome of REM 2 were we to have the technology necessary to achieve it. Unless, however, a technological Singularity occurs, we are unlikely to have the needed technology any time in the near future. That being so, it is very likely that the first WBEs will be created through one of the SR methods. BM&R or SBS are, I think, the expected candidates. Assuming these procedures are successful in creating perfectly functionally isomorphic emulations, what exactly does this achieve?

Is ensuring survival good enough?

As we saw above, BM&R and SBS do not preserve identity. However, there is a Parfitian argument that perhaps preserving identity is *not what matters* in ensuring survival. Hence, we should focus on ensuring survival only. Consider Derek Parfit's (1984) thought experiment on teletransportation.

The person (Tester) enters a Teletransporter and presses a button, at which point a scanner destroys his brain while recording the exact state of all his cells. In a matter of minutes, this information is transmitted by radio to Mars, where the replicator creates a brain and body exactly like Tester's and "he" (or the *new* Tester) wakes up in this new body.

In a sense, we would not be making a mistake in saying that this procedure ensured survival, since the new Tester is an exact functional isomorph of the old Tester. When he wakes up he is privy to all of old Tester's memories, thoughts, beliefs, etc., and, as expected, he believes he is Tester. However, if we take the view of personal identity mapped out earlier, he is *not identical to* Tester 1. Whatever relation new Tester (Tester 2) and old Tester (Tester 1) are in, it is not one of identity. Shoemaker's (1997) perspective is that it would be false to say Tester survives the Teletransporter procedure, but if we say identity is not what matters in survival, then it is perfectly reasonable for Tester to believe the procedure gets him what he wants in wanting to survive. Though this is plausible, I do not see this type of survival as analogous to ordinary survival, since psychological continuity (as perpetuated primarily through immanent causation) seems to be an integral part of ordinary survival.

The Teletransporter case is analogous to the BM&R procedure in all significant respects. In both cases, the initial brain is destroyed during the scanning process and a new one is constructed based on the data and scans acquired. In as much as we can say the Teletransporter case ensures survival, we can say the same thing about the BM&R procedure. The way in which this differs from ordinary survival becomes more evident in a second version of Parfit's Teletransporter case. In this version, the brain is still scanned and recorded and the information is sent to Mars, where a new brain and body are created, etc.; however, the initial brain is not destroyed by the scanning procedure. This would be analogous to SBS. In this scenario, two separate persons wake up following the procedure: one is the initial Tester on earth whose brain was recorded, and the second is an exact functional isomorph of Tester on Mars. So at T2 (post-teletransportation) we have two Testers, both of whom believe themselves to be Tester. Presumably if we told Tester 1 that he is about to die, the fact that Tester 2 survives would not be all that much consolation. For this reason, there is a clear sense in which this is not *as good as* ordinary survival (Parfit 1984).

Ultimately, both the BM&R procedure and the SBS procedure can ensure survival in some sense of the word. But in comparison to ordinary survival where it is the *self* that survives, I think we have reasons to see this second type of survival as more akin to your functionally isomorphic twin surviving.[7] It is very likely that at least the first emulations we see, perhaps even in the next few years, will be more like isomorphic twins of the initial persons. In as much as this might be what we require of the WBE procedure, it does get us what we want. However, some of the significant benefits we would expect to derive from WBE, notably the possibility of immortality and the possibility of living multiple existences, will not be attained.

4 Concluding thoughts

It is possible that WBE will take place within the next few years in some shape or form. However, in the absence of an intelligence explosion (a Singularity), the methods that will be most readily available to us are likely BM&R and, potentially, SBS. Both of these are what I have called structure replication, or SR, methods. In this chapter I have argued that methods reliant on structure replication and reconstruction will not preserve personal identity. I based this on a neo-Lockean definition of personal identity according to which the *self* is a relatively autonomous self-perpetuating substance whose psychological continuity through time is ensured primarily by immanent causation. All SR methods involve too much transeunt causation. This may not be significant from an economics perspective – when examining the potential economic expansion that would come about as a result of WBE (Sandberg and Bostrom 2008) – but it defeats the purpose of seeking immortality if your *self* does not survive. At best, SR methods have the outcome of an exact functional isomorph of *you* surviving.

In order to leave open the possibility of immortality, WBE research should be conducted primarily in the area of cybernetics. My conclusion here is that the only possible method that would preserve personal identity throughout is REM 2, in which the brain is replaced neuron by neuron. This is the only scenario where the process through which psychological continuity is maintained is based primarily on immanent causation.

Acknowledgments

I am grateful to Daniel Stoljar, David Chalmers, Russell Blackford, and Damien Broderick for their extremely helpful comments and feedback during the development of this chapter.

Notes

1 There is a significant distinction between simulation and emulation. *Simulation mimics the outward results, while emulation mimics the internal causal dynamics*. "The emulation is regarded as successful if the emulated system produces the same outward behavior and results as the original" (Sandberg and Bostrom 2008).
2 Note that the thin physical properties shared by the person and the animal body are realizers of thick physical properties – in the sense of guaranteeing their existence – which in turn realize mental states, but that does not mean that these thick properties, once realized, play a role in the body's career. In fact, they are only properties of the person and only significant to the person's career.
3 Shoemaker draws the distinction between immanent and transeunt causation based on W.E. Johnson's (1964) account.
4 *Tester* is a name I will be using for the rest of the chapter.
5 Raymond Kurzweil (2005) defends the view that REM 1 is self-preserving. He argues that this would be no different from a biological process where everything in our bodies changes over time. I claim the Reverse Engineering procedure, if it is carried out in this manner, is actually not all that akin to a biological process because of the amount of transeunt causation involved. In a normal biological process there is nothing outer to your biological body mapping your brain structure and replicating it in order to ensure your psychological continuity. However, if Reverse Engineering were carried out neuron by neuron, this would be close enough to a biological process, in the sense that psychological continuity is still primarily carried through immanent causation.
6 Note that, when the invasive WBE methods are employed, Tester 2 would likely be able to pass a personalized Turing test. Individuals familiar with him would be unable to distinguish the original Tester from his emulation (Sandberg 2013). This is because we are not privy to psychological continuity through direct observation. I will not be discussing the implications of this in this chapter. For further discussion see Sandberg (2013).
7 For an argument against this, see Chalmers (2010).

References

BBC News. 2007. *Mouse brain simulated on computer*, http://news.bbc.co.uk/2/hi/technology/6600965.stm (accessed September 15, 2013).

Blue Brain Project. 2013. *The human brain project*, http://bluebrain.epfl.ch/page-52741-en.html (accessed September 15, 2013).

Chalmers, D.J. 2010. The Singularity: A philosophical analysis. *Journal of Consciousness Studies* 17: 7–65.

Johnson, W.E. 1964. *Logic, Part III: The Logical Foundations of Science*. New York: Dover.

Kurzweil, R. 2005. *The Singularity Is Near: When Humans Transcend Biology*. New York: Viking Adult.

Parfit, D. 1984. *Reasons and Persons*. Oxford: Oxford University Press.

Sandberg, A. 2013. Feasibility of whole brain emulation. In V.C. Muller, ed., *Theory and Philosophy of Artificial Intelligence*. Berlin: Springer, pp. 251–264.

Sandberg, A., and Bostrom, N. 2008. *Whole brain emulation: A roadmap*. Technical Report 2008-3. Oxford: Future of Humanity Institute.

Shoemaker, S. 1997. Self and substance. *Nous* 13(11): 283–304.

Shoemaker, S. 2004. Brown-Brownston revisited. *The Monist* 87(4): 573–593.

Shoemaker, S. 2007. *Physical Realization*. Oxford: Oxford University Press.

Shoemaker, S. 2008. Persons, animals, and identity. *Synthese* 162: 313–324.

Unger, P. 1990. *Identity, Consciousness and Value*. New York: Oxford University Press.

12

The Future of Identity: Implications, Challenges, and Complications of Human/Machine Consciousness

Kathleen Ann Goonan

> *"The question is," said Humpty Dumpty, "which is to be master, that's all."*
>
> (*Lewis Carroll*)

Uploading consciousness is, essentially, a religious vision, updated by science and seeded by the imagination of science fiction, bequeathing one essential question and generating the second: what is consciousness, and what artificial substrate might maintain it? In answer to these questions, science, technology, and science fiction are negotiating one of the most potentially narrative-changing mergers since *Frankenstein* kicked off the genre.

*

Being human has always meant that we desire to live an infinitely long life in a perfect world.

Assuming embeddedness in a conscious environment, as do proponents of uploaded consciousness, has religious antecedents: powerful entities inhabit objects; deities regulate weather; a supernatural agent is our constant companion, creating and reading our minds and regulating events for our immediate benefit; we are divine, with souls, separate from our corruptible material bodies and the world, that can live forever. Our ancestors developed such beliefs to explain our almost visceral apprehension that consciousness

Intelligence Unbound: The Future of Uploaded and Machine Minds, First Edition.
Edited by Russell Blackford and Damien Broderick.

is free-floating. Invisible, like air and water, it sustains, and, at the same time, *is* us, infusing us and flowing between the world and us.

This is one reason, according to philosopher John Searle, that consciousness has never been seriously studied until now: "Humanity has a universal history of embracing dualism, the separation of mind from body" (Searle 2013).

I posit that this integral aspect of what it has always meant to be human is one of the reasons that transferring consciousness to a non-human medium seems a viable goal to transhumanists.

Proponents of the transhumanist vision often gloss over the messy physical details of identity, but we are not only a brain at the top of a body, a soul in a corrupt and useless medium awaiting release.

Instead, scientists such as Eric Kandel have proved that "everything the brain produces, from the most private thoughts to the most public acts, should be understood as a biological process" (Kandel et al. 2000: 1277).

In fact, the entire corporeal body, which rapturous transhuman visions, like the religious dreams on which they draw, conveniently jettison, generates consciousness.

*

Posthumanism, mind uploading, and transhumanism are also fed by science fictional ideas that have been afloat in our culture for over a century.

These religious and science-based visions, derived from two antithetical streams of thought, bump up against heaven, God, immortality, and one another in ways that, despite the religious provenance of this dream, are anathema to religious beliefs, for this is immortality without goodness; an afterlife of perfect economical grace. No matter what your sins might be, you can get in if you meet certain conditions, though the price of admittance has still to be negotiated. Perhaps having the Alzheimer's genes and excellent insurance might get you through the gates of everlasting life. Or you may have to dig into unimaginably deep pockets, take chances on untested new technologies and theories, cross your fingers, and plunge into having your finely sectioned brain preserved in resin – instead of the old-fashioned liquid nitrogen of early cryonics – as is the goal of Henry Markram of the Blue Brain Project (2013), to be resurrected and infused into –

That is one of two crucial questions: the waiting … what?

Science fiction has cued us with images: cloned bodies shrouded in cocoons; cyberspace; computer chips; android or cyborg bodies.

But translating who and what we are into a new substrate that can maintain what is essential to ourselves – identity – in a non-biological environment, requires that biology and machine must not just meet, but merge.

Reducing us to bits and bytes yields information as inert as does cataloging genetic code.

One of the biggest hurdles in this endeavor is that biological scientists and computer engineers are islands of separate, specialized knowledge. These disciplines have few links with one another, although these links are growing, through fields such as biomedical computation, biomechanical engineering, and the all-encompassing field of nanotechnology, for this is the dawn of science of the mind. Massive government funding supports the US Brain Research through Advancing Innovative Neurotechnologies (BRAIN) initiative and the EU Big Brain Project. The vision of both is to begin a conversation between disparate disciplines, which promises not only answers but therapies, technologies, and hard information about the brain and consciousness.

Though computer scientists ignore the realities of biology when envisioning uploading consciousness, neuroscientists find the idea of transferring biological process to a machine problematic, given the complexity and dynamism of life.

> Your brain is built of cells called neurons and glia – hundreds of billions of them. Each one of these cells is as complicated as a city. And each one contains the entire human genome and traffics billions of molecules in intricate economies. (Eagleman 2011: 1)

This is the complicated, ever-moving, and at present unexplained substrate from which consciousness arises, that which we want to preserve, as Buckminster Fuller might put it, as a verb.

When Humpty Dumpty said, "The question is, which is to be master," his subject was the logic of grammar. Changing the subject from language to life – life extended, life transformed, consciousness versus its hidden physicality – gives us a starting point for exploring the questions this subject raises. Uploading consciousness is just as infested with inflection as is language itself; just as fraught with issues of "which is to be master." To be human, one needs to be conscious, but are we the masters of consciousness?

How can we be, if we do not even know what consciousness is? Until lately, lack of hard information about untouchable, dynamic consciousness made theories abstract, unscientific. We could observe what went in and what went out, but we could not know what happened in between.

And in between is what we want to preserve with any uploading project: our sense of self. Our identity. Not only our memories, but the entire reflexive mental and physical gesture-library that makes life feel familiar and gives us automatic responses that are like magic, because they are hidden from our conscious minds. They are the part of us that consciousness evolved to ignore, so we could react with efficacy and speed, the gorilla in the picture of discourse regarding uploading minds: our physical body.

The body is consciousness' blind spot, the parent of who we actually are; the storehouse we build by going through the biological developmental stages of neuron growth, neuron pruning, and change after change to our bodies in a complex communicative dance with the physical world. Seeing, hearing, grasping, perambulating – everything we think and do – is a bodily feedback loop with our surroundings. Consciousness is the child of processes that occur behind the scenes:

> All of these things happen completely underneath the hood of conscious awareness. And it turns out that the conscious part of you … is the smallest bit of what's happening in the brain … It's like the broom closet in the mansion of the brain … When you have an idea, you say, oh, I just thought of something. It wasn't actually you that thought of it. Your brain has been working on that behind the scenes for hours or days … At some point it gets served up to your consciousness and you say oh I'm a genius. But it wasn't really you. (Eagleman 2012)

*

One model for creating artificial consciousness is replicating every fine detail of the brain on computers and setting the model in motion. But can massively detailed full-scale models such as Markram's Blue Brain Project become conscious themselves? "It's really difficult to say how much detail is needed for consciousness to emerge," said Markram. "I do believe that consciousness is an emergent phenomenon. It's like a shift from a liquid to a gas … It's like a machine that has to run fast enough and suddenly it's flying" (Kushner 2009).

In other words, you can't know for sure until the model is finished, and this model is predicated on Markram's death.

Positing consciousness as an emergent property of a sufficiently complex system is not new; Teilhard de Chardin's *The Phenomenon of Man*, with his singularity of the Omega Point portaling the Noösphere, the purely cognitive space towards which all biology is evolving, prefigures the transhuman quest from the point of view of a Jesuit priest.

A related point of view is that an artificial substrate might support and enhance our own feeling of being alive, and provide an environment of agency – a virtual world – in which we can live without fear of biological death. A rich science fictional vision of computer-based possibilities has arisen from writers who are also computer programmers. Greg Egan (1994, 2010) and Ted Chiang (2010) are two of the most interesting writers exploring the philosophical conundrums that might arise when humans are enhanced by, merged with, or live within advanced computational environments.

Are these visions in any way viable, as some transhumanists seem to believe, or are they just intellectual games? Can we transmute ourselves from complex cells to bits and bytes, which then will live?

Probably not.

Like magpies, we create our nest of mind from the fragments of reality our senses meld together into what seems like a seamless present, bounded by a past we think we remember, which informs our actions, and a similarly imagined future that also shapes our choices. Because consciousness has been experimentally demonstrated to be a much more fragmented experience than we think it to be, perhaps we only need snippets of ourselves to feel conscious. Perhaps consciousness is nothing less and nothing more than story, and all we need do to continue to feel conscious is maintain identity through computer-based narrative.

The stone in this conceptual pudding is the fact that identity emerges from emotion, a wilderness we endlessly explore in our lives and in our fictions. The "emotionless computer" cypher in science fiction is logical, polite, puzzled by human emotion, and emphatically alien.

Thus we return to biology. Complexly linked biological systems generate emotions. Emotional development occurs in tandem with our physical growth. The exquisite link between our selves and the world, emotions govern our reactions and decisions and give us infinitely shaded dimensions of love, and fear. Loss of emotional reaction is a symptom of depression, which can lead to suicide. Without consideration of artificial replication of emotions – and from which stage of life would we draw our emotional model? – future artificial or uploaded humans may well abandon the rich nature/nurture stew that is, ultimately, us.

Life is also motion. Not only can you not step into the same river twice, though certain mental processes which we are just on the threshold of understanding make us feel ineluctably as if we are always the same person, we are also rivers; we are not the same person from instant to instant.

The flow of daily life, reconstituted and solidified by one of the most mysterious of human processes, dreams, might somehow serve to keep us surviving by assembling and renewing a somewhat continuous identity. As we theorize the path to artificiality, Philip K. Dick's question "Do androids dream of electric sheep?" might prove to be the most prescient and pressing of questions if we rephrase it as "How can we ensure that androids *will* dream of electric sheep?"

Without wildness in the mix – call it nature, call it all that is other, or all that we do not understand – it seems certain that we would lose serendipity, strangeness, mystery. A self and a world artificially created by humans might promise a heaven of unbounded joy and infinite exploration, but it also seems coincident with the definition of an infantile state and a recipe for dictatorships, mass failures on a huge scale, and thus death, in a different guise. Whether the artificial environment is a sublimed Internet or a free-moving robotic-based AI entity into which our minds might somehow flow, this vision of human evolution has limits as clear as the present limit of organic death. Machines require constant replenishment. Committing to an operating system would be absurd; an incorruptible core personality must be stored somewhere, somehow, to which we can withdraw, to be reborn into the latest gadget. Each complicated step is a weak link.

What is the solution?

I began writing the first novel of my Nanotech Quartet, *Queen City Jazz*, in 1991, after reading Drexler's *Engines of Creation*, which was an instant sensation. Its visionary scenarios of what manipulation of matter on a molecular and even an atomic level might lead to spawned many excited movements. The broad powers of nanotech were, truly, indistinguishable from magic. Nanotechnology was in its infancy then, and we could, and did, let our speculations run wild.

That is the business of writing science fiction, but, in a sense, it is also the business of writing successful science grants, though the scope of the latter is far more limited by the known. But as speculations and theorems accrete, they begin to point to applications and goals.

Nanotechnology has matured. An international array of scientists and engineers investigate the properties of unimaginably small particles, and invent new ones. Applied nanotechnology has generated uncountable applications in electronics, pharmacology, and materials engineering.

The place where nanotechnology meets biology is a fascinating limen. Nanoparticles may not only yield clues to what consciousness is, but have the potential to record and replicate consciousness by entering and shadowing the body and sending a stream of information about the living processes that generate consciousness to a cyborg, which may then replicate it.

Thus, the best approach to life extension and consciousness expansion might lie in our own marvelously complex and entire bodies, meshed with and augmented by tiny bionan machines that become a part of us, rather than the opposite vision of humans migrating into a machine substrate. You might grow your own eternal, artificial self as you gradually become bionic, in stages so tiny that you do not even notice. A swarm of bots, constantly updated and evolving, becomes, over the course time, you – a walking, talking bio-nanotech device, which constantly synchs with information about your original self, reads your DNA, tracks your lifescript, takes your emotional temperature, every insight, flash of anger, and odd, surprising instant of full happiness, and gives you immense powers of memory, emotion, computation, and connectivity.

*

The dream of uploading consciousness will be realized in a future that is, perhaps, almost beyond our ability to imagine, an expanded future of immense intelligence, a frontier that never ends, echoing Anselm's ontological argument of God being "that than which nothing greater can be conceived" (see Halsall 1998), except that we are inventing this divine-like future. Vision, or a hundred visions or models of the future, is always a prime mover in change.

Life extension is a dream as old as humanity. Perhaps, over time, we might improve on biology, or our touchstones might migrate from biology to a new, unlimited, ever-emerging story, thanks to the power of religious dreams from our ancient past.

References

Blue Brain Project. 2013. *The human brain project*, http://bluebrain.epfl.ch/cms/lang/en/pid/56882 (accessed October 6, 2013).

Carroll, L. 1963. *The Annotated Alice, Alice's Adventures in Wonderland & Through the Looking Glass*, ed. M. Gardner. Cleveland and New York: World Publishing.

Chiang, T. 2010. *Story of Your Life and Other Stories*. Easthampton, MA: Small Beer Press.

Dick, P.K. 1968. *Do Androids Dream of Electric Sheep?* New York: Doubleday.

Drexler, Eric K. 1986. *Engines of Creation: The Coming Era of Nanotechnology*. New York: Anchor Books.

Eagleman, D. 2011. *Incognito: The Secret Lives of the Brain*. New York, New York: Pantheon Books.

Eagleman, D. 2012. *Neurologist David Eagleman looks underneath the hood of the brain*, http://www.youtube.com/watch?v=dzMDYCaneXA (accessed October 21, 2013).

Egan, G. 1994. *Permutation City*. London: Millennium.

Egan, G. 2010. *Zendegi*. London: Gollancz.

Goonan, K. 1994. *Queen City Jazz*. New York: Tor.

Halsall, P. 1998. *Medieval Sourcebook: Anselm (1033–1109): Proslogion*, http://www.fordham.edu/halsall/basis/anselm-proslogium.asp#CHAPTER XV (accessed October 6, 2013).

Kandel, E.R., Schwartz, J.H., and Jessell, T.M. 2000. *Principles of Neural Science*. 4th edn. New York: McGraw-Hill.

Kushner, D. 2009. The man who builds brains. *Discover Magazine* (December), http://discovermagazine.com/2009/dec/05-discover-interview-the-man-who-builds-brains (accessed October 6, 2013).

Searle, J. 2013. *TED Talks (July 22): Our shared condition – consciousness.* www.ted.com/talks/john_searle_our_shared_condition_consciousness.html/ (accessed October 6, 2013).

Teilhard de Chardin, P. 2008. *The Phenomenon of Man.* New York: Harper-Perennial.

13

Practical Implications of Mind Uploading

Joe Strout

In this chapter, we take mind uploading as a given, and explore some of the impacts this technology will have on daily life.

1 Physical appearance

Let's begin on the personal scale. It's obvious that once a body is a commodity you can purchase or rent, much like a car or a cell phone, then such attributes as race, gender, and appearance become more a matter of choice than predetermination. However, we can hope that the car analogy doesn't hold too closely; there are only about a hundred different models of cars to choose from in any given year, and even a custom paint job doesn't completely differentiate one car from others of the same model. It would be awkward to show up at a party and bump into three other people with the exact same body shape and facial structure.

However, it's more likely that each body (and face) will be unique, built to order. We can already see the beginnings of such to-order manufacturing in the 3D printing revolution going on now. Provide some pictures of how you want to look, or adjust a large number of parameters – much like creating an avatar in today's video games – and then simply click the "place order" button, and wait for delivery of your completely custom body.

Many people will probably choose at first to have their artificial body match the appearance of their original, biological selves as closely as

Intelligence Unbound: The Future of Uploaded and Machine Minds, First Edition.
Edited by Russell Blackford and Damien Broderick.

possible. However, we do tend to be vain. Why mimic the aged, frail appearance of your biological body's final days, when you can turn back the clock and appear as you did at age 20? But having gone that far, the temptation will be great to make other minor improvements as well: reshape the nose a bit here, adjust the ears there, smooth the skin, and tweak the cheekbones. Similar alterations are already commonly done by celebrities through plastic surgery, but in a post-uploading world, everyone will have access to the same options and more. Everyone can look like a movie star.

The irony will be that, when everyone looks beautiful, perfect looks will come to seem mundane. People may then seek other ways to stand out from the crowd, making themselves unusually large or small, for example, or by adding carefully selected imperfections. Given the often cyclic nature of fashions, there will probably come a time where adopting a "natural" appearance, i.e. looking very ordinary by today's standards, will be regarded as more stylish than perfect movie-star looks.

So far, we've considered only cosmetic changes within the realm of standard human variation. Most people will probably stick to this standard palette; it fits our history and culture, and helps us stay connected to our deep biological past, and our place within the greater animal kingdom. Some, however, are sure to want to explore other possible variations. Inspired by classic fiction or cinema, we are likely to see people shaped (and perhaps behaving) as elves, dwarves, Na'vi, and other fictional races. The sort of people who today put significant effort into learning a fictional language and culture would have the power, and perhaps the motivation, to make those cultures a reality. Will the twenty-second century find entire cities of dwarves living under mountains, or colonies of elves in harmony with the forest? Odd though it seems to us now, such scenarios are quite possible.

Let's push just a bit further along this line of exploration. Our brains are wired for controlling a humanoid body – two arms, two legs, the usual complement of digits, etc. But our brains are also highly plastic, able to adapt to major changes, such as the loss of a limb, or even the addition of one (as demonstrated in monkeys who quickly learn to control a robot arm with only their thoughts). After uploading, it will be possible to build bodies that differ more substantially from the norm. We could become merfolk, replacing our legs with a powerful tail, and live in the oceans. We might add wings to our backs, along with massively expanded chest muscles to drive them, and tiny jet engines to our feet, thus gaining the power of flight. People living in microgravity might replace their legs with a second pair of arms. Or some people might want to try living in the form of an ordinary animal – see what it's like to be a tiger or a whale for a while.

Some restrictions will still apply, of course. An artificial body must be large enough to house the artificial brain, and any support equipment this requires;

we may not see hummingbird-sized people for a very long time. Also, the more different the body plan is from humanoid, the more difficult it will be to learn to control it. Finally, except for customers with very deep pockets, it may be economically impractical to engineer a completely unique body form for just one user. So each basic shape (humanoid, cetacean, etc.) will require enough demand to make it worthwhile to develop.

2 Enhanced senses

However, the plasticity of the human brain raises another interesting possibility. Instead of learning to use a completely different body shape, could we learn to employ entirely new senses? A simple way to do this is to pipe other senses into our existing sensory channels. Artificial eyes might shift automatically to an infrared band in low light, the extended available spectrum appearing as ordinary shades of red, yellow, and blue, like looking through a thermal camera. In the same way, we could be "telepathically" connected to close partners, and hear their subvocalizations through the usual auditory channel.

But these approaches feel like a bit of a cheat. You could get much the same effects now, by wearing special glasses (e.g., night-vision goggles) or hearing aids. We haven't really created any new senses here; we've only directed new information into our existing senses.

Instead, it's more interesting to consider how we could truly extend the range of our senses, or create entirely new ones. Could we perceive infrared and ultraviolet light, even as we still see the standard red, green, and blue we detect today? Could we feel electric fields, sense capacitance, or directly perceive information from social networks without interfering at all with our traditional senses? This might require creating some new neural circuitry. Fortunately, it appears that sensory circuitry in the cortex is fairly standardized, so by the time we have mind uploading, we should have a pretty good idea how to do this. But that would only account for the sensory input; you'd still have to learn to make sense of it all. A significant challenge to say the least, this might well prove too unsettling (or simply too much work) for most people.

3 Travel and duplication

What lifestyle changes might uploading bring? Though these will be many, an important one is changes to travel. Uploading will enable three radical improvements in travel options. First, uploaded bodies could be built to withstand higher acceleration than biological bodies can. This could be important when humanity has spread beyond Earth; many potential launch systems require high G loads, for example.

Second, when travel times are still long – for example, a several-month trip across the solar system – it's not necessary for uploads to experience all that tedium. They could spend the trip in inactive stasis, perceiving no time at all between boarding at one end and disembarking the other. Or they could choose to spend the time active in an artificial reality hosted by the ship's computer (more on these later).

Third, in many cases, it may not be necessary for an upload to ship a physical body from point A to point B at all. Uploading, by its very nature, represents a person as a large but manageable data set. This data can be backed up, restored, and transmitted like any other. So a vacation among the outer planets could be accomplished by putting your Earth body into storage, and transmitting your brain pattern to the destination, where it is loaded into a body you have rented for the duration. At the end of your trip, you return the rental body, and transmit your updated brain pattern back to Earth. In this manner, uploads will be able to travel from place to place at the speed of light, albeit only to places where a receiving station and another body are available.

However, this ability to travel by transmission has an obvious, and disturbing, corollary. Just as with other data, there is no need to delete the original copy after transmitting it somewhere else. In a post-uploading world, people are data, and could be duplicated just as easily as music or videos.

The social implications of personal duplication are profound. In all of human history, it has never before been possible for there to be two or more instances of the same person. Our experience and intuition do not prepare us for this. Duplication ties some thinkers into philosophical knots, leading them to argue that personal identity can't survive uploading at all. Upon closer examination, logical flaws in such arguments are easily found, but they still underlie the most common objections to the very notion of mind uploading.

More serious are the thorny questions that personal duplication will raise for social contracts. If one instance of a person commits a crime, must they all be held accountable? Does a marriage or business contract entered into by one bind them all? If the answer is "no," then duplication offers an easy way out of any contract or consequence. But if it is "yes," then further questions arise: how long must duplicates live separate lives before they legally become separate people? Is there a gray area where the duplicates share some legalities, but not all?

More disturbing still is the likelihood that, if left unchecked, some people will attempt to "go viral." Out of billions of people, there is sure to be one (and probably many) with the inclination and ability to duplicate themselves again and again, forming a population that grows exponentially. Human conflict often arises when people separate themselves into "us" and "them"; but no group has ever been as tightly knit, or easily identified, as a population composed of duplicates of the same person. One can easily imagine this leading to conflict, or even violence, as legions of mental clones vie for control.

Of course, most of the difficulties of personal duplication could be avoided by thoughtful legislation. Perhaps governments will decide to disallow more than one active instance of each person. Backups would certainly be permissible, but to activate a backup would require first showing that the previous active copy was really lost or destroyed. Mistakes would still happen on occasion, resulting in two simultaneously active instances of a person. In that case, some procedure would have to define which instance to suspend, terminate, or exile.

4 Population growth

Let's turn to how mind uploading will affect life on a more global scale. Many people assume that when death is solved, runaway population and overcrowding will result.

It's clearly true that with natural death eliminated, the mortality rate (number of deaths per 1000 people per year) should drop substantially. It will probably never reach zero, as there will always be suicides, religious groups that refuse medical intervention, and so on. In addition, there might be a transition period during the early days of uploading, during which not everyone has equal access to the procedure. But in the long term, we can expect the mortality rate to stabilize very close to zero.

However, mortality is not the only factor in population growth (or decline). The other two important factors are fertility rate and net migration rate.

First consider fertility rate. This is normally expressed as the number of births per woman over her lifetime. This will not be a very useful metric when gender is fluid, lifetimes are essentially unbounded, and reproduction does not always require a womb. Demographers will probably switch to measuring the number of newborns per 1000 people per year, so it is directly analogous to the mortality rate.

The interesting thing about fertility is that it tends to drop as standard of living and education (especially of women) increases. Thirty years ago, the vast majority of the world lived in countries with fertility rates at or above replacement level (that is, enough to compensate for the mortality rate). In 2013, however, 60 percent of the world's population lived in countries with fertility rates below that level. Ignoring immigration, such countries would actually be declining in population (and many of them are, even when immigration is included).

When the mortality rate drops substantially, this balance will shift again. But it's likely that prosperity, education, and equality will all be increasing globally on the same timescale, which suggests that fertility will continue to drop, especially in countries (such as some in sub-Saharan Africa and the Middle East) where fertility rates are still quite high today.

That leaves net migration rate. We'll have more to say about the geographic distribution of humanity in a moment. First, let's consider the Earth as a whole. This has always been, and is still today, a closed system, demographically speaking. No one immigrates to Earth from anywhere else, and no one emigrates away from it either (apart from the handful of astronauts living temporarily on the International Space Station). Thus, on a global scale, net migration is zero, and all that matters is fertility and mortality.

However, this will not always be the case. The solar system is a very big place; the main asteroid belt alone contains enough material to construct parklike space habitats with a total land area hundreds of times that of Earth. When the other planets, dwarf planets, and billions of smaller objects are included, the space and resources available in our star system are, by Earth standards, virtually unlimited. The most difficult part of reaching those riches is the very first part: getting from the ground to Earth orbit. However, the problem of reducing launch cost is primarily operational, not technical. American launch company SpaceX is selling launches for under $1000/pound, a 97 percent reduction compared to launch costs on the Space Shuttle. It seems likely that costs will continue to drop as competition and flight rates increase. At some stage, a tipping point will be reached where costs become low enough to open up new applications, which further increase flight rates and reduce launch costs, until eventually large-scale space settlement becomes practical. So in the long run, Earth population growth will boil down mainly to the balance between fertility and net migration – and given the scale of the solar system, net migration will be dominated by off-world emigration for a very long time.

5 Age and wealth

While the Earth's population might stabilize at some reasonable level, our age distribution will not. Very low mortality and relatively low fertility rates will result in a continuously aging populace. However, aging will not have the same negative implications that it does today. We are used to a world where the elderly are, on average, relatively frail and often ill. A large number of age-related disorders, both physical and mental, combine to make advanced age a challenge, and often a financial drain on savings, pension funds, or younger family members.

That picture changes completely with the advent of mind uploading (or any other cure for senescence). People of advanced age will be no less strong or clear of mind than any young adult; "elderly" will come to mean merely "more experienced." Retirement will be something some people choose when they've saved or invested enough to live off the earnings, and want more time for leisure or personal projects. Others will continue to keep working because they enjoy it, perhaps changing careers every few decades to keep it fresh. So, while the population will indeed grow continuously older, this has none of the distressing consequences that are implied today by the term "aging."

Of greater concern is the distribution of wealth. Already in many countries, wealth is increasingly concentrated in the hands of a relatively small number of multibillionaires and large corporations. The wealthiest 1 percent of Americans in 2012 received almost a quarter of all US income, more than double the proportion received 25 years earlier. Many other countries have similar wealth inequity. It is taken for granted that wealthy individuals will eventually die and have their wealth redistributed to survivors. What happens when death is no longer assured?

This is a complex issue, and we can only scratch the surface here. First, we already have similar issues with corporations, which are immortal entities very similar to natural persons in many respects. Corporations pursue their own interests, and in recent history, often distort the democratic process to their own advantage more than wealthy individuals do. Mind uploading is unlikely to change this fundamental dynamic; with money comes power, and with power comes the temptation (and ability) to accumulate even more. Society will have to deal with this issue regardless.

6 Settling the solar system

We have considered demographic trends that, so far, would apply under any scenario where the problems of senescence and death have been solved. Let's consider now the additional effects of mind uploading on the distribution of humanity.

As already noted in the discussion of travel, the manufactured bodies of uploaded people can be built to withstand a much wider range of environments than evolution has prepared us for. We mentioned building Earth-like space habitats out of the material in the asteroid belt. It could turn out that this is a provincial, short-sighted notion.

With no need to breathe, uploads could live, work, and play quite happily in a vacuum. There could be cities of uploaded people, or entire countries, living on the surface of the Moon, Mars, and the moons of the gas giants.

Living on Mercury would be more challenging. From the surface of Mercury, the Sun is three times bigger in the sky, and a day there lasts two (Mercurian) years (or about six Earth months). All this results in the most dramatic temperature swings in the solar system, from over 400° Celsius during the day, to under 150°C below zero at night. This will limit the choices of materials engineers can use, and make it harder to reject waste heat from mechanisms and actuators. Mercurians may find it easier at first to live underground, venturing out mainly at night or in the early part of each day, before it has grown too hot. Eventually, they are sure to design bodies made entirely of materials that can take the heat, and live on the surface no less comfortably than we do on Earth.

Venus might be even more of a challenge, in part due to an air pressure over 90 atmospheres at the surface, equivalent to being nearly a kilometer underwater on Earth. However, special bodies and other structures built to equilibrate with the atmosphere need not be especially strong, as the many deep-sea fish inhabiting Earth's pelagic zones (1 to 6 kilometers deep) demonstrate. Venus is even hotter than Mercury, at a constant 460°C, year round, everywhere on the surface. Then, of course, there is the sulfuric acid rain to contend with. By our standards today, it's a hellish environment, but it will still probably be easier to build bodies (and everything else we need) suited to that environment than to change the planet to better suit Earthlings. It certainly won't be our first target of settlement, but once we've mastered Mercury, Venus won't seem so daunting. To a properly built inhabitant, a gentle breeze and light rain on Venus will seem no less pleasant than the equivalent weather on Earth.

These are all large rocky bodies in our solar system, and as we've always been planet-dwellers, it was only natural to start with those. However, thinking ahead, we should consider that the surface of a planet might not turn out to be the most desirable place to live. Commerce will thrive on interplanetary travel and shipping, just as today it thrives on international transport, and living at the bottom of a deep gravity well puts you at a disadvantage. What if, instead of converting the asteroids into giant rotating structures with air and artificial gravity, uploaded people simply live in, on, and among them in the microgravity and vacuum of space?

This would require some changes to our bodies of the sort mentioned at the start of the chapter. We would probably want small reaction engines (thrusters) positioned at various points around the body. These might be activated by special gestures such as pointing the toes or flexing the shoulder blades, or they might be hooked more directly into the voluntary motor centers of the brain. In either case, after some practice and experience, controlling them would become second nature, allowing one to flit about in microgravity as confidently as we now walk or swim. There are between one and two million asteroids bigger than a kilometer in diameter in the main belt alone, and hundreds of millions of smaller ones throughout the solar system. Each could be a small but thriving city, adding up to quite a lot of real estate.

The biggest problem with large-scale adaptation to space is handling all the people, plants, and animals that aren't uploaded. While someday we might be able to survive without trees, flowers, and kittens, human life is certainly richer when surrounded by living beings. Since we can't expect to adapt most of these to the diverse environments we'll be living in, we will need to construct biomes that maintain an Earthlike environment just for their sake. On a small scale, individual homes might have small biomes, filled with plants and perhaps some small animals, for people to relax in when not out and about. On a slightly larger scale, there could be enclosed city biome parks that provide homes to a wider variety of terrestrial organisms. Finally, at the upper end of the scale, we might someday construct entire space colonies with a terrestrial environment, not because we'd need them to live, but just to provide nature preserves throughout the solar system. These could host a wide variety of wildlife, tended by park rangers and visited in small numbers by campers, but for the most part left alone. The same sorts of facilities could serve as havens for people who had not yet been uploaded, enabling them to live and work among their uploaded colleagues, though of course these would need spacesuits to exit the biomes.

7 Artificial realities

There is one last, somewhat startling, implication of mind uploading to consider. While uploaded people could adapt their bodies to a wide variety of physical environments, in many cases there seems no reason why a physical body would be needed at all. An uploaded person could live, work, and play in an entirely simulated environment, something like modern video games, but much larger and far more detailed.

Life in such an artificial reality would have advantages and disadvantages. On the plus side, the environment could be whatever the inhabitants wanted it to be; size, gravity, weather, even the laws of physics, could be made to order. Especially tempting might be the forms of real-time, voluntary control over the environment that in the real universe would amount to magic. Telekinesis, teleportation, creating and destroying objects at whim; all these and more would be simple to provide in an artificial reality.

On the other hand, of course, is the basic insecurity of living in a simulated environment. That simulation is being run on a computer that exists in the real universe, and from the inside, one would have no access to that computer, and little control over it. When the computer crashes or goes down for any reason, from the point of view of its inhabitants, the whole universe ceases to exist, taking them with it into oblivion. Backups, and distributed storage and computing, can reduce the risk of physical damage, but not the threat of cyber attacks. Already a multibillion-dollar industry, cybersecurity will become exponentially more important (and difficult) when billions of lives are on the line.

A more subtle problem arises if a significant fraction of the population chooses to live in artificial realities: the risk that the real universe – the one running the simulations – will start to seem less important, maybe even less real, than the artificial ones. While inhabitants could certainly make valuable contributions to such fields as literature, art, and mathematics, they'd be unlikely to contribute much to science or technology, which is grounded on experimental results that can only be obtained in the real universe. This seems like an unhealthy situation, at the very least.

Fortunately, given the great diversity of personality (and potential tweaks to our existing range of moods, desires, biases and goals), there is likely to be a wide range of opinions on artificial realities. Some people will be happy to live there full time, while others will avoid them at all costs; perhaps the largest portion will at first take a moderate stance, using artificial realities for occasional visits and vacations, but living their daily life in the real universe. The obvious risk with that strategy, though, is that people not accelerated to the speed of very fast computers will fall behind their friends and colleagues, as if imprisoned in a slow bubble. The pressure to move into the faster ranks will be immense.

8 Conclusion

We have focused in this chapter on how life after uploading will differ from life today. These differences are substantial: people will be able to alter their shape and appearance, travel at the speed of light, live comfortably throughout the solar system, and even dwell in artificial realities of their own design. It's important to note, however, that these differences are fundamentally superficial. We will laugh, cry, love, despair, strive for goals, and sometimes fall short. We will care for our friends and family, seek reassurance when in doubt, make music, work hard and take breaks, as people have done for thousands of years. In the end, despite all the changes to our bodies, environments, and capabilities – we will still be human.

14

The Values and Directions of Uploaded Minds

Nicole Olson

What values would be adopted by future humans whose minds and bodies are duplicated in – or gradually transformed into – advanced non-biological substrates? Shifting to a new substrate might bring dramatic changes in capacities, indeed the removal of limitations that have, non-trivially, characterized human existence. Post-biological existence implies the possibility of novel sensory and aesthetic modalities. It could open up extraordinary possibilities for movement and form, as well as permitting alterations in cognitive function, including increasing intelligence. Not only would uploading bring a rapid surge in particular kinds of freedom, but choices would become available that are, at present, inconceivable, and vastly more complex than anything yet experienced.

What effect might such a transition have on values? What goals might post-biological persons find worth pursuing? The situation would lack familiar limitations, so how might we anticipate the directions and purposes of uploaded minds?

Looking toward a possible post-biological phase of existence, it is difficult to find a suitable analogy, present-day or past, to reflect or characterize these new values and goals. Imagine the sudden influx of opportunity that comes with winning a $6 million lottery – familiar constraints suddenly removed, and the decision landscape seemingly blown wide open. Though not a perfect analogy, since the lottery winner is still faced with all of the present-day native human biological constraints, it does suggest something of the scale of change.

Intelligence Unbound: The Future of Uploaded and Machine Minds, First Edition.
Edited by Russell Blackford and Damien Broderick.

The purpose of this chapter is to identify some of the unique ways in which uploading relates to transformations in values, as well as to collect, and to some extent integrate, diverse yet overlapping ideas and research relevant to the question of teleology in a transhumanist/posthuman context.

First, what is meant by "values"? To clear up any possible confusion, "values" here is intended to be distinct from "ethics" and "morality." There are common uses of the word in which it is interchangeable with "ethics," for example, "these are my values," or "we have different values," where "values" means a set of beliefs about right and wrong: morality. The word "value," although intricately related to ethics and morality, should be understood to stand for something that is "valuable," where "a value" is something that an agent acts to gain and/or keep. This notion of the concept necessitates a "to whom": an agent for which the achievement and/or retention of the value brings progress toward a particular goal. So statements like "water is valuable" must be qualified both by "to whom" and "for what." It follows that value, in this sense, is neither binary, nor fixed, nor uniform, but relative to the goals and abilities of the agent. Also entailed by this definition is the notion of hierarchy. For example, as the type of biological being that I am, with the particular goals I have now, I can generally say that water is more valuable to me than vinegar, which in turn is more valuable to me than vanilla extract.

1 Uploading as a tipping point in values

In what ways does uploading present a unique scenario with regard to values?

As with the creation of human-level artificial intelligence, uploading can be viewed as a kind of tipping point in an otherwise rather stable and continuous human-technological evolution. Properties that characterize the concept of uploading include: editability, interoperability, scalability, indestructibility, duplicability, etc. Uploading represents a revision of the human-constitutional framework; people would no longer be "playing by the same rules." For one, the materials and data comprising intelligent machines need not be subject to the same kind of frailty endured by flesh-and-blood humans. Not only is radical life extension implied, but so is invulnerability to threats to personhood, as "data" backups could be made and kept on hand in the event that breakdown or disruption occurred, and posthuman bodies would be made of stronger and more resilient materials.

Editability and scalability entail greater capacity for self-improvement. One interesting dimension of scalability is speed; futurists have suggested that uploaded persons might be able to think at speeds one million times faster than today's smartest humans (Yudkowsky 2008: 333). Putting that ratio into perspective, a digital mind running at one million times the human speed would be able to equal a year's worth of thinking (supposing the human set aside no time to sleep, play, or do anything but cogitate) in 32 seconds. All else being equal, even thinking at double the speed of embodied humans would provide a considerable advantage. Truly impressive advantages in speed and editability might not be immediately available. As Kaj Sotala writes: "Digital minds might be developed, then be relatively weak for an extended time, until some hardware or software breakthrough suddenly allowed them to become considerably more powerful" (Sotala 2012: 289). Nevertheless, the move toward uploading represents a dramatic change in the landscape of ability.

In numerous ways, it would alter human values.

2 Enabling leaps upward in motivation hierarchies

It is well documented in the social sciences, in particular the field of microeconomics, that the things humans are motivated by, how we spend our time, what we become preoccupied with, and what we purchase all correlate with variables in our physical and economic circumstances: how healthy we are, how safe from environmental threats and violence, how wealthy, etc. And we understand this phenomenon intuitively. It comes as little surprise to learn that people who are unemployed or undergoing financial struggle are less concerned with whether the coffee they are buying is organic or fair trade. This illuminates a unique relationship uploading holds to values. Uploading, by virtue of the radical nature of the transition, has the potential to accelerate a move "up" in an individual's value hierarchy.

Taking Maslow's Hierarchy of Needs as an example of a motivational hierarchy, uploading can help us satisfy base-level, or fundamental, needs, such as physical safety. Physical pain and suffering and other comfort-related values, prerequisites to being able to focus on higher-level goals, would presumably be eradicated. The leap will be greater or smaller depending on predisposing factors such as age and level of disability prior to uploading, and on differences in the wealth required to invest in enhancement post-uploading. Nevertheless, uploading renders one by default better at surviving, at least within certain physiological dimensions of vulnerability, and hence frees up the individual for the pursuit of self-actualizing/self-developmental goals, creative goals, and recreation.

3 Discarding entire classes of valuable objects

Correspondingly, whether through gradual or all-at-once uploading, there will be entire classes of things currently valued by humans that rather suddenly will cease to have value. Perhaps the best way to imagine this transformation is by analogy to the feeling experienced when cleaning the house after having had a cold for a few days. A box of Kleenex, throat lozenges, a heating blanket, the collection of material objects that felt as though they were one's most prized possessions, quickly become clutter once the illness subsides. Sometimes it is even difficult to identify with one's prior emotions in encountering objects once of high importance. Similarly, recall visiting an old living space, neighborhood, or geographical region, and encountering things that at the time had considerable meaning and significance, but were then more or less forgotten.

Yet even this analogy doesn't approximate the magnitude or gravity of expected value transitions associated with uploading. Uploading is unique in how quickly large classes of materials, objects and habits would become devalued or lose their value entirely. After uploading, most products in the local pharmacy, grocery store, shopping mall, etc. would be of relatively little interest, replaced by a whole new set of desires. There is no precedent in human history for such a radical reformation of value hierarchies.

4 Expanding value hierarchies to include novel phenomena

A further change in value hierarchies would be the introduction and integration of novel phenomena. Recall that values not only have to answer the questions "To whom?" and "For what?" – they are ranked in a hierarchy. But how do we evaluate something unprecedented? Uploading will require us not only to integrate the relative value of familiar experiences or objects and capacities made dramatically stronger, larger, faster, etc., but also of experiences and things that are objectively and subjectively quite novel, and possibly orthogonal to any previous human experience.

As we move into new dimensions of experience, we will be unable to predict some utility functions until we test them, and so our decisions will also be unexpected. Consider how you might evaluate the option of novel sense perceptions. One might assume that greater sensitivity to an expanded light spectrum is desirable, but suppose, as Anders Sandberg does, that when you get your new ultraviolet vision enhancement you realize that "you are not looking at the flowers in the same way." Or perhaps you "realize that you actually prefer your childhood way of looking at the flowers" (Sandberg 2011).

As unprecedented opportunities open up, value hierarchies will be progressively extended or reformulated to include entirely new options. For uploaded persons, the opportunity for novel experience and discovery will seem endless. For instance, the possibility for more robust and interesting body forms suggests that there will be experiments with numerous different configurations of uploads' nervous systems. Robust body forms could enable invulnerability to large predators and micro-organisms on earth, and allow people to live in diverse planetary ecosystems, adapting individual bodies rather than modifying wholesale environments. One day, the question "Would I rather be on Mars than on Kepler-62e?" may be routine.

Even more possibilities will be available once people can live in virtual reality, experiencing data structures in full immersion. Considering the various experiments with environment that are possible with virtual reality, including environments designed to express creative aesthetic sensibility, the permutations and combinations of potential experience might become unlimited.

5 How can we anticipate directionality, or purpose?

It should be clear, then, that in a number of dimensions related to value, uploading entails radical change. In a context of radical degrees of novelty and possibility, however, how can we anticipate directionality or purpose?

Damien Broderick ponders the qualitative experience of the beginning of life as an upload, asking "What would it be like, this reborn life as an upload?" (Broderick 2001: 233). He emphasizes the protective and conservative sensibilities of humans: "Humans love the hint of risk, and the taste of danger and exciting novelty, but we also require stability." At first, in spite of options to become "a bush robot, a glowing Tinkerbelle, or a constantly morphing virtual presence flickering from one computer to another, we'd surely stay much as we are" (Broderick 2001: 233). Broderick fits this analysis into a larger philosophy of life, writing, "Life is the unfolding of narratives out of chaos, and those stories tend to follow a powerful logic, strongly conservative" (2001: 233).

In addition to risk-aversion sensibilities, there will be other particulars of human history that will shape the direction of the future. Robin Hanson, in his presentation at the 2012 Singularity Summit entitled "A tsunami of life:

the extraordinary society of emulated minds," applies standard assumptions from social science, particularly economics, to the scenario of whole brain emulations, asking what such a world might be like. He considers in detail different aspects of how the occupational world would alter. He extrapolates that since the wealthy would be able to afford more computing power, they would be able to run at faster speeds (even if not at the maximum accelerations foreshadowed by Eliezer Yudkowsky). This would be appealing because they would be able to accomplish more in a shorter amount of time, and hence retain their status in the economy. Running faster would also allot more time for leisure: more wealthy uploads might experience a whole day's worth of leisure in a fraction of the subjective time of their less wealthy counterparts. However, since the speed of reaction time is tied to the frequency of body part movements, their bodies would have to be sufficiently small in order to correspond with the speed at which they were thinking. Top management positions, Hanson posits, would be held by "tiny bosses," executives running at 16 times the speed of their subordinates, perhaps, by virtue of being just 1/16th their previous physical size (Hanson 2012).

So the relationship between reaction time and frequency of body movement, combined with the ability to "run" at different speeds, and the demands of larger-scale economic phenomena, could force unexpected choices of body types. While there might be workarounds to resolve this specific relationship between reaction time and frequency of body movement, we can anticipate many such mind-body factors that will encourage one set of preferences over another.

6 Resource availability

Hanson's thought experiment also emphasizes the importance that resource availability has, and will continue to have, on directionality. Often, uploading futures are predicted as landscapes of prodigious abundance, offering unlimited choices. It is common to encounter phrasing such as "the possibilities are limited only by our imaginations," with regard to uploading in particular, and technology-futurism in general. While it is true that technological advancement will yield greater and greater design control over ourselves, the earth, and the universe at large, it is realistic to suspect that at every step of the way we will encounter situations for which options will be restricted by the available resources, either of an individual, or of a group.

As a result, future directions will continue to be motivated, and choices restricted, by the need for efficiency. Incidentals about the natural world, too, will shape the directions we take. Water source locations and paths shaped the direction of our ancient ancestors' lives, especially in the very early days.

An equivalent for an uploading future might be the Interplanetary Transport Network (ITN), a series of paths in the cosmos, or "a collection of gravitationally determined pathways through the solar system that require very little energy for an object to follow" (Interplanetary Transport Network n.d.: para. 1). The ITN provides an example of how incidental attributes of the physical world might provide direction in future situations where otherwise there would be an infinite number of options to choose from. The ITN marks the paths of least resistance for travel in the solar system, and so, in a strictly physical sense, it guides the way. Just as winding rivers directed the paths of our ancestors, influencing where they ended up and what they came into contact with, physical realities in outer space, such as the ITN, may play a role in where we go in the future and how we get there. It seems likely that the economies of power generation and server locations, or the limited supplies of rare materials used to engineer upload substrates, will shape the landscape of available options to uploaded persons.

7 Teleology for uploads

Some futurists theorize a fundamental teleology of human life, and life in general, seeking to elucidate the principles by which a world with dramatically more intelligent agents may evolve.

Ray Kurzweil conceptualizes "the history of evolution – both biological and technological – as occurring in six epochs" (Kurzweil 2005: 14). He divides these epochs as follows: Physics and Chemistry, Biology, Brains, Technology, Merger of Technology and Human Intelligence, The Universe Wakes Up. For Kurzweil, "It is a fair observation that paradigm shifts in the evolutionary process ... each represent an increase in complexity," where complexity is defined as "the minimum amount of meaningful, non-random, but unpredictable information needed to characterize a system or process" (2005: 37–38). He gives the example of DNA (the step between epoch 1 and epoch 2), and how it allows for more complex organisms, because biological information processes could be controlled by the DNA molecule's flexible data storage. Further down the road is the invention of the computer, which "provided a means for human civilization to store and manipulate ever more complex sets of information," and the interconnectedness of the Internet "provides for even greater complexity" (2005: 38). The period of time between uploading/merging with machines and epoch six, then, which Kurzweil defines as the period where "vastly expanded human intelligence spreads through the universe," is especially driven by growing complexity (2005: 15).

However, increasing complexity, according to Kurzweil, is not per se "the ultimate goal or end product of these evolutionary processes" (2005: 38). And since solutions to problems can sometimes mean greater simplicity, complexity is not consistently increased in evolutionary processes. In addressing goals and products, he introduces the concept of "order": "Order is information that fits a purpose. The measure of order is the measure of how well the information fits the purpose" (2005: 38). Order is central, and he defines evolution as "a process of creating patterns of increasing order" (Kurzweil 2005: 14). Different processes have different purposes. To Kurzweil, throughout the evolution of biological life forms, the purpose is to survive. It follows that the fundamental teleology of humans, and of other biological life forms, is to become better and better at surviving, which is a process of increasing order.

If we accept Kurzweil's reasoning and the overarching theory it supports, uploading, or "transcending biology," fits within the past and far future, governed by the same underlying teleological principles. It is not, as sometimes imagined, a kind of deflection point where past order breaks down. Contrast this orderly conception of our world and its processes with one in which human whims are supercharged by vast increases in freedom and power, and we can see that the end of the era of biological constraints is not the end of all underlying patterns of human teleology.

Kevin Kelly provides a similar kind of analysis of the teleology of human life in *What Technology Wants* (2010). Though more descriptive and colorful in some ways than Kurzweil's prospectus, it is sometimes less measured. Tracing humanity back to the origins of life, then forward through the details of human-technological evolution, and then toward greater and greater enhancement, Kelly argues that what life "wants" is increasing efficiency, opportunity, emergence, complexity, diversity, specialization, ubiquity, freedom, mutualism, beauty, sentience, structure, and evolvability (2010: 270).

He details how it is that the inclination toward each of these properties is justified as a governing principle of life. In discussing diversity, he sees examples everywhere, from the total diversity of species on earth to the ever-increasing variety of patent applications and scientific articles. He argues that even though there may be upward and downward local fluctuations, in general, and overall, diversity increases. And the world will continue to diversify, in his view: "From the dawn of creation the tide of diversity has risen, and as far as we can look into the future, it will continue to diverge without end" (2010: 291–292). Similarly, specialization will increase. "Evolution moves from the general to the specific," at both micro and macro-levels. The first version of the cell was a "general-purpose survival-machine blob." But then specialized cell types evolved, and the number of specialized cells has consistently increased over time (2010: 292). At the higher levels, fabrication is becoming more and more specialized, which will continue. "With the advent of rapid fabrication (machines that can fabricate things on demand in quantities of one) specialization will leap ahead so that any tool can be customized to an individual's personal needs or desires" (2010: 296). In general, Kelly believes, "We can forecast the future of almost any invention working today by imagining it evolving into dozens of narrow uses" (2010: 296).

It seems intuitive that post-uploading life will continue the trend of increased complexity, diversity, emergence, beauty, specialization, and freedom. The very nature of the transition seems intrinsically to promote some of these properties. What insight might we glean regarding human directions post-uploading if we apply Kelly's teleological framework? Taking the observed trend of increasing sentience over the course of mammalian evolution, for example, we might infer that post-uploads would aim for ways to expand conscious awareness even further. Or perhaps the assumption that general complexity increases for and around the most vital of beings can be used to predict ever-increasing emotional complexity for uploaded persons. Whether or not Kelly's specific list is accurate and reliable, his overall approach offers a means of anticipating a broad, general teleology, working through the uploading transition and beyond.

8 Conclusion

The transition to a non-biological substrate represents a nonpareil transformation of values. Uploaded persons will surely experience radical transformations in value hierarchies, if not immediately, then as the many novel and exciting details of the future unfold. Given an unprecedented influx of novelty, it is difficult to anticipate new values and directions; however, the underlying patterns of human teleology, coupled with the fundamental values carried forward to the transition, can suggest invariants in values and which directions might be pursued. Would uploaded persons spend most of their time inside or outside virtual reality? Would there be radical diversity in body shape and form, or a concentration of similar morphologies? While many provocative questions remain regarding a post-biological future, some answers seem strongly supported.

References

Broderick, D. 2001. *The Spike: How Our Lives Are Being Transformed by Rapidly Advancing Technologies*. New York: Tor/Forge.

Hanson, R. 2012. A tsunami of life: The extraordinary society of emulated minds. *Singularity Summit*. Lecture conducted by Singularity Institute, New York.

Interplanetary Transport Network. n.d. In *Wikipedia*, en.wikipedia.org/wiki/Interplanetary_Transport_Network (accessed August 1, 2013).

Kelly, K. 2010. *What Technology Wants*. New York: Viking.

Kurzweil, R. 2005. *The Singularity Is Near: When Humans Transcend Biology*. London: Penguin.

Sandberg, A. 2011. The freedom to explore. *Humanity+ @Parsons 2011*. Lecture conducted from Parsons The New School for Design, New York, http://www.youtube.com/watch?v=oqHZ2VPi8_k (accessed October 7, 2013).

Sotala, K. 2012. Advantages of artificial intelligences, uploads, and digital minds. *International Journal of Machine Consciousness* 4(1): 275–291.

Yudkowsky, E. 2008. Artificial intelligence as a positive and negative factor in global risk. In N. Bostrom and M.M. Ćirković, eds., *Global Catastrophic Risks*. New York: Oxford University Press, pp. 308–345.

15

The Enhanced Carnality of Post-Biological Life

Max More

1 Fake fear and loathing of the flesh

Transhumanists and others who foresee ever more radical technological changes expect and recommend the use of advancing technology to change the human condition. They look forward to using new technologies to enhance their bodies and brains and, if possible, eventually transferring themselves to a non-biological platform.

The potential advantages to uploading, or making a gradual transition to a non-biological substrate, are many. Non-biological embodiments – whether located in a single object or distributed across many objects – would not be subject to the weaknesses and aging of biological bodies. While they would not be invulnerable, repairs might be easier and redundancy in storage of personal identity-critical information much easier to achieve. Leaving behind biology and all its evolutionary baggage in the form of the complex machinery of neurons and other cells, we might find it easier to debug problems, remedy shortcomings, and add capabilities. Certainly, the vastly faster transmission speeds in electronic devices will make the pace of neuronal communications appear unbearably slow.

These and other advantages of becoming non-biological should make it easy to understand the appeal. For me, uploading means extending my sensory range, refining myself, and expanding my capabilities. I look forward to multiplying and augmenting my senses. If I live long enough, I intend to exchange my single physical body for a choice of bodies both physical

Intelligence Unbound: The Future of Uploaded and Machine Minds, First Edition.
Edited by Russell Blackford and Damien Broderick.

and virtual. Whether or not this turns out to be possible, it seems eminently sensible and desirable. Yet there are many critics who believe that the desire to move beyond biology is motivated by some ignoble, degenerate, or unhealthy drive.

This criticism takes several, often interrelated, forms. In each case, these critics take it as a given that we post-bios (for want of a better term) reject our bodies. The critics say that we despise our current bodies, or we hate them, or fear them, or are disgusted by them. They sometimes portray us as obese, unhealthy geeks squatting in our parents' basements loathing our bodies, while playing video games all day and dreaming of being bodiless minds, floating unencumbered by physicality in a paradisiacal virtual reality. In this unflattering portrait, the critics may include the claim that we are fearful of our biologically driven emotions and long to become coldly rational minds calculating abstractly forever inside computers.

Is that hyperbole? Setting up a straw man? Unfortunately this absurd and unfounded belief is not at all uncommon. For instance, Athena Andreadis relates how she "finally realized why I balk at cyberpunk and transhumanism like an unruly horse. Both are deeply anhedonic, hostile to physicality and the pleasures of the body, from enjoying wine to playing in an orchestra" (Andreadis 2009). Erik Davis, in *Techgnosis*, attempts to portray us as dualists and Gnostics who look down on the physical world and who have "scant praise for the feelings and intuitions that haunt our sinews" (Davis 1999: 144).

It is easy to dismiss these caricatures for those like me who enjoy pushing our bodies through a hard workout, who delight in good sex, who savor a glass of wine, who relish the feel of sun on our skin. I know so many, many post-bios who do not fit the caricature in the slightest that it's hard to fathom where it comes from. Certainly not from transhumanist philosophy. As I wrote in "True Transhumanism":

> True transhumanism doesn't find the biological human body disgusting or frightening. It does find it to be a marvelous yet flawed piece of engineering, as expressed in *Primo Posthuman* (Vita-More 2011). True transhumanism *does* seek to enable each of us to alter and improve (by our own standards) the human body. It champions what I called *morphological freedom* in my 1993 paper, "Technological Self-Transformation." (More 2010: 144)

The same peculiarly mistaken and unsupported assumption that whoever would upgrade their embodiment must be repelled by their current body arose when I debated Paulina Borsook in the BrainTennis forum on *HotWired*. Borsook, without any basis in what I said or in any published evidence, asserted that transhumanists reject the body and the pleasures of physical sensation. She tried in particular to critique the "cyberculture," a term so broad and vague that it's hard to know whom precisely she had in mind. Probably the claim has something to it if we focus on the most extreme representatives of the hacker stereotype. Certainly there are plenty of people who feel uncomfortable with their bodies and have mixed feelings about them. Some of them, some of the time, may well deny, dislike, or dissociate from their bodies, feeling more comfortable manipulating computerized realities. Most, however, would rather *improve* their bodies than reject them, though they might lack the drive to do so.

2 Beyond either/or thinking

This claim that transhumanists and post-bios loathe their biological bodies remains puzzling. Perhaps these critics actually have no basis for their belief. They just find the desire to trade up from biological bodies so personally unappealing or incomprehensible that they have to *invent* a reason for their rejection and scorn. The actual logic behind their thinking is so blatantly bad that it surely cannot be their true motivation. That logic implies this: wanting to improve on an existing natural condition means you must fear or despise that condition.

On the same basis, if you are thinking about adding more avocado to improve the omelet recipe you used last week, that earlier omelet must now sicken you. Although it seemed rather tasty at the time, clearly you loathe and despise it. Yesterday you were at the gym and set a new personal best. But you think you can do better and you are determined to get stronger. Clearly you must think that you were a loathsome slug yesterday. The leap in logic made by the critic of post-biological life is no less ridiculous.

As I said in "The Philosophy of Transhumanism,"

> Perhaps critics have made a flying leap from the idea of being dissatisfied with the body to hating it, despising it, or loathing it. In reality, transhumanism doesn't find the biological human body disgusting or frightening. It does find it to be a marvelous yet flawed piece of engineering. It could hardly be otherwise, given that it was designed by a blind watchmaker, as Richard Dawkins put it. True transhumanism *does* seek to enable each of us to alter and improve (by our own standards) the human body and champions morphological freedom. Rather than denying the body, transhumanists typically want to choose its form and be able to inhabit different bodies, including virtual bodies. (More 2013: 15)

If I want to improve and refine my body and its senses, to transcend its limitations, that does not mean I despise or loathe it. The false assumption is that either we must uncritically and unconditionally love everything about our physical being, or else we must despise and reject it. This assumption is so baffling, so obviously false, that it surely must result from the culturally ingrained religious tradition that asserts a mind–body dichotomy. The old, influential thread in religious thought of Platonism and Gnosticism holds that you are either festering in the lowly, base physical world – a world deformed by wicked passions and ruled by evil forces – or you have ejected from your physical shell and transcended to a divine realm of non-flesh, non-sensation, pure spirituality.

This dichotomy is false and unsupported by science. Believing in it has historically led to no good and much pain and suffering. Believing in such a flawless ethereal (or anti-physical) realm, whether in Platonic or Christian guise, tends to lead one to dismiss and debase the real, physical world of the senses. Probably many of the critics of post-bio agree with this. Yet their thinking seems to have been so influenced by it that it has strongly shaped their criticism.

The obvious retort is that *even if* there might be such a spiritual dimension, why not *improve* the world of the senses rather than rejecting it? We do not have to choose between rejecting the physical world and accepting it unconditionally. We can continue to alter the physical world, as we always have, building a new virtual or computational layer, a layer still grounded in and inseparable from the physical.

The desire to alter the body technologically and to add virtual experiences and eventually to move entirely beyond biology does not imply a rejection of the body and the senses. We can enjoy our fleshy, sensorial bodies, while seeking to improve on them: to stop and even reverse aging, to extend the senses, to choose our shape and sex, and to expand the range of physical and virtual bodies in which we can live.

It is undeniably true that our biological bodies and brains are not just cognitive engines, they are engines of sense and perception. But emerging and future technologies offer opportunities for improving on and extending our natural senses. Over millions of years, the process of evolution by natural selection gave us senses capable of perceiving medium-size objects in a narrow spectrum moving at slow speeds. Evolutionary pressures resulted in the development of the capacity to taste the difference between substances likely to be poisonous or nutritious. We are relatively good at feeling objects well enough to manipulate those not too much bigger or smaller than our bodies. We sense certain kinds of injuries and pains as well as feelings of satiety and satisfaction. The sensory capacities evolved to suit our survival needs have enjoyable side effects: the same eyes that spot predators also show us the sunset.

It's important to remember that the sensory abilities we possess today evolved in response to our survival needs in primitive environments. We no longer live in those primitive environments, nor have we any reason to limit our sensory abilities to fit past conditions. We can benefit from using advanced technology to augment our senses. We can embrace the sensory qualities of our current bodies while seeking to move beyond the limitations of biological bodies in pursuit of new sensations, a wider perception of the electromagnetic spectrum, more finely tuned senses, upgraded ability to filter incoming sensory data, the ability to see microscopically and telescopically and to amplify our perceptions by using exosomatic instruments. Nothing in this desire for augmentation has anything to do with rejecting what we already have.

3 The distorting lens of the cyborg

Frequently repeated narratives in fiction can exert a powerful influence on our thinking. The almost invariably dystopic futures in science fiction movies probably make us more fearful of our actual future than is warranted. A recurrent trope in science fiction is the cyborg. The salience of the cyborg trope in our minds might be another reason why critics of post-biology assume that we want to do away with emotion, pleasure, and even freedom.

Becoming post-biological does *not* mean becoming like the cyborgs common in fiction. Fictional cyborgs are constructed for the purposes of others. They are invariably intended as weapons, their purpose externally directed and destructive. Their nature allows no room for play, experimentation, or pleasure. Real-life cyborgs are quite different. Those with deep brain stimulation implants, cochlear implants, retinal implants, or pacemakers have chosen to replace defective parts of their biological bodies with non-biological technology not to become more robotic and narrow, but to regain a wider range of function and enjoyment of life.

Don Ihde has written about the cyborg as a Baconian idol (Ihde 2008) that distorts our thinking about the possible human future. He has a point, and he is also correct to note that the mechanical parts of cyborgs wear out. Non-biological embodiments are unlikely to be maintenance-free. That doesn't mean they will not be considerably easier to maintain and repair than the complex, legacy biological systems in which we are embodied today. The unfortunate and undesirable connotations of the cyborg concept are precisely why transhumanists and other post-bios, with few exceptions, avoid the term.

We talk of becoming transhuman, or posthuman, or post-biological, not of becoming cyborgs. While there are more attractive examples in fiction, such as the *Six Million Dollar Man* and the Extremis version of Iron Man, "cyborg" tends to evoke Darth Vader, *Doctor Who*'s Cybermen, *Star Trek*'s the Borg, and Marvel's Deathlok. The Cybermen are a good example of the problem, since they are made unwillingly out of fully biological humans whose wills are utterly bent to the imperialist nature of the collective.

4 The irony of mockery

An interesting peculiarity of harsh criticism of transhumanist and post-bio goals is that it comes both from the highly religious and the harshly anti-religious. The latter is illustrated by a significant portion of responses to my recommending the merger of biology and technology in the secular humanist publication, *Free Inquiry* (More 1994). While some of the many comments expressed interest and sometimes support for the transhumanist goals I expressed, around half of them were angry rejections of becoming anything other than human in a traditional, biologically defined sense.

The irony in this is that those individuals explicitly reject any belief in a transcendent god. They explicitly acknowledge that humans are the result of a blind evolutionary process. This unguided and non-conscious process carries no normative weight. And yet they reacted against the "unnatural" nature of my proposal as if I had offended the sacred word of a higher power.

A different irony accompanies the mocking criticism that often comes from those who preach the truth of a post-mortem heavenly existence as "spirits" or disembodied "souls." There are those who deride the goal of becoming post-biological, despite its clear pragmatic benefits and basis in real science and technology, while they believe in an utterly non-physical realm for which there is no scientific evidence. Virtual bodies are not heavenly bodies, but perhaps they are sufficiently similar in some ways to offend the adherents to pre-scientific worldviews.

At least some of these individuals – those especially infected by the Platonic, Gnostic, and Pauline influences on Christianity – look forward to being released from what they see as the disgusting, corrupting influences of carnality. They may see the potentially endlessly extended senses and experiences of post-biological life as the very opposite of the pure existence of the "afterlife." In this way, their hostility to becoming post-biological is the reverse of those who think post-bios want to mechanize and crush the sensory richness of the human condition.

5 Freedom from biology

Much of the worry about becoming post-biological appears to be rooted in a belief that humans have some unique form of free will and that becoming post-biological would mean giving that up in favor of a mechanized existence that merely simulated free will. That belief assumes that human biology and consciousness possess some special vital property that machines cannot have. Sometimes the view is that post-biological beings might appear to have feeling, awareness, and freedom but that these would be false fronts, covering up the philosophical zombies inside.

Although I don't find the concept of "free will" to be useful or to adequately describe what we find special about human beings, it is not necessary to examine the idea here. What matters is to understand that we are already mechanisms – biological mechanisms that evolution and development have programmed in numerous ways. We are mechanisms who lack all but fragments of our operating manual. (I use the term "mechanism" because "machine" has the stronger implication that someone designed us.) Becoming post-biological involves exchanging a biological mechanism that emerged without conscious planning for a non-biological mechanism whose function and capabilities are completely up to us to design. Our post-biological platforms should enable us to increase our sensory range and our cognitive abilities and to choose our emotional architecture, as I have argued further elsewhere (More 1997, 1998).

Our human bodies and senses are extremely limited, as a glance at the rest of the animal world confirms. Our internal self-awareness is also extremely limited. Our understanding of our own emotions and motivations is poor, as psychologists have experimentally demonstrated. This is because the forces of natural selection rewarded survival and reproductive fitness in early environments, not deep and accurate self-understanding. Our brains evolved in such a way that, when confronted with danger, our limbic system sent signals to our cortex to move us to action. Little would be gained in those stark environments from having equally potent pathways moving in the opposite direction. We have an emotional brain rather than a cognitive brain (Ledoux 1998).

The appeal of altering ourselves with technology and eventually becoming post-biological lies precisely in the desire to move further away from mechanism toward self-control and freedom. Humans remain far too mechanical, too externally determined. The post-biological path offers greatly enhanced morphological freedom (More 1993). This means not only having the ability to choose the form of our embodiment – whether physical or virtual – but also our internal form and function. We call ourselves free, yet consider how little we can directly sense of the inner workings of our bodies and brains. Our hormones and neurotransmitters push us around, setting our moods, altering our energy levels, making us sleepy, slow, and stupid. We find ourselves feeling angry, depressed, anxious, envious, or afraid. When we decide these feelings do not serve us well, we usually find them tremendously hard to alter. Our personalities resist transformation.

As we increasingly incorporate sensors and actuators into our bodies, we will have the option to be far more internally aware. Many people, exemplified by the Quantified Self movement, are already doing this, although using primarily external devices. As we go further and modify or augment or replace various tissues and organs, we will not only be able to sense what is going on within but also modify that activity. This greatly increased ability to understand and modify ourselves has been called "hyperagency" (Sandel 2004) and criticized for expanding our range of choice to unprecedented levels. Many of us, however, will gladly accept the challenge and learn to handle these new choices.

6 Conclusion

I have argued that the desire to improve on the human body and eventually to replace it with post-biological alternatives does *not* imply that we loathe the flesh in which we are currently embodied. It does not mean that we don't take good care of our biological selves. Perhaps some individuals look forward to being coldly calculating disembodied minds. For most of us, though, the appeal of post-biology lies in the opportunities for expanding not only our cognition and sensory richness and for sculpting and refining our emotions but also for deeper self-understanding.

Finally, it should be pointed out that post-biological beings are not truly disembodied. All thinking beings rely ultimately on physical processes, even if those processes are distributed across numerous computational devices. Even the most radical uploading scenarios do not require us to abandon bodies and senses. We can have multiple prosthetic bodies, as well as any number of virtual bodies. Whatever senses are built into the bodies we choose to inhabit, we will also be able to expand our perceptual range enormously by connecting to external sensors. If we can accomplish the transition to post-biological being, the result will not be mechanization and restriction; it will be greater richness of being and existential freedom.

References

Andreadis, A. 2009. *If I can't dance, I don't want to be part of your revolution!*, http://ieet.org/index.php/IEET/more/andreadis20090515/ (accessed October 7, 2013).

Davis, E. 1999. *Techgnosis: Myth, Magic, and Mysticism in the Age of Information*. Three Rivers Press.

Ihde, D. 2008. Of which human are we post? *The Global Spiral*, Metanexus Institute, http://www.metanexus.net/magazine/tabid/68/id/10552/Default.aspx (accessed October 7, 2013).

Ledoux, J. 1998. *The Emotional Brain: The Mysterious Underpinnings of Emotional Life*. New York: Simon & Schuster.

More, M. 1993. Technological self-transformation: Expanding personal extropy. *Extropy #10* 4(2): 15–24.

More, M. 1994. On becoming posthuman. *Free Inquiry* 14 (Fall).

More, M. 1997. *Beyond the machine: Technology and posthuman freedom*. Paper in proceedings of Ars Electronica 1997. (FleshFactor: informationmaschinemensch), Ars Electronica Center, Springer, Wien, New York.

More, M. 1998. Virtue and virtuality (*Von erweiterten Sinnen zu Erfahrungsmaschinen*). In *Der Sinn der Sinne*. Göttingen: Kunst und Austellungshalle der Bundesrepublik Deutschland.

More, M. 2010. True transhumanism. In Gregory R. Hansell and William Grassie, eds., *H+/-: Transhumanism and Its Critics*. Bloomington, IN: XLibris, pp. 136–146.

More, M. 2013. The philosophy of transhumanism. In M. More and N. Vita-More, eds., *The Transhumanist Reader: Classical and Contemporary Essays on the Technology, Science, and Philosophy of the Human Future*. Malden, MA: Wiley-Blackwell, pp. 3–17.

Sandel, M. 2004. The case against perfection. *The Atlantic* (April), http://www.theatlantic.com/magazine/archive/2004/04/the-case-against-perfection/302927/ (accessed October 7, 2013).

16

Qualia Surfing

Richard Loosemore

What will happen to human civilization when we can go *qualia surfing* – collecting new experiences by transferring our consciousness back and forth between different substrates on a whim? As you wake up on a typical morning, your choice of activities for the day might include: becoming a tiger and going off to the jungle for some animal sex; changing into a body that can swim in the atmosphere of Jupiter; floating naked in interplanetary space in a body adapted for hard vacuum, while you stargaze through telescopic eyes that can see beyond the visible spectrum; swimming in a liquid-metal pool at noon on Mercury; porting yourself into a six-inch-tall body so you can go on a *Land of the Giants* expedition; or perhaps visiting a specially designed city where you check your memories at the door and live in a replica of, say, Restoration London or Classical Athens, all the while oblivious to the fact that you are in a simulation.

These activities are exotic enough in themselves, but the aspect I want to focus on here is their long-term implications: how they might seep into every nook and cranny of our culture, redefining what it means to be human. My goal is to produce a quick survey of the different types and degrees of qualia surfing, so we can begin to see the larger picture and appreciate the role that this type of activity will play in our future.

Today, even the most utopian visions of the future contain a worm at their heart: the inevitable decline of humanity into a state of boredom and stagnation. But that depressing picture is partly caused by our failure to understand that we see the world from inside the bodies and minds that we currently

Intelligence Unbound: The Future of Uploaded and Machine Minds, First Edition.
Edited by Russell Blackford and Damien Broderick.

possess, without realizing that when we become free to play with the design of our own minds and bodies, we open up almost infinite numbers of new worlds to explore. With luck, this short chapter will begin to reveal a more optimistic and expansive vision of the future.

The basic version of the qualia surfing idea is that at some point in the future people will freely transfer their consciousness into different substrates (where a *substrate* is either a biological brain or a computer), or modify their existing substrate in various ways, purely because they want to experience the sensations, feelings, points of view, or knowledge that come with being another kind of living creature. I have labeled this "qualia surfing" because the term *qualia* refers to the philosophically inexplicable core properties of our sensations that can be known only to the sentient creature that experiences them – like the redness of the color red that is impossible to convey to someone who is blind. In today's world we seek novelty by finding new patterns or combinations of our existing qualia – we go on vacation to new places and cultures so we can feel a new mix of colors, tastes, sounds, and smells – but in the future we could modify the basic qualia that we experience, so we can know what it is like to perceive the hue of ultraviolet light, or hear what a whale sounds like at infrasound frequencies, or be inside a centaur's body.

1 Fundamentals of qualia surfing

In previous papers (Loosemore 2009, 2012) I have described a theory of consciousness, one implication of which is that new qualia can be built by the right kind of modification to the brain's wiring (another implication of the theory, often taken as a *sine qua non* of mind uploading, is that if the functional machinery of a human brain is copied to another substrate, the consciousness of the original brain truly does exist in the new substrate). If that theory of consciousness is correct (as I will assume from now on), rewiring your brain to experience a new type of color would be relatively straightforward. It would involve building a new set of input pathways in parallel with the existing ones, and ensuring that those pathways end at new primitive concepts at a particular level of the concept system. This would not be a trivial piece of neuroengineering because the new wiring would have to be carefully meshed with the old, but there is no reason in principle why it could not be done by a sufficiently well choreographed nanobot ballet. To get new color qualia, the crucial aspects would be the parallelism of the wiring and the exact location within the brain of the new color concepts.

Similar new wiring could be set up for other senses, giving new primitive sensations in each modality. A simple extension of the auditory system would allow new octaves to be added above and below the normal range – although this would cause only a modest change to the way we experience sounds (we would sense a little more lowness and a little more highness). More dramatic auditory experiences could be generated by installing an entirely new auditory pathway, parallel to the existing one, connected to various kinds of sensor (radar, radio, microwave) in such a way that the signals ended in new sonic primitive concepts. Perceived from the inside, these new "sounds" would have the feel of something that was almost but not quite completely unlike ordinary sound. You could play a microwave version of Stravinsky's *Danses Concertantes* through this new modality, but it might sound both beautiful and – strange – at the same time.

Taste, touch, and smell could all be augmented in analogous ways: with new primary qualia, new degrees of resolution, or extensions to the existing ranges.

One thing that makes hearing different from seeing is that the processing machinery is quite different: a pair of serial channels in the case of sound, compared with a pair of massively parallel channels for the visual input. There are also big differences in the type of analysis done on the signals (among other things, visual input yields a detailed model of a three-dimensional world, whereas sound delivers only limited directionality). This observation leads to ideas about how entirely new channels could be designed, giving significant changes to the subjective experience. What about a five-dimensional sensory system, allowing us to experience spatial relationships directly in a 5D world? The input would have to come from a computer simulation, and the resolution might be limited unless the brain's processing capacity could be augmented considerably – it seems reasonable to suppose that the processing needed would go up rather steeply as the dimensionality increased – but in principle it could be done. Someone could enter a simulated 5D world and feel its layout and processes in ways that only have a vague analogy to the feelings we get in a 3D world.

2 Abstract qualia

Something new happened in that last transition from the idea of new sensory primitives to new perceptions of the dimensionality of space. The person who wakes up with 5D vision will report new color qualia, because the input is coming from new receptors (albeit generated by the computer that is creating the 5D world) – but what's interesting is that she would also report some indescribable qualities in her perception of the new type of space. Would these new feelings in spatial cognition count as new, abstract qualia?

In the traditional philosophical literature the concept of qualia is usually illustrated by simple phenomena like color sensations, the feeling of pain, and so on. But the real meaning of the term is that certain feelings have a quality to them that resists objective description or comparison with other things, and those qualities can just as easily be found in some of the more abstract concepts we experience. If we compare sight and hearing, for example, we can observe that even something as simple as perceiving the *location* of an object is subtly different between the two senses. (To experience this, try walking around an empty room in pitch-black conditions, using the reflected sound of your voice to sense how far away the wall is: the subjective quality of that feeling of closeness is quite distinct from the feeling of distance you get when you can see the wall with your eyes.)

I have raised the subject of abstract qualia because there are some changes that could be made to an uploaded brain that would give sensations of newness over and above the simple sensory qualia. The insertion of a 5D vision system is one example, but if we look at other ways to augment the brain we quickly discover a large array of new possibilities, some of which involve clusters of sensations that do not include new primitive qualia.

3 New bodies

First on the list of these more complex qualia surfing activities would be any that involve a change of body. If nanobots were to create for me a tiger's body with an empty brain inside, the mapping between my original mind structure and the tiger brain would involve a lot of commonality – we both have tongue, and eyes, and four limbs – but the details of how these are shaped and wired into the brain would be very different.

There are two main ways to port my mind into a tiger brain. In the case of olfaction, new brain wiring could be added in parallel to my old human wiring (a parallel set of smell detectors processed by a new set of smell-processing pathways) or, alternatively, my existing brain wiring could be augmented to handle the tiger's more sophisticated smell faculty.

In the first case – new parallel wiring – I would feel a distinct set of new primitive qualia. As a tiger, I could take a big sniff and do some tiger-smelling of the world, but that experience would not resemble the ordinary human smells that I remember from yesterday. However, if my existing pathways were slightly augmented to match the design of the tiger olfactory pathways, I would still recognize the smell of, say, a damp forest, but in some measure it would have a greater detail or richness to it. Which of these modifications is chosen would be a matter of personal preference.

There is a third possibility: throw out all of my old sensory wiring (and not just the sensory wiring but also much of the cognitive wiring) and replace it with the tiger system, leaving the old human concepts intact but not connected to anything. This ought to give rise to a much stronger feeling of being a tiger, but make it harder to experience the side-by-side comparison of human-like and tiger-like existence – I might have vague, ghost-like concepts of what it was like to be a human, but they would vanish at the touch.

After hanging out as a tiger for a while, I would return to my human body. What to do then? Presumably I would want to keep the memories of the tiger episode, but if I revert the wiring to its old state, I could end up with the same class of ghostly, intangible concepts, this time about tigerness. That might not be desirable, so instead I'd probably choose to keep a lot of the old tiger brain wiring, and, just as a human amputee is sometimes convinced that he can reach out with a non-existent limb, I might forever be able to remember those feelings of padding around on big soft feet, or swishing my tail, or extending my claws.

One implication is that collecting experiences as other kinds of creature would mean the gradual accumulation of new brain wiring. Our brains would have to grow to accommodate the machinery needed to re-create the sensations of being tigers, bats, whales, and mermaids. This could get a little expensive on brain real-estate, so presumably we would have the choice to archive some of these experiences: we could keep some faint, ghost-like impressions all the time, but detailed memories of being other creatures could be put away like old photographs in the attic. Memorabilia to be visited occasionally.

Most of the creatures mentioned so far are natural biological types (assuming that mermaids, unicorns, and centaurs are close to normal biology). But qualia surfing could just as easily involve constructed bodies robust enough to be comfortable in the atmosphere of Jupiter, a liquid-metal swimming pool on the surface of Mercury, the surface maelstrom on Venus, or deep interplanetary space.

Simple size modification of an otherwise regular human body would also be possible. There are limits to how small a human-replica body could be made while keeping a human-functional brain inside, but given what we suspect about the redundancy of processing in the brain, it seems likely that we could transfer into, say, a 6-inch-tall person who could explore a *Land of the Giants* re-enactment. Physics would be subtly different at that level because many physical characteristics of the world are not scale-neutral; miniature people would discover that their limbs moved differently, surfaces would be stickier, and falls from apparently fatal heights would be unproblematic (Dusenbery 2011).

Finally, we could also transfer into bodiless computers, to recreate the *Minds* imagined by Iain M. Banks: entities found as the core sentience of houses, spacecraft, planets, and orbitals, but capable of manifesting as androids or drones (Banks 1987).

4 Classic uploading

Everything I have discussed so far involves staying in the real world but changing the form that we take, or the way that we experience it. I hope I have made it clear that even with this real-world restriction the number of different experiences available is vast, almost beyond imagination.

That said, though, we can step things up a level to what might be called the *classic uploading* scenario, where a person's mind is transferred into an entirely virtual body inside a virtual world. Provided that enough computing power is available to support the simulation, this kind of qualia surfing would be just as straightforward as the other kinds. The types of existence, and the types of sensory experience available, would be even more wonderfully diverse – in particular it would be possible to invent worlds in which the laws of physics were different.

There is little that needs to be said about classic uploading, except to suggest that it might be less common in the future than is widely supposed. Disappearing into your own universe will have its attractions, but part of human nature is that we want to have experiences we can share with others of our kind. I suspect that the range of activities chosen by the billions of people who make up our planetary population will eventually look like a thermodynamic distribution, with very many in the cooler (less adventurous, closer to human-normal) parts of the distribution, and then fewer and fewer numbers in the hotter, more exotic types of activity. My guess is that the human race will not suddenly disappear into virtual computer worlds, leaving a silent planet populated only by the robots who manage the host computers.

5 What is our purpose?

Let's pause for a moment to reflect on what it would mean to live in a future in which we were free to spend all of our time engaged in these kinds of pastime. We do the things we do because it gets us as close as possible to being happy – and making ourselves happy means, when all is said and done, the right kind of brain activity. We especially seek the pleasure of new experiences and discoveries, so qualia surfing would give us a supply of novelty that was almost inexhaustible. Would there be limits to this novelty? Could the endless flood of new qualia become passé after a while? New qualia would be unique in ways we can't yet easily comprehend, so there really would be an infinite range of unique experiences to be had, but we must at least consider the possibility that an infinity of new qualia might not be satisfying enough.

Questions about limits to pleasure and boredom in utopia lead straight to questions about what motivation and pleasure really are. We sometimes talk about pleasure as if it were a monolithic thing – your brain either rewards you with a pleasure signal or not (Olds 1956) – but in fact the real mechanism is likely to be more interesting. The exact nature of pleasure and motivation is still an open topic of research, but it seems clear that there is low-level brain wiring that determines what kinds of activities give you pleasure, and what kinds of pleasure you experience when you find them.

Your own personal pleasure landscape is not fixed – it develops through your lifetime, and it is possible to shape it deliberately – but it does remain relatively stable in the short term. The set of things that give you pleasure today is a relatively stable part of who you are; if you happen to be a thrill-seeker, your first thousand years of qualia surfing might be dominated by a search for the most dangerous sports available, but if you are inclined toward the zen patience of a bonsai gardener, you might spend that time growing a giant redwood tree from seed.

How is this relevant to the question of whether qualia surfing might become boring? It is relevant because it opens up one more set of options for self-modification: your motivation system itself can be changed. So a person who is addicted to adrenaline sports might decide that even though an activity like gardening has always seemed tedious, she would consider modifying her own motivation system to make gardening feel pleasurable. That kind of internal change would open up entirely new pleasures, so this meta-level qualia surfing (not changing the qualia directly, but changing your scope for appreciating new qualia) would further expand the landscape of possibilities.

One implication of this motivation-twiddling is that we could select any activity that humans have ever conceived, and even though we dislike that activity right now, we know that by reaching out and pressing a switch or slider we could alter our temperament and feel a delicious thrill at the idea of doing it. Do you find it horrible to imagine changing your sex? In a blink of an eye, you could overcome that feeling and thoroughly enjoy the transformation. Do you want to change yourself to become so passionate about mathematics that you could sit down in a library with a pile of books and slowly work your way through everything mathematical that has ever been written? Any conceivable activity could become pleasurable.

6 Domains

Perhaps the most complete form of qualia surfing would involve a visit to a *domain* – a place where a group of people go to create some way of life or historical epoch, but with the constraint that outside memories are checked at the door. A replica of London at the birth of the Enlightenment, when the very idea of modern science was being created. Or a fantasy domain inhabited by magical creatures. Once again, the range of possibilities is almost endless. The point of going into such a domain would be to experience the genuine thrill of a participant – you would not be a knowing, twenty-first-century interloper watching others experience a fake seventeenth century. The domain could be set up in such a way that you were not, at any time, aware that you were in a simulation, and the key (apart from all the holodeck-like physical technology needed to support the place where this was happening) would be the temporary archiving of your previous memories so that you were not aware of the outside world. After a fixed amount of time you would emerge from the domain and resume your previous existence, but with the memories of your domain experience intact.

Archiving or modification of memories and knowledge would not be limited to domains, of course. Suppose you wanted to live for a while connected to the land, growing your own food, building and maintaining your property with your own hands, and patiently watching the trees grow over a period of thousands of years. Part of that way of life, for you, might involve a decision to temporarily forget the complexities of the world – not just getting rid of outside technology, but reducing the clutter in your mind so you did not even know that such things existed. There would be no need to erase the mental clutter, because it could be archived and then restored from time to time. And then one day, after enjoying the simple life for as long as you wish, you can decide to speed things up again, reload all the memories and jump into the next interstellar starship (or have yourself transmitted there as exabytes of data, to be reassembled at the far end).

The greatest contribution made by these domains would be their capacity to eliminate the idea of stagnation. Yes, a mind that had spent eons looking for every conceivable pleasure might become tired. But a mind that could choose to temporarily forget that it had ever heard Bach's music would have the opportunity to hear it again for the very first time, in different circumstances.

In fact, a person could go into a domain in the form of a baby, and have another chance to rediscover all the things – the music, the art, the first kiss – that had already given them pleasure. But now consider: if substantial numbers of people felt inclined to become babies again (and surely they would), and if substantial numbers of people wanted to marry and have the experience of raising children (and surely they would), why not offer to put the two together in domains where their mutual interests converged? The children would be normal in every respect except that when they finally become adults they would be able to readopt their previous memories, adding one more lifetime to the stock of lifetimes they had already been through. Would this be a steady-state solution to the problem of a human civilization that wants to be as much like it was when it was in the past, but also not continue on the path of exponential population growth? It is possible.

7 The Utopia that came in from the cold

Utopia, for all its theoretical perfection, has almost become a laughing stock. It has acquired a reputation for being a place that would send the human race into a state of bored stagnation and decrepitude. But the picture of qualia surfing sketched here seems to indicate that the range of diversions and pleasures available to the human race would be almost limitless in scope. That picture depends on the ability to choose what experiences to have, what motivations to feel, what memories to keep available, and what environments to explore. And all of that emerges from the simple notion of getting inside the network of neurons, signals, and other machinery of the human brain and either transforming it or moving it to another place.

References

Banks, Iain M. 1987. *Consider Phlebas*. London: Macmillan.

Dusenbery, David B. 2011. *Living at Micro Scale*. Cambridge, MA: Harvard University Press.

Loosemore, R.P.W. 2009. Consciousness in human and machine: A theory and some falsifiable predictions. In B. Goertzel, P. Hitzler, and M. Hutter, eds., *Proceedings of the Second Conference on Artificial General Intelligence*. Amsterdam: Atlantis Press, pp. 120–125.

Loosemore, R.P.W. 2012. Human and machine consciousness as a boundary effect in the concept analysis mechanism. In P. Wang and B. Goertzel, eds., *Theoretical Foundations of AGI*. Amsterdam: Atlantis Press, pp. 283–304.

Olds, J. 1956. Pleasure centers in the brain. *Scientific American* 195: 105–116.

17

Design of Life Expansion and the Human Mind

Natasha Vita-More

Technology undoubtedly alters human nature. Computer-based interfaces and augmentations improve physical performance, and molecular technologies can generate enhanced cognitive characteristics. The more intimate and transparent these interfaces become, the more diverse and expansive human nature becomes. This expansion requires a perceptual system closely intertwined through our cognition of and interactions with the world. Its embodied mind would be a means for prolonging personhood, yet it would not rely on biology. One method to achieve this system would employ a cross-platform, explicitly designed, whole-body prosthetic. To allow for new functions and capacities, this system would evolve continually and integrate persons across substrates and their varied actual material and virtual matter.

In any system where matter comes together, it forms physical objects that act and react to each other. The converging and diverging elements recycle and become something other, altered and unexpected – that is how the world works. In approaching this understanding, I begin by describing two abstractions.

Hans Arp (1886–1966)[1] sought simplicity and elegance in his biomorphic sculpture. The visual approach to his work was arbitrary, yet his technique was quasi-automatic in rasping plaster and engineering bronze castings. His personal belief was based on random chance (famously expressed in Arp 1933); yet he lived in a mechanized world where he felt nature was forgotten. He conjectured that "[s]oon silence will have passed into legend"

Intelligence Unbound: The Future of Uploaded and Machine Minds, First Edition.
Edited by Russell Blackford and Damien Broderick.

through the invention of "machines and devices that increase noise and distract humanity from the essence of life, contemplation, meditation" (Jarski 2007: 456). For Arp, mechanistic noise was both a mental disruption and a looming threat.

By contrast, Antoine de Saint-Exupéry (1890–1944) advocated advancing technology. "The machine does not isolate man from the great problems of nature but plunges him more deeply into them."[2] And plunge he did! In an ill-fated accident during an attempt to break the air-race record for a Paris-to-Saigon flight, Saint-Exupéry and his co-pilot crashed into the Sahara desert. Stranded for days with little water in the intense heat, he found his thinking confused by mirages. This distressing situation became the backdrop for his famed poetic tale *The Little Prince* (*Le Petit Prince*; originally published 1943), and reportedly inspired its plot. In reflecting on the intricacy of technology and the human will to overcome odds, the tale conveys our need to connect on intimate levels, even if connections can obfuscate reason.

Both sets of contrasting relationships offer insights into human nature and technology. Arp's disdain of a mechanized world and the unintended consequence of Saint-Exupéry's flight are components of a larger sphere where chance and reason come together.

1 Beneath the surface

As Donald A. Norman (2002) explains, James Gibson coined the term *affordances* for the actionable properties of relationships between the world and beings (human or otherwise) acting within it (see Gibson 1977). For example, the objects and phenomena we encounter in the world allow or *afford* varying possibilities for interactions. These affordances are shaped by experience and by the forms that information takes, which are not always apparent to our inspection:

> [Affordances] are a part of nature: they do not have to be visible, known, or desirable. Some affordances are yet to be discovered. Some are dangerous. I suspect that none of us know all the affordances of even everyday objects. (Norman 2002)

A goal of expanding life over time, space, and substrate requires that we look beneath the surface of technology and the universal norms placed on human nature to a vision of its future that *could* be realized. For all the emphasis today on mathematical equations, scientific findings, the proportions of aesthetics, and the justification of knowledge, sometimes we are duped into accepting unreliable data. Our memories are frequently selective and our very perceptions often come with built-in misinterpretations. As Gibson notes: "[W]hat there is to be perceived has to be stipulated before one can even talk about perceiving it." (Gibson 1979: 2).

Consider Arp's noise argument. One could say he made two misinterpretations: that noise levels are universal and that "silence has passed into legend" (Jarski 2007: 456). In the first case, the upper end of the human auditory range is around 20,000 Hz, compared to some other animals – dogs, for example – that hear sounds as high as 50,000 Hz, and bats, which can perceive frequencies as high as 100,000 Hz (Giancoli 2005: 323). In the second case, even if hearing is enhanced making us vulnerable to noise, people will create a means to block or prevent mental distractions of all kinds. Consider the Bose Quietcomfort® noise-canceling headset and tiny earbud, reducing about 90 percent of external noise. This type of problem-solving tendency is innate to us and hence also a design component of digital frameworks that deal with the communication chains between user and device.

Digital frameworks and mental models share affordances: they are at once functional physical matter *and* immaterial abstract thought. The processes, like optical illusions such as Saint-Exupéry's mirages, are abstract models that are optimized for our evolution – enhancing the degree of difference we can extract from the world around us. (In this instance, the mental model is associative of the cognitive model for the purposes of comprehension and prediction, focusing on how two or more processes interact, for example, visual search and decision-making). For example, when the perceiver/user applies the information within environments, both physical and immaterial, edge detection is most prevalent (Faaborg 2013). Our minds are always making assumptions about the edges we perceive – using, for example, the Law of Proximity (assigning order to elements, such as "white" space), Law of Closure (the mind completes forms that are visually incomplete), and Law of Similarity (data is distinct in relation to other data) – but it is nevertheless abstract thought that *affords* experience. Further, we must aspire to combine these perspectives with advances in the neuro and cognitive sciences, interface design, storytelling, psychology, and the environmental systems that "support analyses of information structures that are the contents of human symbolic communication and describe the contents of other interactions" (Greeno 1994: 341) that may reside beyond the surface and in-between actions.

2 Fracturing

Thoughts turn into actions as we toggle the hyperlinks between the physical and virtual worlds. Information and communications technology (ICT) is increasingly personalized and ever-present. Yet there is a visible fracturing of the personal and social behaviors of its hybrid users – a process that we might call data-clatter. Because identity is a very complex aspect of human nature, alleviating its fracturing is an everyday practice for most people who are active in cyberspace. For example, carefully assessing how much information is provided in an online profile database, being aware of black-hat hacking trends, and standing up to manipulations of social networking have become common human behaviors.

Although this fracturing takes place, it is essential to protect and preserve our thoughts, even if some are soon discarded and forgotten – like the biological body shedding its cells. In this sense, depending on location, bodily area, and chronological age, we lose somewhere between 30,000 and 40,000 skin cells per hour (Grabianowski n.d.). The mind, however, abandons an uncounted number of thoughts per hour. Now that telepresence is becoming a commercial reality, interface design has been building visual objects that are sufficiently mutable to appear as needed. The MLD Platform[3] is a type of user interface for enhanced user experience that provides a glimpse of how mechanical devices have evolved (e.g., interfaces visually depicted in the films *Minority Report* [2002] and *Iron Man* [2008]).

The questions arise: What do we need to be visible, and what elements of perceptual awareness do we want to expand outside the physical world?

3 Expansion

By "life expansion" I mean increasing the length of time a person is alive and diversifying the matter in which she exists. For human life, the length of time is currently bounded by a single century and its constituent matter is tied to biology. While life expansion seeks the continuation of persons over time and space *and* beyond the physical body, there is no current method for backing up the brain and transferring its processes outside the biological system. And even if this becomes possible, preserving the brain's efficacy will be crucial.

Given this, who might be the target user? Someone whose body is diseased and has ceased to perform; someone who chooses to upgrade; someone who wants to live well past the maximum human life span, if not indefinitely; someone resuscitated from cryonics; and/or someone who opts to exist in cross-platform environments. These users would need a portfolio of bodily systems that will function as interlaced networks. He or she may enjoy uploading, yet want to retain a secure connection with the physical world with the option to download into a bio or semi-bio body.

4 Design

Because design is an iterative process, it reworks and tests concepts to establish their validity. In uncovering what works, what does not, what is missing, and what is successful, and to keep the process going, it resembles life itself. The objectives of life expansion include developing a whole-body prosthesis as both a device for mobility and sensory perception (e.g., wearable technology) and a system that streams cognitive functions.

This platform-diverse body and its collection of apps would support multi-substrate systems. A body of this kind is the key to preserving personhood – the continuation of identity over time and space – and to organize a person's awareness/perception, thinking, and behaviors as performed in multiple substrates. The physical body prosthesis would blend advanced robotics, AI, and hybrid connectivity with digital environments and computer-based systems. The array of human enhancement features developed in its framework for a platform-diverse "Body by Design" (2013) is such an example.[4] Techniques will include robotics, artificial intelligence, brain–computer interfaces, virtual reality, computer science, neuroscience, immersive design and interface design, and whole body prosthetics, including neural prostheses. Materials could include plastics, metal, silicone, fabricated skin and hair, and engineered eyes and other senses. Likely power sources could include portable electricity-generating devices such as batteries or fuel cells, space-based solar power stations, and other methods yet to be determined.

These systems would provide the biosphere for biological systems of humans and the cybersphere for computational systems of digital persons. Autonomy is a necessary starting point because any future body design innovation, in its initial stages, will require autonomy in developing new strategies dedicated to life extension that protects users' independent actions. While persons will be more fluidly networked with each other and their environments, we will need a smart routing system that allows for smooth transitions of the mind between platforms and substrates. A caveat here is that for many people privacy is essential, so even though the fluidity of networked systems is an alluring idea, we might sometimes wish to drop out and find some alone time. These are aspects of a networked mind, as are controversies about human and future human rights such as morphological freedom (More 1993), including those specific to transhumans, posthumans, androids, avatars, etc.

Coming more precisely to the design aspect of the concept, platform-diverse bodies are needed that could function as transportation devices in the physical world as well as memory-storage devices and a docking system for identity or personhood – the aware consciousness/mind. Simply put, not everyone in the future will wish to be an uploaded posthuman. Some may want to exist simultaneously in the physical world and other environments, while others might prefer to travel back and forth between them, as well as into future environments not yet identified. Rather than being limited to one choice or the other, the aim of platform diversity is to develop a platform for users who enjoy both material bodies and virtual embodiment. This would mean that the platform-diverse device or system would have to support interfaces within the biospheric and cybernetic environments.

Building new types of experiences across platforms requires an open-ended approach with emergent relationships between biological cells, nanosystems, and AGI. Here the structure is dynamic and "emerges within a web of movement that spins between the perceiver and the environment" (Braund 2010). Much like avatars in form, but interfacing with the brain, systems will be built that form new structures and methods for transportation and communication in cross-platform environments.

The sexy part of this concept is that the body design's apps and internal and external devices can be developed with a wide-scale array of styles. Already, prosthetic devices for legs and arms have become individualized to meet the user's personal sense of style. Looking a bit deeper into the future of prosthetic devices and networked identity, the need for multi-level usability (in the physical world, virtual world, cybernetic space, etc.) demands a design specifying a smooth transition from human to transhuman to posthuman avatar (Vita-More 2012). Crucially, in emitting or transferring personhood onto and into numerous substrates and platforms, we must safeguard the continuity of identity – our moment-to-moment brain activity and sensory perception experiences that form the narrative memory and behavioral patterns of who we are. Of critical concern is what holds our thoughts together, preventing a fracturing of the mind.

5 Conclusion

Are we now not in the midst of an insurgency to alter ourselves and the environment for prolonging life? This proposition is driven by individual and cultural yearnings to defy death and, beyond simply that, to test out theories and build processes supporting the continuity of persons onto non-biological systems. Continuity does not operate like matter that recycles and becomes something other. We must preserve as much of identity as practicable, or else it will not be ourselves that we prolong.

Nevertheless, we currently exist as a complex biological system of networked cells. The fragility of our biology stands out as the single most important challenge to a person's well-being and sustainability. Every moment, our bodies are degenerating – cells mutate, sometimes for the better, but often to our detriment. And even though modifying biology is argued to be an ethical issue that requires restrictions, we continue to take human biology past the *normal* state that has been determined by universal models. All in all, biology has outperformed its own benchmarks, if not through evolution then though neuropharmaceuticals and internal and external enhancement devices and appendages.

Consider the scenario of mind transfer onto non-biological platforms. Perceptual design will be heightened in providing experiences of what it might be like to be expanded onto diverse systems. Experience design will team up with new interfaces, including the currents of gaming, immersivity, mutable architecture, 3D printing, and the atomization of virtual objects affecting the forms information takes, and into a broader spectrum of approaches. In order to do this, the engineering of identity transfer needs to be enormously advanced and transdisciplinary. It is not just an advance in technology but also an advance in our consciousness – an understanding that will historically affect us.

Notes

1 Jean Arp, formerly Hans Arp, was a German-French sculptor who founded the Dada movement in Zürich (1916).
2 This quotation is available at http://www.editoreric.com/greatlit/authors/SaintExupery.html (accessed October 7, 2013).
3 The MLD Platform (MLD®) uses an optical imaging system for simulating interfaces.
4 "Body by Design" (2013) is a video created by Natasha Vita-More and edited by Kasey McMahon. It is one of the iterative evolutions of the original future body design known as "Primo Posthuman" (developed by Vita-More in 1997).

References

Arp, Jean (Hans). 1933. *According to the laws of chance.* Artwork on display, Tate Museum, London. Image available online, http://www.tate.org.uk/art/artworks/arp-according-to-the-laws-of-chance-t05005 (accessed October 12, 2013).

Braund, Michael J. 2010. *From mechanism to dynamic structure: The reciprocity of ecological perception.* Talk delivered September 2010, British Psychological Society, Oxford University, http://www.academia.edu/1682824/From_Mechanism_to_Dynamic_Structure_The_Reciprocity_of_Ecological_Perception (accessed March 4, 2012).

Faaborg, Alex. 2013. *Presentation at Google I/O conference*, May 15–17, Moscone Center, San Francisco, CA, https://developers.google.com/events/io/sessions /326460111 (accessed July 14, 2013).

Giancoli, Douglas C. 2005. *Physics: Principles with Applications*, 6th international edn. Upper Saddle River, NJ: Pearson Education.

Gibson, James J. 1977. The theory of affordances. In Robert Shaw and John Bransford, eds., *Perceiving, Acting, and Knowing: Toward an Ecological Psychology*. Mahwah, NJ: Lawrence Erlbaum, pp. 67–82.

Gibson, James J. 1979. *The Ecological Approach to Visual Perception*. Boston: Houghton Mifflin.

Grabianowski, Ed. n.d. *How many skin cells do you shed every day?*, http:// health.howstuffworks.com/skin-care/information/anatomy/shed-skin-cells.htm (accessed June 13, 2013).

Greeno, James G. 1994. Gibson's affordances. *Psychology Review* 101(2): 336–342.

Jarski, Rosemarie. 2007. *Words from the Wise: Over 6000 of the Smartest Things Ever Said*. New York: Skyhorse Publishing.

More, Max. 1993. Technological self-transformation. *Extropy #10*, 4(2): 15–24, http://www.maxmore.com/selftrns.htm (accessed November 15, 2013).

Norman, Donald A. 2002. *Affordances and design*, http://www.jnd.org/dn.mss /affordances_and.html (accessed October 7, 2013).

Vita-More, Natasha. 2012. Life expansion media. In Max More and Natasha Vita-More, eds., *The Transhumanist Reader: Classical and Contemporary Essays on the Technology, Science, and Philosophy of the Human Future*. Malden, MA: Wiley-Blackwell, pp. 73–82.

Vita-More, Natasha. 2013. *Body by design*, http://www.youtube.com/watch?v =vVG2MbpHd4o (accessed August 1, 2013).

18

Against Immortality: Why Death is Better than the Alternative

Iain Thomson and James Bodington

1 To be or not to be – forever?

In his saga *A Song of Ice and Fire*, George R.R. Martin proposes a stark but simple choice:

> "What do you say? North or South? Shall I atone for old sins or make some new ones?" (Martin 2011: 24)

Imagine facing the following choice, no less stark or simple. Either you can undergo a quick and painless procedure that will grant you immortality, thereby making it impossible for you to cease to exist subsequently. Or else you can refuse the procedure and continue to exist with your inevitable death in your future, as well as the ineliminable possibility of dying at any moment.[1]

Which would you choose?

We think this overlooked question is crucial for determining whether you are for or against immortality.[2] Why? Imagine any techno-scientific procedure that might actually be able to grant you an immortal existence one day. You might be able to upload your neural net, for example, in some sufficiently dispersed way that you could exist online without the possibility of being accidentally or maliciously deleted. Or you might be able to back up your consciousness continually and store it in a secure location so that, in the event of a catastrophic destruction of your current body (or avatar), your

Intelligence Unbound: The Future of Uploaded and Machine Minds, First Edition.
Edited by Russell Blackford and Damien Broderick.

saved consciousness would be downloaded automatically into cloned, synthetic, robotic, or cybernetic replacement bodies (or parts) which have been made ready for that purpose, allowing you to pick right up where you left off. (Lots of other scenarios remain possible too, though variants on these two seem to be the most popular.) Let us grant, *concesso non dato*, that some such science fiction scenario for achieving immortality could one day become commonplace, a feasible and affordable part of our everyday reality. We would not concede this point ourselves without considering the seemingly insurmountable empirical, ethical, economic, ecological, and other difficulties all such scenarios entail.[3] For the sake of argument, however, let us set such doubts aside so as simply to ask whether such immortality would be desirable if we could achieve it.

Even granting that some techno-scientific procedure capable of bestowing immortality could one day become real, here is the rub. All such procedures could *guarantee* you immortality (completely banishing the threat of involuntary death or non-existence) only by making it *impossible* to permanently delete your dispersed or backed-up self, whether accidentally or deliberately, by malicious strangers or by you yourself. Think about it: If, after undergoing such a procedure, you could ever delete yourself – that is, if you could choose to bring your existence to an end subsequently – then someone else could delete you too, or it could happen by accident. This possibility is ineliminable in principle. If it remains possible for you ever to wipe out your existence, then it remains possible for someone else to do so or for it to happen by accident. In that case, however, you would still be subject to the threat of death and so would not truly be *immortal*. For, "immortal" simply means "not mortal," not subject to death, *mors*. And you are either subject to death or you are not. That mortals are subject to death in varying degrees of intensity, immediacy, etcetera, does not change the fact that, conceptually, there is a fundamental mortal/immortal dichotomy. An "immortal" who can die or permanently cease to exist is not truly *immortal*.[4]

In sum, if you could ever choose to undergo a procedure (such as mind uploading) that would give you true immortality by banishing the threat of death, then after such a procedure you would be unable to die or cease to exist. This means you cannot be rid of the threat of involuntary death while also keeping voluntary death around as an option, should you become hopelessly sick of an existence without end. True immortality, once granted, cannot be rescinded. So, your choice about whether or not to undergo any techno-scientific procedure capable of granting true immortality would be a once and for all time decision.[5] Given this, would you choose mortality or immortality, an existence with or without death?

In thinking about this question, consider the following. Are you so concerned to avoid the apparently eternal nothingness of death that you would instead rush to embrace the eternal "somethingness" of an existence without end, come what may? Or is the vertiginous prospect of actually existing for all eternity, once taken seriously, disconcerting enough to help you overcome what philosophers from Lucretius to Bernard Williams have recognized as our "fear of sheer nothingness" (Williams 1993: 92)?[6] That the alternatives – death or immortality – both seem to be *eternal* makes the decision difficult; eternity is so immeasurably vast as to exceed quantification, if not comprehension. Eternity is not "a long time," any more than infinity is "a large number." Just as infinity is larger than any number, so eternity is longer than any span of time. Eternity cannot end, not because it is outside time but because it is a name for the endlessness of time, just as infinity is a name for the endlessness of number. To become truly *immortal* would be to become endless; similarly, we mortal beings, once we meet our mortality, seem to remain dead for all eternity.

This apparently inexorable endlessness makes it surprisingly difficult to think about what we should prefer to do for eternity, even if the choice is as simple as: "Something or nothing?" And yet, as abyssal as an endless future might be, is it not necessarily *nihilistic* to choose nothing over something? No; only a being who exists can face that choice. Such a being would not be choosing sheer nothingness over something. Instead, the choice would still be between the finite life of a mortal, a life that ends at some point, and the infinite life of an immortal, a life that never ends.[7]

Futurists and philosophers of an immortalist bent often overlook this crucial complication – the fact that immortality would necessarily be endless – in order to argue that immortality would be *desirable*. Instead of trying to confront the full ramifications of a future without death, some simply assume that if you could choose to undergo a techno-scientific procedure granting you immortality, you would still be able to retain the possibility of ending your existence at your own discretion. According to Nick Bostrom, for example, in the future in which immortality is achieved by uploading the mind, death will become a "voluntary" decision (albeit a "regrettable" one [see Bostrom 2003: 37]).

This is a philosophical mistake, however. For the reasons already explained, any mind-uploading scenario that can leave room for the possibility of voluntary death cannot eliminate the possibility of unexpected or unintended death. For, in order to safeguard fully against unexpected or unintended death, it cannot be possible to voluntarily go offline permanently, or else that possibility could also be triggered accidentally or maliciously. (There is simply no way to rule this out with techno-scientific immortality scenarios.) So, any decision about whether or not to become *immortal* by techno-scientific means (including Bostrom's scenario) must be thought of as a version of the choice with which we began: Either you choose to forgo such a procedure and so continue to remain vulnerable to death, or else you choose to undergo the procedure and subsequently live forever, without the possibility of ever ceasing to exist.

Instead of overlooking this crucial complication, a philosopher interested in defending the appeal of immortality can try to deny that it makes a decisive difference. This is the tack John Fischer takes:

> I do not see exactly why the indisputable differences between very long but finite life and immortal life would *make a difference* as regards desirability. I consider this one of the most difficult and challenging issues surrounding immortality. I have argued that, properly understood, immortal life would involve a mix of activities that could propel us into the future with genuine engagement; and I do not see exactly why this engagement would disappear as we move from a very long finite life to an immoral [*sic*, he means *immortal*] life. (Fischer 2009: 17)

Here Fischer suggests that the endless life of an immortal would be just as desirable as the very long but finite life of a long-lived mortal. The problem, however, is that many of us who (under the right circumstances) would love to significantly extend our (currently rather pathetically short) lives by a few decades, centuries, or even millennia nevertheless balk at the prospect of existing for all eternity.

To his credit, Fischer acknowledges that this is "one of the most difficult and challenging issues surrounding immortality." But Fischer sticks to his guns and suggests that his argument that a significantly extended life could be desirable shows that an endless life could be desirable as well: A very long but finite life and an infinite life would both "involve a mix of activities that could propel us into the future with genuine engagement." So, is Fischer right that an endless life could be just as desirable as a very long one? Why do we think, conversely, that being able to die makes a crucial difference? Why would an individual existence that could never come to an end necessarily be bad? These are the questions we will seek to answer in the remainder of this chapter.

2 The finitude of being within the infinitude of time

The "imp" Tyrion Lannister in George R.R. Martin's saga experiences a "grotesque … sense of disproportion" during his brief stay in a giant mansion built for a corpulent tycoon.

> Tyrion Lannister had lived all his life in a world that was too big for him, but in the manse of Illyrio Mopatis the sense of disproportion assumed grotesque dimensions. *I am a mouse in a mammoth's lair*, he mused, *though at least the mammoth keeps a good cellar*. (Martin 2011: 26)

But what monstrous sense of disproportion might a being like us feel if, after aspiring to little more than a century of life, it were suddenly to find itself living forever? How might it feel to live not merely as mice in a mammoth's lair, but as self-conscious beings stretching forever into the infinitude of time? What could continue to get us out of bed in the morning? What sort of "cellar" would we need to discover to help pass the time? And what might we pass the time *toward*? What end could we hope to reach, if our existence were truly endless?

When Fischer argues that the unending life of an immortal would be just as desirable as the finite life of a very long-lived mortal, he is responding to Bernard Williams' "The Makropulos Case: Reflections on the Tedium of Immortality." Inspired by the fictional story of a woman (Elina Makropulos) who has become despondent after a mere 300 years of life extension, Williams argues that an immortal life would necessarily become "meaningless" and "intolerable" for beings like us, leading us inevitably to "boredom and inner death" (Williams 1993: 73, 82). He suggests that, faced with a choice between mortality and immortality, we should not allow our (aforementioned) "fear of sheer nothingness" to override our rational capacities and drive us blindly to embrace an endless life. Instead, we should think about it carefully, asking ourselves: Is the unending life of an immortal one that I myself would actually want? This is a difficult question to think through, as we have seen: How can one think *through* eternity?

Williams' rather ingenious strategy is to argue as follows. We would not happily embrace even an extended life if we knew that this extended life was going to be filled with pain, sickness, and suffering. We might still reluctantly choose to extend a life filled with suffering if there was some very powerful, overriding reason to do so (for instance, if we believed we were close to curing some terrible disease or completing some very important work, or if we had a disabled family member who could not live without us, and so on).[8] But in order for extending my life to be attractive to me in its own right, that extended life itself must be attractive to me. That initially sounds like an obvious tautology, but Williams analyses it as entailing the far from trivial consequence that the entirety of my future life has to be attractive to the person who I am now. In other words, my entire future life must be a life that I would embrace now, given my existing character.

This is a controversial move, however, because it turns on two implicit presuppositions that, once made explicit, are not universally shared. First, it assumes that we know enough about what an immortal life would actually be like to make a meaningful decision now. Second, it assumes that living a meaningful life requires each of us to build and maintain a unified sense of self with a strong and consistent ethical character. (It is this second assumption that would justify our current, ethically mature self in making a decision that will be binding on all our possible future selves.) Today, however, Williams' famous view that no one can have a truly meaningful sense of self without developing and maintaining a robust core of ethical "integrity" is sometimes seen as old-fashioned, and his commitment to such a view (which he shares with Kierkegaard and Heidegger) seems to be getting less popular in our increasingly fractured and fragmented (but only allegedly "postmodern") world.[9] The truth is that our lives often unfold in unpredictable ways, and Fischer forcefully objects (against the second assumption) that it is unreasonable to insist that the self I am now should get the power to reject, ahead of time, the different selves I might become in the future as the result of a series of rational decisions made in response to circumstances I cannot currently envision. (We will come back to this point.)

Fischer's objection to the first assumption is even more forceful: Williams has no argument that an immortal life would be less desirable than the kind of long mortal one that many of us would happily embrace. Here Fischer rather boldly accepts one of Williams' own arguments, but turns it to the opposite conclusion. Williams writes: "perhaps, one day, it will be possible for some of us not to age. If that were so, would it not follow then that, more life being per se better than less life, we should have a reason so far as that went … to live forever?" (Williams 1993: 81) But where Williams would reject both a very long life and an immortal one, Fischer embraces both. We will argue that we should embrace the former and reject the latter. Is Fischer right, though, to embrace immortality?

Even without presupposing that we must maintain a consistent character in order to live a meaningful life, we think we can show that immortality would necessarily be highly undesirable. Our argument will establish the undesirability of an infinite life, but not the undesirability of a very long but finite one. We think there is a crucial difference between the two cases. To anticipate, the crucial difference between existing for a finite and for an infinite stretch of time is this: If it is possible for an event to occur, then even an extremely unlikely event is *certain* to occur, given infinite time. For example, assume that with every keystroke you type, it is possible but astronomically unlikely that the tip of your finger could pass right through the surface of your keyboard. If that were genuinely possible, and you were to keep typing forever (obviously we would have to postulate that neither you nor your keyboard would ever wear out, etc.), then no matter how unlikely that scenario is, it is *certain* to happen eventually.[10]

This is not the case, however, if we assume finite rather than infinite time; so this kind of consideration applies to an immortal life but not to a very long mortal life. The reason we think this generates insuperable problems for immortality is that, given infinite time, various dead-end scenarios that would make an eternal existence into a living hell become inevitable. The converse – eventualities that would turn eternal existence into a kind of permanent heaven that beings like us would desire – is not possible, nor even conceivable (something Williams establishes), and so will never happen even in an infinite life. As a result, there is nothing to stop an endless life from necessarily becoming torturous eventually, which is why we should reject immortality. Or so we will now argue, building on some of Williams' insights and supplementing them with some Kierkegaardian and Heideggerian considerations.

Think of it this way: If I live forever, then either (1) I will remain the same person throughout eternity or (2) I will not. Let us start with alternative 1. If I will remain the same person, then Williams thinks I am doomed to boredom and meaninglessness eventually. Fischer tries to resist this move by arguing for the idea of endlessly "repeatable pleasures" (Fischer 2009: 85), experiences that supposedly could be repeated endlessly without ever ceasing to give us pleasure. As possible examples, Fischer mentions "the pleasures of sex, of eating fine meals and drinking fine wine, of listening to beautiful music, of seeing great art, and so forth" (2009: 85). Unfortunately, we have probably all had the experience of playing our favorite music, watching our favorite film, or reading our favorite book until we could not stand it any longer, and Fischer himself points out that we quickly get sick of even the finest meal if we eat it too often. Williams invokes the suggestive image of "Don Juan in Hell" (Williams 1993: 87), and where an eternal life is concerned, there would probably be a kernel of truth in that cynical old adage, "Show me the most sexually attractive people in the world, and I'll show you someone who is sick of having sex with them."

Fischer suggests that we will not get sick of such experiences if we can vary and space them out sufficiently, so that they can keep us satisfied throughout an endless life. The problem here is that, as Fischer admits, we might not be able to vary and space out such experiences sufficiently to keep them fresh and appealing forever. At some point, we might become permanently sick of such experiences or they might become permanently unavailable to us. And if it is even possible that such experiences might disappear or permanently cease to satisfy us, then, no matter how improbable such an outcome may seem to us now, it will *necessarily* occur, given infinite time.

Fischer responds by asserting that, even if the pleasure of some experiences can become exhausted (or, we would add, if those experiences can become unavailable or otherwise impossible for us to engage in), there are still other meaningful experiences that cannot ever become exhausted. Fischer writes: "surely, the deep and resonant rewards of spiritual and religious experience would not somehow become wooden or etiolated, if part of an endless life" (Fischer 2009: 89). The problem, again, is that there is no way to be so sure about this. (It is difficult not to read Fischer's "surely" as a *denegation*, that is, as a public attempt to exorcise a doubt that in fact reveals it – as in Freud's famous example: "I have no idea what my dream means, Doctor; I only know it was not about my mother.") We cannot eliminate the possibility that we might eventually exhaust the meaning of even the most profound experiences we know of, if we lived forever.

Indeed, Kierkegaard and Heidegger suggest that human beings' most abiding sources of meaningfulness come not from endlessly repeating certain profound experiences – which, sadly, sometimes does wear out their appeal – but, instead, from our struggle to stay true to what those experiences partly disclosed to us in the first place. We keep the meaning of such profound events alive by *struggling* to continue to unfold and so stay true to them in our lives, and such struggles can and sometimes do fail. We take it that this is why Heidegger famously insists that *being is finite*; as far as we can tell, the meaning of such profound experiences is inexhaustible for us mortals, but we have no way of knowing that truly immortal beings might not eventually exhaust their meaning. In our view, the fact that our otherwise tragic finitude makes meaning inexhaustible for us mortals is part of what allows us to embrace our mortality (see Thomson 2011a: 75–77, 217–220).

We think Fischer fails to take seriously the challenge he raises when he mentions Kierkegaard's famous example of the "aesthete" who pursues a complex strategy of "crop rotation," cycling through new experiences in various combinations in hopes of keeping his life endlessly fresh and exciting. Kierkegaard's point is that even such a clever strategy can only postpone the profound disillusionment that comes from the pursuit of novelty, since we can and do get sick of even the most intensely pleasurable experiences. What the aesthete learns from the implosion of this strategy is that we need more from life than the intense feeling of being alive. This catalyzes the aesthete's transformation into a higher "stage" on life's path, namely, the "ethical" sphere of existence, in which his life's meaning comes from his unconditional commitment to some ruling principle (e.g., deontology or consequentialism). But as Aristotle already saw, life at its most demanding requires a skillful responsiveness that transcends the application of all such life-guiding principles. (This is also why consciousness cannot be programmed by traditional means; see Dreyfus 1992.) So unconditional adherence to an ethical principle fails as well, and the implosion of the ethical leads to the "religious" sphere of existence, in which one puts one's unconditional faith in God, who can work miracles to resolve the otherwise irresolvable contradictions that make life absurd and lead us to despair. Because the kind of techno-scientific immortality scenarios we are considering (such as mind uploading) need to obey the rational dictates of programming, they seem to rule out such miracles. So Kierkegaard's solution (or at least the one suggested by his pseudonyms [see Kierkegaard 2009]) is not likely to be of much help here.

So, again, however improbable it might be that we would eventually exhaust even our most profound sources of meaning if we lived forever, if that is possible (and we see no credible way to deny it), then it will necessarily occur, given infinite time. This, we take it, is the deep point behind Williams' assertion that: "Nothing less will do for eternity than something that makes boredom *unthinkable*" (Williams 1993: 87).

Williams' own argument that eternal life would necessarily become boring is not convincing because of his presupposition that living a meaningful life requires us to build and maintain a mature, relatively unchanging ethical character. What remain right about his view, however, are the weaker presuppositions (shared with Heidegger 1962) that beings like us cannot live meaningful lives without some guiding project or hope about the future that can organize our lives and make them meaningful, and that in order for such a guiding hope or life-project itself to be meaningful, it has to be possible for it to succeed or fail. As Williams puts it, "If he can regard this future life as an object of hope, then equally it must be possible for him to regard it with alarm, or depression, and – as in the simple pain case [in which one faces a future filled with overriding pain] – opt out of it" (Williams 1993: 85). Williams shares this basic premise with Heidegger, for whom our defining "commitments are essentially risky" (Haugeland 2013: 186).

Unfortunately (and Williams never makes this point explicit), if it is indeed possible for our defining hope or life-project either to succeed or fail, then, in the eternity of time, it necessarily will either succeed, leaving us first fulfilled and then bored, or else fail, leaving us bereft and hopeless. When the hope that has been making my life meaningful either fails or is fulfilled, then I have to be able to bring that life to an end or else remain trapped in hopelessness forever.

Is this sufficient to show that I must be able to die in order to avoid the torment of eternal hopelessness? Only if we accept Williams' controversial presuppositions that my character must remain unified and that it was my old pursuit of a life project or defining hope that unified my character and made my life meaningful. But why not instead allow – with Kierkegaard, Heidegger, Levinas, Eric Erickson, and others – that a new or transformed life project, and so a new meaningful sense of self, can emerge out of the fulfillment or collapse of my old self's defining hope? When we allow for this possibility of existential rebirth – as we should, since such a death and rebirth of the self happens within even some mortal lives (see Lear 2006; Thomson 2004, 2009), and actuality entails possibility – then we can conceive of an immortal life continuing to be meaningful even after the fulfillment or collapse of its previous life project or defining hope. As a result, an immortal being could conceivably cycle through an endless succession of such selves, each organized into a coherent and meaningful identity by the new life-project born out of the collapse of the old one. This possibility (neglected by Williams) brings us to alternative 2 above, in which I do not remain the same person throughout all eternity.

The problem is that alternative 2 leads us into a dilemma: If I do not remain the same person throughout the infinity of time, then at least one of two undesirable outcomes becomes inevitable. First, it is possible that (2*a*) I will become no self at all; for instance, I might immediately or eventually dissolve into pure flux or meld into oneness with all things as my consciousness is dispersed across time or cyberspace. In such a case, however, I will no longer be "a person but [merely] a phenomenon," as Williams nicely puts it (Williams 1993: 86). Williams' implication is that such a dispersed non-self would not count as an immortal life in any desirable sense, and this seems right to us. Consider: If you are asked whether you would like to undergo a procedure (some mind-uploading scenario, for example) that would make you "one with the universe" – but at the price of losing all the definition and distinctiveness that allows you to exist *as a self* – would you accept that offer?

Why would you, unless you believed the rest of your life was likely to be filled with suffering, or were already convinced (with many Buddhists, Anaximander, and other nihilists) that all finite existence is meaningless? We reject that nihilistic view of a finite human life (and instead believe that many of our lives are full of meaning not despite but because of their finitude [see Thomson 2011a: chs. 3 and 8]). So we think the permanent annihilation of the self is too high a price to pay for immortality. The paradoxical logic of such an exchange reminds us of O. Henry's *The Gift of the Magi*, taken to an absurd conclusion: You can buy immortality, but the cost is the very self that wanted it as well as the possibility of ever having any meaningful sense of selfhood again. Why choose such a self-undermining alternative? (For the same reason, an eternity spent frozen in some amazing feeling would be no better.) Granted, it might well be worth experiencing the *becoming* one with the universe (at least up to the point where such a process can meaningfully be experienced). But at least one of us believes (with Epicurus and Heidegger) that this is what demise will probably be like, anyway, so long as we are awake to experience it, and in so far as it can be meaningfully experienced. (On this view of demise, see Thomson 2013.) So, while it might be worth giving up some life in order to undergo the ultimately paradoxical experience of demise, that is quite different from doing so in order to live forever without a self.

Instead of permanently losing the self through dispersion (into oneness or nothingness), there is a second way I might maintain a meaningful sense of self throughout eternity without remaining the same self forever. Through an unending succession of defining life-projects (in which a new or transformed life-project emerges out of the collapse of my old one, repeatedly giving my life new or renewed purpose), I could (2*b*) cycle through all the selves that are possible for me to become during the endless eternity of time. Here again problems abound, however. For example, if it is possible for me to evolve into someone whom the person I am now would reject as (2*b*1) morally despicable or (2*b*2) otherwise abhorrent, then in the infinity of time such a possibility, no matter how remote, will eventually become an actuality. 2*a* would be one example of 2*b*2; other examples could include all manner of dead-end scenarios in which eternity becomes an endless hell of suffering without hope of remission. For, in order for eternity not to become hopelessly tedious, I could eventually have to pursue the kind of novel experiences that would lead me away from the self I am now, and which could finally prove hopelessly tedious (or otherwise terrible) in turn. (We see no way to rule out such possibilities on principle without reintroducing Williams' untenably strong presuppositions about the unity and stability of the self, which would take us back to the problems of the first alternative, which has already been shown to be a dead end.)

As for 2*b*1, Fischer comes close to biting this bullet when he suggests that, if we can become a person we would now despise one step at a time, where each step toward that self was reasonable given the step that preceded it, then we have no reason to resist becoming that despicable person ahead of time (Fischer 2009: 89–91). Fischer could even argue (though he does not) that, just as even a terribly shameful moment diminishes but does not necessarily ruin an otherwise meaningful mortal life, so a shameful millennium or two might not ruin the life of an immortal. But, again, if an evolution of the self into a person so abhorrent that having become that kind of person would ruin eternity is possible, then, in the infinity of time, it will happen. Here we can feel the force of Williams' point: Who would embrace such an evolution of the self and agree to undergo it ahead of time? How afraid of the nothingness of death would you have to be to choose to embrace a life in which you are doomed to become an evil or otherwise despicable person (by the lights of your own, mature judgment)?[11]

Most of us are familiar with the example of the death camp inmate who is able to survive only so long as he helps his captors murder his fellow prisoners. Obviously the urge to survive at any cost is strong enough that people sometimes do choose such a horrible life, but few of us would argue that they are right to do so, nor would we agree ahead of time to voluntarily undergo such a fate ourselves merely in order to survive. There are fates worse than death, as Socrates famously taught (in the *Apology*), and becoming a person we despise or abhor is a classic example of such a hellish fate. Why would someone choose immortality knowing they were fated to such hells?[12] Why, other than a powerful but irrational fear of nothingness, or a false belief that more life is better even if the addition is bad?

It might still be worth hoping that conscious life (or at least life in some form) will find a way to survive forever. It is unclear how that could possibly happen, given the finitude of matter and the infinitude of time, but it is still early in the game (and some of the axiomatic assumptions of our best science could turn out to be incorrect). Such hope, even if it is ultimately misplaced, might help us continue to find ways of extending the limits of a life worth living. We have argued, however, that the endless life of an immortal would necessarily fail to qualify as a life worth living. So, were we ever to face that choice with which we began, we think living with death remains preferable to the alternative.

Notes

1 We mean "death" here in the ordinary sense (which Heidegger [1962] confusingly calls "demise"), viz., the apparently permanent end of each of our existences that seems to accompany the cessation of our biological life functions. (On the difference between "death" and "demise" for Heidegger, and why we need not fear the latter, see Thomson 2013.)

2 A recent Pew research poll found that when people are asked "whether they, personally, would choose to undergo medical treatments to slow the aging process and live to be 120 or more," 56 percent of US adults say "no" (and only 38 percent say "yes"), despite the fact that 68 percent of those polled believe "most people" would say "yes" (see Pew 2013). The most obvious problem here is that the presumption that life extension will be accomplished by medical procedures that "slow the aging process" suggests an extended old age (with at least some of its attendant health problems) rather than an extension of peak health and fitness (with all their benefits and attractions). But life extension presents some different issues than immortality, and it is the latter that we have chosen to focus on here.

3 Hackers usually stay one step ahead of security, which is one of the reasons we would wager that true immortality will never be empirically achievable by technological means. Another more telling reason is that it is not clear how consciousness can survive infinitely in a universe in which all forms of matter (at least) only exist for finite spans of time. But we recognize that it is much too early in the game to consider such objections decisive, and we feel confident that considerable life extension will be achieved if humanity (or its post-human descendants) survives long enough. Still, we think such life extension may be indefinite but not infinite: Conscious beings will never truly banish the threat of death. We worry, moreover, that the longer we survive the less likely our existences are to continue to resemble the human lives that so matter to us now.

4 Compare the Gods in Wagner's Ring cycle (who are described as immortal but then learn to die) with the "immortal" protagonist in Neil Gaiman's *Sandman* comic series (who arranges for his own death only to have another version of himself reborn). Of course, one might falsely believe oneself to be immortal,

only to find out that one was wrong. (This seems to be what happens to the Gods in the Ring cycle.) Indeed, this seems much more likely than that anyone would ever achieve true immortality. Moreover, even a truly immortal being might still remain subject to "death" in Heidegger's sense; i.e., its particular projects could collapse into meaninglessness (as happens to Dream in *Sandman*). The likelihood of existential world collapse might decrease as one's life-span increases, assuming one learns to cope with disasters better for having gone through them many times. But the opposite is possible too; think of an immortal being exhausted to the point of brittle frailty by an endless existence that has long since grown torturous in its inexorability. All such complications notwithstanding, an immortal cannot die in the ordinary sense.

5 Nietzsche (1974) famously countenances a similar scenario, in which one must decide for all time whether to affirm the endless repetition of one's own life. But Nietzsche's scenario presupposes circular rather than linear time and so leads to paradoxes about free will (among other difficulties) which we need not discuss here.

6 Our fear of nothingness is a "misplaced" but "not unfounded" fear, since it can indeed happen to us that we become nothing while still existing, and this is (for Heidegger) the real source of our anxiety about demise (see Thomson 2013: 281).

7 And one can embrace mortality and reject the quest for immortality as part of the struggle against nihilism. Nietzsche himself taught that if we want to avoid nihilism, then we should learn to embrace our lives in their finitude, rather than believing that our lives must be extended into an immortal beyond in order to be meaningful. But Nietzsche's view presupposes that such immortality is impossible actually to achieve, so that the vain quest for it obscures the meaning inherent in our finite lives. We think Nietzsche is probably right about this, but prefer to take a different tack here so as to make a direct rather than an indirect argument against immortality. (For more on Nietzsche's critique of any appeal to a "transcendent beyond," see Thomson 2011b.)

8 Francis Ford Coppola's beautiful film *Youth Without Youth* (2007) meditates thoughtfully on a version of the second scenario, ultimately suggesting that, in the quest to live a meaningful life, finding love is more important than completing a great work.

9 To be fair, we should note that Williams' "Reflections on the Tedium of Immortality" was originally published in his book *Problems of the Self*, in which he argues for the premises that essay presupposes. On the widely shared understanding of "postmodernity" in terms of the fragmentation of subjectivity (a sense of postmodernity that Heidegger, like Williams, would resist), see Thomson 2011a: ch. 4.

10 The famous empirical objection to Nietzsche's doctrine of eternal recurrence is not apposite here, because it merely points out that an outcome that is not possible – such as the recurrence of a non-recurring pattern like *pi* – will never take place, even given infinite time.

11 Part of what makes Fischer's analogy misleading is that a young person's resistance to future changes in their own character may be arbitrary in a way that

such resistance in a mature person with a stable character need not be. We might even suggest that the "Freudian typo" in the long quotation from Fischer above (his perhaps telling substitution of "immorality" for "immortality") suggests a repressed awareness of the real force of this problem (viz., that an immortal version of our self will eventually become someone whom the self we are now would reject on good moral grounds).

12 We have occasionally used the terms "heaven" and "hell" in a colloquial sense. But if we are right that an immortal life would necessarily be undesirable, then this presents a prima facie challenge to our ordinary conceptions of the Christian "Heaven" as an eternal afterlife. How, exactly, could any kind of endless existence fail to become torturous eventually? In Christian terms, how can Heaven avoid turning into Hell? Of course, theologians may try to bake endless happiness into the very definition of an eternal afterlife, for example, by simply stipulating that being in God's presence is blissfully timeless (a very different conception of "eternity" than the one we have been employing) or otherwise intrinsically satisfying (solutions which risk begging the question), or else by appealing to a mysterious, omniscient, and omnipotent God who would play the ultimate party host, as it were, endlessly varying our experiences or even altering our natures so that we never grow tired of Heavenly existence. Our primary target here has been techno-scientific immortality scenarios, but even with more fantastic scenarios, it is difficult to conceive of an immortal life as attractive without depriving immortal individuals either of their identity or of the knowledge that they are immortal, and this seems fairly telling against the appeal of immortality for a particular individual. (Theologians may also worry that such scenarios risk turning the omnipotent God into a deceiver, benevolent or otherwise. They also need to explain how the existence of such a God could itself fail to become torturous, without falling into a regress.) Here, moreover, one can see why the Christian-affiliated Templeton Foundation awarded Fischer $5 million to develop his argument that immortality is not necessarily bad. For, if he were right, then Heaven need not necessarily become Hell. If we are right, however, then giving individuals an endlessly protracted, immortal existence would inevitably doom them to a living hell.

References

Bostrom, Nick. 2003. *The transhumanist FAQ: A general introduction*, Version 2.1, http://www.transhumanism.org/resources/FAQv21.pdf (accessed September 2 2013).

Dreyfus, Hubert L. 1992. *What Computers* Still *Can't Do: A Critique of Artificial Intelligence*. Cambridge, MA: MIT Press.

Fischer, John Martin. ed. 1993. *The Metaphysics of Death*. Stanford: Stanford University Press.

Fischer, John Martin. 2009. *Our Stories: Essays in Life, Death, and Free Will*. Oxford: Oxford University Press.

Haugeland, John. 2013. *Dasein Disclosed: John Haugeland's Heidegger*, ed. Joseph Rouse. Cambridge, MA: Harvard University Press.

Heidegger, Martin. 1962. *Being and Time*, trans. J. Macquarrie and E. Robinson. New York: Harper & Row. (1st pub. 1927.)

Kierkegaard, Søren. 2009. *Concluding Unscientific Postscript*, trans. Alastair Hannay. Cambridge: Cambridge University Press. (1st pub. 1846.)

Lear, Jonathan. 2006. *Radical Hope: Ethics in the Face of Cultural Devastation*. Cambridge, MA: Harvard University Press.

Martin, George R.R. 2011. *A Dance with Dragons. Book Five of A Song of Ice and Fire*. New York: Bantam Books.

Nietzsche, Friedrich. 1974. *The Gay Science: With a Prelude in Rhymes and an Appendix of Songs*, trans. Walter Kaufmann. New York: Vintage Books. (1st pub. 1882.)

Pew. 2013. Living to 120 and beyond: Americans' views on aging, medical advances and radical life extension. *Pew Research Religion and Public Life Project*, August 6, http://www.pewforum.org/2013/08/06/living-to-120-and-beyond-americans-views-on-aging-medical-advances-and-radical-life-extension/ (accessed August 6, 2013).

Thomson, Iain. 2004. Heidegger's perfectionist philosophy of education in *Being and Time*. *Continental Philosophy Review* 37(4): 439–467.

Thomson, Iain. 2009. Rethinking Levinas on Heidegger on death. *The Harvard Review of Philosophy* 16: 23–43.

Thomson, Iain. 2011a. *Heidegger, Art, and Postmodernity*. Cambridge: Cambridge University Press.

Thomson, Iain. 2011b. Transcendence and the problem of otherworldly nihilism: Taylor, Heidegger, Nietzsche. *Inquiry* 54(2): 140–159.

Thomson, Iain. 2013. Death and demise in *Being and Time*. In Mark A. Wrathall, ed., *The Cambridge Companion to Heidegger's* Being and Time. New York: Cambridge University Press, pp. 260–290.

Williams, Bernard. 1993, The Makropulos case: Reflections on the tedium of immortality. In John Martin Fischer, ed., *The Metaphysics of Death*. Stanford: Stanford University Press, pp. 73–92. (1st pub. in Bernard Williams, *Problems of the Self*. Cambridge: Cambridge University Press, 1973, pp. 82–100.)

19

The Pinocchio Syndrome and the Prosthetic Impulse

Victor Grech

In this book the main emphasis is twofold: on autonomous machine intelligence, and on mind uploading. These can be viewed as two merging paths by which supercomputers and human minds will intersect: independent mentalities arising from devices built first by humans and then flourishing in their own new realm, and machine substrates that house minds which once existed only inside flesh-and-blood bodies. Interesting light is cast on this intersection by the treatment in popular media fiction of two variants: machine intelligence in a humanoid body craving human identity, and the kidnapping of organic minds into a part-machine part-biological cyborg collective where identity is subsumed into a vast hive unity. There are deep roots to this apparent dichotomy, and their exploration in the science fiction franchise *Star Trek* has influenced public attitudes to both AI and mind uploading or capture.

The desire to become human, henceforth referred to as the Pinocchio syndrome, is depicted frequently in literature, a desire eponymously expressed by Pinocchio, a wooden toy boy who wished to become a human boy (Collodi 1883). This desire was also obliquely expressed by Nick Chopper, the Tin Woodman in *The Wonderful Wizard of Oz* (Baum 1899), who was cursed by the Wicked Witch of the East, such that his axe became enchanted and hacked him to pieces. His limbs were replaced by tin prostheses, as was his heart, preventing him from loving his fiancée.

Consequently, his wish for a heart, and hence emotions, indirectly expresses a yearning to reattain his humanity, a desire whose connotations

---

Intelligence Unbound: The Future of Uploaded and Machine Minds, First Edition.
Edited by Russell Blackford and Damien Broderick.

will be amplified later in this chapter. This trope is reiterated in "The Frog Prince," "Beauty and the Beast," "The Little Mermaid," and numerous other tales wherein the main character has his or her humanity cursed away. Indeed, the 2009 Disney movie *The Princess and the Frog* features a song called "When We're Human."

On the other hand, the requirement for prostheses in order for one to continue functioning within society is as old as mythology, as evinced by Hephaestus, the son of Hera and Zeus, who was lame (possibly suffering from clubfoot, a form of talipes, a congenital malformation that causes internal rotation of the foot at the ankle joint), and who walked with the aid of a crutch, a primitive type of prosthesis. He also constructed golden maidens to help him in his labors in his forge, as well as Talos, a giant bronze proto-robot who guarded king Minos' Crete by circling the island's perimeter, throwing rocks with superhuman strength at threatening ships (Hard 2004: 167).

While prostheses might be essential for dealing with medical conditions, Smith and Morra have averred that "our modern western culture has a 'prosthetic impulse' " (2006: 4), an urge to augment the human body, which N. Katherine Hayles refers to as our "original prosthesis we all learn to manipulate, so that extending or replacing the body with other prostheses becomes a continuation of a process that began before we were born" (1999: 3).

The notion of such transhuman transformation was famously mooted by the British scientist J.D. Bernal, who proposed that

> [n]ormal man is an evolutionary dead end; mechanical man […] is actually more in the true tradition of a further evolution. […] Connections between […] minds would tend to become a […] permanent condition until they functioned as dual or multiple organisms. […] But the multiple individual would be, barring cataclysmic accidents, immortal. […] Finally, consciousness itself may end or vanish in a humanity that has become completely etherialized, losing the close-knit organism, becoming masses of atoms in space communicating by radiation, and ultimately perhaps resolving itself entirely into light. (1969: 42–43)

One potential route or intermediate step for such transformation is through cyborg transformation, that is, cybernetic organisms, organic creatures that exploit technology in order to utilize mechanical parts that enhance their abilities. The term "cyborg" was proposed in 1960 by Clynes and Kline, whose article in *Astronautics* was pragmatically blurbed:

> Altering man's bodily functions to meet the requirements of extraterrestrial environments would be more logical than providing an earthly environment for him in space […] Artifact-organism systems […] are one possibility. (1960: 26)

The concept was further popularized by the publication in 1985 of Donna Haraway's "A Manifesto for Cyborgs," and ever since, the cyborg has evolved in diverse disciplines including literature, film, sociology, cybernetics, and medicine. The cyborg questions and assimilates the differences between the sentient and the non-sentient, the human and the non-human, and epitomizes the demolition of the frontiers between social, ethical, legal, and technological issues ranging from disability to genetic engineering to computer privacy (Haraway 1985: 65–108), to "an erasure of individuality and mortality" (Bernal 1969: 47).

Fredric Jameson notes that our potential transhuman transformation, one in which "some altogether unrecognizable 'human nature' would take the place of this one," has caused humanity significant concern (Jameson 2005: 174), an apprehension reflected in science fiction (SF). Smith and Morra have amplified this belief, stating that

> to a perhaps worrying extent, "the prosthetic" has taken on a life of its own. Following closely on the heels of [...] "Cyborg Manifesto" in the 1980's, as well as by developments in the cultural studies of science and technology, science fiction cinema and literature, transplant technology, artificial intelligence, virtual reality, postmodern warfare, and so on – "the prosthetic" has similarly begun to assume an epic status that is out of proportion with its abilities to fulfil our ambitions for it. (2006: 2)

This chapter will show that, while SF has depicted the extreme embrace of the "prosthetic impulse," most notoriously in *Star Trek*'s "Borg," this is used as a warning of the potential Faustian consequences of such tendencies. The *Star Trek* franchise has also highlighted the converse, the Pinocchio syndrome, a reverse prosthetic impulse, most notably in the android Commander Data. (The Pinocchio syndrome described in this chapter is not to be confused with the disease envisioned in *The Pinocchio Syndrome* [2003] by David Zeman; this fictional condition causes paralysis and fusion of the extremities such that they resemble hooves.)

This naturally raises the question of what it means to wish to become human, and SF seems to focus on two aspects: the biological component, that is, the actual replacement of original body parts (limbs, organs, and senses) with human counterparts, and the mental and psychological aspects. Ned Block succinctly summarizes the dilemma, since

> [t]he root of the epistemic problem is that the example of a conscious creature on which the science of consciousness is inevitably based is us (where "us" can be construed to include nonhuman creatures that are neurologically similar to humans). But how can science based on us generalize to creatures that do not share our physical properties? It would seem that a form of physicalism that

> could embrace other creatures would have to be based at least in part on them in the first place, but that cannot be done unless we already know whether they are conscious. (Block 2002: 407)

I will not dwell on the concept of epiphenomenalism, the view that one's actions are not caused by one's thoughts and that we are simply passive spectators laboring under the illusion that we are in command of our behavior and destiny.

The mental and psychological aspects that define humans include at least three components, the desire to acquire "qualia," the presence of intentionality, and application of an Abraham Maslow type of motivational pyramid, with a desire for self-actualization that embraces the desire to attain humanity. These three facets will be briefly described in what follows, and will then be demonstrated through Data in *Star Trek*.

The concept of "qualia" was first presented by Clarence Irving Lewis, who opined that

> [t]here are recognizable qualitative characters of the given, which may be repeated in different experiences, and are thus a sort of universals; I call these "qualia." But although such qualia are universals, in the sense of being recognized from one to another experience, they must be distinguished from the properties of objects. Confusion of these two is characteristic of many historical conceptions, as well as of current essence-theories. The quale is directly intuited, given, and is not the subject of any possible error because it is purely subjective. (Lewis 1956: 121)

The subject and its very definition are fraught with contention, and "we lack a principled basis precisely because we do not have an explanation for the presence of conscious experience even in ourselves" (Levine 2001: 79). The dilemma increases when we consider "the problem of attributing qualia to other creatures, those that do not share our physical organization. I take it that there is a very real puzzle whether such creatures have qualia like ours or even any at all. How much of our physicofunctional architecture must be shared before we have similarity or identity of experience?" (2001: 89). Hence, in this chapter, qualia will be described simply as subjective conscious experiences.

Another relevant concept is *intentionality*: the idea that our mental states such as beliefs, desires, thoughts, and so on, "actually refer to, are about, the world apart from the mind" (Searle 1984: 16). This idea is famously examined by John Searle in the Chinese Room *Gedankenexperiment*. He contends that a machine may respond to, for example, written language, such as Chinese, through a computer program, without actually understanding Chinese, even to the extent of passing a Turing test. Searle calls this "weak artificial intelligence," as opposed to a true comprehension of Chinese, which he calls "strong artificial intelligence," the type of intelligence that is posited in SF (1984: 26–27). Herein, I conceive of intentionality in a way that includes the entirety of what it seems to require or imply: an ability to truly understand, comprehend, and react to surroundings and stimuli, as humans do. The question is then whether we can attribute this to created beings, whether mechanical and computer-powered, or biological.

Arguably, the third aspect is the most important, a Maslow type of motivational hierarchy of personal needs. These are often depicted as a pyramid, with the most basic needs at the bottom, rising to more abstract aspirations at the apex of the pyramid. Briefly, the most basic needs are physiological, "primary drives" absolutely required for survival, such as for air, food, and water (Maslow 1954: 20). Next come safety needs, including a yearning for predictability and protection, such as job security and insurance (1954: 39). The third layer is referred to as love and belonging, and reflects the need for acceptance by others (1954: 43). The fourth level is esteem, the need for self-acknowledgment and self-respect (1954: 45). Self-actualization comprises the apex and implies that even if all of the previous needs are satisfied, it is possible that

> a new discontent and restlessness will soon develop, unless the individual is doing what he, individually, is fitted for […] if he is to be ultimately at peace with himself. What a man can be, he must be. He must be true to his own nature […] man's desire for self-fulfilment, namely, to the tendency for him to become actualized in what he is potentially […] the desire to become more and more what one idiosyncratically is, to become everything that one is capable of becoming. (1954: 46)

Importantly, higher, more abstract levels can overturn needs at lower levels. The Maslow pyramid is frequently but indirectly alluded to in SF, such as Captain Picard's reference to "[t]he potential to make yourself a better man. And that is what it is to be human. To make yourself more than you are" (*Star Trek: Nemesis*). All three components are depicted in the Pinocchio syndrome, as shall be demonstrated.

However, it must be noted from the outset that not all creatures in SF experience the Pinocchio syndrome. A more realistic approach is taken in "Desertion" (1944), a famous short story by Clifford Simak that depicts a metamorphosis of a man and his pet dog, Towser, into alien beings that survive comfortably and enjoy the surface of the planet Jupiter, experiencing incredible sensations – that is, alien and exotic qualia – through alien sensory systems. Each finds himself unwilling to return to his original form. " 'I can't go back,' said Towser. 'Nor I,' said Fowler. 'They would turn me back into a dog,' said Towser. 'And me,' said Fowler, 'back into a man.' "

1 The Pinocchio syndrome in *Star Trek* – Data

Data is a sentient android and a full member of the *Enterprise* starship crew in *Star Trek: The Next Generation*. Data is initially emotionless and possesses a positronic (computer) brain – a term from Isaac Asimov's 1940s robot fiction – with eidetic memory, and is physically much faster and stronger than a man. Although designed to blink, breathe, and have a pulse, Data can actually survive underwater or in a vacuum, and was created in the likeness of his inventor, a Dr. Soong ("Birthright").

Data is the thematic successor of the Vulcan Mr. Spock from the original series of *Star Trek*, the latter being a half-human half-alien hybrid who strove to master his human emotions. However, while Spock is broodingly charismatic, Data is more of a nerdy engineer who lacks Spock's magnetic appeal.

It is made clear from the very first episode of the seven-year series *Star Trek: The Next Generation* that Data has a Pinocchio complex, constantly "endeavoring to become more human" (*Star Trek: First Contact*), a fact pointed out by his superior officer, Riker. When Data is asked "Do you consider yourself superior to us?" he replies "I am superior, sir, in many ways. But I would gladly give it up to be human." To which Riker replies "Nice to meet you … Pinocchio" ("Encounter at Farpoint"). Data "had to search the ship's data banks for the reference, but when he found and accessed it seconds later, even though Riker passed it off as a joke, he was stunned at being compared to the subject of a story about the magical power of love" (Lorrah 1989: 129). Clearly, Data expresses anti-self actualization in that he is superior to humankind in abilities and immortal, and yet still desires to become human.

Data is the main protagonist in several episodes that deliberately explore his quest to become more human. "The Measure of a Man" is one such notable installment wherein Starfleet proposes to disassemble Data so scientists can determine the nature and construction of this unique android, hoping to duplicate him. However, the procedure is hazardous to Data and a legal injunction is brought forward, preventing him from resigning from Starfleet (where Data clearly demonstrates intentionality) and hence avoiding disassembly. The argument that Data is physical Starfleet property is an indefensible proposition since "naturalism (and physicalism) give us no good reason to doubt the consciousness of Commander Data" (Block 2002: 415).

Part of the prosecution's argument is that Data is a machine that can be switched off, with a vivid demonstration during the trial, while declaiming "Pinocchio is broken; its strings have been cut," further dehumanizing Data with the genderless pronoun. His captain, Picard, successfully defends him, vividly declaiming:

> Data is a machine. Do we deny that? No, because it is not relevant – we too are machines, just machines of a different type. […] Data was created by a human; do we deny that? No. Again it is not relevant. Children are created from the "building blocks" of their parents' DNA. Are they property?

In truth, "Our lack of knowledge is no argument against the consciousness of Commander Data" and similar creations (Block 2002: 416).

Sexuality is an inextricable part of humanity, and Data's sexuality is explored in several episodes. In "The Naked Now," Data has sex with the *Enterprise*'s inebriated female security officer, who precedes the intimate encounter by coyly but pointedly asking him: "You are fully functional, aren't you?" to which Data replies "of course, […] in every way, […] I am programmed in multiple techniques, a broad variety of pleasuring," a trope repeated in feminist novels such as Marge Piercy's *He, She, and It* (1991), wherein an artificial being is portrayed as the perfect lover: hygienic, obedient, indefatigable, and considerate.

Readers' assumptions of normative heterosexual relationships are further challenged, with such relationships initiated both by Data and by second parties. In "In Theory," Data deliberately and experimentally cohabits with a human female crewmember, an arrangement that fails as Data cannot respond emotionally. Conversely, in "The Ensigns of Command," an alien humanoid female develops romantic feelings for Data but soon realizes that Data is incapable of any reciprocation.

Data also demonstrates intentionality in his attempts to procreate by fashioning another android, Hephaestus-like and single-handedly crafting a sentient female android. Captain Picard is naturally apprehensive of Starfleet's reaction to this unauthorized fabrication, leading to a humorous dialog about android reproduction. Picard complains, "Data, I would like to have been consulted," to which Data appropriately and correctly replies, "I have not observed anyone else on board consulting you about their procreation, Captain" ("The Offspring"). This attempt eventually fails, however, emphasizing the usual cautionary trope against hubris that SF so frequently enjoins.

Interestingly, Data is offered the option of instantaneously being made human, an offer that he rejects, affirming as his reason that in "this above all, to thine own self be true" ("Hide and Q"). In Jean Lorrah's 1990 tie-in novel *Metamorphosis*, Data actually does become a living and breathing human for a few days, a transformation achieved by alien technology, and the novel explores Data's adaptation to a new life on board the *Enterprise* as an ordinary and emotional human being, before returning back to androidhood.

Data further approaches humanity when he deliberately installs an "emotion chip" that allows him to experience feelings and emotions, thus demonstrating intentionality and attaining qualia. This initially leads him to lose control of his new emotions, to the extent that he actually asks the Captain to be relieved of his duties; his quest for feeling is a double-edged sword (*Star Trek: Generations*). Data's emotions are again highlighted when, during a hazardous situation, he confesses to Captain Picard that he is "feeling… anxiety […] an intriguing sensation […] distracting." Picard advises him to deactivate his emotion chip temporarily, and when Data confirms that he has done so, Picard wistfully remarks "Data, there are times that I envy you."

In the same vein, Data has an android "brother," Lore, another Soong-type android who, under the effects of emotions, becomes evil, causing general mayhem, once again depicting emotions as potentially letting loose latent evil aspects of the psyche in a Jekyll and Hyde confrontation with Data ("Datalore").

2 The prosthetic impulse in *Star Trek* – the Borg

The inverse of the Pinocchio syndrome, the prosthetic impulse, is arguably best exemplified by *Star Trek*'s Borg, who constitute a relentless inhuman tide that threatens to overwhelm every species violently, assimilating all individual beings into the Borg collective, stifling their *élan vital* and incorporating them as part of a hive mind, with an inexorable "insect mentality" (Gross 1995: 179–180). The Borg are cyborg drones ruled by the Borg Queen. Indeed, individual Borg drones do not emit individual life signs; a scan of a Borg vessel cannot result in a head count ("Q Who"). This is perhaps the most terrifying aspect of the Borg Collective; in

> their destruction of the individual and the self […] the Borg destroy freedom of choice, and any ability to act independently of the collective mind. That alteration is allegedly worse than death for the individual involved. (Consalvo 2004: 193)

"The Borg, our most lethal enemy" (*Star Trek: First Contact*) are an uncompromising horde, "profoundly challenging the notion of an embodied and discrete masculine identity, […] penetrated, ungendered and unfamiliar" (Fuchs 1995: 282), inevitably losing the individual's self-actualization (and indeed, selfhood itself) for the gain of the collective.

The Borg were originally purely biological beings, who "evolved to include the synthetic. Now […] use both to attain perfection" (*Star Trek: First Contact*), a process that has been "developing for […] thousands of centuries" ("Q Who"). The collective inhabits spaces that are postmodern in their portrayal of "darkness, warmth, and dampness" (Balinisteanu 2007: 409). The Borg clarion call chillingly evinces the potentially Faustian nature of these prosthetic compulsions:

> We are the Borg. Lower your shields and surrender your ships. We will add your biological and technological distinctiveness to our own. Your culture will adapt to service us. Resistance is futile. (*Star Trek: First Contact*)

The Borg almost poignantly fail to understand the opposition they encounter in their quest for perfection, as they sincerely, almost wistfully, ask "Why do you resist? We only wish to raise quality of life, for all species." The reply "I like my 'species' the way it is," is dismissed by the Borg as "a narrow vision" ("The Best of Both Worlds").

Borg are seen as amoral, "the ultimate users" ("Q Who") who brook no opposition in their drive, viewing guilt ("Day of Honor"), pleasure ("The Raven"), comfort ("Revulsion"), taste ("Year of Hell"), personal opinions ("Vis à Vis"), chance ("Night"), designation ("Drone"), feelings ("Nothing Human"), compassion ("Equinox"), personal plans ("Dragon's Teeth"), practice ("Pathfinder"), feelings, and parents ("Child's Play"), friendship ("Unimatrix Zero") and fame ("Inside Man"), as all being "irrelevant."

The Borg maintain that mundane humanity is "erratic, conflicted, disorganized. Every decision is debated. Every action questioned. Every individual entitled to their own small opinion. You lack harmony, cohesion, greatness. It will be your undoing" ("Scorpion"). However, the Borg are willing to go to great lengths in order to assimilate humanity, despite humanity's perceived limitations: "flawed, weak, organic" (*Star Trek: First Contact*), "physiology inefficient, below average cranial capacity, minimal redundant systems, limited regenerative abilities" ("Dark Frontier"), unequivocally exhibiting an unquenchable desire and drive for the forcible conversion of humanity from individuals into the collective.

An adult human female, designated Seven of Nine, assimilated by the Borg as a child, is recaptured by the *Voyager* Starfleet crew, and slowly divested of her Borg prostheses, thereby regaining her humanity. Seven is "a character on the verge of humanity, whose aspirations to become more human […] illuminate important questions […] a perpetuation of modernity's most highly valued precepts of human nature, namely progress, self-improvement and individualism" (Graham 2002: 153).

At first she complains that she'd have preferred to remain Borg as "the lure of perfection is powerful" ("Drone"), and that "the prospect of becoming human is unsettling" ("Hope and Fear"), but eventually is willing to explore her humanity, exhibiting the full version of the Pinocchio syndrome, entering into complex relationships with her *Voyager* crewmates, and eventually even falling in love. During her time as a Borg drone, Seven had unwittingly "helped assimilate many civilizations" and her work on *Voyager* helps her assuage her guilt and to atone for these misdeeds, an experience she finds "gratifying" ("Dragon's Teeth"). Over the course of the *Voyager* series, Seven embodies Gene Roddenberry's driving idea behind the *Star Trek* concept, "the quest to discern some degree of purpose to the universe amid the complexity and fragility of everyday experience" (Graham 2002: 153).

Other individual Borg units sometimes escape or are rescued from the collective and reattain individuality, and once started on this course, such new individuals pursue their Pinocchio syndrome relentlessly, even to the extent of becoming belligerent toward other, still-assimilated drones ("I Borg").

On the other hand, the different assimilated species that comprise the Borg collective are sometimes shown to revert back to type, violently squabbling over limited resources when their individuality is regained after being freed from the hive mind but stranded on a planet. The only solution, as suggested by a peace-loving human faction, is to re-establish the hive mind, a procedure abetted by the *Voyager* crew, and this restores peace, albeit at the cost of losing individual self actualization ("Unity").

3 Data vs. the Borg

In Jonathan Frakes' movie *Star Trek: First Contact* (1996), "[t]he Borg stand for the ultimate threat to the *Star Trek* vision of human progress and individual integrity" (Graham 2002: 133). The collective, led by the Borg Queen, attempts an invasion of Earth. In this setting

> the Borg Queen figure stands out as a particularly dangerous opponent. She does not simply threaten to overtake human technology, but to assimilate it into what may be a superior technological structure; [...] with reintegration within a collective form of social organization [...] she is not simply driven by instinct, an ungovernable force of nature, but she has a purpose that endows nature with cultural significance. (Balinisteanu 2007: 404)

Data is captured by the Borg and, in a subversion of Data's self-protective inactivation of his emotion chip, the Borg Queen re-engages the chip, causing Data to feel apprehension and even fear, clearly proving that qualia in the form of human-type emotions might not always be desirable (*Star Trek: First Contact*).

The Borg contain biological components, and Data does not. It is almost ironic that Data, a completely artificial being, repudiates the Borg's ideal of perfection via the fusion of the biological and mechanical, stating that "believing oneself to be perfect is often the sign of a delusional mind."

In a reverse prosthetic impulse, the Borg Queen attempts to subvert Data by appealing to his Pinocchio complex, grafting him with biological skin and thereby allowing him to enjoy the sensation of biological touch, a specific quale that initially overwhelms Data. This is unsurprising as "[w]ithout going into the difficult issue of what it is that makes two realizations fundamentally different, we can stipulate that our physical realizations of our conscious states are fundamentally different from Commander Data's physical realizations of his analogs of these states" (Block 2002: 411). When he tries to escape, he wounds his new biological implants and experiences physical pain, another new quale that overpowers him as his "programming was not designed to process these sensations," terminating his escape attempt. The Borg Queen taunts him:

> Is it becoming clear to you yet? Look at yourself, standing there cradling the new flesh that I've given you. If it means nothing to you, why protect it? [...] tear the skin from your limbs as you would a defective circuit. Go ahead, Data. We won't stop you. Do it. Don't be tempted by flesh.

She also promises even more biological grafts and, being herself physically attractive, a "monolithic [...] techno-bodied femme fatale" (Consalvo 2004: 179), has sex with Data and also hints that Data will rule the Borg collective with her as she has "found an equal," blandishments that Data rejects, ultimately aiding in her destruction since clearly, "[t]he Borg represent the antithesis of *Star Trek* values [...] their corruption [...] of the body is achieved by means of invasive technological implants, and the mind by immersion of the individual in a collective consciousness" (Graham 2002: 133). A feminist interpretation of these events is that "the Borg Queen is repudiated as an illegitimate version of the female in order to establish a legitimate version of the male: Picard as warrior and leader and Data as master of reason" (Balinisteanu 2007: 411). Thus, in both physical sensation and in sex, Data attains and experiences new qualia.

4 Discussion

This reading has shown that in *Star Trek*, the Pinocchio syndrome – the wish to somehow attain humanity – has been depicted as a pastiche consisting of the acquisition of a biological human body, in addition to intentionality, as well as the desire to experience qualia. Since most of the beings in SF who express this desire have physical and/or mental powers superior to mundane humanity's, this anthropocentric aspiration is arguably a reverse-self actualization, a negation of the apex of Maslow's pyramid, resulting in the deliberate abandonment of inhuman abilities. However, not all imaginary beings suffer from the Pinocchio syndrome, rejecting anthropocentrism outright upon realizing their superiority to mankind.

We have seen how Data strives to acquire humanity by way of several methods, that is, the occasional appropriation of biological parts, the attainment of qualia, and the clear expression of intentionality. His search for the latter, notably through the implantation and activation of his emotion chip, also demonstrates Daniel Dennett's four properties that are often attributed to qualia. These are that qualia are: (1) ineffable and can only be comprehended through a direct experience; (2) intrinsic; (3) private and impossible to compare interpersonally; and (4) instantly apprehensible to consciousness, such that once experienced, one instantly knows that one has experienced a quale (Dennett 1988: 46).

This syndrome is often depicted in SF, and not just in *Star Trek*, and the regularity with which the desire to become more human (or even fully human) is so frequently restated in SF smacks of overweening hubris in humankind, particularly since this anthropocentric desire is often expressed by beings who are superior, physically and/or mentally, to mere humanity. Its apotheosis is found perhaps most definitively in Isaac Asimov's sentimental "Bicentennial Man," where a 200-year-old repeatedly upgraded robot is granted his wish to die as a human (Asimov 1976).

On the other hand, the dystopic futures that the Borg depict warn against a too trusting embrace of the ultramodern, which may decompose into the "postmodern [...] an aesthetic of decay, exposing the dark side of technology, the process of disintegration. Next to the high-tech, its waste. It is into garbage that the characters constantly step" (Bruno 1987: 63). SF also enjoins us to heed Frankenstein's plight, as such beings

> offer a glimpse of a liberated and empowered humanity, which could be realized thanks to the wonderful possibilities of technology; but so too, they indicate the terrible price of that seductive empowerment in the substitution for our humanity of the qualities and characteristics of the machine. (Fitting 1987: 345)

SF, especially in its visual forms, thus cautions against an exaggerated prosthetic impulse and extreme prosthetic makeovers, leaning more toward the Pinocchio syndrome of anthropocentrism and encouraging us to abandon any Faustian pacts that we might be tempted to make with technology.

This trope is exemplified by the Borg, who through the dispassionate infliction of great pain ("Repentance"), "reproduce themselves by assimilating bodies […] by literal physical penetration" (Fuchs 1995: 282). As in many narratives, the Borg represent a metaphor of what we might become, because "if the Borg are transgressive and integrated, they are also demonized, representing fear of multiple losses, of choice, individual identity and morality" (Fuchs 1995: 298).

These prosthetic impulses can simply start as "a culture inhabited by posthumans who regard their bodies as fashion accessories" (Hayles 1999: 5). However, Baudrillard cautioned against excessive embrace of such artificial additions, averring that

> [w]hen prostheses are introduced at a deeper level, when they are so completely internalized […] when they impose themselves […] as the body's "original" model […] this point means the end of the body […] the individual is now nothing but a cancerous metastasis of his basic formula. (Baudrillard 1993: 119)

This may potentially lead to posthuman subjects comprised of "an amalgam, a collection of heterogenous components […] whose boundaries undergo continuous construction and reconstruction" (Hayles 1999: 7).

Such posthumans, like the Borg, threaten to become the ultimate exemplars of Herbert Marcuse's "one-dimensional man," where "the efficient individual is the one whose performance is an action only insofar as it is the proper reaction to the objective requirements of the apparatus, and his liberty is confined to the selection of the most adequate means for reaching a goal which he did not set" (Marcuse 1978: 142).

In conclusion, SF explores the possibilities of "a future society which blurs the line between human and machine, and it contains philosophical meditations on what it means to be human" (Kellner et al. 1984: 7). The genre also enjoins caution with regard to the android, a sentient embodiment of technology that "inaugurates a crisis of subjectivity. What does it mean to be human in an era wherein human conjoins with machine, biology with technology, nature with manufacture?" thus blurring the implied hierarchy between man and machine (Galvan 1997: 18). With regard to humanity, however, any arguments for or against the modification of the body are almost moot, as "increasingly the question is not whether we will become posthuman, for posthumanity is already here. Rather, the question is what kind of posthumans we will be" (Hayles 1999: 246).

This brief reading has shown that narratives consider potentialities "about the situation of humanity in the age of science. The boundary between humans and machines is broken down" (Schelde 1993: 237), further emphasizing T.H. Huxley's famous assertion in 1866, "[h]ow it is that anything so remarkable as a state of consciousness comes about as a result of irritating nervous tissue, is just as unaccountable as the appearance of Djin when Aladdin rubbed his lamp" (Huxley 1986: 193).

It is hoped that this chapter has made it clear that it would behoove us to cautiously go where no one has gone before.

Acknowledgments

This chapter is adapted, with permission, from an essay that first appeared in *The New York Review of Science Fiction* 284 (April 2012): 16–20.

References

Star Trek episodes and movies cited

Best of Both Worlds, The. June 1990. Dir. Cliff Bole. *Star Trek: The Next Generation*. Paramount.

Birthright. February 1993. Dir. Winrich Kolbe. *Star Trek: The Next Generation*. Paramount.

Child's Play. March 2000. Dir. Mike Vejar. *Star Trek: Voyager*. Paramount.

Dark Frontier. February 1999. Dir. Cliff Bole. *Star Trek: Voyager*. Paramount.

Datalore. January 1988. Dir. Rob Bowman. *Star Trek: The Next Generation*. Paramount.

Day of Honor. September 1997. Dir. Jesús Salvador Treviño. *Star Trek: Voyager*. Paramount.

Dragon's Teeth. November 1999. Dir. Winrich Kolbe. *Star Trek: Voyager*. Paramount.

Drone. October 1998. Dir. Les Landau. *Star Trek: Voyager*. Paramount.

Encounter at Farpoint. September 1987. Dir. Allen Corey. *Star Trek: The Next Generation*. Paramount.

Ensigns of Command, The. October 1989. Dir. Cliff Bole. *Star Trek: The Next Generation*. Paramount.

Equinox. May 1999. Dir. David Livingston. *Star Trek: Voyager*. Paramount.

Hide and Q. November 1987. Dir. Cliff Bole. *Star Trek: The Next Generation*. Paramount.

Hope and Fear. May 1998. Dir. Winrich Kolbe. *Star Trek: Voyager*. Paramount.

I Borg. May 1992. Dir. Robert Lederman. *Star Trek: The Next Generation*. Paramount.

In Theory. June 1991. Dir. Patrick Stewart. *Star Trek: The Next Generation*. Paramount.

Inside Man. November 2000. Dir. Allan Kroeker. *Star Trek: Voyager*. Paramount.

Measure of a Man, The. February 1989. Dir. Robert Scheerer. *Star Trek: The Next Generation*. Paramount.

Naked Now, The. October 1987. Dir. Paul Lynch. *Star Trek: The Next Generation*. Paramount.

Night. October 1998. Dir. David Livingston. *Star Trek: Voyager*. Paramount.

Nothing Human. December 1998. Dir. David Livingston. *Star Trek: Voyager*. Paramount.

Offspring, The. March 1990. Dir. Jonathan Frakes. *Star Trek: The Next Generation*. Paramount.

Pathfinder. December 1999. Dir. Mike Vejar. *Star Trek: Voyager*. Paramount.

Q Who. May 1989. Dir. Rob Bowman. *Star Trek: The Next Generation*. Paramount.

Raven, The. October 1997. Dir. LeVar Burton. *Star Trek: Voyager*. Paramount.

Repentance, January 2001. Dir. Mike Vejar. *Star Trek: Voyager*. Paramount.

Revulsion. October 1997. Dir. Kenneth Biller. *Star Trek: Voyager*. Paramount.

Scorpion. May 1997. Dir. David Livingston. *Star Trek: Voyager*. Paramount.

Star Trek: First Contact. 1996. Dir. Jonathan Frakes. Paramount.

Star Trek: Generations. 1994. Dir. David Carson. Paramount.

Star Trek: Nemesis. 2002. Dir. Stuart Baird. Paramount.

Unimatrix Zero. May 2000. Dir. Allan Kroeker. *Star Trek: Voyager*. Paramount.

Unity. February 1997. Dir. Robert McNeill Duncan. *Star Trek: Voyager*. Paramount.

Vis à Vis. April 1998. Dir. Jesús Salvador Treviño. *Star Trek: Voyager*. Paramount.

Year of Hell. November 1997. Dir. Allan Kroeker. *Star Trek: Voyager*. Paramount.

Publications

Asimov, Isaac. 1976. Bicentennial man. In Judy-Lynn del Rey, ed., *Stellar* 2. New York: Ballantine Books.

Balinisteanu, Tudor. 2007. The cyborg goddess: Social myths of women as goddesses of technologized otherworlds. *Feminist Studies* 33(2): 394–423.

Baudrillard, Jean. 1993. *The Transparency of Evil*, trans. James Benedict. London: Verso.

Baum, Frank L. 1899. *The Wonderful Wizard of Oz*. Chicago: Geo. M. Hill.

Bernal, John D. 1969. *The World, the Flesh and the Devil*. Bloomington: Indiana University Press. (1st pub. 1929.)

Block, Ned. 2002. The harder problem of consciousness. *The Journal of Philosophy* 99: 391–425.

Bruno, Giuliana. 1987. Ramble city: Postmodernism and *Blade Runner*. *October* 41: 61–74.

Clynes, Manfred E., and Kline, Nathan S. 1960. Cyborgs and space. *Astronautics* (September): 26–27, 74–75.

Collodi, Carlo. 1883. *Le Avventure di Pinocchio: Storia di un Burattino*. Florence: Felice Paggi.

Consalvo, Mia. 2004. Borg babes, drones, and the collective: Reading gender and the body in *Star Trek*. *Women's Studies in Communication* 27(2): 177–203.

Dennett, Daniel. 1988. Quining qualia. In A. Marcel and E. Bisiach, eds., *Consciousness in Contemporary Science*. Oxford: Clarendon Press, pp. 42–77.

Fitting, Peter, 1987. Futurecop: The neutralization of revolt in *Blade Runner*. *Science Fiction Studies* 14: 340–354.

Fuchs, Cynthia J. 1995. "Death is irrelevant": Cyborgs, reproduction, and the future of male hysteria. In Chris Hables Gray, ed., *The Cyborg Handbook*. New York: Routledge, pp. 281–300.

Galvan, Jill, 1997. Entering the posthuman collective in Philip K. Dick's *Do Androids Dream of Electric Sheep? Science Fiction Studies* 24: 413–429.

Graham, Elaine L. 2002. *Representations of the Post/Human: Monsters, Aliens and Others in Popular Culture*. New Brunswick: Rutgers University Press.

Gross, Edward, and Altman, Mark A. 1995. *Captains' Logs: The Unauthorized Complete Trek Voyages*. Boston: Little, Brown.

Haraway, Donna J. 1985. A manifesto for cyborgs: Science, technology, and socialist feminism in the 1980s. *Socialist Review* 80: 65–108.

Hard, Robin. 2004. *The Routledge Handbook of Greek Mythology*. London: Routledge.

Hayles, N. Katherine. 1999. *How We Became Posthuman: Virtual Bodies in Cybernetics, Literature and Informatics*. Chicago: University of Chicago Press.

Huxley, T.H. 1986. *Lessons in Elementary Physiology*. London: Macmillan. (1st pub. 1866).

Jameson, Fredric. 2005. *Archaeologies of the Future*. London: Verso.

Kellner, Douglas, Leibowitz, Flo, and Ryan, Michael. 1984. *Blade Runner*: A diagnostic critique. *Jump Cut* 29: 6–8.

Levine, Joe. 2001. *Purple Haze*. Oxford: Oxford University Press.

Lewis, Clarence Irving. 1956. *Mind and the World Order*. New York: Scribner's Sons.

Lorrah, Jean 1989. *Survivors*. New York: Pocket Books.

Lorrah, Jean. 1990. *Metamorphosis*. New York: Pocket Books.

Marcuse, Herbert. 1978. Some social implications of modern technology. In Andrew Arato and Eike Gebhart, eds., *The Essential Frankfurt School Reader*. New York: Urizen Books, pp. 138–161.

Maslow, Abraham H. 1954. *Motivation and Personality*. New York: Harper & Row.

Piercy, Marge. 1991. *He, She, and It*. New York: Fawcett Crest.

Schelde, Per. 1993. *Androids, Humanoids and Other Science Fiction Monsters*. New York: New York University Press.

Searle, John. 1984. *Minds, Brains and Science*. Cambridge, MA: Harvard University Press.

Simak, Clifford. 1944. Desertion. *Astounding Science Fiction* (November): 64–74.

Smith, Marquard, and Morra, Joanne. 2006. *The Prosthetic Impulse*. Cambridge, MA: MIT Press.

Zeman, David. 2003. *The Pinocchio Syndrome*. New York: Doubleday.

20

Being Nice to Software Animals and Babies

Anders Sandberg

For no reason, I reach down and pinch the tail of the mouse. It freezes; eyes narrowed, cheeks puffed, it squeaks an ultrasonic sound I cannot hear. Its fur is erect, whiskers pushed back. When I release the tail, the mouse quickly retreats from me to the far end of the cage, trying to burrow into safety. Did I do something bad? Most people would say that something morally significant occurred: I might have expressed cruelty or indifference, and a living being was in pain and fear for no good reason. If I were a researcher it would be against the rules of ethical animal handling.

What if the mouse were software? I virtually pinch the virtual tail of a complex simulation of a mouse, producing a sequence of signals that make the image on my screen depict a mouse in pain that then retreats from its apparent source. Is the virtual pinch as bad as the real pinch? Should I be banned from treating the simulation that way?

1 Brain emulations

Ever since Hodgkin and Huxley laboriously calculated single nerve action potentials using hand-cranked mechanical calculators in the early 1950s, scientists have attempted to build ever more elaborate and exact computer models of the brain and body. At present the larger simulations involve more than a billion neurons, about the same number as in a small mammalian brain. They are created in order to learn about the real brain by creating

Intelligence Unbound: The Future of Uploaded and Machine Minds, First Edition.
Edited by Russell Blackford and Damien Broderick.

replicas: their behavior can tell us whether or not we have understood the fundamental principles of various systems.

A brain emulation would be a one-to-one simulation where every causal process in the brain is represented, behaving in the same way as the original. It is the apparent logical endpoint of ever larger, ever more data-based realistic models, even if conventional neuroscientists do not pursue it directly. After all, just because the software behaves right does not mean we understand *why* it behaves right. We understand only the low-level function, which might not answer any of the deep questions.

Some researchers have a different ambition: to achieve software intelligence by completely copying into software the functional structure of the nervous systems. Rather than attempting to understand the high-level processes underlying perception, action, emotions, and intelligence, the approach assumes that these would emerge from a sufficiently close imitation of the low-level neural functions (Sandberg and Bostrom 2008, Sandberg 2013). We might get artificial intelligence simply by plagiarizing nature.

But if we are about to explore this realm of software beings, can we do it *right*? Can brain emulations be created and handled ethically?

2 Software animal rights

Opponents of animal testing often argue that much of it is unnecessary and could be replaced with simulations. While this is debatable at present, in the future software might become an adequate replacement. Indeed, since every step could then be controlled and repeated, software might even be *better* for research than real animals.

Unfortunately, developing brain emulations will likely require a significant use of test animals. They would be necessary not only as the templates of the emulation but also for the long chain of experiments providing the necessary understanding of neuroscience, scanning methods, and ways of comparing real and simulated animals. Brain emulation requires us to understand at least one level of the nervous system in sufficient detail to re-create all its functionality. That is a tall research order.

Neuroscientists today use a broad array of species in research, from tiny nematode worms to primates, but also turtles and Amazonian electrical fishes. Early work on brain emulation is likely to focus on simple nervous systems like the nematode *Caenorhabditis elegans*, the British pond snail, or the fruit fly. We already have a complete map of the *C. elegans* nervous system, although we do not know the kind of synapses it uses in most locations. Much neuroscience and tool development will likely also involve such standard vertebrates as mice. This might involve *in vitro* experiments where pieces of neural tissue are studied and scanned, or *in vivo* experiments trying to map neural function to detectable behavior.

Much of the scanning work would avoid normal animal experimentation concerns. There would be no experiment done on the living animal itself, just tissue extraction. It is essentially terminal anesthesia. Here the ethical issues are the treatment of the animal before its demise, whether there is harm done to the animal in killing it, and whether there is a risk of software suffering. The first two issues are dealt with in normal discussions of treatment of lab animals.

Probably, early scans, models, and simulations will often be flawed. Flawed scans would be equivalent to animals with local or global brain damage. Flawed models would introduce systemic distortions, ranging from the state of not having any functioning brain at all to abnormal brain states. Flawed simulations (broken off because of software crashes) would correspond to premature death (possibly repeated, with no memory). By analogy with living animals, it seems that the main worry should be flawed models producing hard-to-detect suffering.

Some success in smaller animals will lead to scanning and simulation of larger and cleverer animals. There are few restrictions on research on invertebrates (except for cephalopods). The rules get progressively stricter as one approaches the higher mammals: research would become increasingly regulated (and more ethically controversial from an animal use perspective). Before moving on to human emulation, the final stages in animal brain emulation would likely involve primates, raising the strongest animal protection issues.

Animal rights activists wishing for emulations to take the place of actual animals must hence swallow the bitter fact that creating emulations will require using lab animals. They might hope, however, that once emulations arrive the need for real animals will entirely disappear. At least to some, this might morally outweigh the short-term moral cost.

3 The moral status of animals

There is a vast literature about what consideration we should give to animals, and we can pose a similar question about what moral claims emulations have on us. Can they be wronged? Can they suffer?

One group of theories argues that animals do not merit moral consideration in themselves, but human actions on them do matter. Immanuel Kant argued that animals lack moral autonomy and hence are not beings whose interests count morally. Our duties toward them are indirect duties toward humanity: being cruel to animals harms our own humanity. Someone who kicks a dog is a cruel person and shows a disregard for other beings unbecoming to a human (Regan and Singer 1989).

This kind of theory does not distinguish between software and animal: if it is bad to pinch the tail of a biological mouse, the same cruel impulse is present in pinching the virtual tail of the emulated mouse. It might be like harming an effigy: it is the intention behind the damage that counts, not that the effigy is broken. Conversely, treating emulations nicely is like treating dolls nicely: it might not be morally obligatory, it might even be slightly silly, but it is compassionate.

A slightly different approach is found in social contract ethics. It is not the intrinsic properties of the creature that matter but the relations we have with it. If we can have the same kind of relationship with an emulated animal as we do with a biological one, it should by this account be treated similarly. Presuming that the ability to form reciprocal relations with other beings depends on some neural substrate that would be successfully emulated, this appears plausible.

Many theories claim that the interests of animals count because animals *do* have some intrinsic property that matters. In a common version, sentience gives moral status: being able to feel pleasure or pain makes you morally relevant no matter what you are. However, telling what is sentient is hard. Typically we rely on an argument from analogy, which looks at similarities between the thing in question and human beings in order to tell whether there is enough functional similarity to justify the conclusion that it can probably experience pain.

However, the argument from analogy runs into trouble with emulations. Software – electrons in a computer – might imitate the functioning of a living organism, but it is a very different kind of *object* from biological wetware. Many doubt that it could have consciousness. We will return to this question.

It is possible to argue for animal rights without recourse to sentience, for example by arguing that animals have beliefs, desires, and self-consciousness of their own and that is what makes them moral patients: they are subjects of a life, and that life has some value, if only to the animal itself (Regan 1983). Like the relationship approach, this seems to grant rights to successful emulations: the maltreated virtual mouse will try to protect itself as best it can. Nonetheless, doubts might remain whether the mere behavior of pain-avoidance *without any experience* is morally important. Accounts of moral patienthood typically assume that experience is fundamental since it ties together the state of affairs involving the agent with a value, the agent's welfare.

4 The moral status of software

Might software have the same moral weight as a real animal, by virtue of being sentient or a being with inherent value?

Whether machines can be built to have consciousness is a perennial component in the AI debate. Opponents of strong AI have often argued against the possibility of any machine (or at least software) having mental states.

Current computational neuroscience does not think it is creating simulations that can have bad experiences. In fact, the assumption that simulations do not have consciousness is often used to motivate such research:

> Secondly, one of the more obvious features of mathematical modelling is that it is not invasive, and hence could be of great advantage in the study of chronic pain. There are major ethical problems with the experimental study of chronic pain in humans and animals. It is possible to use mathematical modelling to test some of the neurochemical and neurophysiological features of chronic pain without the use of methods which would be ethically prohibitive in the laboratory or clinic. (Britton and Skevington 1996)

One reason we might doubt that current simulations have experience is that they are so small, typically a handful of neurons. Intuitively this seems to be too small to produce consciousness or experience. But it is likely not the size of the network that truly matters: there is no reason to think a lot of randomly connected neurons would be conscious either. Conversely Herzog et al. (2007) suggest the "Small Network Argument":

> for each model of consciousness there exists a minimal model, i.e., a small neural network, that fulfills the respective criteria, but to which one would not like to assign consciousness. (2007: 1055)

One way out is to argue that fine-grained consciousness requires at least a mid-sized system, and that small networks only have rudimentary consciousness. Another is to bite the bullet and accept that consciousness might exist in very simple systems. Perhaps phenomenal states are independent of higher-level functions – even thermostats may have simple conscious states (Chalmers 1996). If so, we might have to worry about the moral patienthood of many, many things.

In any case, the largest simulations have reached more than a billion neurons and we are approaching the numbers found in those brains we do find morally relevant. Most such simulations do not have a very sophisticated structure, and this might prevent experience from occurring, but this is just a guess – and many simulations attempt to mirror the overall structure of the brain.

For example, consider the case of Rodney Cotterill's "CyberChild." This is a simulated infant controlled by a biologically inspired neural network and with a simulated body (Cotterill 2003). The network includes neuron populations corresponding to different real brain areas, connected according to standard mammalian brain architecture with learning, attention, and feedback from the body. The body model has muscles allowing it to move, and states like levels of blood glucose, milk in the stomach, and urine in the bladder. The baby needs to get enough milk to keep its blood sugar above a critical level or it "dies." Using its voice and motions it can interact with a user that can feed it milk, and ideally it will learn behaviors that will keep it alive and happy. It is an ambitious project trying to implement a model of consciousness, and the originator was hopeful that it might ultimately develop consciousness.

But a conscious CyberChild would have lived an extremely impoverished life. It would have existed within a world of mainly visual perception except for visceral inputs, hunger, and discomfort from full diapers. Its only means of communication would have been crying and the only possible response would have been the appearance (or not) of a bottle that had to be maneuvered to its mouth. Even if the experience did not have any aversive content, there would be no prospect of real growth or change ever.

This is eerily similar to Metzinger's warning:

> What would you say if someone came along and said, "Hey, we want to genetically engineer mentally retarded human infants! For reasons of scientific progress we need infants with certain cognitive and emotional deficits in order to study their postnatal psychological development – we urgently need some funding for this important and innovative kind of research!" You would certainly think this was not only an absurd and appalling but also a dangerous idea. It would hopefully not pass any ethics committee in the democratic world. However, what today's ethics committees *don't* see is how the first machines satisfying a minimally sufficient set of constraints for conscious experience could be just *like* such mentally retarded infants. They would suffer from all kinds of functional and representational deficits too. But they would now also subjectively experience those deficits. In addition, they would have no political lobby – no representatives in *any* ethics committee. (2003: 621)

Metzinger argues that we should ban all attempts to create or even risk the creation of artificial systems that have phenomenological self-models (his explanation of consciousness). While views might differ between different thinkers on what the particular criterion is for being able to suffer, it is clear that the potential for suffering software should be a normative concern. Nonetheless, as discussed in mainstream animal rights ethics, other interests (such as human ones) can sometimes be strong enough to allow animal suffering. Presumably such interests (if these accounts of ethics are correct) would also permit creating suffering software.

Another classic paper about (machine) consciousness is Dennett's "Why You Can't Make a Computer that Feels Pain" (1978). He argues that creating a machine able to feel pain is nontrivial, largely due to the incoherencies in our ordinary concept of pain. However, he does not rule out the possibility in principle:

> If and when a good physiological sub-personal theory of pain is developed, a robot could in principle be constructed to instantiate it. Such advances in science would probably bring in their train wide-scale changes in what we found intuitive about pain, so that the charge that our robot only suffered what we artificially called pain would lose its persuasiveness. In the meantime (if there were a cultural lag) thoughtful people would refrain from kicking such a robot. (Dennett 1978: 449)

From his perspective we should hence be cautious about whether or not to ascribe suffering to software, since we do not (yet) have a good understanding of what suffering *is* (or rather, what the actual underlying component is that is morally relevant). In particular, successful brain emulations might indeed represent a physiological sub-personal theory of pain, but it might be as opaque to outside observers as real physiological pain. Unfortunately the emulation might still suffer.

Some researchers have suggested probability scales for machine phenomenology based on the intuition that machines built along the same lines as humans are more likely to be conscious than other machines (Gamez 2005). This is similar to the argument from analogy, and brain emulation gets a fairly high score on this scale. Emulations are different from entirely artificial software since the design is deliberately as similar as possible to biological systems deserving of moral consideration, and this should make us more morally cautious.

Since at present there does not seem to be any idea of how to solve the hard problem of consciousness, or how to detect phenomenal states, this seems to push us in the direction of suspending judgment:

> there are the arguments of Moor (1988) and Prinz (2003), who suggest that it may be indeterminable whether a machine is conscious or not. This could force us to acknowledge the possibility of consciousness in a machine, even if we cannot tell for certain whether this is the case by solving the hard problem of consciousness. (Gamez 2008)

The problem of animal experience and moral status is contentious: the problem of emulated experience and status will be even more contentious. Intuitions are likely divergent and there might not be any observations that could settle the differences.

5 Treating emulated animals right

What to do? It seems that a safe moral strategy would be to make the most cautious assumption:

> *Principle of Assuming the Most (PAM)*: Assume that any emulated system could have the same mental properties as the original system and treat it correspondingly.

The fact that we might legitimately doubt whether the emulation is a moral patient does not mean it has a value intermediate between a biological being and nothing, but rather that the actual value is either full or none; we just do not know which. Thus, we should treat the virtual mice the same as the real mice since it is better to treat a simulacrum as a real thing than to mistreat a sentient being, even by mistake.

The principle does not say that we must treat the CyberChild as a real baby. If there are reasons to think that certain mental properties are *not* present, they overrule the principle in that case. An emulated mouse that does not respond to sensory stimuli or lacks most of the brain is clearly different from a normal mouse. The CyberChild, despite its suggestive appearance on the screen, is not an emulation of a human infant but at most a tiny subset of neurons (each area has 20 neurons) in a generic mammalian nervous system. It might still have some form of experience, but it is not the experience of a higher mammal.

Doesn't this principle prevent useful research, like the pain research discussed by Britton and Skevington (1996)? Perhaps not; it is agnostic on whether there are overruling human interests, just as many animal ethics theories do allow experiments if the benefits outweigh the moral costs. It only argues that we should apply such a theory to the software, just in case.

The principle also has the advantage that most of the principles and regulations for animal testing can be imported to the pursuit of brain emulation. Unless there is evidence to the contrary, we should treat emulated animals with the same care as that deserved by the original animal. This means in most cases that practices are equally impermissible in the physical lab and the virtual lab. We can also perform virtual versions of practices that reduce suffering, like sedation and painkillers. Parameters in the simulation can be changed to have the same functional effects that drugs would have in a biological nervous system – or even go beyond them by completely preventing any output from pain-related neurons. It is also possible to run only part of an emulated brain, leaving out pain receptors, pain systems, or systems related to consciousness. That is difficult or impossible in biological animals, but can be done exactly and reversibly in emulations.

Avoiding suffering from experiments is not the only problem in animal experiments: there is an increasing realization that lab animals also need an adequate quality of life in general. In the case of emulations, the problem is that quality of life presumably requires both an adequate simulated body, and an adequate environment for the simulated body to exist in.

This is not going to be much of a problem for the early emulations: worms and snails are unlikely to find a crude VR analogue of their Petri dish or aquarium inadequate. Higher mammals have higher demands of quality of life. Running a brief test in a crude virtual environment might be acceptable, but keeping a mouse, cat, or monkey living in a bare environment or with a crude body for an extended time is not. It can be tricky to figure out what level of resolution is needed. We have no way of estimating the importance rats place on smells, and whether the smells in the virtual cage are rich enough to be adequate. The intricacy of body simulations also matters: how realistic does fur have to feel to simulated touch to be adequate? Modeling the *right* aspects requires a sensitive understanding of the lifeworlds of animals we might prove unable to meet reliably.

One way around the moral hazard might be just to run the experiments and then restore the emulation to the initial state: there is no "free time." But getting good data often requires having animals in a natural state of mind (or body), so they need time to acclimatize to their environment or to behave so the effects of interventions can be seen.

It seems likely that we can develop good practices for treating emulated animals, just as we can develop good practices for treating biological animals. We can approximate enough of the inner life of animals from observations to make some inferences; so too with detecting problems peculiar to their emulated states. In fact, the transparency of an emulation to data-gathering makes it easier to detect certain hazards such as activation of pain systems or behavioral withdrawal, allowing us in principle to backtrack to their causal source. Perhaps we could learn things about the lifeworlds of animals from emulations that we couldn't learn from biological animals.

6 The life and death of emulations

Most animal testing regulations present suffering as the central issue, and hence euthanasia as a way of reducing it. Some critics of animal experimentation argue that, on the contrary, an animal life holds intrinsic value, so ending it is wrong. Emulations throw a spanner into the works by splintering death.

Emulations can have strange existences. They will likely come into being due to the death of a biological organism (since scanning methods are unlikely to be non-destructive). Their existence might consist of periods alternating activity and inert storage of indefinite length. They can be terminated instantly and painlessly. It is possible (due to the multiple realizability of software) to create multiple instances of the same emulation and to terminate them at different times, producing a branching tree of life histories. If ending the identifiable life of an instance is a wrong, then it might be possible to produce a large number of wrongs by repeatedly running and deleting instances of an emulation even if the experiences during the run are neutral or identical.

Another possibility is to run the emulation, make a backup copy of its state, allow some time to pass, delete the running emulation, and replace it with the copy. In this case, it seems that the break in continuity is only observable on the outside: the emulation restored from the backup will continue what it was doing. But there will be a loss of experience of the time between the backup and replacement. It is not clear that much is lost if the interval is very short. Regan (1983) argues that the harm of death is a function of the opportunities of satisfaction it forecloses; in this case it seems that it forecloses the opportunities envisioned by the emulation after the backup copy is made, but it is balanced by whatever satisfaction can be achieved during that time. In fact, the new instance can get the same satisfaction again – the hungry virtual mouse might eat its cheese twice.

A harm that can be reversed is normally seen as smaller than an irreversible harm. Emulation reduces the sting of death by making several of the harms of death completely or partially reversible: suffering while dying, stopping experience, bodily destruction, changes of identity, cessation of existence. Suffering can be abolished using virtual analgesics, experience can be turned on or off by running or stopping the emulation software, the virtual body can be changed without affecting the neural model, the computer hardware "body" can be replaced with other hardware, identity might be modified by software psychosurgery and, perhaps, by the scanning and emulation process, and instances can be deleted and restored from backups. In biological organisms, all these harms are usually bundled together but emulation can separate them. Death forecloses fewer opportunities to emulations.

Some might argue that the problem is not ending emulations, but the fundamental lack of respect for a being. The emulated mouse might not notice anything wrong, but we know it is treated in a disrespectful way.

The reversibility of many forms of emulated death might make emulated life cheaper. In a lifeboat case where we can either give a place in a lifeboat to an animal or to a computer running an emulation of a same-species animal, should we sacrifice the software? If it can be restored from backup, the real loss will be just the lost memories since the most recent backup and possibly some freedom. We might still agree that according to the PAM we should treat the emulation as if it had the same moral weight as the original animal, but in the lifeboat case there is a genuine reason to give priority to the individual without a backup. This reasoning might also carry over to human emulations: the harm from the (total, irreversible) death of one's sole instance is greater than the harm of the death of one's current instance that has a recent backup.

Most people accept that animal life should not be taken wantonly. But cheap death might weaken this: it is easy and painless to end an emulation, and it might be restored with equal ease, with no apparent harm done. If more animals are needed, they can be instantiated up to the limits set by available hardware. Might this lead to a reduction of the value of emulated life? Slippery slope arguments are rarely rationally convincing despite their storytelling: this one depends on our overusing emulated animals and then rationalizing this overuse by an assumed lesser value. But what has been reduced is merely the harm of death, not the value of life. The problem lies in rationalizing something convenient rather than emulation. There is also a much likelier risk that people will treat emulations as unconscious simulacra just because they are software.

7 Ethics of human and animal emulations

Surprisingly, the question of moral status is easier to handle in the case of human emulations than in the animal case, since human emulations can report back about their state.

If a person who is skeptical of brain emulations being conscious or having free will is emulated and, after due introspection and consideration, changes their mind, then that would seem to be some evidence in favor of emulations actually having an inner life. Strictly speaking, however, it would not prove anything stronger than that the processes whereby a person changes their mind are correctly emulated. The emulation *could* still be a functional philosophical zombie lacking consciousness.

If philosophical zombies existed, it seems likely that they would be treated as persons as they took part in human societies. They would behave like persons, they would vote, they would complain and demand human rights if mistreated, and in most scenarios there would not be any way to distinguish the zombies from the humans. They might even invoke the PAM. Hence, if emulations of human brains work well enough to exhibit human-like behavior rather than mere human-like neuroscience, legal personhood is likely to eventually follow, despite the misgivings of skeptical philosophers.

Personal identity is going to be a major issue with brain emulations, both because of the transition from an original unproblematic single human identity to successor identity/identities that might or might not be the same, and because software minds can potentially have multiple realizability. The discussion about how personal identity relates to successor identities on different substrates is already extensive, and I will not add to it here. There are also intriguing questions about how moral obligations carry over when copies are made, and what rights the originals have to dispose of versions of themselves. At the very least, it seems that each running instance is an example of a potential moral agent (as per the PAM), so each ought to be treated well regardless of the existence of other copies.

8 Volunteers and emulation rights

Is it possible to give informed consent to become a brain emulation? The most likely scanning methods are going to be destructive, meaning that they would end the biological life of the volunteer or be applied to donated brains after the person has been declared dead.

Volunteering in the first case is a form of unusual assisted suicide, where a possible outcome is another life. Due to the uncertainty about the mental life of software there is no guarantee that there will be any experience "after," even if the emulation technology looks perfect. There will also be the usual considerations about personal identity and continuity, but no doubt volunteers will tend to have views on these compatible with an emulation being *them* in a sense that matters.

From a legal standpoint this might be problematic, even in liberal jurisdictions. While ending one's life in order to escape pain is increasingly accepted, doing it for science is not. The Nuremberg code states that "No experiment should be conducted, where there is an a priori reason to believe that death or disabling injury will occur."

There might be an opening if the emulation researchers themselves volunteer. The code continues: "except, perhaps, in those experiments where the experimental physicians also serve as subjects." But at least at present, extreme self-experimentation is not well regarded. Some experiments may produce such lasting harm that they cannot be justified by any social value of the research (Miller and Rosenstein 2008). No doubt some people will think the possibility of reaching a posthuman state with fundamentally open-ended evolutionary possibilities might actually have a sufficiently high value. The resulting debate will no doubt be both acrimonious and fascinating.

One volunteer group who would seem better placed to take part in brain emulation research is terminal patients, who might prefer this particular form of "suicide" to a guaranteed death. An analogy can be made to the use of experimental therapies by the terminally ill, where concerns about harm must be weighed against uncertainty about the therapy, and where the vulnerability of patients makes them exploitable – it is not hard to imagine brain emulation being oversold by enthusiastic developers.

In the case of post-mortem brain scanning, the legal and ethical situation is easier. There is no legal or moral person in existence, just the preferences of a past person and the rules for handling anatomical donations. This also means that a successful brain emulation based on a person would exist in a legal limbo: the law would lack the resources to regard it as more than an unusual product resulting from a legitimate anatomical donation. It would not be regarded as a person, and current views would hold it to be the property of whatever institution performed the experiment.

Just as in the zombie case, a highly successful human brain emulation could probably convince a liberal society that it was a thinking, feeling being with moral agency, and hence entitled to various rights. The PAM would support this: even if one doubted that the being was "real," the moral risk of not treating a potential moral agent well would be worse than the risk of treating non-moral agents better than needed. It is another matter whether this would be convincing enough to have the order of death nullified and the emulation regarded as the same *legal* person as the donor.

The risks of ending up a non-person in the eyes of the law, possibly being used against one's will for someone else's purposes, ending up in a brain-damaged state, or waking up in a disorientingly alien future might not deter volunteers. Similar risks certainly do not deter people from signing contracts for cryonic preservation today, although they are fully aware that they will be stored as non-person anatomical donations and might be revived in a future with greatly altered moral and social views. Given that the alternative is certain death, cryonic preservation appears to many to be a rational choice.

9 Handling of flawed and distressed versions

Whatever the moral problems in the case of experimental animals, they are worse for attempted human emulations. The process might produce distressed minds that have rights yet have an existence not worth living, or that lack the capacity to form or express their wishes. For example, they could exist in analogs to persistent vegetative states, dementia, schizophrenia, or chronic pain. Many of these are of course parallel to current cases in medical ethics.

When can you "pull the plug" of an emulation? It might seem easy to argue that when we are ethically forbidden from pulling the plug of a counterpart biological human, we are forbidden from doing the same to the emulation. This unfortunately might lead to a situation where we have a large number of emulation "patients" requiring significant resources, yet not contributing anything to refining the technology nor having any realistic chance of a "cure."

Fortunately, a running emulation can be stopped and its state stored for possible future instantiation. This way at least ongoing painful or meaningless experience is stopped and no resources wasted, but it leads to questions about the right to eventual revival of the now frozen emulations. What if they were left on a shelf forever, without ever restarting? That would be the same as deletion. But do they in that case have a right to be run at least occasionally, despite their lacking any detectable benefit from the experience?

Persons might write advance directives about the treatment of their emulations. This appears equivalent to normal advance directives, although the reversibility of local termination makes pulling the plug less problematic. It is less clear how to handle directives to terminate more subtly deranged emulations. While a person might not currently wish to have a version with a personality disorder become the successor, at the point where the emulation comes into being it will potentially be a moral subject with a right to its life, and might regard its changed personality as the "correct" one.

10 Time and communication

Emulations will experience and behave on a timescale set by the speed of their software. The speed at which their body and world simulations are run relative to the outside world can be changed, depending on available hardware and software. Current large-scale neural simulations are commonly run with slowdown factors between a thousand and a hundred, but there does not seem to be any reason precluding emulations running faster than biological brains: a millionfold increase does not seem impossible.

Nick Bostrom and Eliezer Yudkowsky have proposed a Principle of Subjective Rate of Time: "In cases where the duration of an experience is of basic normative significance, it is the experience's subjective duration that counts" (Bostrom and Yudkowsky, forthcoming). On this account, frozen states do not count at all. Conversely, very fast emulations can rapidly produce a large amount of positive or negative value if they are in extreme states: they might count for more in utilitarian calculations than slower minds.

Is there a right for a human emulation to run in real time, so it can interact with the outside world? Speed does not matter to it as long it interacts only with a virtual world and other emulations set to the same speed. But if its speed diverges from that of biological people, communication with them will become troublesome or impossible. Participation in social activities depends on interaction, and it might be made impossible if human activities flash by faster than the emulation can handle. Conversely, a very fast emulation would be isolated from them by their (apparently) glacial slowness. Hence it seems that if emulated persons are to enjoy human rights (which typically hinge on interactions with other persons and institutions) they will need access to real-time interaction, or at least "disability support" if they cannot function quickly enough.

All this suggests that emulated humans will have a right to contact with the world outside their simulation. As Robert Nozick's (1974: 42–45) experience machine thought experiment demonstrates, most people seem to want to interact with the "real world," although that might just mean the shared social reality of meaningful activity rather than the physical world. Since the virtual world is contingent upon the physical world, and asymmetrically affected by it, restricting access only to the virtual is not enough if the emulated people are to be equal citizens of their wider society.

11 Vulnerability and self-ownership

Software is amazingly fragile compared to biological bodies. The software and data constituting brain emulations and their mental states can be instantly erased or changed by anybody with access to the system on which they are running. Brain emulations would not be self-contained, and their survival would depend upon hardware over which they might not have any control. They could be subjected to undetectable violations such as illicit copying. From an emulation perspective software security is identical to personal security.

They also have a problematic privacy situation, since not only can an emulation's behavior be perfectly documented by the very system it is running on, but also its complete brain states are (in principle) open for inspection. Whether that information can be interpreted in a meaningful way depends on future advances in neuroscience, but it is not unreasonable to think that by the time human emulations exist many neural correlates of private mental states will be known. This would put emulations in a precarious situation.

These considerations suggest that the ethical way of treating software people would be to require strict privacy protection of their computational processes, and that they have legal protection or ownership of the hardware on which they are running. The computer is, in a sense, an emulation's physical body. Can this be squared with actual technological praxis (for example, running emulations as distributed processes in the Cloud) and economic considerations (suppose an emulation ran out of funds to pay for its upkeep)? That remains to be seen.

Even if emulations are granted personhood and adequate property rights in their hardware, they might still find the ownership of parts of themselves to be complicated. It is not obvious that an emulation can claim to own the brain scan that produced it: it was made at a point in time when the person did not legally exist. The process might also produce valuable intellectual property, for example useful neural networks that can be integrated in non-emulation software to solve problems. If so, a problem emerges as to who has a right to the property and any financial proceeds from it. Already there have been legal battles over property rights to cells extracted from patient's bodies and turned into lucrative products. Cervical tumor cells taken from Henrietta Lacks in 1951, the year she died, aided in the development of polio vaccine and other treatments and major discoveries. HeLa cell cultures are still alive in labs, effectively immortal. Lacks' genome has been sequenced, and concerns from her family prevailed in August 2013 when the unremunerated family "decided that it wanted the data to be available under a restricted-access system [linking] individuals' genetic make-up to traits and diseases. Researchers would apply for permission to acquire the data and agree to use them for biomedical research only, and would not contact Lacks family members" (Callaway 2013). Emulations might have even weaker legal protections unless they managed to add enough fine print to their anatomical donation papers.

Conversely, essential sub-systems of the emulation software or hardware could be licensed or outright owned by other parties. Does a right to life or self-ownership trump conventional property rights? Even if it does, the human owners might still want fair compensation and look to assistance from the law. Would it be acceptable for owners of computing facilities to slow down or freeze non-paying emulations? Should this be allowed by a future legal scheme of self-ownership for emulations?

12 The big picture

We have seen that it is possible to develop brain emulations ethically. But is it a good idea in itself?

Leaving aside fiction, which has been exploring the topic ingeniously for at least half a century, the small amount of research on the social impact of human brain emulation suggests it could be massively disruptive. In particular, simple economic models predict that copyable human capital produces explosive economic growth and population increase but also that wages plummet toward Malthusian levels (Hanson 1994, 2008). Economies that can harness emulation technology productively might have a huge strategic advantage over latecomers. It is not hard to imagine emulation technology leading to arms races, increasing inequality, disruption of the old order, and the violent emergence of new centers of power. There would be concerns for human rights, triggers of xenophobia, and volatile religious and philosophical views.

Even if emulation did not lead to conflict, it might still lead to bad outcomes. For example, long-run competition between copyable minds might produce beings optimized only for work, spending all available resources on replication and optimizing away everything that actually gives life value. If emulations are zombies, a humanity tempted by cybernetic immortality might gradually trade away its consciousness.

Conversely, the technology might drastically reduce the harms of death. Given that 160,000 people now die worldwide every day, this might be a *massive* moral good. Non-biological humans might have minuscule ecological footprints and would not need to devour other living creatures. They would be immune to many of the threats to biological humans. If the human species split into two, the joint risks might be significantly reduced, even if emulations had their own worries about power outages and computer viruses. Software minds would have a far better shot at colonizing space than biological minds, and could even be transmitted to receiver bodies without requiring spacecraft. The precious eggs of Earth might be put into more than one basket.

The world available to posthuman, upgradeable minds might contain modes of being more valuable than anything a human could experience – just as our art, games, science, and spirituality have value that other mammals cannot grasp.

Unfortunately, these considerations do not lend themselves to comparison. They all depend on speculative scenarios, and their probabilities and magnitude cannot easily be compared. Rather than offering a rationale either for going ahead or for stopping emulation, they give reasons for assuming that – were it to succeed – it will matter enormously. The value of information that helps determine the correct course of action is equally significant.

We are still far, far away from a race toward posthumanity. But we are close enough to the virtual mice that we should start thinking about how to care for them.

References

Bostrom, Nick, and Yudkowsky, Eliezer. Forthcoming. The ethics of artificial intelligence. In William Ramsey and Keith Frankish, eds., *The Cambridge Handbook of Artificial Intelligence*. Cambridge: Cambridge University Press.

Britton, Nicholas F., and Skevington, Suzanne M. 1996. On the mathematical modeling of pain, *Neurochemical Research* 21(9): 1133–1140.

Callaway, Ewen. 2013. Deal done over HeLa cell line, *Nature News*, http://www.nature.com/news/deal-done-over-hela-cell-line-1.13511 (accessed October 8, 2013).

Chalmers, David J. 1996. *The Conscious Mind: In Search of a Fundamental Theory*. New York and Oxford: Oxford University Press.

Cotterill, Rodney. 2003. CyberChild: A simulation test-bed for consciousness studies. In Owen Holland, ed., *Machine Consciousness*. Exeter: Imprint Academic.

Dennett, Daniel C. 1978. Why you can't make a computer that feels pain. *Synthese* 38: 415–456.

Gamez, David. 2005. An ordinal probability scale for synthetic phenomenology. In R. Chrisley, R. Clowes, and S. Torrance, eds., *Next-Generation Approaches to Machine Consciousness: Proceedings of the AISB05 Symposium on Next-Generation Approaches to Machine Consciousness*. Hatfield, UK: University of Hertfordshire, pp. 85–94.

Gamez, David. 2008. Progress in machine consciousness. *Conscious Cognition* 17(3): 887–910. (Epub. June 14.)

Hanson, R. 1994. If uploads come first: The crack of a future dawn. *Extropy* 6(2): 10–15.

Hanson, R. 2008. Economics of the singularity. *IEEE Spectrum, pp.* 37–42.

Herzog, Michael H., Esfeld, Michael, and Gersner, Wulfram. 2007. Consciousness and the small network argument. *Neural Networks* 20(9): 1054–1056. doi: 10.1016/j.neunet.2007.09.001.

Metzinger, Thomas. 2003. *Being No One*. Cambridge, MA: MIT Press.

Miller F.G., and Rosenstein, D.L. 2008. Challenge experiments. In E.J. Emanuel, C. Grady, R.A. Crouch, et al., eds., *The Oxford Textbook of Clinical Research Ethics*. Oxford: Oxford University Press, pp. 273–279.

Nozick, Robert. 1974. *Anarchy, State, and Utopia*. New York: Basic Books.

Regan, Tom. 1983. *The Case for Animal Rights*. Berkeley: University of California Press.

Regan, T., and Singer, P., eds. 1989. *Animal Rights and Human Obligations*, 2nd edn. Englewood Cliffs, N.J.: Prentice Hall.

Sandberg, Anders. 2013. Feasibility of whole brain emulation. In Vincent C. Müller, ed., *Philosophy and Theory of Artificial Intelligence*. Berlin: Springer, pp. 251–264.

Sandberg, A., and Bostrom, N. 2008. *Whole Brain Emulation: A Roadmap*. Oxford: Future of Humanity Institute, Oxford University.

21

What Will It Be Like To Be an Emulation?

Robin Hanson

The next big epochal change is likely to be the arrival of "artificial intelligence": machines intelligent enough to substitute wholesale for human workers. A good guess about the origin of such machines is that the first ones, arriving within roughly a century, will be uploaded humans – whole brain emulations (Hanson 1994, 2008; Sandberg and Bostrom 2008), or "ems."

> **Definition:** An *em* results from taking a particular human brain, scanning it to record its particular cell features and connections, and then building a computer model that processes signals according to those same features and connections. A good enough em has roughly the same input-output signal behavior as the original human. One might talk with it, and convince it to do useful jobs.

Rather than debate the feasibility or timing of ems, or ponder their implications for the philosophy of mind or identity, this chapter will seek realistic social implications. In what sort of new social world might ems live, and what will it be like to *be* an em?

1 Why think about ems now?

We take far more effort to study the past than the future, even though we can't do anything about the past. But modest efforts have often given

Intelligence Unbound: The Future of Uploaded and Machine Minds, First Edition.
Edited by Russell Blackford and Damien Broderick.

substantial insights into our future, and we would know much more about the future if we tried harder. If policy matters, then the future matters, because most policy effects happen in the future. And unless we are ridiculously self-centered, the distant future matters the most, since with continuing growth we expect that the vast majority will live there.

If, within decades, enormous changes will happen, policy analyses that ignore such shifts might be irrelevant or badly misdirected. So it's important to try to foresee any big upcoming changes, and their likely consequences. My analysis takes the somewhat unusual approach of using basic social theory, in addition to common sense and trend projection, to forecast future societies.

Understanding our descendants also helps us to understand our place in history. We define ourselves in part by how we differ from our neighbors in time.

2 Life among the ems

For some portion of the next century, the world still looks much like ours. Then a few firms start making cheap mind-emulating machines able to substitute wholesale for human workers. States or nations that do not prohibit those machines quickly get fantastically rich, and then dominate the world economy.

Billions of ems, perhaps trillions, are now found in cities packed dense with computer hardware. Such cities are very hot, even glowing, covered and pressurized, and arranged as a vast three-dimensional lattice, rather than as separate buildings, pulling winds of hot air into tall clouds overhead.

Em cities are likely toxic to ordinary humans, who, controlling most of the rest of the Earth, mostly live comfortably on their em-economy investments. While ems could easily buy the rest of the Earth, they don't care enough to bother, beyond ensuring energy, raw materials, and cooling for their cities.

While some ems work in tiny robotic bodies, most do so in virtual offices, and almost everyone plays in virtual reality. Here is the surprising thing: either way, ems think and feel like humans. Their world looks and feels to them much as ours looks and feels to us. Like humans, ems remember a past, are aware of a present, and anticipate a future. Ems can be happy or sad, eager or tired, fearful or hopeful, proud or shamed, creative or derivative, compassionate or cold. Ems have friends, lovers, bosses, and colleagues. Em mental and psychological features might differ from the human average, but, despite some eccentrics, are usually near the range of human variation.

Ems reproduce by making copies who remember exactly the same past, but then diverge afterward with differing experience. Typically, whole teams of copies will work and socialize together, and then retire together from the workforce. Often, hundreds of similar teams are made at once. Most ems remember formerly being in another team, and agreeing to let this copy be made so he or she can join the new team. Ems feel grateful to exist, and mostly accept their place in the world.

As with us, most em choices are Either/Or: shall I spend my personal budget of time and money to do this, or that? An em might pick an entertainment to watch (or participate in), or a friend to be with. But for ems, bigger life choices can be Add/And: shall I allow another me to have a new life? Big choices are often made jointly with copies, teammates, and investors. Teams are tightly bound, like traditional working-class work groups, with lots of insults, teasing, and profanity to express and test emotional strength.

On the upside, most ems have office jobs, and work and play in spectacular high-quality virtual realities without hunger, severe cold or heat, grime, physical illness, or intense pain – unless those are chosen deliberately. Unlimited lifespans are possible. On the downside, em wages are so low, for reasons we'll consider in a moment, that most barely scrape by while working hard for half or more of their waking hours (assuming that ems still need sleep and dreaming time). And their extended lifespans induce greater wealth inequality among ems.

After a short time, most ems, due to strong selection pressures, are copies of the thousand or fewer humans best suited for em jobs. These thousand-or-so copy "clans" are the smartest, most cooperative, hardest-working people comfortable with often splitting off a short-term "spur" copy to do a several-hour task and then end (die), or maybe retire to a much slower speed. At any one time, most working ems (weighing by count or speed) are spurs.

3 The culture of ems

An em would trust its clan of copies more than other groups and may get clan-based life coaching, drawn from the experiences of millions of similar copies. Since clans might be legally liable for member actions, they regulate member behavior to protect clan reputation, making ems pretty trustworthy. To avoid nepotism, inefficiency, and social weirdness, most workplaces would avoid having ems from the same clan take on many different roles. Em firms would be bigger, with more managers, more meetings, and narrower job descriptions.

Em minds run at many different speeds, with higher speeds giving higher status; different speeds have different cultures, and fast cultures fragment into local cultures. The cost to run an em is nearly proportional to its speed over a wide range, making the cost of a subjective minute of em experience nearly independent of speed. Because of different speeds, one-em one-vote won't work, though speed-weighted voting might do. The politics of em city-states and firms might reflect shifting coalitions of clans, perhaps coordinated by widely watched one-copy-per-clan "reality show" social gatherings.

To allow romantic relations when there is unequal demand for male vs. female workers, the less demanded gender might run more slowly, and periodically speed up to meet with faster mates. Em sex would be only for recreation; ems would have superb bodies, and most would have impressive minds. But few would have the youthful personality or wealth that men and women today find sexually attractive.

The em economy might double every month or week, a growth driven less by innovation and more by population increase. While this em era might last for only a year or two, for a typical em running a thousand times as quickly as a human, it would last for subjective millennia. To such ems, their world seems more stable than our world seems to us. Bosses and software engineers run even faster, some at a million times human speed.

Em industries include security, emergency response, training, law, finance, news, entertainment, politics, education, software, computer and communication hardware, energy, cooling, transportation, manufacturing, construction, and mining. Em tasks, to the extent that these have not already been taken over by smart but not human-level AIs, include designing, marketing, selling, purchasing, managing, negotiating, administration, testing, monitoring, diagnosis, repair, cleaning, driving, accounting, assembling, packing, installation, mixing, sorting, and fitting (to the extent that these tasks have not been totally automated).

Faster ems with physical but non-biological bodies have proportionally smaller embodiment; a typical em operating a thousand times quicker than a human would stand 2 millimeters tall. Physical ems see a mix of reality and virtual overlays. Most long-distance physical travel is "beam me up" electronic travel, though done with care to avoid mind theft. Compared to humans, ems are far less fearful of the death of their particular copy. But the risk of mind theft is a frightful evil, being a plausible route to personal destitution, torture, or worse, and a serious threat to the economic order. While some ems offer themselves as open source and free to copy, most ems work hard to prevent or mitigate mind theft, a cause that evokes great moral feelings and charity efforts.

Humans today reach peak productivity around the age of 50. Most ems are near their age of peak productivity, perhaps 60 or more. Older minds become less flexible, and must eventually retire to an indefinite life of leisure at a much slower speed, sometimes as low as one thousandth of human speed. The subjective lifespans of both humans and slow em retirees depend mainly on the stability of the em civilization; a collapse or revolution might kill them. Ems would be wary of allowing theft from retirees and humans, as that might threaten the institutions ems use to keep peace among themselves.

4 Em identity

Ems focus their identity less on individual personalities and abilities, and more on being part of a particular team. While copy clans coordinate to show off common clan abilities, individual ems focus on showing their identities, abilities, and loyalties as team players. Teams prefer to socialize internally, to reduce team productivity variance. Instead of trying to cure a depressed or lovesick em, that individual can be reverted to a version from before the problem appeared. For larger problems, whole teams might be reverted or replaced.

Team members can often read the surface of each other's minds. In general, ems specialize in dealing either with high transparency or high opacity of associates' minds. Ems can mistrust their own experiences, suspecting that unusual experiences might be simulations designed to test their loyalty or extract a secret. Many schemes are tried to avoid being fooled by a simpler automated mimic.

By having one em plan and train, and then split into many copies who do the related tasks, ems find it easier to prepare for and coordinate tasks. For example, a single em can conceive of a software or artistic design and vision, and then split into an army who execute that vision. Childhood and job training are similarly cheaper; copies of young humans' minds are rare but pampered.

Larger projects can also be completed more often on time, if not on budget, by speeding up the ems who work on lagging parts. More generally, em firms are larger and better coordinated, because fast bosses can coordinate more, and because employee clans with strong financial and reputational interests less often game employee evaluations.

Even if most ems work hard much of the time, and will probably end or retire soon, they usually remember a long history of succeeding against the odds, with long stretches of leisure and training punctuated by short intense work periods. Such self-deception is easier for ems because when things really matter spurs can convince them to do what is practical without explaining why. To most ems, it seems good to be an em.

5 Inequality

How unequal would ems be from one another?

During humankind's forager era, the main units of organization were bands of roughly 20 to 50 people, and smaller family units. Foragers did differ in personal property or prestige, but lacking larger units foragers did not have inequality analogous to our unequal towns, firms, or nations. Over the million-year-plus forager era, however, foragers had great inequality of lineages, in the sense that almost all lineages became extinct.

The farmer era saw larger units of organization, such as clans, towns, nations, and empires. While empires sometimes became nearly as large as feasible, transportation limits weakened their influence on local behavior. Towns were usually much smaller than nations, and firms were smaller still. While most farmers lived in rather small towns, with the emergence of industry people aggregated evenly across feasible city sizes.

For most products today, market shares are relatively concentrated within transport-cost-limited market areas; for each type of product, a small number of firms supply most customers.

Power laws often well describe the upper tails of the distributions of how such items are grouped into units. In such cases, a power of 1.0 describes a uniform distribution of items across feasible unit sizes. Powers greater than 1.0 describe more equal distributions, where most items reside in small units, and powers less than 1.0 describe less equal distributions, where most items are clumped into fewer, larger units. Compared to some reference-sized unit, for a power of 1.0 a unit twice the size is half as frequent. For a power greater than 1.0, such double-size units are less frequent, and with a power less than 1.0 they are more frequent.

In all eras so far, family names have been distributed relatively equally, with a power of about 2.0. In the late farmer era, towns were distributed with a power of about 1.4 (Nitsch 2005), roughly the power that describes today's individual wealth distribution (Davies et al. 2008). Today, nations, firms within nations, and cities within nations, are all distributed with a power of about 1.0 (Axtell 2001; Eeckhout 2004; Giesen et al. 2010). Product suppliers are usually more clumped, with a power less than 1.0.

Em-era clans probably clump much more unequally than did prior-em-era families; most ems, as noted, might come from a dozen to a thousand clans. Labor markets become much more like today's product markets, with a few clans supplying most workers in any given skill area. Clans coordinate to prevent the theft of their members, and to ensure that they can profit from training investments. Fixed costs of training and marketing create concentration and market power, though not net profits after paying for fixed costs. Because virtual reality meetings greatly cut the commuting congestion that limits city sizes today, em cities and nations are also likely to be much more unequal, with most ems found in a few very large city-states.

Em firms would probably continue to be distributed evenly across feasible firm sizes. Even so, because a larger economy could support larger firms, typical firm size would increase. Today in a world of 7 billion people, firms are spread evenly between, roughly, one and 1 million employees. The middle firm size, where half of workers are in larger firms, is about 1000. For every factor of 100 increase in the size of the largest feasible firm, there should be about a factor of 10 increase in the size of the average-size firm.

Em wealth would also probably be more unequal, because of both indefinite em lifespans and the em capacity to run at different speeds. Today, cities and firms can spread uniformly across all feasible sizes due to their indefinite lifespans; if a city or firm continues to succeed, it can grow, regardless of its age. In contrast, while wealthy individuals today often consistently grow their wealth over their lifespan, their children usually fail to continue the same growth pattern. Rags-to-riches-to-rags in three generations is, after all, a common scenario. With indefinite em lifespans, however, successful ems could continue their winning financial habits indefinitely. This should tend to distribute wealth more evenly across all feasible wealth sizes, rather as firms and cities are distributed evenly today across feasible sizes.

The tendency of em minds to become inflexible with experience, however, could somewhat reduce this effect, especially if rich ems do not reduce their speed. On the other hand, the ability to run at many different speeds will expand the possible range of em wealth. While very poor humans must starve, very poor ems can run at very slow speeds or be archived at negligible cost.

A power of 1.0 for the distribution of em wealth would make wealth more unequal than today, both because this is a more unequal power, and because a richer em world can make feasible both higher and lower wealth levels. While today's richest person holds ~0.02 percent of the world's wealth, the richest em may hold a much larger fraction, perhaps ~2 percent. The exact fraction, however, might depend on em wealth-sharing arrangements. For example, some em clans might agree to share much of their wealth internally.

6 War

Today the frequency of war, civil war, and criminal violence tends to fall as nations get richer, have older citizens, and sit more toward the extremes of democracy and autocracy (Magee and Massoud 2011). The fact that most ems would be near peak-productivity subjective age suggests that their attitudes toward war would be more like that of a typical 50-year-old, who today is less supportive of war. The fact that ems would be poorer in many ways, however, might push for more war. Other relevant factors might include em gender imbalances, reduced calming effects from raising children, productivity tweaks that might increase aggressiveness, and a generally more competitive world.

Having ems concentrated in a few very large, dense cities should reduce the frequency of small wars. After all, wars within cities are very destructive of the value that cities produce, and cities have many other ways to help discourage and settle internal disputes. Wars were especially common in the farming era because valuable loot could be seized, and because farm land quickly returned to full productivity even after all-out war burned crops and buildings to the ground.

Wars between big cities are a greater concern, in part because some cities might beat others in economic competitions. Nuclear weapons could still threaten to destroy entire cities in a single strike. To a kilo-em, however, running at a thousandfold speed-up, a nuclear missile that gave 15 minutes of objective warning time would give 10 days of subjective warning, making it much easier to respond flexibly. In contrast, lasers and directed-energy weapons would still have apparently instantaneous effects on city-scale distances. To mega-ems, however, such light-speed weapons would seem to have substantial delays on such scales.

Em soldiers would hardly fear the death of any one copy, as they could easily revert to a recent backup copy. The material resources lost when a copy (or a city) is destroyed, however, would still sting. Wars of attrition would be accounted less by deaths than by resources destroyed.

7 Clans

How would clans organize?

Each of us today is part of many organizations: neighborhoods, firms, clubs. But we rely most on our families when we seek strong long-term bonds and trust. It is in families that we mainly share resources, let ourselves be most vulnerable, and seek help in bad times. Humans evolved to trust families more than others because of closer genetic relations, and we have developed many family-specific adaptations to complement such trust.

Today, identical twins are even more closely related than other family members. Because of the rarity of such twins, humans have probably evolved few adaptations specific to twinning. Even so, the bonds and trust between identical twins are usually even stronger than between other siblings and parents.

Ems will have access to a new and tighter unit of organization: clans of copies of the same original person. Compared to families or even identical twins, ems will have yet stronger reasons to trust and bond with fellow clan members. This makes em copy clans a natural unit of finance, reproduction, legal liability, and political representation.

Clans with billions or more members would likely split into sub-clans of millions or thousands, at least for many purposes. The tree structure of their copy ancestry is a natural basis for such sub-clan grouping. During the farming era, ancestry trees of family clans were often a basis for legal liability, political coalitions, and much else. Relative to em clans, em sub-clans would be more similar to each other in jobs, hobbies, friends, personality, and shared memories.

Law usually tries to deter crime via small chances of big punishments. It can be especially hard, however, to impose big punishments cheaply on short-lived ems (such as spurs). Giving spurs a longer fast life to suffer judicially imposed retributive torture, for example, could be expensive. For such ems it can make sense to use vicarious liability, i.e., to have legal liability apply to an associated unit with deeper pockets. In principle, this could be any sponsor willing to take on the liability, but in practice it probably would be the sub-clan containing this em. The em would care more about harming its sub-clan, and the sub-clan would know better how to discourage liability-inducing events.

Holding closely related copies responsible might seem more legitimate if archived versions could be tested in simulation to see if they would behave similarly given a similar criminal opportunity, at least for situations where behavioral inclinations seem relevant. Em clan liability is similar to the way that farmer societies often made larger family units liable for the crimes of family members. In response, clans legally liable for member behavior would seek to regulate problematic behaviors, and seek sufficient powers in order to manage clan reputations. Ems in clans that more strongly manage their reputations are likely to be more predictable and reliable.

Since political regimes become unstable when members do not accept their legitimacy, and since we tend to accept and defer to internal decisions of families more than to those of other kinds of groupings, farmer-era city and regional politics often used families as the first unit of grouping. Accordingly, ancient politics was often the politics of shifting coalitions of family clans (Braekevelt et al. 2012). This remains true in the Middle East and Asia (Sailer 2003).

For ems, it makes more sense to use clans as the first unit of political organization. If most ems constitute from a dozen to a thousand clans, the politics of an em city-state might naturally be the politics of shifting coalitions of em copy clans. Clans whose root ems were raised together as children might tend to ally more with each other, and childhood cohorts might be chosen with this prospect in mind. To encourage clan loyalty, clans could also try to anticipate and coordinate to prevent situations where clan members compete over friends, lovers, or jobs. For example, different sub-clans might be prevented from competing for the same jobs or teams. In a clan-dominated era, people whose basic personality makes it harder to coordinate and compromise with copies of themselves might suffer a serious competitive disadvantage.

8 Intelligence unbound

Merely being faster will make ems seem smarter in many ways. Even if we control for speed, however, ems would be smarter than humans because of stronger selection, both in choosing ems from among humans, and in selecting mental tweaks for the emulation process. Ems might also find ways to get smarter by expanding their mental hardware, perhaps by increasing the number or size of many simple repeating brain circuits. And some ems might choose to lower their brain hardware costs by getting dumber, via reducing the number or size of such circuitry.

We expect smarter workers to accomplish more with the same resources, to make fewer and less consequential mistakes, to master a wider scope of tasks and skills, to communicate effectively with a wider range of fellow workers doing different jobs, to adapt to changing circumstances faster and better, and to learn specific and specialized roles faster and better.

How these changing capacities would change the mix of jobs and careers will vary by profession and industry. In more stable, slower-changing environments, the gains from making fewer mistakes and better learning specific skills should allow a finer division of labor into more specialized, more interdependent roles. By contrast, in uncertain and rapidly changing environments, the abilities to master more skills and adapt faster should matter more; em organizations should be able to function effectively in a wider range of such environments, using smaller teams of less specialized workers.

By being smarter, ems should become better at innovation, em bosses should be able to manage simultaneously a wider range of subordinates, em jobs could be redesigned more often, and em careers should last longer before em minds become too fragile to compete effectively.

But note: while these changes are non-trivial, they are also not radical. A society full of creatures much smarter than we are could remain quite recognizable and understandable to humans. It need not create a horizon of visibility beyond which we cannot see. Some claim that a world of much smarter creatures would quickly become a world run by a single dominant mind. I've explained my reasons for disagreeing with that elsewhere (Hanson and Yudkowsky 2013), but even if it happened, such a world would differ primarily in its concentration of power, not in the intelligence of its creatures.

9 Conclusion

The analysis in this chapter suggests that lives in the next great era might be as different from what we are accustomed to as ours are from farmers' lives, or farmers' from foragers'. Some readers, living industrial-era lives and sharing industrial-era values, will be disturbed to see a forecast of em-era descendants with choices and lifestyles that appear to reject many values they hold dear. Such readers might be tempted reject this scenario, and fight to prevent it, perhaps preferring a continuation of the industrial era to the arrival of such a different epoch.

But I advise such readers to first try hard to see this new era in some detail from the point of view of its typical residents. See what they enjoy and find meaningful, consider what fills them with pride, and listen to their criticisms of your era and values. Understand how disturbed foragers were by many aspects of farmers' lives, and farmers by many aspects of our industry-era lives. And then decide.

References

Axtell, Robert L. 2001. Zipf distribution of US firm sizes. *Science* 293: 5536

Braekevelt, Jonas, Buylaert, Frederik, Dumolyn, Jan, and Haemers, Jelle. 2012. The politics of factional conflict in late medieval Flanders. *Historical Research* 85(227): 13–31.

Davies, James B., Sandström, Susanna, Shorrocks, Anthony, and Wolff, Edward N. 2008. *The world distribution of household wealth*, UNU-WIDER Discussion Paper 2008/03, February.

Eeckhout, Jan. 2004. Gibrat's law for (all) cities. *American Economic Review* (January): 1429–1451.

Giesen, Kristian, Zimmermann, Arndt, and Suedekum, Jens. 2010. The size distribution across all cities – Double Pareto lognormal strikes. *Journal of Urban Economics* 68(2): 129–137.

Hanson, Robin. 1994. If uploads come first: The crack of a future dawn. *Extropy* 6(2): 10–15.

Hanson, Robin. 2008. Economics of the Singularity. *IEEE Spectrum* (June): 37–42.

Hanson, Robin, and Yudkowsky, Eliezer. 2013. *The Hanson–Yudkowsky AI-Foom Debate*. Berkeley, CA: Machine Intelligence Research Institute.

Magee, Christopher, and Massoud, Tansa. 2011. Openness and internal conflict. *Journal of Peace Research* 48: 59–72.

Nitsch, Volker. 2005. Zipf zipped. *Journal of Urban Economics* 57(1): 86–100.

Sailer, Steve. 2003. Cousin marriage conundrum: The ancient practice discourages democratic nation-building. *The American Conservative* (January 13): 20–22.

Sandberg, Anders, and Bostrom, Nick. 2008. *Whole Brain Emulation: A Roadmap*, Oxford: Future of Humanity Institute, Oxford University, www.fhi.ox.ac.uk/brain-emulation-roadmap-report.pdf (accessed October 26, 2013).

Afterword

Linda MacDonald Glenn

This book is a wonderful illustration for a proposition by William Arthur Ward (1970):

> *The adventure of life is to learn. The purpose of life is to grow. The nature of life is to change. The challenge of life is to overcome. The essence of life is to care. The opportunity of life is to serve. The secret of life is to dare.*

Yes. Life, with all that the future holds, is a true adventure. Adventures can be exhilarating and galvanizing but they can also be unnerving and, sometimes, downright frightening. Our colleagues attempt to augur the adventure: what fundamental changes lie in store for humanity in a world where the merger of human and machine seems inevitable? Whether or not their prognostications are accurate remains to be seen, but their reflections are about growing, changing, overcoming, caring, serving, and daring, all the elements of a hale and hearty life, as Ward suggests.

In the first essay, "How Conscience Apps and Caring Computers will Illuminate and Strengthen Human Morality," James Hughes tackles moral enhancement, daring humanity to care and serve with exocortical facilitation and software. While he expresses concerns about the voluntariness of their use, he envisions "a robust, evolving ecosystem of moral enhancement tools" that would help the average (read: unsaintly) person retain compassion and mindfulness, and new levels of moral self-control and consistency.

Intelligence Unbound: The Future of Uploaded and Machine Minds, First Edition.
Edited by Russell Blackford and Damien Broderick.

In "Threshold Leaps in Advanced Artificial Intelligence," Michael Anissimov focuses on the exponential growth of AI and urges readers to stretch their imagination beyond what most people think of as AI (i.e., human-like intelligence) and to apply intelligent engineering and computational power, raised to the *n*th degree, to biologically inspired designs. Anissimov's approach is somewhat reminiscent of Robert Freitas' "Sentience Quotient," which is a "sliding scale of cosmic sentience universally applicable to any intelligent entity in the cosmos," based on computational power (Freitas 1984). But the comparison ends there. Freitas' use of the word "sentience" departs from traditional philosophical use of the term, and perhaps the word "sapience" would be more appropriate; although Anissimov ponders the implications of exponential computer power, he leaves the philosophical ponderings to his other colleagues.

In "Who Knows Anything About Anything About AI?" Stuart Armstrong and Seán ÓhÉigeartaigh look at the various methods of prediction (causal models, non-causal models, the outside view, philosophical arguments, and expert judgments) and analyze their accuracy. Their assessment of the methods leads to a realization that there are limits to what can truly be known (aka "unknown unknowns"), but that we must continue to strive for accuracy. My hope is that this team might combine their analytical skills with the science of networking, as described by Albert-László Barabási (2002), and the wisdom of Malcolm Gladwell in *Outliers* (2008). Perhaps they might overcome the shortcomings they rightly point to in current methods and develop an entirely new one that becomes the standard for prediction models.

In their chapter "Nine Ways to Bias Open-Source Artificial General Intelligence Toward Friendliness," Ben Goertzel and Joel Pitt propose that an open-source AGI can and should be biased toward friendliness, and they offer nine ways to do just that. They take Eliezer Yudkowsky's notion of Coherent *Extrapolated* Volition a step further, and proffer that, with human collaboration, through a collective interactive process, Coherent *Blended* Volition can be designed. This blending process is already present in what the authors term the "Global Brain" (the composite, self-organizing information system comprising humans, computers, data stores, the Internet, mobile phones, and other communication systems) and supports deep sharing and collective engagement among human participants. Along the lines of "transparency is the best disinfectant," Goertzel and Pitt recommend that the development of the AGI be tightly linked with the Global Brain. Other useful suggestions include the creation of an "AGI Nanny" and the fostering of deep, consensus-building interactions and commensurability between divergent viewpoints. This resembles my call in a 2003 article,

"Biology at the Margins of Personhood," where I discuss evolving notions of personhood and their implications.

In "Feasible Mind Uploading," Randal Koene details developments at the intersection of neuroscience, the connectome, and artificial intelligence that hold the promise of one form of immortality: mind uploading (or whole brain emulation). Koene argues that the notion of uploading a mind means that we want to take that which we think embodies or generates ourselves, the feeling of being, the experience of existence – and to capture it in a new physical state or keep it going while replacing the physical mechanisms that are generating it. The potential reconstruction of a mind outside the biological framework conjures up a possible future with a "library of personages." Instead of reading biographies or autobiographies, imagine checking out the thoughts, memories, and experiences of an Albert Einstein or a Marie Curie. It is a concept that melds nicely with the "extended mind thesis" in philosophy, where the mind is seen as encompassing every level of the cognitive process, including the use of external aids, such as our smartphones and digital devices (Clark and Chalmers 1998).

David Chalmers, one of the original philosophical proponents of this thesis, probes the different possible methods of mind uploading in "Uploading: A Philosophical Analysis." His chapter is the first of several that consider issues relating to self-identity and destructive uploading, gradual uploading, and non-destructive uploading. His analysis here is drawn from his more general work on the Singularity (Chalmers 2010), which has prompted considerable debate among philosophers of mind and others concerned with the nature and preconditions of consciousness. His writings take Scottish philosopher David Hume's concept of self and his analogy of the Ship of Theseus to new levels and into the modern era.

By contrast, Massimo Pigliucci's "Mind-Uploading: A Philosophical Counter-Analysis," contends that consciousness and self-identity are inherently biological phenomena. Pigliucci subscribes to John Searle's (2008) "biological naturalism" position, and attempts to refute the notion that the concept of self-identity can be independent from the substrate, as that results in a form of dualism. He rejects destructive uploading as constituting a form of suicide, a mere simulation of the original self, and rejects uploading in a non-destructive manner as mere duplication, not preservation of identity.

In their jointly authored contribution, "If You Upload, Will You Survive?", it seems as if Joseph Corabi and Susan Schneider pick up where Pigliucci left off and ask the further question, if uploading of a particular sort does not preserve identity, is the upload at least a *continuation* of the original? Corabi and Schneider draw some lessons from earlier debates about cloning, examine the debate following Chalmers' previous consideration of gradual uploading, and argue for a negative answer to their posed question. For Corabi and Schneider, spatiotemporal discontinuity issues, together with the assumption that the biological brain is destroyed (albeit gradually), defeat the possibility that you could survive mind uploading.

In his chapter, "On the Prudential Irrationality of Mind Uploading," Nicholas Agar contemplates the pros and cons of strong artificial intelligence, and argues that uploading should not replace the option to maintain a biological substrate. If uploading the mind results in death of the biological substrate, this may deny a future in which technologies compatible with the survival of a biological brain can rejuvenate our bodies and enhance our powers of thought. On Agar's assumptions, an approach grounded in decision theory necessitates that we say no to the prospect of mind uploading.

Mark Walker argues for the opposite view in "Uploading and Personal Identity." He distinguishes between token and type identity, argues persuasively that preservation of either identity is a worthy goal, and suggests that there are considerable advantages (or at least apparent advantages) to being uploaded, including immortality and enhancement.

Naomi Wellington takes a refreshingly different approach to this ongoing debate in her chapter, "Whole Brain Emulation: Invasive vs. Non-Invasive Methods." She examines five emulation methods, draws a distinction between Structure Replication and Structure Reconstruction and (on the other hand) Reverse Brain Engineering, and asserts that a distinction between invasive vs. non-invasive terminology is more useful in teasing out the complex issues of identity and selfhood. After a detailed explanation of currently proposed methods, Wellington concludes that the only possible method that would preserve personal identity throughout would be a very gradual emulation process, where the brain is replaced neuron by neuron. Alternatively, we might need to rely on an intelligence explosion associated with a technological singularity, which might produce possibilities that we can't now even imagine.

Kathleen Ann Goonan urges us not to be too quick to abandon our corporeal existence in her chapter, "The Future of Identity: Implications, Challenges, and Complications of Human/Machine Consciousness." In one of my favorite passages in the book, Goonan offers a vision in which advanced technology is used to transform us gradually, from within:

> Thus the best approach to life extension and consciousness expansion might lie in our own marvelously complex and entire bodies, meshed with and augmented by tiny bionan machines that become a part of us, rather than the opposite vision of humans migrating into a machine substrate. You might grow your own eternal, artificial self as you gradually become bionic, in stages so tiny that you do not even notice.

This is consistent with Raymond Kurzweil's view of the Singularity (Kurzweil 2005) and the gradual uploading argument developed by Chalmers. A similar vision to Goonan's is also illustrated masterfully in Mark Stiegler's 1989 short story "The Gentle Seduction" (reprinted in Stiegler 1990); this is required reading for anyone interested in elevating the human condition.

Shifting from these tough questions of identity and survival, Joe Strout's chapter "Practical Implications of Mind Uploading" paints a colorful future where such characteristics as race, gender, and appearance become much more matters of choice – rather than predetermination – and you can order your own custom-built body. But then, how will we distinguish each other, or ourselves, as individuals? As Strout points out, "The irony will be that, when everyone looks beautiful, perfect looks will come to seem mundane." He goes well beyond the cosmetic level, describing possible "mer-folk" who would thrive in the ocean, winged individuals able to take flight, and the ultimate enhancement of our senses. Strout imagines the extraordinary lifestyle changes that uploading, duplication, virtual (or artificial) reality, extreme life extension, and intergalactic space travel might bring. Throughout this uplifting piece, he maintains that even these changes are fundamentally superficial, and that we will retain our humanity, so long as we continue to love, laugh, cry, and care for one another.

Nicole Olson's contribution is similarly uplifting. In "The Values and Directions of Uploaded Minds," Olson notes that post-biological existence entails the possibility of novel sensory and aesthetic modalities. More importantly, she asks how our values and the meaning of our lives will change with such dramatic change in our abilities. She anticipates that, in a manner akin to Maslow's hierarchy of needs, what we consider valuable will change: uploading and departing from biological substrates will enable humans to leap upward in motivational hierarchies. Although she doesn't state this explicitly, she hints that in leaping upward we might eventually create an entirely new set of needs and transcend Maslow's highest level of self-actualization. But this leads to a question that reads like a Zen koan: If you can transcend self-actualization, was there truly ever a self to actualize? Or transcend?

Max More, a renowned transhumanist philosopher, offers his own version of a radical future for human minds and bodies, encouraging us to embrace "The Enhanced Carnality of Post-Biological Life." In this spirited and passionate chapter (in which the first subtitle is "Fake fear and loathing of the flesh"), More contests the misleading stereotype of flabby technogeeks who putatively dream of living in a virtual world. In particular, he rebuts the notion that, if you seek to improve something, you must loathe it in its current form. He argues that we should enjoy our corporeal pleasures, yet seek to improve on them. In particular, we have every reason to stop the aging process and even reverse it, to regain a wider range of function, enhance our enjoyment of life, and expand the range of physical entities in which we can live. On More's approach, it is rational and good to seek freedom from the restraints and limitations of our current biological structures. Personally, as someone who has enjoyed running, hiking, and dancing most of her life and is now coping with degenerative knee problems, I appreciate and sympathize with these sentiments; regenerative nanomedicine cannot arrive quickly enough for me!

And yet, we do fear losing what we think is the essence of humanity, and we cling to the idea that being human is the ultimate ideal; Victor Grech dubs this "The Pinocchio syndrome" in his chapter. He delves into Greek mythology, such as the story of the crippled god Hephaestus, who requires a prosthesis for mobility, then probes the implications of our current popular culture. Grech examines such characters as Commander Data, a sentient android who is a full member of the *Enterprise* crew in *Star Trek: The Next Generation*. As Grech demonstrates, contemporary science fiction deals with issues of property vs. personhood and the age-old philosophical question of what it means to be human. Perhaps, indeed, the most important question to ask is not even "What does it mean to be human?", but rather "What sort of (post) humans do we want to be?"

I would posit that we'd want to retain our ability to empathize, no matter what else about us might be transformed, since there is evidence that a lack of empathy results in sociopathic behavior (Baron-Cohen 2011) and all the destruction this entails. However strange our descendants might be, or we might become, if transformed by technology, empathy will always be needed to maintain social contracts and sustain a peaceful coexistence. One way to encourage this might be through what Richard Loosemore describes in his optimistic and imaginative chapter, "Qualia Surfing". Loosemore explains that "the term *qualia* refers to the philosophically inexplicable core properties of our sensations that can only be known if you are the sentient creature that experiences them." After describing a plethora of potential playgrounds for our consciousness, he goes on to ruminate, "but part of human nature is that we want to have experiences that we can share with others of our kind," and that the experience of qualia surfing would cause us to pause and reflect on the purpose and meaning of existence.

Natasha Vita-More, the original designer of *Primo Posthuman Body* (a platform-diverse design for posthuman beings) counsels us, in "Design of Life Expansion and the Human Mind," that the important question to ask is what we need to be visible and what elements of perceptual awareness do we want to expand outside the physical world. In another of my favorite passages in *Intelligence Unbound*, Vita-More reflects that a goal of "expanding life over time, space, and substrate requires that we look beneath the surface of technology and the universal norms placed on human nature to a vision of its future that *could* be realized."

Part of that vision is a healthy, joyful extended lifespan – but does that mean we should strive for immortality? In "Against Immortality: Why Death is Better than the Alternative," Iain Thomson and James Bodington present the important distinction between an indefinite life span and immortality; they cite Heidegger's dictum that "being is finite," and Kierkegaard's point that one "can only postpone the disillusionment that comes from pursuit of novelty." From a Nietzschean viewpoint, they explain, "one can embrace mortality and reject the quest for immortality, as part of the struggle against nihilism."

Thomson and Bodington acknowledge the urge to extend fleeting lives, while insisting that eternity is also a fearful prospect:

> The problem […] is that many of us who (under the right circumstances) would love to significantly extend our (currently rather pathetically short) lives by a few decades, centuries, or even millennia nevertheless balk at the prospect of existing for all eternity.

This sentiment is understandable and something that we have long struggled with as a species; in the words of Percy Bysshe Shelley, "Lift not the painted veil which those who live Call Life." There is comfort in the thought that, when we have learned all we can on this Earth, and served whatever purpose we might have, we return to No-thing-ness or Everything-ness (or, if you prefer, to the Cosmos, Eternity, the Universe, the Multiverse, or God).

Thus the Buddhist monk Thich Nhát Hạnh (2002) writes that we are afraid to die because we are afraid we will become nothing when we die. But rather than seeing death as an end to life, he teaches, we should see our lives as a temporary manifestation, like a parenthesis in a sentence that is eternity, or like a wave that is part of the larger ocean. On this account, death can teach us valuable lessons about impermanence and the interconnectedness of all things.

And what of those entities that we might yet create as possible extensions of ourselves, such as brain emulations? What, if any, duties do we owe to them? Anders Sandberg, in the chapter "Being Nice to Software Animals and Babies," notes that much has been written about what moral consideration we should give to animals, and argues that we ought to pose a similar question about emulations. He submits that a digital imitation of the functioning of a living organism is different from biological wetware; indeed, he accepts that many of us would doubt whether it could experience consciousness. Nonetheless, Sandberg proposes that a safe moral strategy would be to make the most cautious assumption. This would be: "Assume that any emulated system could have the same mental properties as the original system and treat it correspondingly." The concept of sentience is not objectively verifiable (Glenn 2003), and Sandberg takes this into account. Since we cannot know whether or not a simulation is a moral patient, he avers that "we should treat the virtual mice the same as the real mice since it is better to treat a simulacrum as a real thing than to mistreat a sentient being, even by mistake."

In his chapter "What Will It Be Like To Be An Emulation?", Robin Hanson explores somewhat further how these extensions of ourselves might turn out. He visualizes a future world that still looks much like ours, but contains cities of emulations ("ems" for short). The title is evocative of Thomas Nagel's celebrated and oft-cited article "What Is It Like To Be A Bat?" Either question is perplexing, making novel demands on our imaginations – as Nagel explains:

> My point is […] that even to form a *conception* of what it is like to be a bat (and a fortiori to know what it is like to be a bat) one must take up the bat's point of view. If one can take it up roughly, or partially, then one's conception will also be rough or partial. Or so it seems in our present state of understanding. (Nagel 1974: 442)

Hanson takes the em's point of view and speculates that it might be more like ours than we first imagine. *That* is a matter for us to ponder:

> Here is the surprising thing […] ems think and feel like humans. Their world looks and feels to them much as ours looks and feels to us. Like humans, ems remember a past, are aware of a present, and anticipate a future. Ems can be happy or sad, eager or tired, fearful or hopeful, proud or shamed, creative or derivative, compassionate or cold. Ems have friends, lovers, bosses, and colleagues. Em mental and psychological features might differ from the human average, but, despite some eccentrics, are usually near the range of human variation.

Here, I can't help thinking of Nick Bostrom's (once more, celebrated and oft-cited) paper "Are We Living in a Computer Simulation?" (2003). Again, the title is in the form of a question – and it is a challenging one. We might create brain emulations, but who is to say that we ourselves are not emulations? Like the flowers and produce of master gardeners who take delight in cultivating and nurturing their terrain and bringing new things into existence out of seemingly nothing, perhaps we are the product of another civilization's creative impulses. If this might be so, it lends strength to Sandberg's proposition that we ought to treat emulations as we would like to be treated.

Coming full circle, our distinguished editors Damien Broderick and Russell Blackford have shared their own perspectives about notions of self and identity, as well as the present and future of minds and machines melding together. Whether one takes the viewpoint that there is no true "self," or that identity can be maintained through a change of substrate, or that our creations are persons as opposed to property (Glenn 2003), as Broderick notes, "these topics remain genuinely controversial, even philosophically troubling, so it is necessary to approach the topics carefully, exploring the pros and cons." And as Blackford comments, there is still much to consider; this book raises more questions than answers, which is appropriate in such a new field. It has been an honor and a pleasure getting to work with such esteemed editors and contributors.

A final word. This book lays out just some of the choices that lie ahead for humanity. The potential use for neuro-rehabilitation in the criminal justice system is an area that is just beginning to be considered (Persson and Savulescu 2013), and could easily fill an entire separate treatise. Earlier, I mentioned regenerative nanomedicine – that it cannot arrive too quickly. Research in this field is making tremendous strides and holds out hope for extended healthy lifespans; some of the most promising research is based upon the convergence of biology and nanotechnology (Glenn and Boyce 2012). There are many possibilities for the human future, some of them alluring and some of them quite frightening. Still, we must choose.

We can choose to be satisfied with humanity's current lot, or we can choose to improve our situation. I choose to close with the words of the author with whom I began this afterword: "To try is to risk failure. But risks must be taken, because the greatest hazard in life is to risk nothing" (Ward 1970).

References

Barabási, Albert-László. 2002. *Linked: The New Science of Networks*. Cambridge, MA: Perseus.

Baron-Cohen, Simon. 2011. *Zero Degrees of Empathy: A New Theory of Human Cruelty*. London: Penguin.

Bostrom, Nick. 2003. Are we living in a computer simulation? *Philosophical Quarterly* 53: 243–255. doi: 10.1111/1467-9213.00309.

Chalmers, David J. 2010. The Singularity: A philosophical analysis. *Journal of Consciousness Studies* 17(9–10): 7–65.

Clark, Andy, and Chalmers, David J. 1998. The extended mind. *Analysis* 58: 7–19.

Freitas, Robert A. Jr,. 1984. Xenopsychology. *Analog Science Fiction/Science Fact* 104 (April): 41–53, http://www.rfreitas.com/Astro/Xenopsychology.htm (accessed November 17, 2013).

Gladwell, Malcolm. 2008. *Outliers: The Story of Success*. New York: Little, Brown.

Glenn, Linda MacDonald. 2003. Biology at the margins of personhood: An evolving legal paradigm. *Journal of Evolution and Technology* 13(1) (March), http://jetpress.org/volume13/glenn.html (accessed November 27, 2013).

Glenn, Linda. M., and Boyce, Jeanann S. 2012. Regenerative nanomedicine: Ethical, legal, and social issues. *Methods in Molecular Biology* 811: 303–316. doi: 10.1007/978-1-61779-388-2_19.

Hạnh, Thich Nhát. 2002. *No Death, No Fear: Comforting Wisdom for Life*. New York: Riverhead.

Hume, David. 1739. *A Treatise of Human Nature*. Available at http://files.libertyfund.org/files/342/0213_Bk.pdf (accessed November 20, 2013).

Kurzweil, Ray. 2005. *The Singularity Is Near: When Humans Transcend Biology*. New York: Viking.

Nagel, Thomas. 1974. What is it like to be a bat? *Philosophical Review* 83(4): 435–450.

Persson, I., and Savulescu, J. 2013. Should moral bioenhancement be compulsory? Reply to Vojin Rakic. *Journal of Medical Ethics*. March 22 (Epub ahead of print). doi:10.1136/medethics-2013-101423.

Searle, J. 2008. Biological naturalism. In M. Velmans and S. Schneider, eds., *The Blackwell Companion to Consciousness*. Malden, MA: Blackwell, pp. 325–334.

Stiegler, Marc. 1990. *The Gentle Seduction*. New York: Baen Books.

Ward, William Arthur. 1970. *Fountains of Faith: The Words of William Arthur Ward*. Anderson, SC: Droke House.

Index

Intelligence Unbound: The Future of Uploaded and Machine Minds, First Edition.
Edited by Russell Blackford and Damien Broderick.